MEDIEVAL ICONOGRAPHY

GARLAND MEDIEVAL BIBLIOGRAPHIES
VOLUME 20
GARLAND REFERENCE LIBRARY OF THE HUMANITIES
VOLUME 1870

GARLAND MEDIEVAL BIBLIOGRAPHIES

THE MEDIEVAL CONSOLATION
OF PHILOSOPHY
An Annotated Bibliography
Noel Harold Kaylor, Jr.

THE ROMAN DE LA ROSE
An Annotated Bibliography
Heather M. Arden

MEDIEVAL VISIONS
OF HEAVEN AND HELL
A Sourcebook
Eileen Gardiner

SIR GAWAIN AND
THE GREEN KNIGHT
*An Annotated Bibliography,
1978–1989*
Meg Stainsby

BEOWULF SCHOLARSHIP
*An Annotated Bibliography,
1979–1990*
Robert J. Hasenfratz

THE MEDIEVAL CHARLEMAGNE
LEGEND
An Annotated Bibliography
Susan E. Farrier
Dutch materials treated by
Geert H. M. Claassens

THE LYRICS OF THE TROUVERES
A Research Guide (1970–1990)
Eglal Doss-Quinby

THE PILGRIMAGE TO
SANTIAGO DE COMPOSTELA
*A Comprehensive,
Annotated Bibliography*
Maryjane Dunn
and Linda Kay Davidson

MUSIC AND POETRY IN THE
MIDDLE AGES
*A Guide to Research on French
and Occitan Song, 1100–1400*
Margaret L. Switten

MEDIEVAL ICONOGRAPHY
A Research Guide
John B. Friedman
and Jessica M. Wegmann

MEDIEVAL ICONOGRAPHY
A RESEARCH GUIDE

JOHN B. FRIEDMAN
AND JESSICA M. WEGMANN

GARLAND PUBLISHING, INC.
A MEMBER OF THE TAYLOR & FRANCIS GROUP
NEW YORK AND LONDON
1998

Copyright © 1998 by John B. Friedman and Jessica M. Wegmann
All rights reserved

Library of Congress Cataloging-in-Publication Data

Friedman, John Block, 1934–
    Medieval iconography : a research guide / by John B. Friedman and
Jessica M. Wegmann.
        p.   cm. — (Garland medieval bibliographies ; vol. 20) (Garland
reference library of the humanities ; vol. 1870)
    Includes index.
    ISBN 0-8153-1753-0 (alk. paper)
    1. Arts, Medieval—Themes, motives—Sources—Bibliography.
I. Wegmann, Jessica M. II. Title. III. Series. IV. Series: Garland reference
library of the humanities ; vol. 1870.
Z5933.F75   1998
[NX449]
016.700'9'02—dc21   97-42974
                                                                            CIP

Please note that Entry 822 on page 174 has been omitted

Printed on acid-free, 250-year-life paper
Manufactured in the United States of America

In loving memory of Dr. Thomas G. Wegmann, father, academic, mentor, who instilled in me a passion for the quest for knowledge

and

For Lawrence J. Ross, May 11, 1926- January 23, 1996, scholar, teacher, iconographer

CONTENTS

Introduction   ix

Abbreviations   xv

PART ONE

Chapter One: Art   1

Chapter Two: Other Tools   101

PART TWO

Chapter Three: Learned Imagery   119

Chapter Four: The Christian Tradition   189

Chapter Five: The Natural World   247

Chapter Six: Medieval Daily Life   341

Index   413

INTRODUCTION

The present volume aims to help the researcher locate visual motifs, whether in medieval art or in literature, and to understand how they function in yet other medieval literary or artistic works. This process, as we understand and practice it ourselves, is not the same thing as "source hunting" for it is not an artist's sources which are usually very interesting in themselves, but rather the way the artistic imagination combines or modifies them to express something which may be peculiar to that artist's time and place.

So too, the key word in the title "iconography" we use here in a somewhat different way than was the case in the early part of this century, where it often meant the simple identification of figures in an artistic composition. Thus, for example, a wall painting's "iconography" was "explained" when the generic figure of a saint had been identified as Antony by means of his familiar pig. In the sense we intend it, however, iconography pertains more to the symbolism or less apparent content of a work, which can often be difficult to determine and which allows us, once we understand it, partially to recover the universe of early works of art as that universe was understood and inhabited by the artist and his audience.

We believe that there is no book in English quite like the one we offer here. Robert Kaske's *Medieval Christian Literary Imagery* (1988) was really concerned not so much with visual images as these would have been understood by the eye of a medieval person, but rather with the use of patristic writing to clarify metaphors and images in medieval poetry. While there are many areas where our work overlaps with his, we try for the most part to focus on how visual images from one work of art can help to make understandable similar images in another. The recent *ICONCLASS: An Iconographic Classification System*, by H. van de Waal tends towards the older phenomenological approach; by going through the New and Old Testaments scene by scene, it offers alphabetical indices of iconography with related bibliographies.

We hope, however, that the researcher who uses this Guide—whom we envision as the advanced undergraduate, the graduate student, or the

literary scholar challenged by a complex visual idea—will find it a
resource, not a collection of ready made interpretations. Let us say, then,
that the student is puzzled by the duplicity of the fox in a medieval
poem, or by a scene of a fox lying on its back, legs in the air, while birds
fly over it, in a woodcarving or in a medieval manuscript miniature. We
aim to provide a select list of studies on this animal to make clear to our
readers how the poet or artist is using the fox in a "field" of its traditional
symbolism and connotations, obvious, perhaps, in the fourteenth century
but less so today. We have listed important books and articles enabling
the student to grasp the intellectual and historical background of a given
image, and we have offered occasional cross references to similar
concepts treated elsewhere in the Guide. In a few cases we have provided
headnotes on the development of particular images in order to call
attention to the importance of a visual idea like that in which man is
understood as an upside-down tree.

   Obviously, a guide such as this must be limited in scope and
undoubtedly there will be some users who will wish for coverage of other
topics. On the great movements of Western medieval art, we have
mentioned only a fraction of the studies available. Yet we have tried to
treat relatively recent studies of a general or overview-providing sort,
whose bibliographies can in turn, help the user to locate useful material.
We have not, in the main, evaluated the works we mention, except to
indicate that sometimes they are coffee table books, always a sore point
with a scholar who sees a good plate of an interesting image in one and
then turns to the Illustration Credits only to find no location or other
identifying information for the picture. We have also tried to mention
when an item, though useful, is really focussed on art of a time earlier or
later than the Middle Ages. Though the annotations have been kept as
short as possible to allow for broad rather than deep coverage, we have
often indicated when a book has received an easily accessible review.

   A word about the Guide's structure is in order here. We have arranged
our material into two Parts containing six chapters. Part One is concerned
with tools rather than themes. Its purpose is to guide the student to works
which will place a wall painting in context, or tell where a famous
illuminated manuscript is located, or offer a hand-list of stained glass
window fragments in the United States, or provide a list of the sorts of
source books to which medieval artists and their learned audiences might
have gone to see how Venus should be traditionally depicted rising from
the sea with roses on her skin, a conch shell in her hand, and doves flying
over her head. Thus Chapter One is called Art and it broadly covers

various aspects of medieval art understood as the tools of investigation, such as the theory of iconography, genres like woodcarving, sculpture, and manuscript painting, periods like Anglo-Saxon, and countries—Bohemia or England. We have listed what may seem an inordinately large number of manuscript catalogues because illuminated manuscripts are one of the iconographer's greatest resources and collections of them are often elusive. Chapter Two is called Other Tools; it offers a guide to works which are not in themselves visual but which medieval artists may have consulted or been influenced by, such as encyclopaediae offering the physical descriptions, habits, and oddities of animals, plants, and insects, and exempla and sermon collections containing illustrative stories like those using the fox as a symbol of duplicity. This class of books, moreover, is a good guide to how an image might have been "received" by a medieval audience, since such works tend to have been compiled out of fossilized traditions and received opinions about things.

Part Two of the Guide is chiefly concerned with themes in both learned and popular culture. Chapter Three, Learned Imagery, treats traditions, works, concepts, and persons of interest to educated medieval people, such as alchemy, mythology, astrology, Alexander the Great, or the legend of the philosopher Aristotle ridden about like a horse by a woman named Campaspe or Phyllis, widely interpreted as an allegory of reason subjected to passion. A variety of *topoi* or familiar common places of a visual sort are touched on as well. Chapter Four, The Christian Tradition, treats the Bible and figures and situations in it, as well as the vast body of glosses, exegesis, and legend which was copied into the medieval Bible in the course of manuscript transmission. Subjects like the imagery of apocryphal works associated with the New and Old Testaments, and figures with a distinctive history of representation, such as Antichrist, or Job, or Mary Magdalene, receive detailed treatment. Chapter Five,The Natural World, covers what we might broadly call "natural history": medieval scientific conceptions; animals, listed as specific terrestrial, aerial, and marine creatures as well as imaginary forms of life, like the griffin or barnacle goose; members of the plant kingdom; and geographical features such as cliffs and mountains. Books like herbals and bestiaries are also studied in themselves. The last chapter of the Guide, Medieval Daily Life, treats a great variety of subjects somewhat more popular in appeal than those touched on in Chapter Three. These include baths, beauty and ugliness, costume, fools and madness, magic, and ships.

Admittedly, there is an idiosyncratic character to many of these selections, and in large part, the Guide reflects an individual scholar's pursuits, over some thirty years, of solutions to problems in the relation of literature and art. An example of both the limitations and, it is hoped, the strengths of iconographic investigation can be drawn from item 1700, which embodies such a search extending over sixteen years.

In 1960, during a graduate seminar in Jacobean drama offered by the late Lawrence J. Ross at Johns Hopkins University, one of us was vividly impressed by Ross's explanation of the subtle use of the cushion's apparent symbolism of lust and assignation in John Webster's play *The Duchess of Malfi*. In this work, the Duke of Brachiano desires a married woman, Vittoria Corombona, who is innocent of the Duke's obsession, and through go-betweens arranges an interview with her. The stage directions for the scene are these: "Re-enter Brachiano. Zanche [a Moorish waiting woman] brings out a carpet, spreads it, and lays on it two fair cushions." The Moorish bawd and the oriental opulence seemed to control the sense of the cushions and indeed, of the scene itself, making it clear to the audience, if not to Vittoria, the nature and eventual outcome of the Duke's interest.

Some years later, and now a teacher myself, I was queried by an eager undergraduate in a seminar on Chaucer's *Troilus and Criseyde* about why Pandarus, the poem's bawd figure, rushes to fetch a cushion to place under Troilus' knees as he kneels by his lady's bed. I remembered this chronologically later use of cushions by Webster and determined to investigate what Pandarus' cushion might have suggested to the poem's audience. The result of my finding was embodied in the article mentioned above (item 1700), but the process of research led me to the solution of yet another puzzling element in Webster's assignation scene, the seraglio-like carpet spread by Zanche. It seems that cushions in one of Juvenal's satires were associated with the decadent "east" and especially with Sardanapalus, a self-indulgent and lustful eastern ruler. Thus in answering for myself the student's question about Pandarus I was able to explain something about Webster. The recognition of the rich context which an object or person or situation from another time may bring to us with the right historical coaxing, and the desire to make this type of information available, led to the beginnings of the present Guide.

We should like to thank the University of Illinois at Urbana-Champaign, its Inter-Library Loan staff and the Graduate College and Department of English for aid in the preparation of this book. Charles D. Wright, Lorraine K. Stock, and my wife, Kristen M. Figg, were especially helpful in offering advice on the book's preparation and production.

ABBREVIATIONS

AAQ   Architectural Association Quarterly

AB   Art Bulletin

AC   Archaeologia Cantiana

AFH   Archivum Franciscanum Historicum

AHR   The American Historical Review

AJ   Archaeological Journal

AJA   American Journal of Archaeology

AK   Archiv für Kulturgeschichte

AKB   Aachener Kunstblatter

Annales ESC   Annales economies, sociétés, civilisation

Archive   Archiv für das Studium der neueren

    Sprachen und Literaturen

Arv   Arv; Tidskrift för Nordisk Folkminnesforskning

AQ   Art Quarterly

AR   American Recorder

ARCSE   Annals of the Royal College of Surgeons of England

BAEPE   Boletin de la Asociacion Europea de Professores de Español

BB   Bulletin of Bibliography

BGPTM *Beiträge zur Geschichte der Philosophie und Theologie des Mittelalters*

BHM *Bulletin of the History of Medicine*

BHR *Bibliothèque d'humanisme et renaissance*

BIAB *Bulletin de l'institut archéologique bulgare*

BJRL *Bulletin of the John Rylands Library*

BLR *Bodleian Library Record*

BM *Burlington Magazine*

BMHBA *Bulletin du Musée Hongrois des Beaux-Arts*

BMMA *Bulletin of the New York Metropolitan Museum of Art*

BMon *Bulletin Monumental*

BMQ *British Museum Quarterly*

BMRAH *Bulletin des Musées Royaux d'art et d'histoire*

BQR *Bodleian Quarterly Record*

CA *Cahiers archéologiques*

CAIEF *Cahiers de l'association internationale des études françaises*

C&M *Classica et Medievalia*

CC Corpus Christianorum

CC SL Corpus Christianorum: Series Latina

CCC *Canterbury Cathedral Chronicle*

CCM *Cahiers de civilisation médiévale*

CD *Comparative Drama*

CF *Classical Folia: Studies in the Christian Perpetuation of the Classics*

CG *Colloquia Germanica. Internationale Zeitschrift für germanische*

  Sprach-und Literaturwissenschaft

CHR *Catholic Historical Review*

CJ *Classical Journal*

C&M *Classica & Mediaevalia*

CP *Classical Philology*

CR *The Chaucer Review*

CVMA Corpus Vitriarum Medii Aevi

DA *Les dossiers de l'archéologie*

DAEM *Deutsches Archiv für Erforschung des Mittelalters*

DAI *Dissertation Abstracts International*

DOP *Dumbarton Oaks Papers*

DS *Dante Studies*

DSR *Downside Review*

EDAM Early Drama, Art and Music Monographs Series

EE *Environmental Ethics*

EF *Etudes françaises*

EG   Etudes germaniques

EETS Early English Text Society

ELR   English Literature Review

ERB   Etudes romanes de Brno

FF Forschungen und Fortschritte

Florilegium   Florilegium: Carleton University Annual Papers on Classical
    Antiquity and the Middle Ages

FMR   Franco Maria Ricci

FS   Frümittelalterliche Studien

GBA   Gazette des Beaux-Arts

GM   Geographical Magazine

HSCP   Harvard Studies in Classical Philology

HT   History Today

HTR   Harvard Theological Review

IJS   International Journal of Symbology

JAAC   The Journal of Aesthetics and Art Criticism

JAMS Journal of the American Musicological Society

JBAA   Journal of the British Archaeological Association

JEGP   The Journal of English and Germanic Philology

JFH   Journal of Forest History

JHI Journal of the History of Ideas

JIPCS Journal of the International Playing Card Society

JKMA Jaarboek van het Koninklijk Museum voor Schone Kunsten te Antwerp

JMRS The Journal of Medieval and Renaissance Studies

JMS Journal of Medieval Studies

JPC Journal of Popular Culture

JPGMJ The J. Paul Getty Museum Journal

JQR Jewish Quarterly Review

JRAI The Journal of the Royal Anthropological Institute

JTS Journal of Theological Studies

JWAG Journal of the Walters Art Gallery

JWCI Journal of the Warburg and Courtauld Institutes

L'AA L'Année archéologique

LEP Les Etudes Philosophiques

LJ Literaturwissenschaftliches Jahrbuch

LM Les langues modernes

LMA Le Moyen Age

LMAM Le Moyen Age maintenant

LMAR Le monde alpin et rhodanien

LMS   London Medieval Studies

LQ   Library Quarterly

LR   Les lettres romanes

LSE   Leeds Studies in English

LV   L'Art vivant

M&H   Medievalia et Humanistica

MA   Medium Aevum

MAcad   Michigan Academy

MAHL   Mélanges d'archéologie, d'histoire, et de littérature

MEFRMA   Mélanges de l'Ecole Française de Rome: Moyen Age

MH   Medical History

ML   Mittellateinisches Jahrbuch

MLR   Modern Language Review

MN   Miscellanea Neerlandica

MINF Mémoires de l'Institute National de France: Académie des

   Inscriptions et Belles-lettres

MIOG Mitteilungen des Instituts für Öesterreichische Geschichtsforschung

MJGK   Mainfrankisches Jahrbuch für Geschichte und Kunst

MJK   Marburger Jahrbuch für Kunstwissenschaft

MRIL Memorie del Reale Istituto Lombardo di Scienze e Lettere : Classe di Lettere, Scienza Morali e Storiche

MM Miscellanea Medievalia

MMAIBL Monuments et mémoires de l'Académie des Inscriptions et Belles Lettres

MQ Music Quarterly

MeR Medioevo Romanzo

MR Marche romane

MRS Medieval and Renaissance Studies

MS Mediaeval Studies

MSM Mémoires de la Société d'Agriculture, Commerce, Sciences et Arts de la Marne

MSNAF Mémoires de la Société Nationale des Antiquaires de France

MSNH Mémoires de la Société Néo-philologique à Helsingfors

NA Norfolk Archaeology

N&Q Notes and Queries

NM Neuphilologische Mitteilungen

NNAS Norfolk and Norwich Archaeological Society

OZKD Öesterreichische Zeitschrift für Kunst und Denkmalopflege

PAAAS Proceedings of the American Academy of Arts and Sciences

PLC   Princeton Library Chronicle

PLPLS   Proceedings of the Leeds Philosophical and Literary Society

PMLA   Publications of the Modern Language Association of America

PQ   Philological Quarterly

PSAL   Proceedings of the Society of Antiquaries of London

*PSIASNH   Proceedings of the Suffolk Institute of Archaeology, Statistics,
       and Natural History*

*PSANHS   Proceedings of the Somerset Archaeological and Natural History
       Society*

RA   Revue archéologique

RAEPE   Revista de la Asociacion Europea de Profesores de Español

RER   Revue des études Rabelaisiennes

RES   Review of English Studies

RF   Romanische Forschungen

RFHS   Revue française d'héraldique et de sigillographie

RLC   Revue de littérature comparée

RMAL   Revue du Moyen Age latin

RP   Romance Philology

RR   The Romanic Review

RSH   Revue des sciences humaines

RSL *Recherches de science religieuse*

RUO *Revue de l'Université d'Ottawa*

SAC *Surrey Archaeological Collection*

SAQ *South Atlantic Quarterly*

SATF Société des Anciens Textes Français

 SC Sources Chrétiennes

S&C *Scrittura e Civiltà*

SEU *Studia Ethnographica Upsaliensia*

SFQ *Southern Folklore Quarterly*

SH *Scientia Historia*

SHi *Social History*

SI *Studies in Iconography*

SJ *Stadel Jahrbuch*

SM *Studi Medievali*

SMRH *Studies in Medieval and Renaissance History*

SN *Studia Neophilologia*

SP *Studies in Philology*

SQ *Shakespeare Quarterly*

SS *Scandinavian Studies*

TAPA *Transactions of the American Philological Association*

TAPS Transactions of the American Philosophical Society

TCBS Transactions of the Cambridge Bibliographical Society

TSE Tulane Studies in English

UTQ University of Toronto Quarterly

VBW Vorträge Bibliothek Warburg

VC Vigiliae Christianae

WS The Walpole Society

WUS   Washington University Studies

WZR   Wissenschaftliche Zeitschrift der Universität Rostock, gesellschafts-
und sprachwissenschaftliche Reihe

YAJ Yorkshire Archaeological Journal

YLS Yearbook of Langland Studies

YWES   Year's Work in English Studies

ZDADL Zeitschrift für deutsches Altertum und deutsche Literatur

ZDK Zeitschrift für katolische Theologie

ZFSL Zeitschrift für französische Sprache und Literatur

PART ONE

Chapter One: Art

GENERAL REFERENCE

1. Aurenhammer, Hans. *Lexikon der christlichen Ikonographie.* 1 vol.
   Vienna: Bruder Hollinek, 1959-1967.
   Only one volume of this work has appeared so far; it treats, with
   representative pictures and bibliography, persons, images, and events
   up through the word "Christus."

2. Beigbeder, Olivier. *Lexique des symboles.* Introduction à la nuit des
   temps, no. 5. Paris: Zodaique, 1969.
   Follows *L'introduction au monde des symboles* from the same
   series, expanding upon the subject matter there by discussing a
   number of different themes in the iconography of Romanesque art.
   These are arranged alphabetically so that the book functions as an
   encyclopaedia of sorts, with plates and diagrams of how such themes
   are represented, especially in medieval sculpture.

3. *Bibliographie zur Symbolik, Ikonographie und Mythologie.*
   Internationales Referateorgan. Edited by Manfred Lurker, et
   al. 28 vols. to date. Baden-Baden: Valentin Koerner, 1968—.
   An analytic bibliography of iconographical and mythological motifs,
   ranging widely. The annotations are in German. With author and
   theme indices for each volume.

4. Bréhier, Louis. *L'art Chrétien: Son dévelopement iconographique des origines à nos jours.* Paris: Henri Laurens, 1928.
   Organized chronologically from the first century AD up until modern times, this substantial volume provides a good overview of the subject, supplemented by 290 engravings and six plates.

5. Cabrol, F., et al. *Dictionnaire d'archéologie chrétienne et de liturgie.* 15 vols. Paris: Letouzey et Ané, 1907-1953.
   Covers virtually all topics relating to the history and art of early Christianity. Pictures of related objects, places, and the like appear in each article along with bibliographies, now somewhat dated.

6. Champeaux, Gerard de, and Dom Sébastien Sterckx. *Introduction au monde des symboles.* Introduction à la nuit des temps, no. 3. Paris: Zodaique, 1966.
   Introduction to the study of symbolism in the art of the Romanesque period, with many plates from different types of art works. Sections focus on the following subjects: the sky, simple figures, temple and cosmos, high places, man, and trees.

7. Didron, A. *Histoire de iconographie chretiénne: Dieu.* Paris: Imprimerie Royale, 1843.
   Looks at iconography in Christian art from the ninth through the seventeenth centuries with line drawings of the art works it discusses and specific sections on elements of divine and Trinitarian representations, such as the nimbus, glory, and halo.

8. Garnier, François. *Thesaurus iconographique: Système descriptif de représentations.* Paris: Le Léopard d'or, 1984.
   This work attempts to apply scientific principles of taxonomy to the classification of iconography. It is in its present form a prolegomenon to a larger work still to come. Much of the book is devoted to the system of classification to be used and how the different rubrics are intended to be comprehensive, with various

subheadings. These rubrics comprise a vast body, a,s for example, the rubric agriculture is broken down into hunting, fishing, agricultural architecture and the like. All of this is illustrated with pictures, chiefly woodcuts and engravings, of the sixteenth century or later, so the book's utility for medievalists is at present limited. The cross referencing and subcategories seem to us rather cumbersome and reminiscent of the eighteenth-century "Encylopédistes." Possibly the greatest utility of the work lies in its indices, where a great variety of very specific words, such as "alouette," or lark, are keyed to the representations. This is followed by a table of illustrations and finally by a set of high quality black-and-white illustrations (some medieval) from manuscripts, ivories, textiles, sculpture, and the like, which illustrate the descriptive system set forth.

9. *International Repertory of the Literature of Art. A Bibliographic Service of the Getty Art History Information Program.* Malibu: J. Paul Getty Museum, 1975-89.
   This work contains annotated entries on various aspects of medieval art, as for example Annunciations or Rhenish lime wood sculpture. It has indices of authors and subjects. The format is that of a CD-ROM. It is available as one laser disc, requiring at least an IBM 386, though a 486 or higher is recommended; four MB of RAM; six MB of drive space; and either Windows 3.X or Windows 95. A VGA or better, SVGA color display is recommended as is a mouse.

10. Kirschbaum, Engelbert, et al., eds. *Lexikon der christlichen Ikonographie.* 8 vols. Rome: Herder, 1968-76.
    Treats Christian themes, names, and concepts, with plates and extensive bibliographies. Each topic, such as Adam and Eve, is broken down into categories such as sources, early representations such as catacomb frescos, and typological treatments in both New and Old Testament works. Volume Eight on the Iconography of Saints is especially useful as it contains registers of festivals and attributes.

11. Künstle, Karl. *Ikonographie der christlichen Kunst.* Freiburg-im-Breisgau: Herder, 1928.

A standard iconography handbook with bibliographies and 388 plates.

12. Lowrie, Walker. *Art in the Early Church.* New York: Pantheon, 1947.
    A very informative book with chapters on tomb art, churches, monumental arts of other types, Bible illustrations, industrial arts, and civil and ecclesiastical dress.

13. Lurker, Manfred. *Bibliographie zur Symbolkunde.* 3 vols. Baden-Baden: Heitz, 1964-68.
    Volume One of this work deals with lexica, periodicals, and the like. The entries are only sparsely annotated and range widely over many cultures, both of the east and west. Volume Two treats elements, plants, animals, man, and symbols of various kinds. Volume Three is a somewhat more broadly based form of Volume Two. There are author and subject indices.

14. Marle, Raimond van. *Iconographie de l'art profane au Moyen Age et à la Renaissance et la decoration des demeures.* Vol.1: *La vie quotidiennne.* The Hague: Martinus Nijhoff, 1931. Vol.2: *Allégories et symboles.* The Hague: Martinus Nijhoff,1932.
    A large and not easily found but extremely useful guide to the iconography of medieval daily life. Many plates and a focus on Netherlandish art. Volume One covers such topics as the life of the nobility, fishing, hunting, warfare, and teaching and the university, as well as rural life and the labors of the months, vineyards, animals, gardens, and peasants. Volume Two treats more abstract matters such as philosophical and ethical allegories of the virtues and vices, the wheel of fortune, and the pageants of and triumphs of monarchs allegorized, as well as the subjects of death and love allegorized.

15. Morey, Charles Rufus. *Medieval Art.* New York: Norton, 1942.
    An informative general history of medieval art with some illustrations and sections on early Christian, Byzantine, Romanesque, and early and late Gothic art.

16. *Répertoire d'art et d'archéologie (de l'époque paléochrétienne à 1939)*. Reprint. Nendeln, Liechtenstein: Kraus, 1989.
Contains a section on medieval iconography with an annotated bibliography and cross references to similar objects, places, or concepts. Runs from 1910 to 1989.

17. Rushforth, G. McN. *Medieval Christian Imagery as Illustrated by the Painted Windows of Great Malvern Priory Church, Worcestershire, Together with a Description and Explanation of the Ancient Glass in the Church.* Oxford: Clarendon, 1936.
Includes a great number of plates of these Gothic windows and describes in detail the provenance of their iconography with excursions to parallels in other art forms.

18. Schmidt, O., et al. *Reallexikon zur deutschen Kunstgeschichte.* Stuttgart: J. B. Metzlersche Verlagsbuchhandlung, 1937—.
An encyclopaedia—still in the process of completion—dealing with all aspects of German art. Some treatment of the Middle Ages. In-text plates and bibliographies with each article.

19. Tervarent, Guy de. *Attributs et symboles dans l'art profane, 1450-1600: Dictionnaire d'un language perdu.* 2 vols. Travaux d'humanisme et Renaissance, no. 29. Geneva: Droz 1958-9.
Alphabetically arranged according to topics, for instance chariots pulled by wolves, with references to the theme in emblem books and in art historical studies. Numerous excellent plates.

20. *Thesaurus des images médiévales pour la constitution de bases de données iconographiques.* Paris: Ecole des hautes études en sciences sociales,1993.
As the title suggests, an image data-base.

AESTHETICS

21. Bruyne, Edgar de. *Etudes d'esthétique médiévale.* 3 vols. Reprint.
    Geneva: Slatkine, 1975.
    This book, while a fascinating introduction to medieval esthetics,
    should be used with great caution, as many of the passages in
    medieval texts the author adduces in support of his arguments are
    not, in fact, to be found in those authors. Divided as follows:
    Boethius to Duns Scotus, Romanesque, and Gothic.

22. Tatarkiewicz, Wladyslaw. *History of Aesthetics.* Vol. 2: *Medieval
    Aesthetics.* Edited by C. Barrett. The Hague and Paris:
    Mouton; Warsaw: PWN—Polish Scientific Publishers, 1970.
    Surveys ideas on aesthetics in the Middle Ages beginning with the
    Bible and Church Fathers and moving chronologically through the
    different periods, citing passages (some long) from a number of
    major figures (as for instance Augustine, Boethius, Isidore, Albert
    the Great, Duns Scotus) and dealing with such topics as music, visual
    arts, poetics, philosophical aesthetics, and the like. Indices.

ANGLO-SAXON

23. Alexander, J. J. G. Preface. *Anglo-Saxon Illumination in Oxford
    Libraries.* Bodleian Picture Books Special Series, no. 1. Oxford:
    The Bodleian Library, 1970.
    Provides plates from Bodleian manuscripts ranging in date from the
    late ninth century up to the end of the eleventh century. The majority
    of the manuscripts illustrated are religious or liturgical texts coming
    from monastic scriptoria. The plates are accompanied by a preface,
    description, and select bibliography.

24. Bailey, Richard N. *England's Earliest Sculptors.* Toronto: Pontifical Institute,1996.
Overview of Anglo-Saxon sculpture with forty-one plates. Studies Continental influence and interaction, with an annotated bibliography.

25. Bryce, Derek, ed. *Symbolism of the Celtic Cross.* Felinfach, Dyfed: Llanerch Enterprises, 1989.
Illustrated with drawings, this book explores the symbolism of images on Cetic crosses, decribing the Pictish tradition behind them. Treats fish, Chi-Ro, swastika, spiral, plait, animal and vegetable motifs, as well as different forms of the cross such as the Manx.

26. Cassidy, Brendan, ed. *The Ruthwell Cross: Papers from the Colloquium Sponsored by the Index of Christian Art, Princeton University, 8 December, 1989.* Index of Christian Art Occasional Papers, no. 1. Princeton Univ. Press, 1992.
Miscellaneous papers dealing with the history and iconography of this eighth-century stone cross in the Scottish border country. Includes a bibliography of the Ruthwell Cross compiled by Brendan Cassidy and Katherine Kiefer.

27. Deshman, Robert. *Anglo-Saxon and Anglo-Scandinavian Art: An Annotated Bibliography.* Boston: G. K. Hall, 1984.
Covers all forms of art (other than coins and architecture) made between the last third of the ninth century to about the first quarter of the twelfth century.

28. Dodwell, C. R. *The Canterbury School of Illumination 1066-1200.* Cambridge: Cambridge Univ. Press, 1954.
Begins before the Norman Conquest and follows the Canterbury style of illumination up to the end of the thirteenth century. Has 291 photographs, a select bibliography, an index, and appendices containing a handlist of manuscripts illuminated at Canterbury.

29. Gameson, Richard. *The Role of Art in the Late Anglo-Saxon Church.* Oxford Historical Monographs. Oxford: Clarendon, 1995.

Gameson explains that "this work explores the role of the visual arts in the English church (and especially in its monastic sector) from the reign of Alfred the Great (871-99) to the generation after the Norman conquest," providing "interrelated quite sharply focused studies, which collectively define some of the parameters of the field as a whole, while casting a clear light on particular areas in it" (1). These chapters cover the illustration of texts, inscriptions, visual language, repetition of motif and image and their possible implications, pictorial narrative, composition, and decoration. Finishes with broader perspectives on monastic art generally. Some plates, bibliography, and indices.

30. Karkov, Catherine, and Robert Farrell, eds. *Studies in Insular Art and Archaeology.* American Medieval Studies, no. 1. Oxford, OH: Miami Univ. School of Fine Arts, 1991.
    This collection of essays relating to English and Irish art and archaeology is reviewed and analyzed by Carol Neuman de Vegvar in *Speculum* 68, no. 4 (October 1993): 1148-9.

31. Nordenfalk, Carl. *Celtic and Anglo-Saxon Painting: Book Illumination in the British Isles 600-800.* New York: George Braziller, 1977.
    An album of color plates each accompanied by a description along with an introduction and bibliography on the subject.

32. Schapiro, Meyer. "The Religious Meaning of the Ruthwell Cross." *AB* 26 (1944): 232-45.
    Examines the iconography of the figures carved on the Ruthwell Cross and their relation to the inscriptions. Places the cross in the context of similar works of art in the period. Some illustrations.

33. Spearman, R. Michael, and John Higgitt, eds. *The Age of Migrating Ideas: Early Medieval Art in Northern Britain and Ireland.* Stroud, Gloucestershire: Alan Sutton, 1993.
    Articles by several contributors consider such broad areas as the migration of artistic ideas, centers of patronage and production, Insular manuscripts, metalwork, and sculpture. Many illustrations.

34. Stevick, Robert D. *The Earliest Irish and English Bookarts: Visual and Poetic Forms Before A.D.1000*. Philadelphia: Univ. of Pennsylvania Press, 1994.
Studies form in the book arts of English and Irish monastic communities from the seventh through the tenth centuries. Looks at works such as the Books of Kells and of Durrow and the Lindisfarne, Echternach, and St. Gall Gospels.

35. Webster, Leslie, and Janet Backhouse, eds. *The Making of England: Anglo-Saxon Art and Culture, AD 600-900*. London: The British Library,1991.
This informative and thorough book includes selections by many specialists in different areas such as manuscripts, coinage, metalwork, and sculpture. Contains 100 color and 150 black-and-white illustrations.

36. Wilson, David M. *Anglo-Saxon Art from the Seventh Century to the Norman Conquest*. Woodstock, NY: Thames and Hudson, 1984.
A survey of Anglo-Saxon art updating Sir Thomas Kendrick's two-volume study from the 1960's. A good general treatment with numerous illustrations. Indices.

ANTIQUE HERITAGE

37. Adhémar, Jean. *Influences antiques dans l'art du Moyen Age français*. Studies of the Warburg Institute, no. 7. London: The Warburg Institute, 1939.
Looks generally at medieval knowledge of late antique art, with discussion of the study of the classics in the Middle Ages. Many plates.

38. Ainalov, D.V. *The Hellenistic Origins of Byzantine Art.* Translated by Elizabeth and Serge Sobolevitch. Edited by Cyril Mango. New Brunswick, NJ: Rutgers Univ. Press, 1961.
     Treats authoritatively Alexandrian and Syrian manuscript miniatures, pictorial reliefs, the Hellenistic background of Byzantine fresco painting, and the relationship of Constantinople and the East, among other topics. Many plates and index.

39. Baltrusaitis, Jurgis. "Quelque survivances de symboles solaires dans l'art du Moyen Age." *GBA*, 6th ser., 17 (1937): 75-82.
     Examines the iconographical heritage of the round sun-like figure surrounded by apostles in the depiction of the Pentecost in a pericope manuscript in the Munich State Library.

40. Erzgräber, Willi, ed. *Kontinuität und Transformation der Antike im Mittelalter.* Sigmaringen: Jan Thorbeke, 1989.
     A collection of essays by various hands focussing on the antique heritage of medieval literature and music though with some discussion of art. Some articles from this collection are mentioned under items 770f.

41. Weitzmann, Kurt. *Illustrations in Roll and Codex: A History of the Origin and Method of Text Illumination.* Studies in Manuscript Illumination, no. 2. Princeton Univ. Press, 1947.
     An authoritative general study of the subject, mainly in late antiquity and the early Middle Ages, with numerous illustrations and index. Treats the relation of literature and the representational arts, text and content of miniatures, and picture cycles, among other subjects.

42. _____. *Ancient Book Illumination.* Martin Classical Lectures, no. 16. Cambridge, MA: Harvard Univ. Press, 1959.
     Discusses mostly illumination but with some medieval examples of didactic treatises, codices containing epics, and other literary forms. Includes numerous plates.

ARCHITECTURE

General

43. Coldstream, Nicola. *The Decorated Style. Architecture and Ornament 1240-1360.* London: The British Library, 1994.
Studies the English decorated style which was popular from the reign of Henry III through that of Edward III. This style is of particular interest here from the way it fused architecture with other forms of ornament, such as polychrome stone work, stained glass, sculpture, and heraldic motifs. Though chiefly a style employed in churches and cathedrals it is also to be found in more secular and domestic contexts. Includes ten color plates and 120 black-and-white illustrations and a select bibliography.

44. Colvin, Howard. *Architecture and the Afterlife.* New Haven and London: Yale Univ. Press, 1991.
Starts with megaliths and tumuli, and proceeds through the Roman, medieval, and Renaissance periods, describing and analyzing architecture created with an interest in the afterlife. Numerous plates. Reviewed by James F. O'Gorman in *Speculum* 69, no. 2 (April 1994): 446-7.

45. Heydenreich, Ludwig H. *Architecture in Italy, 1400-1500.* Revised by Paul Davies. New Haven, CT: Yale Univ. Press, 1995.
Covers major works of Italian late medieval and early Renaissance architecture, with seventy-five color and 120 black-and- white plates.

46. Krautheimer, Richard. *Introduction à un 'iconographie de l'architecture médiévale.'* Paris: Gerard Monfort, 1993.
Argues that medieval architects emphasized different features in their plans for construction than did those since the Renaissance. More important than function, design, and the like, were the religious implications of architectural forms. Makes the important point that

Romanesque forms were often associated with the Old Law and Gothic forms with the New. This small book is a development of an article published in English in 1942 in *JWCI*. Some plates.

47. Lampl, Paul. "Schemes of Architectural Representation in Early Medieval Art." *Marsyas* 9 (1961): 6-13.
    Treats the different ways architectural forms were represented in medieval manuscript illumination. Has a number of plates.

48. Lavedan, Pierre. *Représentation des villes dans l'art du Moyen Age.* Paris: Vanoest, 1954.
    With numerous plates, this book examines such subjects as urbanization by region, conceptions of space, and realistic as opposed to fantastic depictions of cities. Includes indices of the names of cities and of the cities represented in the illustrations.

49. Platt, Colin. *The Architecture of Medieval Britain: A Social History.* New Haven, CT: Yale Univ. Press, 1991.
    Relates formal architecture to English social values and ways of life. With 201 black-and-white and 179 color plates.

50. Rodley, Lynn. *Byzantine Art and Architecture: An Introduction.* Cambridge: Cambridge Univ. Press, 1994.
    A good general overview with 286 black-and-white plates.

51. Smith, Earl Baldwin. *Architectural Symbolism of Imperial Rome and the Middle Ages.* Princeton Univ. Press,1956.
    Investigates such architectural features as city-gates and palace entrances and their royal and divine significance in the popular imagination.

52. Thurley, Simon. *The Palaces of Henry VIII: Architecture and Court Life 1460-1547.* New Haven, CT: Yale Univ. Press, 1993.
    Treats royal buildings and decoration in a wealth of detail. 150 black-and-white pictures and 70 color plates.

Castles

53. Cornelius, Roberta D. "Le Songe du Castel." *PMLA* 46, no.1 (1931): 321-32.
    This work considers allegorical castles and treats some of their "visual" details but is chiefly concerned with a French poem of about 1300 published here for the first time and considered as an example of a medieval castle allegory. The work uses the castle as a metaphor rather more than as a form of architecture.

54. DeVries, Kelly. *Medieval Military Technology*. Peterborough, Ontario and Lewiston, NY: Broadview Press, 1992.
    With sections on arms and armor, artillery, fortifications and warships, this book is an excellent introduction to the subject. Not art historical in orientation, but useful for understanding miniatures containing military iconography. Reviewed by Bradford B. Blaine in *Speculum* 69, no.2 (April 1994): 452-4.

55. King, David J. Cathcart *Castellarium Anglicanum: An Index and Bibliography of the Castles in England, Wales, and the Islands*. 2 vols. Millwood, NY: Kraus, 1983.
    An inventory listing structures such as town walls, fortified monasteries, and defenses of secular and religious communities erected between 1051 and 1547. Castles are listed alphabetically with one chapter assigned to each county. Each castle is classified and described and bibliographical information is provided. Volume One covers castles and their distribution in Angelsey-Montgomery and includes an introduction offering a definition and description of a typical castle. Volume Two covers castles in Norfolk, Yorkshire, and the islands.

56. Oman, Charles. *Castles*. London: The Great Western Railway, 1926.
    Covers the castles of Wales, and the English counties along the Welsh borders, Somerset, Devon, and Cornwall. Each castle is described and pictures and drawings are given. The introduction provides a good overview of castles generally.

57. Pounds, N. J. G. *The Medieval Castle in England and Wales: A Social and Political History.* Cambridge: Cambridge Univ. Press,1990.
Divided into three parts treating the castle in early English feudalism, in the thirteenth century, and in the high Middle Ages, the informative text is supplemented by a number of illustrations. Reviewed by Charlotte Goldy in *Speculum* 68, no. 4 (October 1993): 1197-9.

Cathedrals and Churches

58. Anderson, M. D. *The Imagery of British Churches.* London: Murray, 1955.
A rather general introduction to the popular understanding of medieval imagery especially that found in churches and cathedrals, rather than its doctrinal and aesthetic aspects. Covers approaches of the parish craftsmen and parishioner, the structure and plan of churches, Old and New Testament subjects, heaven, hell, saints, and similar iconographic topics. Index but few plates.

59. Lehmberg, S. E. *The Reformation of Cathedrals. Cathedrals in English Society, 1485-1603.* Princeton Univ. Press, 1988.
Chronicles the development of English cathedrals as Tudor social institutions, focussing more on their social function and hierarchical structure than on their architecture. Includes many plates, and charts containing information on cathedral music, colleges of canons, prebendaries, deacons, and the like.

60. Meulen, Jan van der, et al. *Chartres: Sources and Literary Interpretation: A Critical Bibliography.* Reference Publications in Art History. Boston: G. K. Hall, 1989.
Particularly useful in this annotated bibliography may be Chapter Five: Iconographic Studies, covering the comprehensive program, the architectural program, the sculptural program, the stained glass

and mural programs, and a section arranged by iconographic theme (regardless of medium); and Chapter Seven: The Cathedral in the Literature of Art, proceeding again by medium and then by period. Plates.

ARTISTS, FEMALE

61. Miner, Dorothy. *Anastaise and Her Sisters, Women Artists of the Middle Ages*. Baltimore: Johns Hopkins Univ. Press, 1974.
    Considers records and representations of various female artists, mostly nun-illuminators.

62. Monson, Craig A., ed. *The Crannied Wall: Women, Religion, and the Arts in Early Modern Europe*. Ann Arbor: Univ. of Michigan Press, 1992.
    A collection of essays detailing how religious women participated in the religious life of late medieval Europe. The authors discuss their presence in music, drama, and the formulation of iconography, in the context of similar art works of the period. Some illustrations.

ATTITUDES TO AND DESCRIPTIONS OF ART

63. Eco, Umberto. *Art and Beauty in the Middle Ages*. Translated by Hugh Bredin. New Haven, CT and London: Yale Univ. Press, 1988.
    A study of medieval aesthetic doctrines.

64. Holt, Elizabeth Gilmore, ed. *Literary Sources of Art History: An Anthology of Texts from Theophilus to Goethe.* Princeton Univ. Press, 1947.
A useful guide to medieval attitudes towards the fine arts. The section on the Middle Ages includes selections by Raul Glaber, Leo of Ostia,Theophilus, Bernard of Clairvaux, and Abbot Suger, Letters on how Chartres was built, Gervase of Canterbury, Villard de Honnecourt, William Durand, Duccio, and Cennino Cennini.

65. James, M. R., ed. "Pictor in Carmine." *Archaeologia* 94 (1951): 141-66.
Provides the preface (and a translation of it) from this "largest known collection of types and antitypes intended to be used by artists"(141) that explains how artists should treat serious Biblical matters rather than such subjects as fantastical beasts. James then discusses the plan of the work, copies of it available, possible sources also dealing with this topic, a few works of art that may have been influenced by it, and finishes by reproducing the long table of contents of "Pictor."

66. Pépin, J. "*Vt scriptura pictura*: Un thème de l'esthétique médiévale et ses origins." *From Augustine to Eriugena: Essays on Neoplatonism and Christianity in Honor of John J. O'Meara.* Edited by F.X. Martin and J. A. Richmond. Washington, DC: Catholic Univ. of America Press,1991, pp. 168-82.
Looks at different councils and patristic writings, and examines the history of the idea throughout the Middle Ages that pictures may function in place of scripture to instruct the illiterate.

67. Ratkowitsch, Christine. *Descriptio Picturae: Die literarische Funktion des Beschreibung von Kunstwerken in der lateinischen Grosdichtung des 12. Jahrunderts.* Vienna: Österreichische Akademie der Wissenschaften,1991.
Treats a group of writers— Walter of Chatillon, Alan of Lille, John of Hautville, and Joseph of Exeter— who offer ecphrases or literary descriptions of works of art. One plate and a bibliography. Reviewed by Christine Smith in *Speculum* 69, no. 2. (April 1994): 555-7.

68. Rudolph, Conrad. *The Things of Greater Importance: Bernard of Clairvaux's "Apologia" and the Medieval Attitude Towards Art.* Philadelphia: Univ. of Pennsylvania Press, 1990.
    Treats medieval attitudes towards the visual arts by way of Bernard of Clairvaux's "Apologia" and the early twelth-century controversy over art. Considers the early patristic period to 1153.

69. Wirth, K.-A., ed. *Pictor in Carmine. Ein Handbuch der Typologie aus dem 12. Jahrhundert. Nach der Handschrift des Corpus Christi College in Cambridge, MS 300.* Berlin: Mann,1989.
    An edition of the famous treatise in the Corpus Christi College, Cambridge manuscript containing the largest known collection of types and antitypes intended to be used by artists. Its strictures as to how artists should treat serious Biblical matters rather than grotesques make it one of the key contemporary aesthetic statements about Romanesque and early Gothic art.

COLLECTIONS, GENERAL

70. Bruzelius, Caroline, and Jill Meredith, eds. *The Brummer Collection of Medieval Art.* Durham, NC and London: Duke Univ. Press, 1991.
    Articles by different authors each showing some aspect of, or work in, this collection of forty- two major art objects at Duke University. This collection is analyzed in *Speculum* 68, no.4 (October 1993): 1243.

71. Gillerman, Dorothy W., ed. *Gothic Sculpture in America.* Vol.1: *The New England Museums.* Publications of the International Center of Medieval Art, no. 2. New York and London: Garland, 1989.

Describes each work in New England collections in detail, giving provenance, history, and a picture, as well as bibliography on that piece.

72. Stones, Alison, and J. Steyaert. *Medieval Illumination, Glass, and Sculpture in Minnesota Collections.* Minneapolis: Univ. of Minnesota Press, 1978.
Excellent overview of a variety of art works which can be examined in Minnesota.

COLLECTIONS OF ILLUMINATED MANUSCRIPTS

General

73. Fitzgerald, Wilma. *Ocelli Nominum. Names and Shelf Marks of Famous/Familiar Manuscripts.* Subsidia Mediaevalia, no. 19. Toronto: Pontifical Institute of Medieval Studies, 1992.
This invaluable work serves as a guide to the often confusing popular names of many manuscripts, such as the Lindisfarne Gospels or the Luttrell Psalter and tells where they are presently to be found, as well as locating the present whereabouts of many manuscripts which have been sold in recent years, like those once in the famous Ludwig Collection but now in the J. Paul Getty Museum in Malibu, CA.

74. Krochalis, Jeanne, and Jean F. Preston. *Teachers' Guide to Finding Western Medieval Manuscripts.* Kalamazoo, MI: Medieval Institute Publications, 1988.
A sixty-six-page bibliography of useful works and suggestions for beginnning researchers in this area.

75. Mokretsova, I. P., and V. L. Romanova. *Les manuscrits enluminés français du XIII siècle dans les collections soviétiques 1200-1270*. Moscow: State Publishing Company, 1984. Offers a large number of black-and-white and color plates from a variety of manuscripts, psalters, missals, Bibles, and bestiaries, now in Russia. This work is in Russian with French summaries of the descriptions.

76. Narkiss, Bezalel, and Gabrielle Sed-Rajna. *Index of Jewish Art: Iconographical Index of Hebrew Illuminated Manuscripts*. 3 vols. Jerusalem: The Israel Academy of Sciences and Humanities, 1983. The introduction explains that "the present index sets out to be complementary to the Princeton Index of Christian Art in a field that the latter, by definition, had to leave out of its scope: a comprehensive iconographical Index of Jewish Art" (9 of the guide to the series). The aim of this section of the index on Hebrew Illuminated Manuscripts is to "list systematically all subjects and their iconographic representations in Hebrew manuscripts from the 9th century . . . up to the 16th" (10). The three volumes completed as of the publication of this guide cover altogether eight manuscripts ranging in date from 1300 through the sixteenth century. Each volume consists of a collection of loose cards, each bearing the plate of one illumination and describing it. The guide contains the iconographical index keyed in to the plates.

77. Winter, Patrick M. de. *La bibliothèque de Philippe le Hardi, duc de Bourgogne (1364-1404): Étude des manuscrits à peintures d'une collection princière à l'époque du style gothique international*. Paris: CNRS, 1985. Studies the library of this famous patron of manuscript illuminators and ateliers, and talks of his methods of commissioning books.

Specific Collections, Owners or Manuscripts by Country or City

(These titles are mostly self-explanatory and do not

usually need description.)

[Aachen]

78. Euw, A. von, and J. Plottzek. *Die Handschriften der Sammlung Ludwig, II*. Cologne: Das Museum,1979-1985.
    Details the manuscripts once in this famous collection but now mostly dispersed to the J. Paul Getty Museum, Malibu, CA.

[Aberdeen]

79. James, Montague Rhodes. *A Catalogue of the Medieval Manuscripts in the University Library, Aberdeen*. Cambridge: Cambridge Univ. Press, 1932.

[Aberystwyth]

80. *Handlist of Manuscripts in the National Library of Wales*.4 vols. Aberystwyth: Council of the National Library of Wales,1940-1986.

[America]

81. Ricci, Seymour de, and W. J. Wilson. *Census of Medieval and Renaissance Manuscripts in the United States and Canada*. Reprint. New York: Kraus, 1961; and *Supplement,* New York: Bibliographical Society, 1962.

[Australia]

82. Manion, Margaret M. *Medieval and Renaissance Illuminated Manuscripts in Australian Collections*. Melbourne and New York: Thames and Hudson,1984.

[Baltimore]

83. Randall, Lilian M. C., et al. *Medieval and Renaissance Manuscripts in the Walters Art Gallery*. Vol. 1: *France 875-1420;* Vol. 2:

France: 1420-1540. Baltimore and London: Johns Hopkins Univ. Press in association with the Walters Art Gallery, 1992. Reviewed by Paul Binski in *Speculum* 69, no. 4 (October 1994): 1256-7.

[Cambridge, England]

84. James, Montague Rhodes. *A Descriptive Catalogue of the Manuscripts of the Library of Corpus Christi College Cambridge.* 2 vols. Cambridge: Cambridge Univ. Press, 1912.

85. _____. *A Descriptive Catalogue of the Western Manuscripts in the Library of Clare College.* Cambridge: Cambridge Univ. Press, 1905.

86. _____. *The Western Manuscripts in the Library of Emmanuel College, a Descriptive Catalogue.* Cambridge: Cambridge Univ. Press, 1904.

87. _____. *A Descriptive Catalogue of the Manuscripts of the Library of Eton College* Cambridge: Cambridge Univ. Press, 1895.

88. _____. *A Descriptive Catalogue of the Manuscripts in the Fitzwilliam Museum.* Cambridge: Cambridge Univ. Press, 1895.

89. _____. *A Descriptive Catalogue of the McClean Collection of Manuscripts in the Fitzwilliam Museum.* Cambridge: Cambridge Univ. Press, 1912.

90. _____. *A Descriptive Catalogue of the Manuscripts in the Library of Gonville and Caius College.* Cambridge: Cambridge Univ. Press, 1907-1914.

91. _____. *A Descriptive Catalogue of the Manuscripts in the Library of Jesus College, Cambridge.* 3 vols. London and Cambridge: Cambridge Univ. Press, 1895.

92. _____. *A Descriptive Catalogue of the Manuscripts in King's College.* Cambridge: Cambridge Univ. Press, 1895.

93. _____. *A Descriptive Catalogue of the Manuscripts in the Library of Pembroke College, Cambridge.* Cambridge: Cambridge Univ. Press, 1905.

94. _____. *A Descriptive Catalogue of the Manuscripts in the Library of Samuel Pepys, Cambridge.* Part 2.1: *Medieval Manuscripts.* London: Sidgwick and Jackson, 1923.

95. _____. *A Descriptive Catalogue of the Manuscripts in the Library of Peterhouse.* Cambridge: Cambridge Univ. Press, 1899.

96. _____. *A Descriptive Catalogue of the Western Manuscripts in the Library of Queen's College, Cambridge.* Cambridge: Cambridge Univ. Press, 1905.

97. _____. *A Descriptive Catalogue of the Manuscripts in the Library of Sidney Sussex College, Cambridge.* Cambridge: Cambridge Univ. Press, 1895.

98. _____. *A Descriptive Catalogue of the Manuscripts in the Library of St. John's College.* Cambridge: Cambridge Univ. Press, 1913.

99. _____. *A Descriptive Catalogue of the Western Manuscripts in the Library of Trinity College, Cambridge.* 4 vols. Cambridge: Cambridge Univ. Press, 1900-1904.

100. _____. *A Descriptive Catalogue of the Manuscripts in the Library of Trinity Hall.* Cambridge: Cambridge Univ. Press, 1907.

101. Luard, H. R. *A Catalogue of the Manuscripts Preserved in the Library of the University of Cambridge.* Reprint. Munich: Kraus; Hildesheim: G.Olms, 1980.

[Cambridge, MA]

102. Light, Laura. *Catalogue of Medieval and Renaissance Manuscripts in the Houghton Library, Harvard University.* Vol.1 : *MSS Latin.* Binghamton, NY: State Univ. of New York Press, 1996.

[Canterbury, England]

103. Woodruff, Charles Everleigh. *A Catalogue of Manuscripts Books (which are preserved in study X, Y, Z and in the Howly-Harrison collection) in the Library of Christ Church, Canterbury.* Canterbury: Cross and Jackman, 1911.

[Chicago]

104. Saenger, Paul. *A Catalogue of the Pre-1500 Western Manuscript Books at the Newberry Library.* Chicago: Univ. of Chicago Press, 1989.

[Claremont, CA]

105. Dutschke, C. W., et al. *Medieval and Renaissance Manuscripts in the Claremont Libraries.* Berkeley: Univ. of California Press, 1986.

[Denmark]

106. Mackeprang, M., et al. *Greek and Latin Illuminated Manuscripts X-XIII Centuries, in Danish Collections.* Copenhagen: Levin and Munksgaard, 1917.

[Dublin]

107. Colker, Marvin L. *Trinity College Library Dublin: Descriptive Catalogue of the Medieval and Renaissance Latin Manuscripts.* Aldershot, Hampshire: Scolar Press,1991.

108. Millar, Eric G. *Library of A. Chester Beatty: A Descriptive Catalogue of the Western Manuscripts.* 2 vols. London: Oxford Univ. Press, 1927 and 1930.

[Edinburgh]

109. Anon. *Index to Manuscripts in Edinburgh University Library.* 2 vols. Boston: G.K. Hall, 1964. With supplement, 1981.

110. Borland, C. A. *Descriptive Catalogue of the Western Mediaeval Manuscripts in Edinburgh University Library.* Edinburgh: Edinburgh Univ. Press, 1916.

[England]

111. Narkiss, Bezalel, et al. *Hebrew Illuminated Manuscripts in the British Isles: A Catalogue Raisonné: The Spanish and Portuguese Manuscripts.* 2 vols. Oxford and New York: Oxford Univ. Press, 1982.

[Florence]

112. Bandini, A. *Catalogus codicum manuscriptorum Latinae Bibliothecae Mediceae Laurentianae.* Reprint. Leipzig: Zentral-Antiquariat der Deutschen Demokratischen Republik, 1961.

[France]

113. Génévoix, A.-M., et al. *Bibliothèques de manuscrits médiévaux en France. Relevé des inventaires du VIIIe au XVIIIe siècles.* Paris: CNRS, 1987.

[Glasgow]

114. Young, John, and P. Henderson Aitken. *A Catalogue of the Manuscripts of the Hunterian Museum in the University of Glasgow.* Glasgow: J. Maclehose, 1908.

[Hereford]

115. Bannister, A. T. *A Descriptive Catalogue of the Manuscripts in the Hereford Cathedral Library*. With an Introduction by M. R. James. Hereford: Wilson and Phillips, 1927.

116. Mynors R. A. B., and Rodney Thomson. *Catalogue of the Manuscripts of Hereford Cathedral Library*. Cambridge: D. S. Brewer; Rochester, NY: Boydell and Brewer, 1995.

[Lincoln]

117. Thomson, Rodney M. *A Catalogue of the Manuscripts of Lincoln Cathedral Chapter Library*. Woodbridge, Suffolk and Wolfeboro, NH: D. S. Brewer, 1989.

118. Wooley, R. M. *Catalogue of the Manuscripts of Lincoln Cathedral Chapter Library*. London: Oxford Univ. Press, 1927.

[Liverpool]

119. *A Guide to the Manuscript Collections in the Liverpool University Library*. Liverpool: Liverpool Univ. Press, 1962.

[London]

120. *A Catalogue of the Harleian Manuscripts in the British Museum*. London: British Museum, Department of Manuscripts, 1808.

121. *A Catalogue of the Lansdowne Manuscripts in the British Museum with Indexes of Persons, Places and Matters*. Reprint. Hildesheim and New York: G. Olms, 1974.

122. *Catalogue of Manuscripts in the British Museum*, n.s., no. 1. Part I: *Arundel* and Part II: *Burney*. London: British Museum, 1834.

123. *Catalogue of Stowe Manuscripts in the British Museum.* London: British Museum, 1895.

124. James, Montague Rhodes. *A Descriptive Catalogue of Fifty Manuscripts from the Collection of Henry Yates Thompson.* Cambridge: Cambridge Univ. Press, 1898.

125. _____. *A Descriptive Catalogue of the Second Series of Fifty Manuscripts (51-100) in the Collection of Henry Yates Thompson.* Cambridge: Cambridge Univ. Press, 1902.

126. _____, and Claude Jenkins. *A Descriptive Catalogue of the Manuscripts in the Library of Lambeth Palace.* 5 vols. Cambridge: Cambridge Univ. Press, 1930-32.

127. Scott, E. J. L. *Index to the Sloane Manuscripts in the British Museum.* London: Printed by order of the Trustees, 1904.

128. Smith, Thomas. *A Catalogue of the Manuscripts in the Cottonian Library Deposited in the British Museum.* Edited by C. G. C. Tite. Translated by Godfrey E. Turton. Cambridge: D. S. Brewer, 1984.

129. Warner, George F., and Julius P. Gilson. *Catalogue of Western Manuscripts in the Old Royal and King's Collections.* 3 vols. London: The Trustees of the British Museum, 1921.

[Los Angeles, CA]

130. Ferrari, Mirella. *Medieval and Renaissance Manuscripts at the University of California, Los Angeles.* Edited by Richard H. Rouse. Berkeley: Univ. of California Press, 1991.

[Manchester]

131. Fawtier, Robert. "Hand-list of Additions to the Collection of Latin Manuscripts in the John Rylands Library, 1908-1920." *BJRL* 6 (1921): 186-206.

132. James, Montague Rhodes. *A Descriptive Catalogue of the Latin Manuscripts in the John Rylands Library of Manchester.* 2 vols. Manchester: Manchester Univ. Press, 1921.

133. Tyson, Moses. "Hand-list of the Collection of English Manuscripts in the John Rylands Library, 1928." *BJRL* 13 (1929): 152-219.

[Milan]

134. Kirsch, Edith W. *Five Illuminated Manuscripts of Giangaleazzo Visconti.* University Park, PA and London: Pennsylvania State Univ. Press, 1991.

135. Luzzatto, Aldo, and Luisa Mortara Ottolenghi. Parts 1 and 2. *Hebraica Ambrosiana. Catalogue of Undescribed Hebrew Manuscripts in the Ambrosian Library.* Milan: Edizioni il Polifilo, 1972.

[New Haven]

136. Babcock, Robert G., et al. *Catalogue of Medieval and Renaissance Manuscripts in the Beinecke Rare Book and Manuscript Library, Yale University.* Vol. 4. *MSS 481-485.* New York: State Univ. of New York Press, 1997.
This catalogue treats manuscript fragments in the Beinecke Library dating from the seventh to the sixteenth centuries; it continues the Shailor volumes noted below.

137. Shailor, Barbara. *Catalogue of Medieval and Renaissance Manuscripts in the Beinecke Rare Book and Manuscript Library, Yale University.* Vol. 1: *1-250*; Vol. 2: *251-500.* Binghamton, NY: State Univ. of New York Press, 1987. Vol. 3: *The Marston Manuscripts.* Binghamton, NY: State Univ. of New York Press, 1992.
Volume Three is reviewed by John B. Friedman in *M&H,* n.s., 21 (1994): 145-52.

[New York]

138. Terrien-Somerville, Beatrice, ed. *Medieval and Renaissance Manuscripts at Columbia University: Papers Presented at a Symposium Sponsored by the Columbia University Graduate School of Arts and Sciences Interdepartmental Committee on Medieval and Renaissance Studies, March 31, 1990.* New York: Columbia Univ. Libraries, 1991.
A collection of essays relating to Columbia University manuscript holdings.

[New Zealand]

139. Manion, Margaret, et al. *Medieval and Renaissance Manuscripts in New Zealand Collections.* Melbourne: Thames and Hudson, 1989.

[Oxford]

140. Alexander, J. J. G., and Elzbieta Temple. *Illuminated Manuscripts in Oxford College Libraries, The University Archives, and the Taylor Institute.* 3 vols. Oxford and New York: Oxford Univ. Press, 1985.

141. Black, W. H. *A Descriptive, Analytical and Critical Catalogue of the Manuscripts Bequeathed unto the University of Oxford by Elias Ashmole.* Oxford: Oxford Univ. Press, 1845.

142. Coxe, Henry O. *Catalogus Codicum Manuscriptorum qui in Collegiis Aulisque Oxoniensibus Hodie Adservantur.* Oxford: e typographeo academico, 1852.

143. Macray, William. *Catalogus Codicum Manuscriptorum Bibliothecae Bodleianae, Bibliothecae Bodleianae Partes quintus, fasciculus primus Viri Munificentissimi Ricardi Rawlinson.* Oxford: Oxford Univ. Press, 1868.

144. _____. *Catalogi Codicum Manuscriptorum Bodleianae Pars Nona codices a viro clarissimo Kenelm Digby.* Oxford: Oxford Univ. Press, 1893.

145. _____. *Partes Quintae Fasciculus secundus* Oxford: Oxford Univ. Press, 1878.

146. Madan, Falconer, et al. *Summary Catalogue of Western Manuscripts in the Bodleian Library at Oxford.* Reprint. Munich: Kraus-Thomson,1980.

147. Mynors R. A. B. *Catalogue of the Manuscripts of Balliol College, Oxford.* Oxford: Clarendon, 1963.

148. Pächt, Otto, and J. J. G. Alexander. *Illuminated Manuscripts in the Bodleian Library, Oxford.* 3 vols. Oxford: Clarendon, 1963-73.

149. Vaughan, R., and John Fines. "Handlist of Manuscripts in the Library of Corpus Christi College, not described by M. R. James." *TCBS* 3, no.2 (1960): 113-23.

[Paris]

150. Omont, Henri Auguste. *Miniatures des plus anciens manuscrits grecs de la Bibliothèque Nationale de VIe au XIVe siècle.* Paris: H. Champion, 1929.

[San Marino, CA]

151. Dutschke, C.W., et al. *Guide to Medieval and Renaissance Manuscripts in the Huntington Library.* San Marino, CA: Huntington Library, 1989.

[Urbana, IL]

152. Friedman, John B. "Resources for Scholars: Medieval Manuscripts at the University of Illinois at Urbana-Champaign." *LQ* 57, no.1 (January 1987): 70-80.

[Utrecht]

153. Horst, K. van der. *Illuminated and Decorated Medieval Manuscripts in the University Library, Utrecht: An Illustrated Catalogue.* Cambridge: Cambridge Univ. Press, 1989.

[Vienna]

154. Pächt, Otto, and Dagmar Thoss. *Die illuminierten Handschriften und Inkunabeln der Österreichischen Nationalbibliothek: Flämische Schule* II. 2 vols. Vienna: Österreichische Akademie der Wissenschaften, 1990.
    Reviewed by Anne Van Buren in *Speculum* 68, no. 4 (October 1993): 1187-90.

[Worcester, England]

155. Floyer, J. *Catalogue of Manuscripts in the Chapter Library of Worcester Cathedral.* Worcester: The Cathedral, 1906.

DECORATIVE AND DOMESTIC ARTS

General

156. Barral i Altet, X. *Artistes, artisans, et production artistique au Moyen Age*. Vol. 3: *Fabrication et consommation de l'oeuvre. Colloque internationale CNRS Université de Rennes II—Haute-Bretagne. 2-6 mai, 1983*. Paris: Picard, 1990.
Contains items 162,164, and 186.

157. Evans, Joan. *Pattern: A Study of Ornament in Western Europe, 1180-1900*. Vol. 1: *The Middle Ages*. Reprint. New York: Da Capo, 1976.
Covers a wide range of topics, for example, Gothic decoration, arcades, and tracery, canopies, animals, plants, heraldic motifs, and textile patterns.

158. Winter, Patrick M. de. *European Decorative Arts 1400-1600: An Annotated Bibliography*. Reference Publications in Art History. Boston, MA: G. K. Hall, 1988.
Organized according to medium and then by country and region, this work is a most valuable guide.

Alabasters

159. Cheetham, Francis. *English Medieval Alabasters with a Catalogue of the Collection in the Victoria and Albert Museum*. Oxford: Phaidon,1984.
The best general treatment of the subject, with many magnificent plates of the carvings chiefly at the Victoria and Albert Museum. Arranged according to the representation of subject, for example, the Sacred Face, this lengthy catalogue has a plate and description of each work of art. There is an excellent introduction to the medium of alabaster and its economic and geographical backgrounds.

160. Ramsay, Nigel. "La production et exportation des albâtres anglais médiévaux double." *Artistes, artisans, et production artistique* (item 156), pp. 609-19.
A general overview of the trade with only one plate.

Brasses

161. Clayton, Muriel. *Catalogue of Rubbings of Brasses and Incised Slabs.* London: Victoria and Albert Museum, 1929.
     A *catalogue raisonné* of this important medium, chiefly bourgeois and English. Many plates.

162. Emmerson, Robin. "Design for Mass Production: Monumental Brasses Made in London ca. 1420-1485." *Artistes, artisans, et production artistique* (item 156), pp. 133-71.
     Very useful overview article on the funerary brass trade, accompanied by a large number of rubbings and enlarged details of faces, hems, and letters used on these. Helpful in identifying other productions of the London workshops.

163. Kent, J. P. C. "Monumental Brasses: A New Classification of Military Effigies *ca.* 1360 *ca.* 1485." *JBAA* 12 (1949): 70-97.
     Studies the brasses depicting armed knights common in English churches.

164. Norris, Malcolm. *Monumental Brasses, the Craft.* London: Faber and Faber, 1978.
     Basic study of the purpose, manufacture, and patronage of funerary brasses. Extensive bibliography.

165. Stephanson, Mill. *A Revised List of Monumental Brasses in the British Isles.* London: Monumental Brass Society, 1977.
     A slender handlist identifying and briefly describing funerary brasses in England by church and county. Some plates.

166. Trivick, Henry H. *The Craft and Design of Monumental Brasses.* London: J. Baker; New York: Humanities Press, 1969.
     Eighty-five plates and bibliography.

Cards, Images on

167. Allmagne, Henri-René d'. *Les cartes à jouer de XIVe au XXe siècle.* 2 vols. Paris: Librairie Hachette,1906.
This vast repertoire of playing card motifs goes through France by region and time period, providing very detailed information on the manufacture, appearance, and imagery of playing cards. There are plates of the cards themselves as well as of art works depicting cards being manufactured or various card games being played.

168. Berti, Giordano, and Andrea Vitali, eds. *Le Carte di Corte: I tarocchi. Gioco e magia alle corte degli estensi.* Bologna: Nuova Alfa Editoriale, 1987.
A collection of essays by various authors on the history and symbolism of the images on tarot cards. Many plates.

169. Dummett, Michael (with the assistance of Sylvia Mann). *The Game of Tarot from Ferrara to Salt Lake City.* London: Duckworth, 1980.
Discusses the history of, and, in great detail, the changing rules of the game in many different localities, from its origins until the present day, with numerous annotated illustrations. Index.

170. Hargrave, Catherine Perry. *A History of Playing Cards and a Bibliography of Cards and Gaming: Compiled and Illustrated from the Old Cards and Books in the Collection of the United States Playing Card Company in Cincinnati.* Reprint. New York: Dover, 1966.
Discusses the history of playing cards from as early as they can be traced, proceeding by country (mostly European) and starting in the Middle Ages, but covering also Japan, China, India, and America, supplemented by numerous plates from the collection described in the subtitle and going back as early as the fourteenth century. Lengthy bibliography and indices.

171. Hoffman, Detleff, and Margot Dietrich. *Tarot, Tarock, Tarocchi mit italienischen Farben*. Leinfelden-Echterdingen: Deutsches Spielkartenmuseum, 1988.
Excellent background guide to the images on tarot cards. Many illustrations.

172. Kaplan, Stuart R. *The Encyclopedia of Tarot*. New York: U. S. Games Systems, 1978.
Iconographical in focus, this historical overview of the game of tarot examines chronologically and by subject depicted, plates of different cards throughout the ages. Contains much material from the medieval and Renaissance periods including an interesting section detailing the "Earliest References to Playing Cards." Bibliography and index.

173. Merlin, Romain. *Origine des cartes à jouer*. Paris: the author, 1896.
This general history is divided by country and each section proceeds chronologically, many beginning with some information about the medieval period and including plenty of black-and-white and color plates and interesting contemporary quotations about cards and card playing. The lengthy bibliography is organized by topic (collections of cards, designs on them, and types of cards such as tarot). Indices.

174. Pinder, E. *Charta lusoria. Spielkarten aus aller Welt u. 6 Jahrhunderten*. Biberach: Basoderm, 1961.
General guide to the imagery of playing cards, with a world focus. Not specifically interested in late medieval decks.

175. Psichari, Michel. "Les jeux de gargantua." *RER* 6 (1908): 16-37.
Discusses various card games (in particular one called "flux") and the terminology used in these games in the fifteenth and sixteenth centuries, with quotations from numerous works about them.

176. Schreiber, W. L. *Die ältesten Spielkarten und die aus das Kartenspiel Bezug habenden Urkunden des 14. und 15. Jahrhunderts*. Strassburg: Heitz, 1937.
Background on late medieval playing card imagery.

177. Séguin, Jean-Pierre. *Le jeu de cartes.* Paris: Hermann, 1968.
This volume discusses the origins and development of cards and card games, the art on the cards, the technique of making them, cards as depicted in art works, cards used for purposes other than for playing, and the players. Ranges up until the present day but does include many examples from the medieval and Renaissance periods. Includes throughout numerous plates of cards and of art works showing card playing as well as interesting quotations and facts about card playing in particular periods at different locations. Concludes with a subject chronology and a bibliography.

Ceramic and Tessarae

178. Eames, Elizabeth. *English Medieval Tiles.* Cambridge, MA: Harvard Univ. Press, 1985.
An introduction to medieval ceramic tiles. Includes an extensive bibliography and a catalogue of many surviving tiles. Several plates of pavements in color.

179. _____. *English Tilers.* Medieval Craftsmen Series. Toronto and Buffalo: Univ. of Toronto Press, 1992.
An introduction to the making and decorating of medieval tiles, both the practical roof tiles and the more elaborate floor tiles. Many plates. Reviewed by Robert Calkins in *Speculum* 69, no. 2 (April 1994): 421-3.

180. _____."Inlaid Tile Mosaic from Chertsey Abbey, Surrey, and Related Sites." *Catalogue of Medieval Lead-Glazed Earthenware Tiles in the Department of Medieval and Later Antiquities.* London: The British Museum, 1980, pp.141-71.
Studies the ceramic tiles of Chertsey Abbey depicting the story of Tristan and Iseult and Richard Lionheart.

181. James, Montague Rhodes. "Rare Medieval Tiles and Their Stories." *BM* 42 (1923): 32-37.

Studies the depiction on some early fourteenth-century English tiles
of the nine episodes of the Infancy of Christ, tracing the sources of
the Infancy Gospels in the Middle Ages. With plates.

182. Lejeune, Rita. "La légende du roi Arthur dans
    l'iconographiereligieuse médiévale." *Archaeologia* 14 (1967):
    51-5.
    Studies the floor mosaic of Otranto Cathedral, *ca.* 1165, depicting
    Alexander the Great and King Arthur.

183. Loomis, Roger Sherman. *Illustrations of Medieval Romance on
    Tiles from Chertsey Abbey.* New York: Johnson Reprint Corp.,
    1967.
    Discusses a group of thirteenth-century tiles illustrating the Tristan
    story. Accompanied by drawings rather than photographs of the tiles.
    He discusses their iconography, provenance, and the previous
    scholarship on the subject. Also useful is a list of Tristan
    illustrations.

184. Norton, Christopher. "The Production and Distribution of Medieval
    Floor Tiles in France and England." *Artistes, artisans, et
    production artistique* (item 156), pp. 101-30.
    An overview of tile making and distribution in France and England,
    with numerous plates. The types of tiles discussed do not have
    narrative illustrations.

Drawings

185. Evans, Michael W. *Medieval Drawings.* London: Paul Hamlyn,1969.
    Consists mostly of plates of the drawings, each described as in a
    catalogue. Contains a thorough introduction to the subject of drawing
    as an art form and its evolution in the Middle Ages.

186. Heimann, Adelheid. "Three Illustrations from the Bury St. Edmunds

Psalter and Their Prototypes: Notes on the Iconography of
Some Anglo-Saxon Drawings." *JWCI* 29 (1966): 39-59.
Examines the development and iconography of three forms that
appear in the psalter: personification of Vita and Mors, the figure of
the Creator, and the figure of the woman with evil children. With
plates.

Enamel

187. Boehm, Barbara D., and Elisabeth Taburet-Delahaye. *Enamels of
     Limoges, 1000-1350*. New York: Metropolitan Museum, 1996.
     A catalogue of the exhibition held in Paris at the Louvre and at the
     Metropolitan Museum of Art. Many color and black-and-white
     plates.

188. Chamot, M. *English Mediaeval Enamels.* Monographs on English
     Medieval Art. London: Ernest Benn, 1930.
     Provides a catalogue of works of probable English provenance in this
     material. Contains fifty-three plates.

189. Gauthier, Marie-Madeleine. *Emaux du Moyen Age occidental.*
     Fribourg: Office du Livre, 1972.
     Treats enamel work from its Roman origins through Romanesque
     and Gothic art. Deals with enamel on gold, copper, and silver
     supports. With numerous plates.

190. Mitchell, H. P. "English Enamels of the Twelfth Century." *BM* 47
     (1925): 163-70 and 49 (1926): 161-73.
     Part one describes "English enamelling of about the third quarter of
     the twelfth century in a highly characteristic style of drawing
     distinguished by figures in expressive and even exaggerated action,
     with clinging draperies, owing not a little to Byzantine influence."
     (BM 49 {1926}:161). Part two discusses and provides examples of

another style of English enamels from this same period more typical of the "normal manner of English figure drawing" (161). Plates.

191. Stratford, Neil. *Catalogue of Medieval Enamels in the British Museum*. Vol. 2: *Northern Romanesque Enamel*. London: British Museum Press, 1993.
      Offers a catalogue of enamels in the British Museum along with plates, an introduction, and a section on the techniques of Northern Romanesque enamels. There is also a technical appendix on the composition of the glazes.

Glass

A great many medieval churches have now been studied in the *Corpus Vitrearum Medii Aevi* series. Listed in detail here are some major collections of glass in the United States as well as some of the churches whose extensive iconographical programs have been published.

192. Brown, Sarah, and David O'Connor. *Glass-Painters*. Medieval Craftsmen Series. Toronto and Buffalo: Univ. of Toronto Press, 1991.
      Using guild records and costings, this work treats the persons responsible for the design, construction, and erection of medieval stained glass windows. Reviewed by Robert Calkins in *Speculum* 69, no. 2 (April 1994): 421-3.

193. Caviness, Madeline H. *The Early Stained Glass of Canterbury Cathedral, circa 1175-1220*. Princeton Univ. Press, 1977.
      Considers among other things iconographic programs and Biblical and hagiographic subjects. Many plates, and diagrams of window placement.

194. _____. *The Windows of Christ Church, Canterbury*. CVMA, no. 2. London: Published for the British Academy by Oxford Univ. Press, 1981.

Considers the iconographic programs and Biblical and hagiographic subjects of these windows. Many plates of the windows and diagrams of window placement. 224 pages of plates, bibliography, and index.

195. _____, ed. *Medieval and Renaissance Stained Glass from New England Collections:Catalogue of an Exhibition Held at the Busch-Reisinger Museum. Harvard University April 25-June 10, 1978.* Medford, MA: Tufts Univ. Press, 1978.
Pictures and lengthy descriptions of glass and an introduction. Good assortment of plates.

196. _____, and Evelyn Ruth Staudinger, eds. *Stained Glass before 1540: An Annotated Bibliography.* A Reference Publication in Art History. Boston MA: G. K. Hall, 1983.
Covers techniques of glass painting, conservation and restoration, collections and sales of stained glass. The book is arranged by regions and has indices.

197. _____, et al. *Stained Glass before 1700 in American Collections: Mid-Atlantic and Southeastern Seaboard States.* CV Checklist, no. 2. Studies in the History of Art, no. 23. Monograph Series, no.1 Washington, DC: National Gallery of Art, 1987.

198. _____. *Stained Glass before 1700 in American Collections:: Midwestern and Western States.* Washington, DC: National Gallery of Art, 1989.

199. _____, et al. *Stained Glass before 1700 in American Collections: New England and New York.* CV Checklist, no.1. Studies in the History of Art, no. 15. Monograph Series, no. 1. Washington, DC: National Gallery of Art, 1985.

200. Evans, David. *A Bibliography of Stained Glass.* Cambridge, England: D. S. Brewer, 1982.
Arranged alphabetically by author, with general and topographical indices.

201. French, Thomas, and David O'Connor. *York Minster: A Catalogue of Medieval Stained Glass: The West Windows of the Nave.* CVMA, no. 3. New York and London: Oxford Univ. Press, 1987.
Considers iconographic programs, and Biblical and hagiographic subjects. Many plates and diagrams of window placement.

202. Fritzsche, Gabriela. *Die mittelalterlichen Glasmalerien im Regensburger Dom.* 2 vols. CVMA, no. 13. Berlin: Deutscher Verlag für Kunstwissenschaft, 1987.
Studies the medieval windows in this cathedral, with numerous reproductions.

203. Husband, Timothy B. *The Luminous Image: Painted Glass Roundels from the Lowlands, 1480-1560.* New York: Metropolitan Museum of Art, 1995.
A *catalogue raisonné* with twenty-one color and many black-and-white plates.

204. _____. *Stained Glass before 1700 in American Collections: Silver Stained Roundels and Unipartite Panels.* CV Checklist, no. 4. Studies in the History of Art, no. 39. Monograph Series, no. 1. Washington, DC: National Gallery of Art, 1991.

205. Marks, Richard. *Stained Glass in England during the Middle Ages.* London: Routledge, 1993.
A luxurious and thorough study of the art, manufacturing techniques, and patronage of stained- glass windows in England, with thirty color and 200 black-and-white plates. Bibliography.

206. Newton, Peter. *The County of Oxford: A Catalogue of Medieval Stained Glass.* CVMA, no. 1: *Great Britain.* Oxford: Published for the British Academy by Oxford Univ. Press, 1979.
Treats some of the windows in Oxford churches.

Ivory

207. Beckwith, John, et al., eds. *Ivory Carvings in Early Medieval England 700-1200*. Arts Council of Great Britain. London: Victoria and Albert Museum, 1974.
Ivories from the Franks casket to 1200 are considered. Each is pictured and described.

208. Bergman, Robert P. *The Salerno Ivories: Ars Sacra from Medieval Amalfi*. Cambridge, MA and London: Harvard Univ. Press, 1980.
An account of Old and New Testament representations in eleventh-century South Italian ivories.

209. Cutler, Anthony. *The Hand of the Master. Craftsmanship, Ivory, and Society in Byzantium (9th-11th Centuries)*. Princeton Univ. Press, 1994.
Considers the Byzantine use of ivory for icons and provides reproductions of numerous examples.

210. Dalton, O. M. *Catalogue of the Ivory Carvings of the Christian Era in the British Museum*. London: The British Museum, 1909.
A very useful *catalogue raisonné* in English of a great variety of different ivory objects down through the seventeenth century with full iconographic descriptions. Excellent plates.

211. Gaborit-Chopin, Danielle. *Ivoires du Moyen Age*. Fribourg and Paris: Office du Livre, 1978.
A history of ivory work beginning in antiquity and continuing up through the end of the Middle Ages. Many plates and a catalogue of ivories and a bibliography at the back.

212. Goldschmidt, Adolph. *Die Elfenbeinskulpturen aus der Zeit der karolingischen und sachsischen Kaiser*. 4 vols. Berlin: Deutscher Verlag für Kunstwissenschaft, 1914-26.
Standard reference work on ivory carving for the earlier Middle Ages. Many plates.

213. Kurt Weitzmann. *Die Byzantischen Elfenbeinskulpturen des x.-xiii jahrhunderts.* 2 vols. Reprint. Berlin: Deutscher Verlag für Kunstwissenschaft, 1979.
    Arranged as a *catalogue raisonné* of ivories in major collections throughout the world, but with thematic divisions so that Adam and Eve, Joshua, and other Old Testament figures are treated all together. Has numerous plates.

214. Koechlin, Raymond. *Les ivoires gothiques français.* 2 vols. Reprint. Paris: F. De Nobele, 1968.
    Volume One discusses different types of ivories and gives their date and provenance. Volume Two is a catalogue. Each volume treats both religious and secular ivories.

215. Longhurst, Margaret H. *Catalogue of Carvings in Ivory: Victoria and Albert Museum.* Part I: *Up to the Thirteenth Century.* London: Published under the authority of the Board of Education,1927.
    An introduction is followed by a description of each item,with plates at the back.

216. _____. *English Ivories.* London:G. P. Putnam's Sons,1926.
    A catalogue with an historical introduction and plates at the back.

217. Molinier, Emile. *Catalogue des ivoires. Musée National du Louvre.* Paris: Librairies Imprimeries Réunies, 1896.
    Treats the great collection of ivory carving in the Louvre. Now somewhat dated.

218. Volbach, Wolfgang Fritz. *Die Elfenbeinbildwerke (Staatliche Museen zu Berlin: Die Bildwerke der deutschen Museums).* Berlin and Leipzig: Walter de Gruyter, 1923.
    Essentially a catalogue of a large number of ivory objects, pyxes, combs, diptychs, and the like from the early Christian through the Byzantine, Romanesque, Gothic, Renaissance, and Baroque periods in German museums. Accompanied by numerous extremely high quality black-and-white plates.

219. _____. *Elfenbeinarbeiten der Spätantike und des frühen Mittelalters*. Reprint. Mainz am Rhein: Von Zaberg, 1976. Catalogues 260 ivory carvings, pyxes, combs, diptychs, and the like in various great collections. Accompanied by 116 extremely high quality black-and-white plates and a fairly extensive bibliography, mostly of works in German.

220. Williamson, G. C. *The Book of Ivory*. London: F. Muller, 1938. General study for the beginner.

Jewelry and Gold Work

221. Cherry, John. *Goldsmiths*. Medieval Craftsmen Series. Toronto and Buffalo: Univ. of Toronto Press, 1992. Reviewed by Robert Calkins in *Speculum* 69, no.2 (April 1994): 421-3. Introductory study of the making and significance of plate and jewelry. Some plates.

222. Lightbown, Ronald W. *Mediaeval European Jewellery: With a Catalogue of the Collection in the Victoria & Albert Museum*. London: Published by the Victoria and Albert Museum, 1992. This magnificent book with many plates, some in color, and with detailed discussions of many forms of medieval jewelry was reviewed by Denise Allen in *Speculum* 69, no. 4 (October 1994): 1208-11.

223. Winston-Allen, Anne. *Stories of the Rose: The Making of the Rosary in the Middle Ages*. University Park, PA: Pennsylvania State Univ. Press, 1997. Develops the spiritual, literary, and artistic dimensions of the rosary in the Middle Ages. 35 plates.

Tapestry

224. Ackerman, Phyllis. *Tapestry: The Mirror of Civilization.* Reprint New York: AMS, 1970.
In this history of tapestry, beginning with Egyptian examples, the author surveys the different periods of medieval tapestry and looks at the form in other countries such as Mexico and Peru as late as the nineteenth century. With black-and-white plates, selective bibliography, and index.

225. Cavallo, Adolfo. *Medieval Tapestries in the Metropolitan Museum of Art.* New York: Metropolitan Museum of Art, 1993.
A *catalogue raisonné* of sixty-four tapestries in the Metropolitan Museum, with introductory chapters on the manufacture of tapestries, on their use in domestic architecture and on their design. Extremely detailed individual entries and many plates. Reviewed by Jeffrey Hamburger in *Speculum* 71, no. 2 (April 1996): 402-4.

226. Geijer, Agnes. *Albertus Pictor, målere och pärlstickare.* Stockholm: Pettersons, 1949.
Treats the ecclesiastical embroidery of this very important Swedish artist and its motifs, with twelve pages of plates.

227. Göbel, Heinrich. *Tapestries of the Lowlands.* Translated by R. West. New York: Brentano's, 1924.
More than half this volume consists of plates of tapestries or of pictures representing tapestry-making technique. Although much of the volume concentrates on later tapestry making, there are sections on, and mention thoughout of, medieval tapestry making. Describes in detail the techniques of tapestry making, the completion of the tapestry, and the interpretation of tapestry hanging before proceeding through the various counties of Lowland countries to look at particular tapestries and at evidence of the industry as a whole in these.

228. Hulst, Roger-A. d.' *Choix de tapisseries flamandes du XIVe au XVIe siècle.* Brussels: Cultura, 1961.

Standard introduction to the great tapestry making centers of the region, with numerous color and black-and-white plates of such scenes as apocalypses, Alexander the Great, scenes from the Passion of Christ, and some extremely interesting and detailed boar hunting scenes reflecting contemporary practice.

229. Hunter, George Leland. *The Practical Book of Tapestries.* Philadelphia and London: J. B. Lippincott, 1925.
Divided into specific sections according to the imagery, materials, period, and provenance of tapestries. Examines Gothic religious allegories in tapestry, Gothic country life and narrative tapestries. Indices and plates.

230. _____. *Tapestries and their Origins, History and Renaissance.* New York: John Lane, 1912
Covers Gothic and Renaissance tapestries from different production centers. Treats the Gobelin tapestries and discusses technical features like high and low warp and weaving methods. Many plates and index.

231. Joubert, Fabienne. *La Tapisserie.* Typologie des sources du Moyen Age occidental, no. 67. Turnhout: Brepols, 1993.
Like other volumes in this series, Joubert's provides an excellent overview of its subject. It begins with a lengthy and useful annotated bibliography of works concerning tapestries. An essay on the subject treats general topics such as authorship, authenticity, dating, tapestry as a source of history, and the use of iconography in tapestries.

232. Jourdain, M. A. *The History of English Secular Embroidery.* London: Kegan Paul, Trench, Trübner, 1910.
Very informative on Saxon through Tudor embroidery, though only a short section is devoted to the early phases of the subject. Proceeds chronologically, then discusses specifics like emblems, stamp work, needlework copies of pictures, and the like.

233. King, Donald. *Opus Anglicanum: English Medieval Embroidery.* London: Arts Council of Great Britain, 1963.

Catalogue of an exhibition held at the Victoria and Albert Museum in 1963.

234. Muntz, E. "Tapisseries allégoriques inédités ou peu connues." *MMAIBL* 9 (1902): 95-121.
Examines the theme of combat between personified virtues and vices in a number of narrative tapestries in famous French collections, with an account of the appearance of this very popular theme in tapestry generally.

235. Staniland, Kay. *Embroiderers.* Medieval Craftsmen Series. Toronto and Buffalo: Univ. of Toronto Press, 1991.
A general introduction to wall hangings, altar clothes, and costume. The author examines the techniques of embroidery, appliqué, quilting, and the like and the way in which embroiderers moved from country to country. Reviewed by Robert Calkins in *Speculum* 69, no. 2 (April 1994): 421-23.

236. Thomson, W. H. G. *A History of Tapestry.* London: Hodder and Stoughton, 1930.
Good general introduction for the beginner.

DIAGRAMS AND SCHEMATA

237. Obrist, Barbara. "Le diagramme isidorien de l'année et des saisons: Son contentu physique et les représentations figuratives." *MEFRMA* 108, no.1 (1996): 95-164.
Extremely learned and thorough study, with many plates of different diagrams of the *homo/annus/mundi* variety.

238. Teyssèdre, Bernard. "Un example de survie de la figure humaine dans les manuscrits précarolingiens. Les illustrations du *De natura rerum* d'Isidore." *GBA* 102 (1960): 19-34.

Many examples from medieval manuscript illustration of the human body enclosing or being enclosed by the cosmos.

ICONOGRAPHY

239. Alexander, Jonathan J. G. "Iconography and Ideology: Uncovering Social Meanings in Western Medieval Christian Art." *SI* 15 (1993): 1-44.
Treats how medieval Christian art can be read to reflect back to medieval society its own ideological values. Theoretical in orientation, the piece ties plates from numerous visual sources to a number of historical and cultural practices.

240. Anderson, Flemming G., et al. *Medieval Iconography and Narrative: A Symposium.* Odense: Odense Univ. Press, 1980.
Papers on various topics in medieval iconography and narrative read at the 19-20 November,1979 symposium at Odense University.

241. Braider, Christopher. *Refiguring the Real: Picture and Modernity in Word and Image, 1400-1700.* Princeton Univ. Press, 1993.
A theoretical study in which manuscript painting becomes a metaphor for literary and philosophical expression. Many plates.

242. Camille, Michael. *The Gothic Idol: Ideology and Image-Making in Medieval Art.* Cambridge: Cambridge Univ. Press, 1989.
A thorough study of what medieval people perceived as idols with numerous illustrations. Sections on pagan, Saracen, and Jewish idols follow "Gothic Idols," comprising idols of the church, of society, and of the mind.

243. Cassidy, Brendan, ed. *Iconography at the Crossroads: Papers from the Colloquium Sponsored by the Index of Christian Art. Princeton University 23-24 March 1990.* Index of Christian Art Occasional Papers, no. 2. Princeton Univ. Press, 1993.

Essays by different authors, among them Michael Camille, John Fleming, Keith Moxey, and Herbert Kessler on the subject of iconography, many focussing on, or discussing, the medieval period. Index.

244. Collins, Patrick J. *The N— Town Plays and Medieval Picture Cycles*. EDAM Monograph Series, no. 2. Kalamazoo, MI: The Medieval Institute, 1979.
Studies the presence in English cycle plays of certain motifs or abstract ideas made visual.

245. Davidson, Clifford. *Visualizing the Moral Life: Medieval Iconography and the Macro Moralities*. New York: AMS, 1989.
Studies the plays in the Macro Manuscript in the Folger Library from the point of view of their iconography and visual effects. Sections on themes involving sowing and reaping, castles, and alienation and reconciliation in drama. Plates and index.

246. Duchet-Suchaux, Gaston, ed. *Iconographie médiévale: Image, texte, contexte*. Paris: CNRS, 1990.
A collection of rather miscellaneous essays not really bearing on iconography as a subject so much as treating images of various kinds in illuminated manuscripts. Reviewed by Marcia Kupfer in *Speculum* 68, no. 3 (July 1993): 748-50.

247. Durand, Paul, and Didron, M. *Manuel d'iconographie chrétienne, grecque et latine*. Burt Franklin Research and Source Works Series, no. 45. New York: Burt Franklin, 1963.
The notes an eighteenth-century Byzantine monk, Dionysius, took on medieval wall paintings. He looked at iconographic representations of specific figures, the saints, the feasts of Mary, the Parables, and the Passion, as well as technical matters such as the fabrication and application of colors.

248. Esmeijer, Anna C. *Divina Quarternitas: A Preliminary Study in the Method and Application of Visual Exegesis*. Assen: Van Gorcum, 1978.

Concerned with visual exegesis as a technique in the Middle Ages, especially as related to various quadripartite forms such as the heavenly Jerusalem or the Four Rivers of Paradise. Numerous plates of these motifs in world maps and the like. In Dutch with an English summary.

249. Gurevich, Aaron J. *Das Weltbild des mittelalterlichen Menschen.* Munich: Beck, 1982.
    Originally published in Russian in 1972, this study treats the philosophical and visual universe of the Middle Ages, with a number of plates of cosmological schema. Each section, for example, microcosm and macrocosm, is followed by a bibliography, chiefly of German works.

250. Heckscher, William S. *Art and Literature: Studies in Relationship.* Edited by Egon Verheyer. Saecula Spiritualia, no. 17. Durham NC: Duke Univ. Press; Baden-Baden: Valentin Koerner, 1985.
    Consists of Hecksher's selected writings, miscellaneous in character, but all dealing with iconography, such as "Pagan Antiquity in Mediaeval Settings" and "Aphrodite as a nun."

251. Hermerén, Göran. *Representation and Meaning in the Visual Arts*: *A Study in the Methodology of Iconography and Iconology.* Lund Studies in Philosophy, no.1. Lund: Berlingska Boktryckeriet, 1969.
    A theoretical book with no illustrations, explaining how to interpret such concepts as allegory, depiction, and meaning in works of art.

252. Keller, John E., and Richard P. Kinkade. *Iconography in Medieval Spanish Literature.* Lexington: Univ. of Kentucky Press, 1984.
    Emphasizes the relation of (chiefly Spanish) art to the literature. Numerous plates and a selected bibliography. In spite of its English title, most of the essays are in Spanish.

253. Ladner, Gerhart B. *Images and Ideas in the Middle Ages: Selected Studies in History and Art.* 2 vols. Los Angeles, CA, and New York: The Center for Medieval and Renaissance Studies and the Kress Foundation, 1983.

A collection of articles in English, German, and Italian treating images and iconoclasm, symbols and images, the iconography of portraits, and the like.

254. Mâle, Emile. *L'art religieux du XIIe siècle en France: Etude sur les origines de l'iconographie du Moyen Age.* Paris: Armand Colin, 1953.
An history of twelfth-century religious art with numerous illustrations focussing on iconography. Covers such topics as the birth of monumental sculpture and the influence of illuminated manuscripts; influences of Eastern and Byzantine art on that of the west; influences of liturgy and liturgical drama; Suger; the saints; pilgrimage routes through Italy, France, and Spain; and encyclopaediae and their relation to art.

255. _____. *L'art religieux du XIIIe siècle en France: Etude sur l'iconographie du Moyen Age et sur ses sources d'inspiration.* Paris: Armand Colin, 1948.
This work studies the thirteenth century from the same perspective as the work by this author cited above. It is divided into sections such as nature, science, morality, and history.

256. _____. *L'art religieux de la fin du Moyen Age en France. Étude sur l'iconographie du Moyen Age et sur ses sources d'inspiration.* Paris: Armand Colin, 1949.
Studies the end of the Middle Ages in France from the same perspective as the two volumes mentioned above by this author. Sections on French iconography and Italian art, religious art and theater, the cult of saints, the theme of a combat between vices and virtues, death and the tomb, the end of the world and the Last Judgment.

257. Manion, Margaret M., and Bernard J. Muir, eds. *Medieval Texts and Images. Studies of Manuscripts from the Middle Ages.* Chur, Switzerland and Sidney, Harwook: Academic Publishers and Craftsman House, 1991.
Treats themes and visual topoi.

258. Marrow, James. "Symbol and Meaning in Northern European Art of the Late Middle Ages and the Early Renaissance." *Simiolus* 16 (1986): 150-69. Followed by a "Response to James Marrow," pp. 170-72, by Craig Harbison.
    Discusses the way in which modern critics *do* and the ways in which they *should* analyze medieval art, its iconography and function, with examples.

259. Nichols, Stephen G., Jr. *Romanesque Signs: Early Medieval Narrative and Iconography.* New Haven and London: Yale Univ. Press, 1983.
    Treats the way public and monumental art programs and narrative literature intersected from the eleventh century onward, and how sacred and heroic views of Charlemagne and Roland were used in the representation of contemporary kings and emperors.

260. Pernoud, Régine. *Couleurs du Moyen Age.* Images du Monde, no.1. Geneva and Paris: Editions Clairefontaines, 1987.
    Contains some theoretical discussion of images and some excellent plates of images from medieval manuscripts like encyclopaediae.

261. Pickering, F. P. *Essays on Medieval German Literature and Iconography.* Cambridge: Cambridge Univ. Press, 1980.
    This book is more generally useful to the iconographer than its title would suggest, as it ranges widely over medieval literature and art, touching on such topics as the Gothic treatment of the figurative Christ, fate and fortune, and the image of Byzantium in Western art.

262. Réau, Louis, *Iconographie de l'art Chrétien.* 6 Vols. Paris: Presses Universitaires de France,1955-59.
    Basic reference work for research in iconography. The first part is a general introduction to the subject, with discussion of many types of iconography: animal, human, liturgical, canonical and apocryphal books of the Bible, and saints and their cults. Part Two examines more specifically the two Testaments. Part Three is concerned in greater detail with the iconography of the saints, their patronage of various towns and cities and their attributes.

263. Schapiro, Meyer. *Words and Pictures: On the Literal and the Symbolic in the Illustration of a Text.* Approaches to Semiotics Paperback Series, no. 11. The Hague, Paris: Mouton, 1973.
A brief treatment of how European artists "invented" their images from the Middle Ages to the eighteenth century. Among the topics treated are representations of Exodus and frontal and profile representations of figures. Includes many plates and an index.

264. Schreckenberg, Heinz, and Kurt Schubert. *Jewish Historiography and Iconography in Early and Medieval Christianity.* Compendia Rerum Iudaicarum ad Novum Testamentum, no. 3. Jewish Traditions in Early Christian Literature, vol. 2. Aasen/Maastricht: Van Gorcum; Minneapolis: Fortress, 1992.
In Part One, Schreckenberg examines the portrayal of the Jewish historian Josephus in early Christian texts and in medieval Christian art. In Part Two, Schubert treats "Jewish Art in the Light of Jewish Tradition"; "The Holiness of the Synagogue and Its Figurative Decoration"; "Jewish Programmatic Painting: The Dura Europos Synagogue"; "Jewish Influence on Earliest Christian Paintings: The Via Latina Catacomb"; and "Jewish Traditions in Christian Painting Cycles: The Vienna Genesis and the Ashburnham Pentateuch." Each section is arranged by image discussed, such as Adam and Eve driven from Paradise or Jacob's dream at Bethel. Includes numerous plates and a bibliography.

265. Simonds, Peggy Munõz. *Iconographic Research in English Renaissance Literature: A Critical Guide.* New York: Garland Publishing, 1995.
Though later in emphasis than the period covered in the present guide, this volume offers useful pointers, especially in emblem literature, for the medievalist iconographer.

266. Smith, Earl Baldwin. *Early Christian Iconography and a School of Ivory Carvers in Provence.* Princeton Monographs in Art and Archeology, no. 6. Princeton Univ. Press, 1918.
Treats such themes as the Virgin in the Temple, the Annunciation at the Spring, the Nativity, the appearance of the star to the Magi

and their Adoration, the Massacre of the Innocents, Christ among the Doctors, the Baptism, the Miracles at Canna, Entry into Jerusalem, and Last Supper, with tables and plates at back showing works of art in which these figures are represented.

267. Straten, Roelof van. *ICONCLASS Browser System & Bibliography.* Version 2.0.Leiden/Utrecht: ICONCLASS Research and Development Group, 1991, 1994.
This is a computerized data collection for IBM Windows 3.1 machines drawn from *ICONCLASS* (item 271). In format it consists of seven computer disks and a browser user's and bibliography user's guide.

268. _____. *An Introduction to Iconography, Symbols, Allusions, and Meaning in the Visual Arts.* Translated by Patricia de Man. Langhorne, PA: Gordon and Breach,1994.
A small volume which seeks to acquaint the beginner in art history with the fundamentals of iconography. It is divided into a theoretical section (heavily indebted to Erwin Panofsky in methodology) and a practical section. The latter offers the main textual sources for religious and classical subjects and themes in chiefly northern European Renaissance art. Though the Middle Ages are treated, the medievalist will find information most generally where the same theme or subject has been rehandled in later art. The last part of the "practical' section makes much use of *ICONCLASS* (item 271). Straten's book is reviewed by Brendan Cassidy in *SI* 17 (1996): 432-5.

269. Szonyi, György E., ed. *European Iconography East and West: Selected Papers of the Szeged International Conference, June 9-12, 1993.* Symbola et Emblemata, no. 7. Leiden: Brill, 1995.
Eighteen papers on such topics as iconography and ideology, iconography and history, and emblems.

270. Trapp, J. B. "Iconography." *John Milton: Introductions.* Edited by John Broadbent. London: Cambridge Univ. Press, 1973, pp. 162-85.

Not by any means limited to Milton: this essay touches upon the following topics, images and myths, continuity and change, Creation and the Fall , the iconography of Adam and Eve, and of fallen angels. Sometimes these topics are treated very generally and at other times specifically with references to particular works of art.

271. Waal, van de Henri, et al. *ICONCLASS*: An Iconographic Classification System. Koninklijke Nederlandse Akademie van Wetenschappen Amsterdam: North-Holland Publishing Co., 1973-85.
This is a seven- volume system for classifying iconographic themes and motifs rather like that of a library cataloguing system and lending itself to computerization. It offers thematic bibliographies and a key word index. The great utility of this work is that the subjects are given alpha-numeric codes, so that the problems involved in indexing them by name are somewhat lessened.

272. Wittkower, Rudolf. *Allegory and the Migration of Symbols.* New York: Thames and Hudson, 1987.
A collection of this author's essays on various topics related to iconography. Contains items 273, 646, 755, 832, 862, 1445,1478, and 1832.

273. _____. "Interpretation of Visual Symbols." *Allegory and the Migration of Symbols* (item 272), pp. 174-87.
An excellent account of how images such as beards can be interpreted in early works of art.

MANUSCRIPT ILLUMINATION

General

274. Alexander, J. J. G. *Medieval Illuminators and Their Methods of Work*. New Haven: Yale Univ. Press, 1992.
Perhaps the best introduction to the subject. The first part deals with contemporary sources of information about, and technical aspects of, the art of manuscript decoration, as well as programs and marginal instructions for the illuminator. Later chapters consider illuminators from the early Romanesque period through the fifteenth cenury. As the author develops his topics he uses two or three manuscript miniatures or decorated initials to explain or illustrate the point being made. The book also contains appendices with artists' contracts, both the originals and in translations and a handlist of manuscripts still retaining preliminary drawings in the margins for the actual pictures. Many black-and-white and some color plates and an extensive bibliography. Reviewed by John B. Friedman in *M&H*, n.s., 21 (1994): 145-52.

275. Ancona, P. D', and E. Aeschlimann. *The Art of Illumination: An Anthology of Manuscripts from the Sixth to the Sixteenth Century*. Translated by Alison M. Brown with Additional Notes on the Plates by M. Alison Stones. London: Phaidon, 1969.
A short introduction tracing the development of European miniature paintings accompanies this attractive collection of annotated black-and-white and color plates. Bibliography.

276. Backhouse, Janet. *The Illuminated Manuscript*. Oxford: Phaidon, 1979.
A sumptuous selection of pictures of medieval manuscript illumination spanning 900 years with descriptions of the plates represented and some account of their history and importance.

277. Binski, Paul. *Painters*. Medieval Craftsmen Series. Toronto and Buffalo: Univ. of Toronto Press, 1991.
Explores medieval painting in the church as well as in domestic architecture. Seeks to reconstruct the processes involved in creating works of art from a social and economic standpoint. With many plates. Reviewed by Robert Calkins in *Speculum* 69, no.2 (April 1994): 421-3.

278. Branner, Robert. *Manuscript Painting in Paris during the Reign of Saint Louis*. Berkeley and Los Angeles: Univ. of California Press, 1977.
Treats the rise of manuscript ateliers, among other subjects pertaining to the development of teams of illuminators under the king's patronage.

279. Brown, Michelle P. *Understanding Illuminated Manuscripts: A Guide to Technical Terms*. Malibu, CA: J. Paul Getty Museum in association with the British Library, 1994.
Treats definitions and descriptions of terms used by and of scribes and illuminators, as well as techniques, processes, and materials in medieval manuscript painting. Arranged alphabetically according to term, with plates illustrating terms under discussion.

280. Brownrigg, Linda, ed. *Making the Medieval Book: Techniques of Production*. Los Altos Hills, CA: Anderson-Lovelace, The Red Gull Press, 1995.
Essays by various hands on the technical aspects of the handmade manuscript.

281. Bühler, Curt F. *The Fifteenth-Century Book: The Scribes, the Printers, the Decorators*. Philadelphia: Univ. of Pennsylvania Press, 1960.
Three lectures, each on one of the three subjects in the title. Some plates.

282. Byrne, Donal. "Manuscript Ruling and Pictorial Design in the Work of the Limbourgs, the Bedford Master and the Boucicaut Master." *AB* 66 (1984): 118-36.
Discusses the effect of ruling on the proportioning of the miniatures, treating mainly books of hours. Many plates.

283. Cahn, Walter. *Romanesque Bible Illumination.* Ithaca, NY: Cornell Univ. Press, 1982.
A thorough treatment, using plates of antique, Carolingian, Mozarab, Anglo-Saxon, and Ottonian illumination. Treats the programs of illustrations for various books of the Bible such as Samuel, Kings,

Psalms, and the prophets, as well as the artists and patrons of these manuscripts. Ends with a selected illustrated catalogue of Bibles written and illuminated from about 1000 to the beginning of the thirteenth century. Includes a selective bibliography and an index.

284. Calkins, Robert G. *Programs of Medieval Illumination.* The Franklin D. Murphy Lectures, no. 5. Lawrence: Helen Foresman Spencer Museum of Art and Univ. of Kansas Press, 1984.
Includes two lectures of particular interest to the medievalist. "The Golden Age of Imperial Illuminated Manuscripts" treats the development of decorative programs in early gospel books even when the illuminations were not always narrative scenes or figurative representations. "Fields and Fortresses in the Très Riches Heures" concerns this manuscript's program of calendar scenes and their relation to the socio-economic and administrative issues of Jean de Berri's age. Both lectures have many plates.

285. Davis-Weyer, Caecilia. *Early Medieval Art, 300-1150.* Sources and Documents in the History of Art Series. Englewood Cliffs, NJ: Prentice Hall, 1971.
This work treats medieval artists' materials, such as parchment, panels, pigments and their preparation, and the application of gold leaf as well as general processes such as underpainting, incaustic, and fresco application.

286. Delaissé, L. M. J. "Towards a History of the Medieval Book." *Miscellanea André Combes.* Edited by Antonio Piolanti. Vol. 2: *Studi Medievali.* Cathedra Sancti Thomae Pontificiae Universitatis Lateranensis, no. 4. Rome: Pontificiae Università Lateranense and Paris: Librairie Philosophique J. Vrin, 1967-68, pp. 27-39.
Examines the state of scholarship on the medieval book at the time, considering what has been done and what approaches should be taken.

287. Diringer, David. *The Illuminated Book: Its History and Production.* London: Faber and Faber, 1967.

Considers ancient book production before proceeding to an extensive study, by century and type, of the production of medieval manuscripts. Plates.

288. Donati, Lamberto. *Bibliografia della miniatura.* 2 vols. Florence: L.S. Olschki, 1972.
Extensive bibliography of illuminated manuscripts of Italian provenance. Volume Two consists of plates.

289. Farquhar, James Douglas. *Creation and Imitation: The Work of a Fifteenth-Century Manuscript Illuminator.* Nova University Studies in the Humanities, no. 1. Fort Lauderdale: Nova Univ. Press, 1976.
Uses some Bruges workshop manuscripts to generalize about the work of a fifteenth-century Flemish master. Considers creation and imitation in workshop practice. Many plates from a select group of fifteenth-century manuscripts, codicological descriptions, selected bibliography, and index.

290. Grabar, André, and Carl Nordenfalk. *Early Medieval Painting from the Fourth to the Eleventh Century.* Lausanne, Switzerland: SKIRA, 1957.
Contains a large number of color plates and treats early medieval bookpainting, as well as murals and mosaics. There are indices of manuscripts, names, and places.

291. Hamel, Christopher de. *Scribes and Illuminators.* Medieval Craftsmen Series. Toronto and Buffalo: Univ. of Toronto Press, 1992.
Examines the successive stages in the production of a manuscript. Treats the roles of stationers and booksellers, and the importance of exemplars, patrons, prices, and the like from the eleventh to the fourteenth century. Reviewed by Robert Calkins in *Speculum* 69, no. 2 (April 1994): 421-3.

292. Herbert, J. A. *Illuminated Manuscripts.* Burt Franklin Bibliographical Series, no. 11. New York: Burt Franklin, 1958.

First published in 1911, this work is an art historical study of illuminated manuscripts divided according to place and time. It treats only the vellum codex from classical antiquity through the age of print. Some plates.

293. Hindman, Sandra. "The Illustrated Book: An Addendum to the State of Research in Northern European Art." *AB* 68 (1986): 536-42.
Chiefly a critical introduction to the scholarship on the illustrated book, discussing strengths and weaknesses of various recent approaches.

294. Leroquais, Victor. *Les psautiers manuscrits latins des bibliothèques publiques de France*. Mâcon: Protat Frères, 1940-41.
A basic study of the psalter, both illuminated and not, with examples drawn from a variety of French collections.

295. Middleton, Henry J. *Illuminated Manuscripts in Classical and Medieval Times: Their Art and Technique*. Cambridge: Cambridge Univ. Press, 1892.
Similar in makeup to Diringer's book noted above, un-technical and easy to use. Plates.

296. Mitchell, Sabrina. *Medieval Manuscript Painting*. Compass History of Art Series. New York: Viking, 1965.
Comprised chiefly of color plates. Opens with a discussion of Romanesque, Gothic, and International Style manuscript illumination. Among the subjects treated are manuscripts commissioned by René d'Anjou and books painted by Jean Fouquet.

297. Mombello, Gianni. *La tradizione manuscritta dell'Epistre Othea di Christine de Pisan. Prolegomeni all'edizione deo testo*. Memorie dell'Accademia delle Scienze di Torino, Classe di Scienze morali, Storiche et Filologiche, 4th ser., vol. 16. Turin: Accademia delle Scienze, 1967.
This is the standard treatment of the manuscript tradition associated with this work.

298. Morgan, Nigel. "Aspects of Colour in English and French Manuscript Painting of the Late 13th Century." *Europäische Kunst um 1300, Akten des XXV. Internationalen Kongresses für Kunstgeschichte. Wien, 1983.* Edited by Gerhard Schmidt and Elisabeth Liskar. Vienna: H. Bohläu,1986, pp. 111-16.
Studies the use of color—particularly yellows and greens—to model drapery forms in tones of light and shade.

299. Nash, Susie. *Manuscript Illumination in Amiens between France and Flanders in the Fifteenth Century.* London: British Library, 1996.
This study of book painting in the Burgundian territories focusses on the important illuminator Simon Marmion and the city of Amiens as a center for book production and export. Studies a group of manuscripts made there with eight color and seventy black-and-white illustrations.

300. Pächt, Otto. *Book Illumination in the Middle Ages: An Introduction.* London: Harvey Miller; New York and Oxford: Oxford Univ. Press, 1986.
Excellent introduction to the subject with chapters on pictorial decoration, initials, and Bible, psalter, and apocalypse illustration. Numerous plates, select bibliography, and index.

301. Pirani, Emma. *Gothic Illuminated Manuscripts.* Translated by Margaret Crosland. London: Hamlyn, 1970.
A beautifully produced small book consisting chiefly of color plates. The bulk of the work treats the different schools of illumination in Italy, France, Germany, Bohemia, and England.

302. Robb, David M. *The Art of the Illuminated Manuscript.* The Philadelphia Art Alliance. Cranbury, NJ: A. S. Barnes, 1973.
Treats illumination by regional styles and origins. Studies Byzantine, Carolingian, Ottonian, and earlier and later Gothic art up through the fifteenth century. Many plates and a bibliography, index and an appendix on special types of illuminated manuscripts such as liturgical, service, and devotional books.

303. Toubert, Hélène. *Mise en page et mise en texte du livre manuscrit.* Edited by Henri-Jean Martin, and Jean Vézin. Paris: Editions du Cercle de la Librairie—Promodis, 1990.
This extremely useful work by various hands surveys the structural history of the handmade book from the oldest Egyptian papryi down to the age of print. Especially valuable are the various essays on the Biblical, classical, legal, and university texts and the various forms of miniature placement: marginal, full page, and the like. Virtually all the manuscripts treated are French, from French collections. Many color and black-and-white plates.

By Country of Origin

[Armenia]

304. Mathews, Thomas F., and Roger S. Wieck, eds. *Treasures in Heaven: Armenian Illuminated Manuscripts.* New York: Pierpont Morgan Library and Princeton Univ. Press, 1994.
Treats the background of Armenian manuscript painting. Many plates.

[Bohemia]

305. Beyerle, K. "Astronomische Handschriften im Böhmischen Königshofe." *MIOG* 39 (1922-23): 34-40.
Considers some important Aratus manuscripts containing im ages of the constellations, with many high-quality plates.

306. Drobná, Zoroslava. "K problematice bible boskovské" *Umeni* 13, no. 2 (1965): 127-38.
A study of the Boskowitzer Bible, one of the great monuments of Bohemian manuscript illumination, with some plates of miniatures and a German summary.

307. Dvorakova, Vlasta, et al. *Gothic Mural Painting in Bohemia and Moravia 1300-1378.* London: Oxford Univ. Press, 1964.
     A collection of articles by four authors on different aspects of this topic, each dealing with a very specific region or time period within that stated in the title. About half the volume consists of plates. Includes also a catalogue, organized by the churches in which the wall paintings are found; an iconographical index; and a bibliography.

308. Frinta, Mojmír. "The Master of the Gerona Martyrology and Bohemian Illumination." *AB* 46 (1964): 283-306.
     Disputes the notion of the first two decades of the fifteenth century as a period of esthetic stagnancy in Bohemian painting and finds that the productions of Bohemian ateliers rivalled the works of the best Franco-Flemish artists. Numerous plates.

309. Hermon, Sharon. "Illuminated Manuscripts of the Court of King Wenceslas IV of Bohemia." *Scriptorium* 9 (1967): 115-24.
     Discusses the characteristics and techniques of thirteenth- and fourteenth-century Bohemian manuscript illumination, looking at some particular manuscripts and with a special interest in emblematic figures and the unique borders of these manuscripts.

310. Kletzel, Otto. "Studien zu böhmischen Buchmalerie." *MJK* 7 (1933): 1-76.
     Though primarily about the late fourteenth-century St. Florian and Zittau missals, this study treats canon pages of various Bohemian missals, the "te igitur" motif, and the use of acanthus, with such a large selection of excellent plates that it serves as a good overview of Bohemian manuscript illumination of this period.

311. Krása, Josef. *Die Handschriften König Wenzels IV.* Vienna: Forum, 1971.
     A study of Wenceslas and the manuscripts he commissioned. Treats not only the Bibles but also the astronomical manuscripts. The important symbolism of bathing and bath houses common in the illumination of these codices is also discussed. There is as well a detailed study of Bohemian manuscript illumination comprising

Chapter Four. Many color and black-and-white plates and a chronological list of manuscripts made for Wenceslas complete the work.

312. Krofta, Jan, et al. *Les primitifs de Bohème, l'art gothique en Tchécoslovaquie 1350-1420.* Brussels-Rotterdam: Palais des Beaux Arts, 1966.
Three essays in French by well-known scholars of Bohemian art on the relationship of the Netherlands to Bohemian sculpture and painting under the house of Luxembourg, accompany this beautiful collection of plates of various works of Bohemian art, each with its own description.

313. Kutal, Albert. *Gothic Art in Bohemia and Moravia.* Feltham: Hamlyn,1972.
Standard study of medieval Bohemian painting by an eminent authority. Many plates and a bibliography of works mostly in Czech.

314. Matejcek, Antonín, and Jaroslav Pesina. "La miniature tchèque." *L'Art vivant* 4, no. 78 (March 1928): 215-19.
Describes the distinctive style of Czech miniatures in comparison to other national styles and influences.

315. _____. *La peinture gothique tchèque, 1350-1450.* Prague: Melantrich, 1950.
A preface and an essay on the subject, as well as a bibliography precede this large catalogue of works. Each black-and-white or color plate is described.

316. Pesina, Jaroslav, et al. *Ceské umeni Gotické 1350-1420.* Prague: Academia, 1970.
A *catalogue raisonné* of Bohemian art with numerous excellent black-and-white plates and an extensive bibliography.

317. Schmidt, G. "Neues Material zur Österreichischen Buchmalerei der Spätgotik in slowakischen Handschriften." *OZKD* 18 (1964): 34-40.

Useful collection of high quality plates drawn from important manuscripts like the Vienna Missal and Prayerbook.

[England]

318. Alexander, J. J. G. *Insular Manuscripts from the 6th to the 9th Century*. A Survey of Manuscripts Illuminated in the British Isles. Vol. 2. London: Harvey Miller, 1978.
A catalogue with numerous plates, some in color. Introduction to this period in manuscript painting, index, and motif index, and also a detailed analysis of the manuscripts in the catalogue, which lists them according to the type of book, school of illumination, or region of origin. Extensive bibliographies accompany each catalogue entry.

319. Harrison, F. *English Manuscripts of the Fourteenth Century c.1250-1400*. London: The Studio, 1937.
An introduction discussing general background and history as well as specific genres such as the illustrated apocalypse, bestiary, and psalter. The book also considers illuminators and their patrons as well as such technical issues as pigments and painting techniques. There are twenty-four color plates taken from some of the monuments of fourteenth-century English manuscript painting, each with a detailed description.

320. Kauffmann, C. M. *Romanesque Manuscripts 1066-1190*. A Survey of Manuscripts Illuminated in the British Isles. Vol. 3. Edited by J. J. G. Alexander. London: Harvey Miller, 1975.
Similar to item 318 for the later period.

321. Kuhn, Charles L. "Herman Scheerre and English Illumination of the Early Fifteenth Century." *AB* 22 (1940): 138-56.
Treats the influence of this very important Continental illuminator on English manuscript painting of the fifteenth century and how this influence is felt in a sudden change in style. Many plates.

322. Marks, Richard, and Nigel Morgan. *The Golden Age of English Manuscript Painting: 1200-1500*. London: Chatto and Windus, 1981.

The bulk of this book is comprised of forty plates with commentaries. They are preceded by an introduction, list of manuscripts, and selected bibliography.

323. Millar, Eric G. *English Illuminated Manuscripts from the Xth to the XIIIth Century.* Paris and Brussels: Les Editions G. van Oest, 1926.
Surveys the art of book illumination in England from the tenth century to the year 1300. Proceeds chronologically, providing descriptions of the one hundred plates. The work ends with a handlist of English illuminated manuscripts and an index.

324. _____. *English Illuminated Manuscripts of the XIVth and XVth-Centuries.* Paris and Brussels: Les Editions G. van Oest, 1928.
Considers the East Anglian and International styles of miniature painting, concentrating on famous examples from such deluxe manuscripts as the Ormsby, Gorleston, Queen Mary, and Luttrell Psalters, as well as works of Walter de Milemete, the Bohun manuscripts, and the Sherborne Missal. Many excellent black-and-white plates.

325. Morgan, Nigel. *Early Gothic Manuscripts [I] 1190-1250,* and *[2]1250-1285.* A Survey of Manuscripts Illuminated in the British Isles. Vol. 4. Edited by J. J. G. Alexander. 2 vols. London: Harvey Miller, 1982.
Similar to item 318 for the later period.

326. Rickert, Margaret. *Painting in Britain: The Middle Ages.* Baltimore, MD: Penguin, 1954.
Proceeds chronologically from Hiberno-Saxon of the seventh through the ninth centuries up to the last chapter on the painting of the end of the Middle Ages. Each chapter deals with one period, providing the historical background and a discussion of the painting. Very informative and detailed, with numerous plates.

327. Sandler, Lucy Freeman. *Gothic Manuscripts 1285-1385.* A Survey of Manuscripts Illuminated in the British Isles: Vol. 5. Edited by

J. J. G. Alexander. 2 vols. London: Harvey Miller, and Oxford
Univ. Press 1986.
Similar to item 325 for the later period.

328. Saunders, Elfrida O. *English Illumination.* 2 vols. Florence:
Pantheon,1928.
A history of illumination with sections on the Celtic, Anglo-Saxon,
and Romanesque periods. Treats issues such as the transition from
Romanesque to Gothic as well as genres like bestiary and
apocalypse, and styles like East Anglian and International Gothic.
Has a bibliography and a large number of plates in Volume One.
Plates comprise all of Volume Two.

329. Scott, Kathleen. *Later Gothic Manuscripts- The Fifteenth Century.*
A Survey of Manuscripts Illuminated in the British Isles. Vol.6.
Edited by J. J. G. Alexander. London: Harvey Miller, 1997.
Similar to item 327 for the later period

330. Temple Elzbieta. *Anglo-Saxon Manuscripts 900-1066.* A Survey of
Manuscripts Illuminated in the British Isles. Vol. 2. Edited by J. J.
G. Alexander. London: Harvey Miller, 1976.
Similar to item 325 for the earlier period.

331. Turner, D. H. *Early Gothic Illuminated Manuscripts in England.*
London: British Museum, 1969.
A description of the early Gothic style and its development, touching
on a number of different manuscripts, for which color or black-and-
white plates are included, mostly from manuscripts in the collections
of the British Library.

[France]

332. Meiss, Millard, et al. *French Painting in the Time of Jean de Berry:*
The Late Fourteenth Century and the Patronage of the Duke. 2
vols. National Gallery of Art: Kress Foundation. Studies in the
History of European Art, no. 2. London and New York:
Phaidon, 1969.

Treats Jean de Berry in detail, his life, his role as a patron of illuminated books, as well as his portraits, arms and emblems. Other sections treat artists associated with him, like the Parement and Brussels Initials masters, Beauneveu, and specific manuscripts like the Petites Heurs, Vatican Bible, Brussels Hours and Grands Heures. The whole is accompanied by tables of historical events, genealogies, discussion of Jean's children, and inventories of his possessions. There is a bibliography and index. Volume Two is comprised of plates.

333. _____. *French Painting in the Time of Jean de Berry: The Limbourgs and Their Contemporaries.* 2 vols. National Gallery of Art: Kress Foundation Studies in the History of European Art. London and New York: Phaidon, 1974.
Treats the illustration of secular history and the response to antiquity in early fifteenth-century Paris. The biographies of the Limbourgs, such as are known, are given and their great manuscripts, the Belles Heures, and Très Riches Heures are studied in some detail. Appendices, bibliography, and index complete Volume One while Volume Two is comprised of plates.

334. _____. *French Painting in the Time of Jean de Berry: The Boucicaut Master.* National Gallery of Art: Kress Foundation Studies in the History of European Art, no. 3. London: Phaidon, 1968.
The second half of the volume consists of plates accompanying the discussion of the Boucicaut Hours. Topics touched on are the relation of the Boucicaut master to others in the workshop, the dated manuscripts which can be associated with him, and his relation to Jacques Coene. There is a catalogue of manuscripts and a variety of appendices on different aspects of this painter's life and times followed by a bibliography and index.

335. Thomas, Marcel. *The Golden Age: Manuscript Painting at the Time of Jean Duke of Berry.* Translated by Ursula Molinaro and Bruce Benderson. New York: George Braziller, 1979.
Forty plates drawn from great manuscripts with commentaries, introduction, and select bibliography.

[Germany]

336. Amira, Karl. *Die Dresdener Bilderhandschrift des Sachsenspiegels.*
     Leipzig: Hiersemann, 1902-06.
     Studies an important codex of this illustrated popularizing custumal
     law manuscript.

337. Beer, Ellen J. *Beiträge zur oberrheinischen Buchmalerei in der
     ersten Halfte des 14. Jahrhunderts, unter besonderer
     Berücksichtigung der Initialornamentik.* Basel: Birkhäuser,
     1959.
     Studies the illuminated manuscripts of Austrian origin made in the
     early fourteenth century and focusses on illuminated and decorated
     initials. Sixty-nine plates.

338. Brandl, Rainer. "Art or Craft? Art and the Artist in Medieval
     Nuremberg." *Gothic and Renaissance Art in Nuremberg, 1300-
     1550.* Munich-New York: Prestel-Verlag, Metropolitan Museum
     of Art, 1986, pp. 51-60.
     Discusses artistic activity and artists' guilds in this important
     German city.

339. Früehmorgen-Voss, Hella. *Text und Illustration im Mittelalter:
     Aufsätze zu den Wechselbeziehungen zwischen Literatur und
     bildender Kunst.* Edited by Norbert Ott. Munich: Beck, 1975.
     A collection of the author's earlier essays on a variety of topics
     devoted to manuscript studies of the illustrative programs of
     medieval romances, especially those with Tristan illustration. Ott
     gives a useful handlist of known representions of Tristan and Iseult
     in medieval art. **See also Tristan.**

340. Holter, Kurt, and Karl Oettinger. *Les principaux manuscrits à
     peintures de la Bibliothèque Nationale de Vienne.* Paris: Bulletin
     de la société française de reproductions de manuscrits à
     peintures,1937.

This work concerns the most important illuminated manuscripts in the Austrian National Library.

341. Koehler, Wilhelm. *Die Karolingischen Miniaturen.* Vol. I: *Die Schule von Tours.* Vol. 1: *Die Ornamentik.* Berlin: Deutscher Verein für Kunstwissenschaft, 1930. Vol. 2: *Die Bilder.* Reprint. Berlin: Deutscher Verein für Kunstwissenschaft, 1935.
A general introduction to Carolingian miniature painting with plates and index.

342. _____. *Die Karolingischen Miniaturen.* Vol. II: *Die Hofschule Karls des Grossen.* Berlin: Deutscher Verein für Kunstwissenschaft, 1958.
Treats manuscripts of courtly commissioning.

343. _____. *Die Karolingischen Miniaturen.* Vol. III: *Die Gruppe des Wiener Krönungs-Evangeliars—Metzer Handschriften.* Berlin: Deutscher Verein für Kunstwissenschaft, 1960.
Treats the great gospel books of this period.

344. _____, and Florence Mütherich. *Die Karolingischen Miniaturen.* Vol. IV: *Die Hofschule Kaiser Lothar— Einzelhandschriften aus Lotharingien.* Berlin: Deutscher Verein für Kunstwissenschaft, 1971.
Treats Ottonian illuminated manuscripts.

345. Koschorreck, Walter, and Wilfried Werner, eds. *Die grosse Heidelberger Liederhandschrift. Faksimile-Ausgabe in 12 Lieferungen.* Frankfurt: Insel, 1975, 1978.
Facsimile of this famous illuminated manuscript.

346. Mayr-Harting, Henry. *Ottonian Book Illumination: An Historical Survey.* 2 vols. London: Harvey Miller, 1991.
The first volume covers social and political themes depicted in Ottonian book illumination and the second is organized according to the different manuscripts it discusses. Both intersperse numerous plates with discussion of the subjects depicted in them and both include a chronology of the political history of the Ottonian period,

table of principal Ottonian illuminated books, bibliography, indices of iconography, and of manuscripts, and a general index.

347. Mittler, Elmar, and Wilfried Werner, eds. *Codex Manesse: Katalog zur Ausstellung vom 12. Juni bis 4. September 1988 Universitatsbibliothek Heidelberg.* Heidelberg: Braus,1988.
     Detailed survey of the contents of this richly illustrated codex.

348. Müller, Ulrich, and Wilfried Werner, eds. *Die Grosse Heidelberger 'Manessische' Liederhandschrift.* Göppingen: Alfred Kümmerle, 1971.
     A photographic facsimile of the Heidelberg Manesse codex, with a very brief introduction and no commentary.

349. Mutherich, Florence, and Joachim E. Gaehde. *Carolingian Painting.* New York: George Braziller, 1976.
     Excellent introduction to the subject with many color and black-and-white plates and an extensive bibliography.

350. Schmidt, Gerhard. *Die Malerschule von St.Florian. Beiträge zur suddeutschen Malerei zu Ende des 13. und im 14. Jahrhundert.* Graz: H. Böhlaus, 1962.
     Discusses the important center for book illumination at St. Florian and describes some of the books made there. Plates and bibliography.

351. Schmidt-Wiegand, Ruth, ed. *Eike von Repgow, Sachsenspiegel: Die Wolfenbuettler Bilderhandschrift Cod. Guelf. 3.1, Faksimile, Text-und Kommentarband.* Berlin: Akademie, 1992.
     A facsimile edition of this manuscript, including a transcription of the original Middle High German text and a parallel modern German translation.

352. _____. *Text-Bild-Interpretation: Untersuchungen zu den Bilderhandschriften des Sachsenspiegels.* 2 vols. Munchen: W. Fink, 1986.
     Volume One is a study, by various authors, of the intellectual and artistic backgrounds of this fascinating work containing popularized custumal law. The last section also deals with the heraldry of the

manuscripts. Volume Two consists of plates of the miniatures in manuscripts of this work. Includes bibliographical references, a handlist of manuscripts, and detailed indices.

353. Stange, Alfred. *Deutsche Malerei der Gotik.* Berlin and Munich: Deutscher Kunstverlag, 1934-58.
General introduction to German Gothic painting of all types.

354. Walther, Ingo F., and Gisela Siebert, eds. *Codex Manesse: Die Miniaturen der Grossen Heidelberger Liederhandschrift.* Frankfurt am Main: Insel, 1988.
Study and reproduction of the miniatures. Includes bibliographical references.

[Italy]

355. Stevenson, T. B. *Miniature Decoration in the Vatican Virgil: A Study in Late Antique Iconography.* Tübingen: Ernst Wasmuth, 1983.
Treats this famous illuminated Virgil manuscript, now Vatican Library MS Lat. 3225, and one of some twenty codices of classical Latin authors written in rustic capitals. Provides an iconographic analysis of the miniatures and argues that this as well as similar books are Italian and date from the late fourth or early fifth centuries. Includes plates of miniatures from the codex as well as from a number of iconographically related art works.

[Netherlands and Flanders]

356. Byvanck, Alexander William. *La miniature dans les Pays-Bas septentrionaux.* Paris: Les éditions d'art et d'histoire, 1937.
One of the most important treatments of the miniatures of Flemish manuscripts.

357. _____, and G. J. Hoogewerff. *Noord-Nederlandsche miniaturen in handschriften der 14e, 15e en 16e eeuwen.* 3 vols. 's-Gravenhage: Martin Nijhoff, 1922-25.
Catalogue-handlist of illustrated and illuminated Flemish manuscripts and their miniatures. See Item 376.

358. Courtens, André. *Romanesque Art in Belgium.* Translated by J. A. Kennedy. Brussels: Vokaer, 1969.
     Treats the earliest art forms in this region in various media. Plates.

359. Cutler, Charles. *Northern Painting: From Pucelle to Breughel.* New York and Chicago: Holt, Rinehart, and Winston, 1968.
     General introduction to the painting, chiefly panel, of northern Europe. Plates and bibliography.

360. Delaissé, L. M. J. *A Century of Dutch Manuscript Illumination.* Berkeley: Univ. of California Press, 1968.
     An extended essay largely on "Dutch style," whose dominant characteristic is "a deep sensibility in regard to the visible aspects of nature." Argues too that events in Flanders in the 1490's were predated by developments in Utrecht and Guelders.

361. Dogaer, Georges. *Flemish Miniature Painting in the 15th and 16th Centuries.* Amsterdam: B. M. Israël B.V., 1987.
     An introduction which goes through all the different schools and artists of the period, providing for each a short discussion, plates, bibliography, and a finding list of manuscripts. Probably the single most useful introduction to Netherlandish book painting.

362. Eemans, Marc. *Les trésors de la peinture flamande.* Brussels: Meddens, 1963.
     Touches on the great examples of late medieval and early Renaissance Flemish work, chiefly panel.

363. Fierens, M. Paul, et al. *L'art en Belgique du Moyen Age à nos jours.* Brussels: La Renaissance du Livre, 1947.
     Provides a chronological history of architecture, sculpture, and painting in Belgium beginning with the eleventh century and supplemented with numerous plates and index. Of particular interest is the section by Jacques Lavalleye," La peinture et l'enlumineure des origines à la fin du XVe siècle."

364. *Fifteenth-Century Flemish Manuscripts in Cambridge Collections.* *TCBS* 10, no. 2 (1992).
A special issue of this journal with essays by different authors on Flemish art with plates and bibliography. The work concludes with general and iconographic indices.

365. Geurts, A. J., ed. *Ontsluiting van middeleeuwse handschriften in de Nederland.* Nijmegen: Alfa, 1987.
Deals with the state of manuscript studies in the Netherlands based on papers given in 1984 and 1988 in Nijmegen and Groningen.

366. Gibson, Walter S. *Hieronymous Bosch: An Annotated Bibliography.* Reference Publications in Art History. Boston, MA: G. K. Hall, 1983.
Organized by the focus of the particular study but includes indices of authors, paintings, and drawings attributed to Bosch, and subjects and symbols in the works.

367. Goffin, Arnold. *L'art religieux en Belgique: La peinture des origines à la fin du XVIIIe siècle.* Paris and Brussels: Librairie Nationale d'art et d'histoire, G. Van Oest, 1924.
Proceeds chronologically from the Middle Ages up through the eighteenth century. Begins with the characteristics of medieval painting, symbolism, the birth of realism, Saint Francis of Assisi and religious realism, the influence of the cycle plays on art, mural paintings, guilds, artistic centers, Belgian artists serving French princes and their works, and the *Très Riches Heures* of the Duc de Berry. With black-and-white plates.

368. Harbison, Craig. "Realism and Symbolism in Early Flemish Painting." *AB* 66 (1984): 588-602.
Examines the sources of the move toward realism in Flemish painting beginning around the fifteenth century. Discusses particularly the different approaches of Van Eyck, Campin, and Van der Weyden as to how the visible world operates, especially their views on the place of symbolism. With plates.

369. Hindman, Sandra. *Text and Image in Fifteenth-Century Illustrated Dutch Bibles.* Corpus Sacrae Scripturae Neerlandicae Medii Aevi. Miscellanea, no. 1. Leiden: Brill, 1977.
Treats such topics as the religious and historical background for, and place of, the first "history" Bibles in the Dutch Biblical tradition, and narrative illustrations, and pictorial realism in the miniature cycles in these works. Bibliography, index, and numerous plates.

370. Horst, K. van der, ed. *Masters and Miniatures. Proceedings of the Congress on Medieval Manuscript Illumination in the Northern Netherlands. (Utrecht, 10-13 December, 1989).* Doornspijk: Davaco, 1991.
Important collection of articles on illuminated and illustrated manuscripts, chiefly Netherlandish, by many authorities. Numerous plates.

371. Kaufmann, Thomas Da Costa, and Virginia Roehrig Kaufmann. "The Sanctification of Nature: Observations on the Origins of Trompe l'Oeil in Netherlandish Book Painting of the Fifteenth and Sixteenth Centuries." *JPGMJ* 19 (1991): 43-64.
Examines the rise of interest in *trompe-l'oeil* painting in the late fifteenth and early sixteenth centuries and such devices as casting shadows, and the illusion of objects piercing the page or being attached to it by a thread or a pin, or objects depicted as close to their actual size to create the illusion that the objects depicted are lying on the page. Also treats the practice in illuminated Ghent-Bruges manuscripts of storing pilgrim badges and flowers acquired on pilgrimage within a book of hours, often by pinning or sewing.

372. Korteweg, Anne S., ed. *Kriezels, aubergines en takkenbossen. Randversiering in Noordnederlandse handschriften uit de vijftiende eeuw.* 's-Gravenhage: Rijksmuseum Meermano-Westreenianum/Koninklijke Bibliothek, 1992.
A study of the decorative pen work flourishing in medieval manuscripts, chiefly Flemish, with a great many fine plates.

373. Lane, Barbara G. *Flemish Painting outside Bruges, 1400-1500: An Annotated Bibliography.* Reference Publications in Art History. Boston, MA: G. K. Hall, 1986.
Though this book does not consider manuscript painting, it is a valuable resource for the study of late medieval Netherlandish panel painters, such as Robert Campin and his Mérode Altar Piece. Van Eyck, Petrus Christus, Memling, and their followers are not treated here but in other bibliographies in this series.

374. Liebaers, Herman, et al., eds. *Flemish Art: From the Beginnings to Now.* Antwerp: Mercatorfonds, 1988.
A large anthology of Flemish art organized chronologically and by medium with numerous plates. Each section is written by a different specialist in that area.

375. Marrow, James H. "Dutch Manuscript Painting in Context: Encounters with the Art of France, the Southern Netherlands and Germany." *Masters and Miniatures* (item 370), pp. 53-88.
Argues that Dutch manuscript painting of this period is based overwhelmingly upon the imitation of Flemish manuscript painting.

376. _____. "Prolegomena to a New Descriptive Catalogue of Dutch Illuminated Manuscripts." *MN* 1 (1987): 295-309.
Discusses a replacement volume for the standard work by Byvanck-Hoogewerff mentioned above.

377. _____, et al., eds. *The Golden Age of Dutch Manuscript Painting.* New York: George Braziller, 1990.
Essays on Dutch manuscript painting of the very late fourteenth to the very early sixteenth centuries with an introduction by Marrow. Numerous plates, bibliography, and index.

378. Mély, F. de. *Les primitifs et leurs signatures: Les miniaturistes.* Paris: Geuthner, 1913.
Discusses the changes in and meanings of the signatures of miniature painters from the year 817 chronologically up until the sixteenth century with numerous black-and-white plates. Index.

379. Mundy, E. James. *Painting in Bruges, 1470-1550: An Annotated Bibliography.* Reference Publications in Art History. Boston, MA: G. K. Hall, 1985.
   Despite the title of this work it does not treat manuscript paintings, but focusses on the famous panel painters like Hans Memling.

380. Oliver, Judith. *Gothic Manuscript Illumination in the Diocese of Liège (c.1250-c.1330).* Louvain: Uitgeveri Peeters, 1989.
   Studies manuscripts produced by workshops—often for export—in this important book center.

381. Smits, K. *De Iconografie van de nederlandsche primitieven.* Amsterdam: de Spieghel, 1933.
   Though this work does not deal with manuscript illuminations, it considers the Flemish use of typical iconography of God, Old Testament scenes, Christ and Mary, the saints, and the Four Last Things as these appear in painters like Robert Campin. Many plates and a useful finding list.

382. Upton, Joel M. *Petrus Christus: His Place in Fifteenth-Century Flemish Painting.* University Park, PA and London: Pennsylvania State Univ. Press, 1990.
   Analysis of the art of this fifteenth-century painter and his historical context with numerous plates, bibliography, and index.

383. Wilson, Jean C. "Marketing Paintings in Late Medieval Flanders and Brabant." *Artistes, artisans, et production artistique* (item 156), pp. 621-27.
   Discusses the export trade of manuscripts, guild restrictions, illuminators' marks and the like.

Cycles of Illustration

384. Bober, Harry. "An Illustrated Medieval School-Book of Bede's *De Natura Rerum.*" *JWAG* 19-20 (1956-57): 65-97.

Describes and analyzes the Walters Art Gallery "cosmography," Walters MS 73, with plates of its unusual illustrations and discussion of its composition and sources. Bober discusses the illustrations and identifies the manuscript as a medieval scientific compendium, though very different in its more abstract character from the scenic and figural presentations of typical medieval book painting.

385. Laborde, Alexandre de. *Les manuscrits à peintures de la Cité de Dieu de Saint Augustin.* 3 vols. Paris: Pour la société des bibliophiles français, E. Rahir, 1909.
Facsimile and study of this illustrated vernacular version of the *City of God.*

386. Pächt, Otto. *The Rise of Pictorial Narrative in Twelfth-Century England.* Oxford: Clarendon, 1962.
This major study of the topic treats Anglo-Saxon narratives, the twelfth-century Renaissance, pictorial representations, and litugical drama. Index and plates.

387. Smeyers, M. *La miniature.* Typologie des sources du Moyen Age occidental, no. 8. Turnhout: Brepols, 1974.
Though, like other works in this series, this volume has no plates, it introduces the beginner to most aspects of medieval illumination such as techniques, workshops, iconographic motifs, and *mises-en-page.* Concise bibliography.

388. Smith, Sharon O. Dunlap. *Illustrations of Raoul de Presles' Translation of St. Augustine's City of God between 1375 and 1420.* New York: Garland, 1983.
Study of this important vernacular version of the *City of God* with eighty-one plates.

Horae, or Books of Hours

389. Backhouse, Janet. *Book of Hours*. London: The British Library, 1985.
      A small introductory volume with thirty color and forty-four black-and-white plates from various books of hours, chiefly in the British Library.

390. Donovan, Claire. *The de Brailes Hours: Shaping the Book of Hours in Thirteenth-Century Oxford*. Toronto Medieval Texts and Translations, no. 7. Toronto and Buffalo: Univ. of Toronto Press, 1991.
      Treats a very early book of hours illuminated by the well-known Oxford painter, William de Brailes. While not a facsimile, this detailed study of a single manuscript with an introduction is important for the issue of female ownership and commissioning of manuscripts. Reviewed by Jeffrey Hamburger in *Speculum* 68, no. 4 (October 1993): 1103-5.

391. Harthan, John. *Books of Hours and Their Owners*. London: Thames and Hudson, 1977.
      An introduction to the evolution, contents, decoration, and social aspects of books of hours combined with a collection of color plates and descriptions of a large number of examples. A select reading list and index complete this volume.

392. Leroquais, Victor. *Les livres d'heures manuscrits de la Bibliothèque Nationale*. 2 vols. and supplement. Paris: Imprimerie Nationale, 1927-43.
      Basic guide to the book of hours as a devotional medium, focussing on those in the collections of the Bibliothèque Nationale.

393. Saenger, Paul. "Books of Hours and the Reading Habits of the Later Middle Ages." *The Culture of Print: Power and the Uses of Print in Early Modern Europe*. Edited by R. Chartier, Translated by L. Cochrane. Cambridge: Cambridge Univ. Press, 1989, pp. 141-73.

Examines the role of books of hours in daily life, looking at representations of prayers and reading in some illustrations in texts. No plates.

394. Soleil, F. *Les heures gothiques et la littérature pieuse aux XVe et XVIe siècles.* Geneva: Slatkine Reprints, 1965.
This general introduction, originally published in 1882, treats books of hours down to the end of the fifteenth and the beginning of the sixteenth centuries. The author concentrates on several highly illuminated volumes like the hours of Simon Vostre. Numerous plates.

395. Wieck, Roger S., et al. *Time Sanctified. The Book of Hours in Medieval Art and Life.* New York: George Braziller in association with the Walters Art Gallery, Baltimore,1988.
A collection of essays divided up into chapters on various aspects of the book of hours' relation to medieval cultural and religious life. An important source for any study of *horae*, with numerous plates and including a catalogue of manuscripts, concordance of shelf marks, list of books for further reading, and index of artists.

Marginalia

396. Camille, Michael. *Image at the Edge: The Margins of Medieval Art.* Cambridge, MA: Harvard Univ. Press, 1992.
A provocative treatment of marginalia. Many unusual plates. Reviewed by Jeffrey Hamburger in *AB* 75 (June1993): 319-27.

397. Randall, Lilian M. C. "Humour and Fantasy in the Margins of an English Book of Hours." *Apollo* 84 (December 1966): 482-88.
Examines the illustrations in an early fourteenth-century book of hours in the Walters Art Gallery, and discusses how they are related to the text and wittily comment on it. Some plates.

398. _____. *Images in the Margins of Gothic Manuscripts*. Berkeley and Los Angeles: Univ. of California Press, 1966.
This standard work is a detailed examination of the marginalia in a number of manuscripts in American and European libraries, with introductory essay, many plates, and an index of themes and types. Bibliography.

399. Varela, Gerardo Boto, and Joan Molina Figueras. "Satire et comique dans l'illustration marginale: Un manuscrit du gothique international catalan." *Flanders in a European Perspective: Manuscript Illumination around 1400 in Flanders and Abroad. Proceedings of the International Colloquium, Leuven, 7-10 September 1993*. Edited by Maurits Smeyers and Bert Cardon. Leuven: Uitgerij Peeters, 1995, pp. 155-70.
Examines various animal-grotesque human encounters in marginalia. Several plates.

Specific Studies, Films, and Facsimiles of Illuminated Manuscripts

Facsimiles of various books of hours in English collections are available from World Microfilms, 2-6 Foscote Mews, London W9 2HH, Tel: 071-266-2202, Fax: 071-266 2314. At the time of this writing, the Cambridge University Library and the British Library collections are not represented, while those of the Oxford colleges, Trinity College, Dublin, Lambeth Palace, and Lincoln Cathedral are.

400. Backhouse, Janet. *The Bedford Hours*. London: British Library, 1990.
Examines the overall design of this early fifteenth-century horae, discussing the historical background of its production and patronage. Sixty color and black-and-white plates.

401. _____. *The Isabella Breviary*. London: The British Library, 1989.
Selection of plates reproducing leaves of this manuscript with an introduction and bibliography.

402. _____. *The Madresfield Hours: A Fourteenth-Century Manuscript in the Library of Earl Beauchamp.* Oxford: Roxburghe Club, 1975.
Introduction, general description of the manuscript and of its text, decoration, and history, accompanied by numerous plates. A useful appendix contains a handlist of twenty-four books of hours made for English owners between 1240 and the mid-fourteenth century.

403. Brown, T. J. "The Salvin Horae." *BMQ* 21 (1959): 8-12.
Treats a thirteenth-century illuminated English book of hours briefly, no plates.

404. Cazelles, Raymond, et al., eds. *The 'Très Riches Heures' of Jean, Duke of Berry.* Translated by Victoria Benedict. New York: George Braziller, 1969.
A collection of facsimile plates of the calender and other pages from this manuscript at the Musée Condé, at Chantilly. All the miniatures and many of the text decorations are included. These pages are accompanied by detailed commentaries on their iconographic meaning. Includes preface, introduction, and selective bibliography.

405. Egbert, Donald D. "The Grey-Fitzpayn Hours: An English Gothic Manuscript of the Early Fourteenth Century Now in the FitzWilliam Museum, Cambridge, MS 242." *AB* 18 (1936): 527-38.
Examines the history, importance, and composition of this manuscript with several plates.

406. Hamburger, Jeffrey F. *The Rothschild Canticles, Art and Mysticism in Flanders and the Rhineland circa 1300.* New Haven, CT: Yale Univ. Press, 1990.
An early fourteenth-century compendium whose mix of image and text for the devotional use of nuns in Flanders and the Rhineland was very important for the understanding of mystical writing and painting in those regions. Provides a lengthy analysis of the codex, focusing on iconography, along with a selected bibliography, index of manuscripts, and general index, followed by a photographic

facsimile of the entire Rothschild Canticles and numerous plates
from similar manuscripts for comparison.

407. Hassall, William O. *The Engelbert Book of Hours: Master of Mary
      of Burgundy: M.S. Douce 219-220.* Illuminated Medieval
      Manuscripts in Microform Ser. 1. The Bodleian Library, no. 4.
      Oxford: Oxford Microform Publications, 1978.
      This is one of the most magnificent examples of the Ghent-Bruges
      school of illumination, and at present the film is the only means by
      which to see this manuscript, as it is no longer available for direct
      consultation. Preface and introduction in a little booklet is
      accompanied by a facsimile of the manuscript on microfiche. Other
      manuscripts reproduced in this series are 1) The Romance of
      Alexander, MS Bodley 264; 2) The Douce Apocalypse, MS Douce
      180; 3) The Ormesby Psalter, MS Douce 366; 4) The Bible
      Moralisée MS Douce 270b; 5) The Franciscan Missal, MS Douce
      313; 6) Bede's Life of St. Cuthbert, MS Univ. Coll. 165; 7) Herbal
      and Bestiary, MS Bodley 130; 8) Terence, Comedies, MS Auct.
      F.2.13; and 9) The Macregol or Rushworth Gospels, MS Auct. D.
      2.19.

408. Hattinger, Franz. *The Duc de Berry's Book of Hours.* Orbis pictus,
      no. 10. Berne: Hallwag,1962.
      An introduction followed by nineteen color plates of the twelve
      calender leaves, each with an accompanying description and
      commentary.

409. Inglis, Eric. *The Hours of Mary of Burgundy: Codex Vindobonensis
      1857, Vienna, Österreichische Nationalbibliothek.* Manuscripts
      in Miniature. London: Harvey Miller, 1995.
      A very high-quality facsimile of this magnificent codex.

410. Mâle, Emile, ed. *Les Heures d'Anne de Bretagne, Bibliothèque
      Nationale MS latin 9474. Verve: Revue artistique et littéraire*
      4, nos.14-15 (1943-46).
      Contains numerous black-and-white and color plates of miniatures
      from this work of *ca.* 1500 painted by Jean Bourdichon, along with
      a description and historical study.

411. Malo, Henri. *Les Très Riches Heures du Duc de Berry.* Paris: Verve, 1945.
A facsimile edition with some commentary.

412. Meiss, Millard. *The De Lévis Hours and the Bedford Workshop.* Yale Lectures in Medieval Illumination. New Haven, CT: Yale Univ. Library, 1972.
Describes and analyzes this manuscript and others from the same workshop, with numerous plates.

413. _____ , and Marcel Thomas. *The Rohan Master: A Book of Hours. Bibliothèque Nationale, Paris (M.S. latin 9471).* New York: George Braziller, 1973.
Reproduces the miniatures and a good number of pages of the text of this early fifteeenth-century manuscript with commentaries on the plates by Marcel Thomas and an introduction by both authors. The work concludes with lists of related manuscripts and selective bibliography, accompanied by an introduction and list of related manuscripts. Bibliography.

414. _____ , and Edith W. Kirsch. *The Visconti Hours.* New York: George Braziller, 1972.
Beautifully presented color facsimile of plates from the manuscript with commentaries.

415. Plummer, John. *The Hours of Catherine of Cleves.* New York: George Braziller, 1967.
A facsimile edition with extensive notes and commentary and a selective bibliography.

416. Porcher, Jean. *The Rohan Book of Hours.* The Faber Library of Illuminated Manuscripts, no. 4. Edited by Walter Oakeshott. London: Faber and Faber, 1959.
An introduction to the work with eight color plates, each with a detailed description.

417. Rorimer, James, and Margaret Freeman. *Les Belles Heures du Duc de Berry*. London: Thames and Hudson,1959.
      Reproduces in facsimile thirty-two illuminations with descriptions.

418. Spencer, Eleanor P. *The Sobieski Hours: A Manuscript in the Royal Library at Windsor Castle*. Roxburghe Club. London: Academic Press, 1977.
      All the miniatures are reproduced along with pictures of the binding. Discusses textual history, miniatures, the three illuminators, and codicology of the manuscript. Bibliography.

419. Turner, D. H., ed. *The Hastings Hours: A 15th-century Flemish Book of Hours Made for William, Lord Hastings, Now in the British Library [Add.MS. 54782]*. London: Thames and Hudson, 1983.
      Color plates reproduced from the manuscript, accompanied by commentaries, history, and description of the manuscript.

MODEL BOOKS

420. Lehmann-Haupt, Hellmut, ed. *The Göttingen Model Book*. Columbia, MO: Univ. of Missouri Press, 1978.
      Edition of an important late medieval German illuminators' model book.

421. Scheller, Robert W. *Exemplum: Model-Book Drawings and the Practice of Artistic Transmission in the Middle Ages (ca. 900-ca. 1470)*. Translated by Michael Hoyle. Amsterdam Univ. Press, distributed by Univ. of Michigan Press, 1995.
      Studies the use of models and cartoons for the transmission of scenes and figure types in medieval manuscripts. Fourteen color plates, 265 black-and-white figures, and a *catalogue raisonné* of thirty-six model books. Reviewed by Jeffrey Hamburger in *Speculum* 72, no. 1 (January 1997): 217-19.

MONUMENTAL ART

By Country of Origin

[Bohemia]

422. Kramár, Vincent."La peinture et la sculpture du IVe siècle en Bohème." *LV* 4, no. 78 (March 1928): 202-15.

A good art historical overview and general introduction to the period, discussing the various styles and later influence of Bohemian art in the fourteenth century, with a number of illustrative plates of sculpture and architecture.

[England]

423. Evans, Joan. *English Art: 1307-1461.* Oxford: Clarendon, 1949.

This volume in the Oxford History of English Art studies the origins of the "decorated" and perpendicular styles in English architecture and treats such topics as art after the plague, the art of the great English houses, funeral effigies, canopied tombs, and the art of chantries and colleges. There is a bibliography and index as well as numerous plates.

[France]

424. Williamson, Paul. *Gothic Sculpture, 1140-1300.* New Haven, CT: Yale University Press, 1996.

General introduction to the sculpture of such cathedrals as Chartres, Amiens, and Reims. 261 black-and-white and 125 color plates.

[Netherlands]

425. Morand, Kathleen. *Claus Sluter: Artist at the Court of Burgundy.*
     Austin: Univ. of Texas Press, 1991.
     Includes a catalogue of Sluter's work with plates but also deals with
     the life, cultural, and artistic environment in the Netherlands of this
     late thirteenth- and early fourteenth-century monumental sculptor.
     Reviewed by Stephen K. Scher in *Speculum* 68, no. 4 (October
     1993): 1180-3.

Funerary Art (Including Early Christian)

426. Bovini, Giuseppe. *I Sarcofagi paleocristiani della Spagna.* Vatican
     City: Pontifical Institute of Christian Archaeology, 1954.
     This book is a *catalogue raisonné* of often richly decorated
     sculptured stone sarcophagi, both pagan and Christian, arranged by
     city of location and offering brief descriptions, followed by half
     tones of the principal sculptural motifs and brief bibliographies.

427. Camille, Michael. *Master of Death. The Lifeless Art of Pierre
     Remiet, Illuminator.* New Haven, Yale Univ. Press, 1996.
     Studies the imagery of death in Remiet's painting and provides a
     good overview of funerary iconography generally. 145 black-and-
     white and forty-five color plates.

428. Colvin, Howard. *Architecture and the Afterlife.*
     General study of the role of tombs in church architecture See item
     44.

429. Fiero, Gloria K. "Death Ritual in Fifteenth-Century Manuscript
     Illumination." *JMH* 10 (1984): 271-94.
     As explained in her summary, "the iconography of death ritual that
     emerged after 1375 was actually a manifestation of the popular need
     to assert the restoration of social and religious traditions that had

been suspended during the period when the Black Death ravaged western Europe" (271). Plates.

430. Gardner, A. *Alabaster Tombs of the Pre-Reformation Period in England.* Cambridge: Cambridge Univ. Press, 1940.
Covers the alabasterers' guilds, tomb chests, and weepers, and the various types of effigies to appear on the chests, listing them by place and describing the particular features of their iconography.

431. Kirsch, G. P. *Le catacombe romane.* Rome: Pontifico Istituto di Archeologia Cristiana, 1933.
A small guide book to the catacombs beneath the city of Rome arranged according to the cardinal directions. Each entry is accompanied by black-and-white photographs of the catacomb and its principal frescos and inscriptions. An introduction discusses catacombs generally. Select bibliography.

432. Llewellyn, Nigel. *The Art of Death:Visual Culture in the English Death Ritual c.1500-1800.* The Victoria and Albert Museum. London: Reaktion Books, 1991.
Looks at the iconographical representations of death in paintings, sculpture, engravings, clothing, jewelry, and a number of other different types of surviving artifacts with numerous plates, select bibliography, and index.

433. Pfister, Kurt. *Katakomben malerei.* Potsdam: Gustav Kiepenheuer, 1924.
An introduction to the frescos of the Roman catacombs, arranged as a series of thirty high-quality color and black-and-white lithographic plates with modest commentary.

434. Richmond, Velma Bourgeois. *Laments for the Dead in Medieval Narrative.* Duquesne Studies, Philological Series, no. 8. Pittsburgh, PA: Duquesne Univ. Press, 1966.
Treats the importance of laments for the dead for medieval narrative. Discusses general characteristics, elements of style, and the like, with an anthology of passages. No plates or treatment of visual motifs, but useful as a survey.

435. Styger, Paul. *Die Römischen Katacomben.* Berlin: Verlag für
     Kunstwissenchaft, 1933.
     This monumental volume considers the Roman catacombs from the
     second through the fourth centuries and contains a number of maps,
     plans, and very high quality black-and-white photographs of the
     frescoes and inscriptions.

436. Wilpert, Josef. *I sarcofagi cristiani antichi.* Roma: Pontificio Istituto
     di Archeologia Cristiana, 1929-36.
     The standard work on the catacombs, with two volumes of plates
     and an atlas.

Sculpture

437. Adeline, Jules. *Les sculptures grotesques et symboliques (Rouen et
     environs).* Rouen: E. Auge, ND.
     Collects a large number of drawings of grotesques, mostly from
     Rouen. Each is described and there is some discussion of the
     production of grotesques by medieval artists.

438. Anderson, Jørgen. *The Witch on the Wall: Medieval Erotic
     Sculpture in the British Isles.* Copenhagen: Rosenkilde and
     Bagger; London: George Allen and Unwin, 1977.
     Anderson explains, "this work presents a catalogue of primitive,
     mainly medieval carvings from church and castle walls in the British
     Isles, Western France and Normandy, especially a figure known
     under a curious, and never satisfactorily explained name of
     'Sheela-na-gig.' The commentary attempts to show the development
     of the 'walking vagina' motif from its limited use on Romanesque
     corbels and capitals in France to a remarkable independence in
     England and Ireland during the later Middle Ages, and it also
     indicates a possible purpose for the figures, based on their
     architectural function, their consistent application on quoins, and
     above doorways" (7). A fascinating collection of plates depicting

erotic sculpture, many of women exposing or touching their genitals, but also on other topics, with interesting commentary, on such subjects as "the evil-averting influence of the vulva."

439. Bond, Francis. *Fonts and Font Covers*. Reprint. London: Waterstone, 1985.
Covers methods of baptism, the baptistry as a space, and types of fonts and their materials, as well as carved fonts and their covers, arranged by century. With bibliography, numerous plates, and indices of places and things.

440. Coldstream, Nicola. *Masons and Sculptors*. Medieval Craftsmen Series. Toronto and Buffalo: Univ. of Toronto Press, 1991.
Focuses somewhat more on the master mason than on the sculptor and how the masons were involved in the design as well as the fabrication of buildings. Treats masons' records, building contracts and accounts, inscriptions, masons' self-portraits, and their personal marks. Discusses who the masons were, how they organized their guilds, the role of their patrons, and how they designed and built cathedrals and castles. Reviewed by Robert Calkins in *Speculum* 69, no. 2 (April 1994): 421-3.

441. Swarzenski, Hanns. *Monuments of Romanesque Art: The Art of Church Treasures in North-Western Europe*. Chicago: Univ. of Chicago Press, 1967.
Gathers a large number of plates with an introduction and indices to the plates of iconographic motifs, names, places of origin, present locations, materials, techniques, and objects.

442. Weir, Anthony, and James Jerman. *Images of Lust: Sexual Carvings on Medieval Churches*. London: B. T. Batsford, 1986.
Covering such subjects as Sheela-na-gig, mermaids, centaurs, and other hybrid monsters, disgust for the flesh, priapic figures, gestures, and postures, female exhibitionists, and the distribution of carvings with sexual themes. With numerous plates and line drawings, bibliography, and index.

Sculpture by Country of Origin

[Denmark]

443. Mills, James. *An Iconographic Index to Danmarks Kirker: 1100-1600*. Part I: *Jutland to Date*. Revised Edition. Kalamazoo, MI: Medieval Institute Publications, 1991.
    An iconographical index to the Danmarks Kirker series (an inventory of older churches in Denmark put out by the National Museum in Copenhagen). Arranged by iconographic subjects, (Old Testament, Virgin Mary, The Passion, Saints, allegories and the like); each entry refers the reader to what church and location the image appears at, in what volume and page of Danmarks Kirker the description and illustration may be found, as well as dates, and workshops if known. Index of Artisans and Workshops. To be used in conjunction with the whole collection.

444. _____, *Medieval Danish Wooden Sculpture: Roods*. Part I: *1100 A. D -1400 A. D*. Glen Head, NY: Aggersborg Press, 1991; and Part II: *1400 A. D.- 1600 A. D*. Glen Head, NY: Aggersborg Press, 1992.
    Each volume begins with a similar introduction and a discussion of the Danmarks Kirker series (an inventory of older churches in Denmark put out by the National Museum in Copenhagen), then provides chronological descriptions of the different rood screens found in the various churches, most of them accompanied by plates, which make up the greater portion of these two volumes. This is chiefly a catalogue.

[England]

445. Anderson, M. D. *The Choir Stalls of Lincoln Minster*. London: The Friends of Lincoln Cathedral, 1951.
    Plates and discussion of these gothic carvings on a variety of religious subjects and including many animals and monsters, with a catalogue of them at the end.

446. Cave, C. J. P. "The Bosses on the Vault of the Quire of Winchester Cathedral." *Archaeologia* 76 (1927): 161-78.
A detailed list of these ninety-seven wooden bosses, representing a variety of different figures and carved in the early 1500's on the roof of the presbytry of Winchester Cathedral, with plates.

447. Gardner, Arthur. *English Medieval Sculpture.* Cambridge: Cambridge Univ. Press 1951.
Introduction to the topic with numerous plates. Proceeds chronologically from Pre-Conquest sculpture to the late Gothic and Perpendicular period.

448. MacLean, Sally-Beth. *Chester Art: A Subject List of Extent and Lost Art Including Items Relevant to Early Drama.* Early Drama, Art, and Music Reference Series. Kalamazoo, MI: The Medieval Institute, 1982.
Treats depictions of Christ, the Virgin, apostles, saints, and the like in the Chester region, and discusses where and why the images appear in its medieval art. Appendices on St. Weburgh's cult and shrine, musical instruments, and Chester Cathedral misericords as well as a select bibliography and index complete the volume. Numerous plates.

449. Prior, Edward A., and Arthur Gardner. *An Account of Medieval Figure-Sculpture in Britain.* Cambridge: Cambridge Univ. Press, 1912.
A thorough introduction to the subject extending from 650 AD up through the sixteenth century. Treats materials, iconographic subjects, and the role of the medieval sculptor in the art of the period. As well, the major developments and styles are examined chronologically. Covers such subjects as fonts, tombs, and marble effigies.

450. Richardson, James S. *The Medieval Stone Carver in Scotland.* Edinburgh: Edinburgh Univ. Press, 1964.
Treats the Roman inheritance, the Norman infiltration, the monastic expansion, and the high Gothic period. Numerous plates.

451. Stone, L. *Sculpture in Britain: The Middle Ages.* Middlesex: Penguin, 1955.
   Very general survey for the beginner, with many plates.

[France]

452. Bridaham, Lester Burbank. *Gargoyles, Chimères, and the Grotesque in French Gothic Sculpture.* Reprint. New York: Da Capo, 1969.
   A large collection of identified plates organized by type with a five-page introduction. Bibliography.

453. Evans, Joan. *Art in Mediaeval France, 987-1498.* London: Geoffrey Cumberlege, Oxford Univ. Press, 1948.
   Sections treat the Benedictines, Augustinian Canons, mendicant orders, king and court, and villagers. Half of this volume consists of plates. Index.

454. Forsyth, Ilene H. *The Throne of Wisdom: Wood Sculptures of the Madonna in Romanesque France.* Princeton Univ. Press, 1972.
   Considers wooden sculpture of the Virgin holding the Christ child in her lap. Contains numerous plates each described in a register of principal examples of such sculptures up through the twelfth century.

455. Gardner, Arthur. *Medieval Sculpture in France.* Cambridge: Cambridge Univ. Press, 1931.
   Like his book on England, this one treats a variety of cathedral and other forms of sculpture chiefly during the Gothic period. Plates.

[Germany]

456. Baxandall, Michael. *The Limewood Sculptors of Renaissance Germany, 1475-1525.* New Haven, CT and London: Yale Univ. Press, 1980.
   Treats pre-Reformation south German wood sculpture, covering the functions of the sculpture, the material, the markets, identities of carvers when known, sculptural types of the period, all accompanied by numerous plates, a select bibliography, and an index.

457. Osten, Gert van der, and Horst Vey. *Painting and Sculpture in Germany and the Netherlands: 1500-1600.* New Haven, CT: Yale Univ. Press, 1995.
Though a little late for the period of this guide, the work is a good general introduction to high Gothic German art. With 307 illustrations.

[Italy]

458. Crichton, G. H. *Romanesque Sculpture in Italy.* London: Routledge and Kegan Paul, 1954.
An art history organized by area and by school, with numerous plates, bibliography, and index.

459. Pope-Hennessy, John W. *Italian Gothic Sculpture.* London: Phaidon, 1955.
Treats the most important works of Italian sculpture, with some plates.

460. Seymour, Charles, Jr. *Sculpture in Italy: 1400-1500.* New Haven, CT: Yale Univ. Press, 1996.
General introduction with 160 in-text illustrations.

461. Stiénnon, Jacques, and Rita Lejeune. "La l égende arthurienne dans la sculpture de la cathédrale de Modène." *CCM* 6 (1963): 281-96.
Examines the iconography of the Arthurian legend in this cathedral's sculpture, with plates.

462. White, John. *Art and Architecture in Italy: 1250-1400.* New Haven, CT: Yale Univ. Press, 1996.
Overview and general art history with 300 black-and-white and seventy-five color plates.

[Spain]

463. Gaillard, Georges. *La sculpture romane espagnole.* Paris: Hartmann, 1939.

Spanish Romanesque sculpture of all sorts treated here, with plates.

464. Moralejo, Serafin. "Artes figurativas y artes literarias en la España medieval: Romanico, Romance y Roman." *AEPE* 32-33 (1989): 61-70.
     Examines the historical and social changes reflected in Romanesque sculpture and twelfth-century literature to explain how the epic imagination was represented in sculpture. Numerous line drawings of different medieval Spanish sculptural works.

465. Porter, Arthur Kingsley. *Spanish Romanesque Sculpture.* 2 vols. Florence: Pantheon, 1928.
     Thorough treatment by a great authority, and *catalogue raisonné*. Now somewhat dated.

[Sweden]

466. Norström, Folke. *Mediaeval Baptismal Fonts: An Iconographical Study.* Acta Universitatis Umensis. Umeå and Stockholm: Almqvist and Wiksell International, 1984.
     Divided according to iconographical depiction into the following subject headings: the fountain of life, death and resurrection, rebirth and baptism, prototypes and symbols of baptism, symbols of the eucharist, old and new Adam, and vices and virtues. Contains numerous plates, chiefly of Swedish fonts, and indices of persons and places.

WALL AND PANEL PAINTING

General

467. Harris, Elizabeth Lee. "The Mural as a Decorative Device in Medieval Literature." Diss. Nashville: Vanderbilt Univ., 1935.
     Though this work has no pictures or indices, it does talk about the way wall paintings—which the writer calls murals—are seen in

literature. In a group of descriptive and analytic essays Harris considers the backgrounds of the "mural" in classical wall painting and then moves to medieval examples. Most of the work concerns references to wall paintings in the French romances, in Dante, and in Chaucer and his successors.

WALL AND PANEL PAINTING

By Country of Origin

[Austria]

468. Lanc, Elga. *Die Mittelalterlichen Waldmalereien in Wien und Niederösterreich.* Corpus der Mittelalterlichen Waldmalereien Österreichs. Vienna: Österreichischen Akademie der Wissenschaften, 1983.
An art historical introduction to wall painting is followed by an alphabetically arranged register of Austrian churches with wall paintings, each with floor plan, list of subjects, and bibliography. Some in-text color plates and a large number of black-and-white plates complete the volume.

[England]

469. Keyser, C. E. *A List of Buildings in Great Britain and Ireland Having Mural and Other Painted Decoration, of Dates Prior to the Latter Part of the Seventeenth Century.* London: Eyre and Spottiswode,1883.
After an historical introduction comes an index of objects, subjects, saints, and the like. Each wall painting is described and dates given.

470. Tristram, E. W. *English Mediaeval Wall-Painting: The Thirteenth Century.* Oxford: Oxford Univ. Press,1950.
Plates and a *catalogue raisonné.*

[Italy]

471. Blume,   Dieter. *Wandmalerei   als   Ordenspropaganda:
     Bildprogramme im Chorbereich franziskanischer Konvente
     Italiens bis zur Mitte des 14. Jahrhunderts.* Worms:
     Werner'sche, 1983.
     Examines a number of wall painting programs in Italian churches
     associated with Franciscan convents and considers how scenes of
     the life of Francis and the like were used for propaganda purposes
     to further the order's interests during the height of the secular-
     mendicant controversy. 100 pages of black-and-white plates.

[Sweden]

472. Cornell, Henrik. *Albertus Pictor, Sten Stures och Jacob Ulvssons
     Malere.* Stockholm: Almqvist and Wiksell,1981.
     This volume on one of the most important of medieval Scandinavian
     painters offers a wealth of information on Albertus Pictor and his
     relation to the *Biblia Pauperum.* Themes and subjects like Sampson
     slaying the lion are also treated. Each church is analyzed, area by
     area, with fifty-four black-and-white plates and bibliography.

473. Lundberg, Erik. *Albertus Pictor.* Stockholm: Sveriges allmanna
     konstforenings publikation, 1961.
     General study with a few plates and church plans.

474. Pulsiano, Phillip J., and Kristen Wolf, eds. *Medieval Scandinavia.
     An Encyclopedi*a. New York: Garland, 1992.
     The preface explains that the work is intended for students lacking
     Scandinavian languages but needing a tool for the study of medieval
     Scandinavia, by which is meant Denmark, Finland, Iceland, Norway,
     and Sweden from the period of the Migration to the Reformation.
     Many plates of works of art. Reviewed by Roberta Frank in
     Speculum 71, no. 1 (January 1996): 195-6.

475. Söderberg, Bengt G. *Gotlandska kalk malningar 1200-1400.* Visby:
     Foreningen Gotlands Fornvanner, 1971.
     Church wall paintings in Jutland, with plates and bibliography.

476.   _____. *Svenska kyrkomalningar fran medeltiden.* Stockholm:
         Natur och Kultur, 1951.
         General study of Swedish medieval wall painting with 164 church
         plans and sixty-two plates, some in color.

WOOD CARVING

By Country of Origin

[England]

477.   Bond, Francis. *Screens and Galleries in English Churches.* London:
         Oxford Univ. Press, 1908.
         Treats medieval English rood screens and their carvings. Some
         plates.

478.   _____. *Wood Carvings in English Churches.* 2 vols. London:
         Oxford Univ. Press, 1910.
         General study of rood screens, misericord carvings, and bench ends,
         some plates.

479.   Cave, C. J. P. *Medieval Carvings in Exeter Cathedral.* London:
         Penguin, 1953.
         Amateur's guide to the various figural carvings in this building.
         Some plates.

480.   _____. *Roof Bosses in Medieval Churches. An Aspect of Gothic
         Sculpture.* Cambridge: Cambridge Univ. Press, 1948.
         Study and *catalogue raisonné* of the carved figural bosses which
         are used to hide the rafter joints in many medieval English churches.
         Many plates.

481. Cox, Charles J. *Bench Ends in English Churches.* London: Humphrey Milford: Oxford Univ. Press, 1916.
     Detailed treatment of the bench end as an architectural feature with sections on types of seats, seat constructions, and pews and galleries generally. The volume is organized as a catalogue according to region with an analysis and description of the style in each region. Useful index of persons, places, and subjects.

482. _____. *Pulpits, Lecterns and Organs.* London: Humphrey Milford. Oxford Univ. Press, 1915.
     Thorough, informative book with many plates. Treats preaching and the pulpit, and medieval stone and wood pulpits down to the Reformation. Other sections touch on lecterns, and eagles of brass, wood, and stone, as well as gospel and reading desks, organs and their wooden cases. There are indices of places and things.

483. Gardner, Arthur. *Minor English Wood Sculpture 1400-1550.* London: Tiranti, 1958.
     Small guide book with black-and-white plates of representative carvings.

484. Goulburn, Edward Meyrick. *The Ancient Sculptures in the Roof of Norwich Cathedral which Exhibit the Course of Scripture History from the Creation to Solomon and from the Birth of Christ to the Final Judgment.* Reprint. London: Autotype Fine Art Co., 1971.
     Though previously virtually unobtainable, this study of the roof and cloister bosses in Norwich Cathedral is now reprinted with thirty pages of plates reproducing the extremely high quality originals. While much of what the author says about these bosses is now very much out of date, the book remains one of the few convenient sources of photographs of the entire program.

485. Grössinger, Christa. "English Misericords of the Thirteenth and Fourteenth Centuries and their Relationship to Manuscript Illuminations." *JWCI* 38 (1975): 97-108.
     Compares images in English misericords with those in manuscript initials with detailed examples.

486. Kraus, Dorothy, and Henry Kraus. *The Hidden World of Misericords*. New York: George Braziller, 1975.
A useful book of plates with descriptions and some analyses, treating iconographic patterns, outstanding French collections, and misericords of other countries.

487. Phipson, Emma. *Choir Stalls and Their Carvings: Examples of Misericords from English Cathedrals and Churches*. London: B. T. Batsford, 1896.
Listed by cathedral or church, the stalls and their carvings are described in detail with some sketches for each church. Introductory essay as well.

488. Remnant, G. L. *A Catalogue of Misericords in Great Britain with an Essay on their Iconography*. Oxford: Clarendon, 1969.
Organized by area with an iconographical index and one of proper names. Numerous plates.

489. Sheridan, Ronald, and Anne Ross. *Grotesques and Gargoyles: Paganism in the Medieval Church*. Boston: New York Graphic Society, 1975.
Divided according to type of representation, such as giants, creatures devouring heads, hermaphrodites, and centaurs. With many plates and commentary on the plates.

490. Smith, J . C. D. *A Guide to Church Woodcarvings: Misericords and Bench-ends*. Newton Abbot: David and Charles, 1974.
A general guide to exploring the subjects carved on the wooden seating of medieval churches. Treats daily life, subjects from romances, bestiary themes, and the like. Many plates.

491. Smith, M. Q. "The Roof Bosses of Norwich Cathedral and Their Relation to the Medieval Drama of the City." *NNAS* 32, no.1 (1958): 12-20.
Attempts to prove a relationship between the cathedral bosses and the contemporary religious drama of Norwich. From Smith's evidence, it is possible to reconstruct in greater detail than before

the form and content of the cycle. Most useful for its treatment of the order and grouping of subjects and iconographic themes in the bosses.

492. Tracy, Charles. *English Gothic Choir-Stalls 1200-1400.* Woodbridge, Suffolk and Wolfeboro, NH: Boydell, 1987. Discusses the different styles of choir stalls in different schools and regions. About half of this large volume is comprised of plates. Also includes select bibliography and index.

493. _____. *English Medieval Furniture and Woodwork.* London: Victoria and Albert Museum, 1988. A catalogue with plates and select bibliography of the medieval furniture in the Victoria and Albert Museum, both ecclesiastical and domestic. Further sections treat doors, corner posts, screens, chests, and coffers, and their imagery.

494. Whittingham, Arthur Bensly. *Norwich Cathedral Bosses and Misericords.* Norwich, 1981. Plates and discussion of the bosses and their iconographic programs.

495. _____. *The Stalls of Norwich Cathedral.* Norwich: Cathedral Chapter, 1961. Brief illustrated guide to the choir stall carvings.

496. Wright, Peter Poyntz. *The Rural Bench Ends of Somerset: A Study in Medieval Woodcarving.* Amersham, England: Avebury, 1983. Complemented by numerous plates and an index, this book includes particular sections on the carvers, their methods and their influences. Treats major categories of imagery such as pelicans, green men, birds, symbols, quadrupeds, people, and miscellaneous designs.

Chapter Two: Other Tools

ENCYCLOPAEDIAE AS SOURCES FOR IMAGERY

General

497. Chibnall, Marjorie. "Pliny's *Natural History* in the Middle Ages."
  Empire and Aftermath: Silver Latin II. Edited by T. A. Dorey.
  London and Boston: Routledge and Kegan Paul, 1975, pp.
  57-78.
  Discusses the popularity of this ancient encyclopaedia and the
  reasons for this popularity in the Middle Ages, looking specifically
  at some of the work's contents and how they may have been
  interesting to medieval readers and scholars.

498. Collison, Robert. *Encyclopaedias: Their History throughout the
  Ages: A Bibliographical Guide with Extensive Historical Notes
  to the General Encyclopaedias issued throughout the World*

from 350 B. C. to the Present Day. New York and London: Hafner, 1966.
Chapter Two, "The Middle Ages," may be useful to the medievalist. With a chronology of encyclopaediae, bibliography, and index.

499. Goldschmidt, Adolph. "Frümittelalterliche illustrierte Enzyclopäiden." *VBW* [1923-1924] (1926): 215-26.
Treats early medieval encyclopaediae like that of Rhabanus Maurus. Plates from Rhabanus Maurus, the *Liber Floridus*, and the *Hortus Deliciarum*.

500. Saxl, Fritz. "A Spiritual Encyclopaedia of the Later Middle Ages." *JWCI* 5 (1942): 82-142.
In describing the illustrations of two related fifteenth-century German manuscripts, Saxl discusses "The Politico-Apocalyptic Group" of illustrations contained therein, "The 'Macabre' Group" (including the *Debate Between Body and Soul* and the Wheel of Fortune), "Allegorical Figures with Commentary," "Pictures without Commentary," "The Tree of Virtues and Vices and Other Diagrams," "The Encyclopaedic Tradition," "The Gradual Formation of the Collectanea," "The Revival" (of this tradition in manuscript compiling), "The Wellcome Apocalypse," and "Luther." Each section discusses the two manuscripts in light of the tradition in contemporary manuscript illustration with a number of plates. This article includes two appendices by Otto Kurtz.

501. Weijers, Olga. *Dictionnaires et répertoires au Moyen Age: Une étude du vocabulaire.* Civcima: Etudes sur le vocabulaire intellectuel du Moyen Age, no. 4. Brepols: Turnhout, 1991.
A history of dictionary and repertory making with a focus upon how medieval writers themselves described and discussed these projects. For the student of the medieval encyclopaedia this work's greatest utility is its coverage of the history of alphabetical classification, analytic devices like marginal renvoi, and indices and tabulae. Bibliography and indices.

Individual Encyclopaediae by Compiler or Title

[Alexander Neckam]

502. Holmes, Urban Tigner, Jr. *Daily Living in the Twelfth Century, Based on the Observations of Alexander Neckam in London and Paris.* Madison, WI: The Univ. of Wisconsin Press, 1966. This book, which leads the reader on a fictional journey with Alexander Neckam from Dunstable to Paris, draws upon many sources dating from 1150-1200, chiefly from Alexander's own encyclopaedia, quoting from a number of them and discussing others in extensive notes, to depict daily life in the period. Very useful for descriptions of domestic objects and processes. Index.

503. Hunt, R. W. *The Schools and the Cloister: The Life and Writings of Alexander Nequam (1157-1217).* Edited and Revised by Margaret Gibson. Oxford: Clarendon, 1984. Discusses the life, works, and influence of this late twelfth- or early thirteenth-century author. Appendices provide editions and manuscripts of his works and sermons. Indices.

[Bartholomaeus Anglicus]

504. Byrne, Donal. "The Boucicaut Master and the Iconographical Tradition of the *Livre des Propriétés des Choses.*" *GBA,* 6th ser, 92 (1978): 149-64. Examines the iconography of two manuscripts of this text thought to be illustrated in the workshop of the Boucicaut Master. Plates.

505. _____. ."Rex imago Dei: Charles V of France and *the Livre des Propriétés des Choses.*" *JMH* 7 (1981): 97-113. Studies the frontispiece of the royal exemplar of the fourteenth-century French translation of Bartholomaeus's *De Proprietatibus Rerum.* Argues that "the textual additions of the translator and the iconography of this frontispiece reveal a new conception of the meaning and usage of the encyclopaedia as well as a concerted attempt to draw this authoritative work into the orbit of royal aims and aspirations" (97).

506. Edwards, A. S. G. "Bartholomaeus Anglicus' *De Proprietatibus Rerum* and Medieval English Literature." *Archiv* 222 (1985): 121-8.
 Discusses the influence of this thirteeth-century work which "established itself as *the* standard medieval encyclopedia" (121) in medieval English literature generally and provides a number of quotations from specific works.

507. Greetham, D. C. "The Concept of Nature in Bartholomaeus Anglicus (Fl. 1230)." *JHI* 41 (1980): 663-77.
 Examines the conflicting views of nature and natural phenomena in *De Proprietatibus Rerum*—including animals, angels, and the Chain of Being—with the assumption that these views influenced not only the learned but also the common people.

508. Long, James R. *Bartholomaeus Anglicus. On the Properties of Soul and Body: De Proprietatibus Rerum Libri III et IV.* Toronto Medieval Latin Texts, no. 9. Toronto: Institute of Mediaeval Studies, 1979.
 Critical edition of these two books (one dealing with the nature and properties of the rational soul, the other with the human body) from this popular and influential thirteenth-century encyclopaedia, edited from Bibliothèque Nationale MS Latin 16098, with introduction and bibliography.

509. Seymour, M. C. *Bartholomaeus Anglicus and His Encyclopedia.* Aldershot, Hampshire and Brookfield, Vermont: Variorum, 1992.
 Follows up the English edition of Bartholomaeus which the author published in 1975-88, and attempts to make Bartholomaeus more accessible for modern readers by commenting on the sources of each of his different works. Extensive bibliography of primary sources, *index manuscriptorum*, and of the early printed editions.

510. _____, et al., eds. *On the Properties of Things: John Trevisa's Translation of Bartholomaeus Anglicus De Proprietatibus Rerum. A Critical Text.* 3 vols. Oxford: Clarendon, 1975-88.
 A critical edition of this popular and much-copied Middle English translation of Bartholomaeus Anglicus's work done by John Trevisa at the close of the fourteenth century.

[Bede]

511. Bober, Harry. "An Illustrated Medieval School-Book of Bede's *De Natura Rerum*."
     Cited above as item 384.

[Brunetto Latini]

512. Barrette, Paul, and Spurgeon P. Baldwin, trans. Brunetto Latini, *Li Livres dou Tresor (The Book of the Treasure)*. Garland Library of Medieval Literature, ser. B, no. 90. New York: Garland, 1993.
     Makes this important early vernacular encyclopaedia by one of Dante's mentors accessible to the English reader.

513. Holloway, Julia Bolton. *Brunetto Latini: An Analytic Bibliography*. London and Wolfeboro, NH: Grant and Cutler, 1986.
     Collects studies of the work and influence of this encyclopaedist.

[*Compendium Philosophiae*]

514. Bouard, Michel de. *Une nouvelle encyclopédie médiévale: Le Compendium Philosophiae*. Paris: E. de Boccard, 1936.
     Discusses this medieval encyclopaedia so popular in the thirteenth and fourteenth centuries and includes excerpts from the work itself.

[Honorius of Autun]

515. Flint, Valerie I. J., ed. "Honorius Augustodunensis, *Imago Mundi*." *AHDLMA* 49 (1982): 7-153.
     Standard edition and study of this important early encyclopaedia.

[Isidore of Seville]

516. Fontaine, Jacques. In item 592.
     The two articles on Isidore as encyclopaedist are the following: "Isidore de Seville et la mutation de l'encyclopédisme antique" and

"Cassiodore et Isidore: L'évolution de l'encyclopédisme latin du VIe au VIIe siècle."

[Konrad of Megenberg]

517. Sollbach, Gerhard E. *Das Tierbuch des Konrad von Megenberg.*
Dortmund: Harenberg, 1989.
A study of the British Library MS Royal 12. F. xiii codex of the natural history of this important vernacular writer. Some color plates.

[Lambert of Saint Omer]

518. Derolez, Albert. *Lambertus qui librum Fecit. Een codicologische studie van de Liber Floridus-autograaf (Gent, Universiteitsbibliotheek, handschrift 92).* Verhandelingen van de Koninklijke Academie voor Wetenschappen, Letteren en schone Kunsten van België, Klasse der Letteren 40, no. 89. Brussels: Paleis der Academien, 1978.
Detailed codicological analysis of the Ghent manuscript with a number of plates and full English summary. Index and select bibliography.

519. _____, ed. *Liber Floridus Codex Autographus Bibliothecae Universitatis Gandavensis.* Ghent: Ghent Univ. Press, 1968.
Luxurious facsimile edition with many color plates of the original diagrams and miniatures.

520. Lefevre, Yves. "Le *Liber Floridus* et la littérature encyclopédique au Moyen Age." *Liber Floridus Colloquium: Papers Read at the International Meeting Held in the University Library, Ghent on 3-5 September 1967.* Edited by Albert Derolez. Ghent: E. Story-Scientia, 1973, pp. 1-9.
Examines the place of the early twelfth-century *Liber Floridus* in the medieval encyclopaedia tradition, its composition, and its treatment of the marvellous.

521. Poesch, Jesse. "The Beasts from Job in the *Liber Floridus* Manuscripts." *JWCI* 33 (1970): 41-51.
Studies the adaptations from Job iconography on the part of the *Liber Floridus* illuminator.

522. Swarzenski, Hanns. "Comments on the Figural Illustrations." *Liber Floridus Colloquium*, Item 520, pp. 21-30.
A thorough investigation into the iconography of the early twelfth-century *Liber Floridus* illustrations. Thirty-four plates.

[Rabanus Maurus]

523. Amelli, A. M., ed. *Miniature sacre e profane dell' anno 1023 illustranti l'encylopedia medioevale di Rabano Mauri.* Monte Cassino: Tipo-Litografia di Montecassino, 1896.
A color facsimile edition of the important illustrated Monte Casino manuscript. A brief preface describes the plates.

524. Berrurier, Diane O. le. *The Pictorial Sources of Mythological and Scientific Illustration in Hrabanus Maurus' De Rerum Naturis.* New York: Garland Dissertations in Fine Arts, 1978.
Examines sources for the pictures in the five extant illustrated copies of this work (of eleventh to fifteenth century) with sections on "The Monsters," "Astronomical Illustrations," and "Botanical Illustrations." More than half of this large volume consists of plates and bibliography.

[Thomas of Cantimpré]

525. Friedman, John Block. "Thomas of Cantimpré. *De Naturis Rerum.* Prologue, Book III and Book XIX." *Cahiers d'études médiévales II. La science de la nature: Théories et pratiques.* Montreal: Bellarmin; Paris: J. Vrin, 1974, pp. 107-54.
An edition, with introduction, of portions of a thirteenth-century Latin encyclopaedia. The two books are chosen because of how "they illustrated the striking association in the author's mind of natural history with theology and preaching techniques" (107).

[Vincent of Beauvais]

526. Aerts, W. J., and M. Gosman, et al., eds. *Vincent of Beauvais and Alexander the Great: Studies on the Speculum Maius and Its Translations into Medieval Vernaculars.* Groningen: Egbert Forsten, 1986.

Seven articles in English and German on the subject.

527. Brincken, Anna-Dorothee von den. "Geschichtsbetrachtung bei Vincenz von Beauvais. Die Apologia Auctoris zum *Speculum Maius*." *DAEM* 34 (1978): 410-99.
A German introductory study of the extremely long and detailed preface of Vincent to his encyclopaedia outlining his sources, method, and purpose, followed by a good Latin text of the preface established from the best manuscripts.

528. Duchenne, M. C., et al. "Une liste des manuscrits du *Speculum Historiale* de Vincent de Beauvais." *Scriptorium* 42 (1987): 286-94.
Useful for finding illuminated manuscripts of the historical part of the encyclopaedia.

529. Lusignan, Serge. *Préface au Speculum Maius de Vincent de Beauvais: Réfraction et diffraction.* Cahiers d'études médiévales, no. 5. Montreal: Bellarmin; Paris: Vrin, 1979.
Lusignan describes his own book as a "preface" to the preface of the largest medieval encyclopaedia, an introduction to the history and meaning of the *Speculum Maius*. He discusses the life and works of Vincent generally and gives an edition of his *Libellus totius operis apologeticus*. Bibliography.

530. _____, et al., eds. *Vincent de Beauvais: Intentions et réceptions d'une oeuvre encyclopédique au Moyen-Age. Actes du colloque de l'Institut d' études médiévales (l'Université de Montréal) 27-30 avril, 1988.* Paris and Montreal: Vrin, 1990.
Essays by various hands on this great encyclopaedia.

531. Paulmier-Foucart, Monique. "L'atelier Vincent de Beauvais: Recherches sur l'état des connaissances au Moyen Age d'après une encyclopédie du XIIIe siècle." *LMA* 85 (1979): 87-99.
A report from a group organized in 1974 to study and provide an edition of the *Speculum Maius*. This article explains what the work is, the author's intention in his *Libellus apologeticus,* and the relationship of the Table of Jean de Hautfuney to the *Speculum.*

532. *Spicae, Cahiers de l'Atelier Vincent de Beauvais.*

Four volumes of this work have so far appeared. The articles most useful for the iconographer are Jean Schneider, "Orientation bibliographique." 1 (1978): 6-30; Monique Paulmier-Foucart, "Les 'flores' d'auteurs antiques et médiévaux dans le *Speculum Historiale.*" 1 (1978): 31-70 and 2 (1980): 9-16 and the same author's "Etude sur l'état des connaissances au milieu du XIIIe siècle: Nouvelles recherches sur la genèse du *Speculum Maius* de Vincent de Beauvais." 1 (1978): 91-122 and Jean Hautfuney, ed. "Tabula super *Speculum Historiale* fratris Vincentii." 2 (1980): 5-262 and 3 (1981): 5-208.

EXEMPLA

533. Bataillon, Louis-Jacques. "Similitudines et exempla dans les sermons du XIIe siècle." *The Bible in the Medieval World: Essays in Memory of Beryl Smalley.* Edited by Katherine Walsh and Diana Wood. Oxford and New York: B. H. Blackwell, 1985, pp. 191-205.
    Treats in an authoritative way the use of exempla by some university sermon writers. Among other chapters in this interesting collection are "Beryl Smalley and the Place of the Bible in Medieval Studies, 1927-84," by R.W. Southern.

534. Berlioz, Jacques, and Marie Anne Polo de Beaulieu, eds. *Les exempla médiévaux. Introduction à la recherche. Suivie des tables critiques de l'index exemplorum de Frederic C. Tubach.* Carcassone: GARAE/Hesiode, 1992.
    A collection of studies on medieval exempla.

535. Bremond, Claude, et al. *L'Exemplum.* Typologie des sources du Moyen Age occidental, no. 40. Turnhout: Brepols, 1982.
    A standard bibliographical study in this series, with a full definition and treatment of *exempla*, their collections, types, historical evolution, scholarship and modern editions. Part Two then examines the structure of the *exemplum* in Jacques de Vitry, and, Part Three, the *exemplum* in the sermon.

536. Crane, Thomas Frederick, ed. *The Exempla or Illustrative Stories from the Sermones Vulgares of Jacques de Vitry.* New York: Burt Franklin, 1980.
A critical edition of the exempla from these thirteenth-century sermons in Latin. Each one is explained in English before analysis. Extensive notes examine the influence of the exempla upon medieval preaching.

537. Gilman, Sander L. *The Parodic Sermon in European Perspective: Aspects of Liturgical Parody from the Middle Ages to the Twentieth Century.* Wiesbaden: Steiner,1974.
Mock sermons and parodies of them were an important source of imagery. Extensive bibliography.

538. Levy, B. J. *Nine Verse Sermons by Nicholas Bozon: The Art of an Anglo-Norman Poet and Preacher.* Medium Aevum Monographs, n.s., 11, London: Society for the Study of Mediaeval Languages and Literature, 1981.
Bozon was an important source of medieval exempla.

539. Mosher, Joseph Albert. *The Exemplum in the Early Religious and Didactic Literature of England.* New York: AMS Press, 1966.
Reprint of a dated but still useful study of exempla collections. Index.

540. Tubach, Frederic C. *Index Exemplorum: A Handbook of Medieval Religious Tales.* Helsinki: Suomalainen Tiedeakatemia Akademia Scientiarum Fennica,1969.
An annotated handbook of (5400 found in 37 collections) instructive medieval religious stories, arranged alphabetically according to "the most concrete act . . . the most memorable event or the most clearly profiled actor or thing" (517) with another long index of smaller topics referring the reader to the annotations. Very useful.

541. Welter, J.-Th. *L'exemplum dans la littérature religieuse et didactique du Moyen Age.* Bibliothèque d'histoire ecclésiastique de France. Paris and Toulouse: E -H. Guitard, 1927.
Studies the origin and development of the exemplum in religious and didactic literature up to the end of the twelfth century, then turns

to its expansion in the thirteenth and fourteenth centuries,and its decline in the fifteenth, discussing a large number of different medieval works. With a list of manuscripts containing exempla in an appendix. Bibliography and index.

542. Wenzel, Seigfried. *Macaronic Sermons: Bilingualism and Preaching in Late-Medieval England.* Ann Arbor, MI: Univ. of Michigan Press, 1994.
A study of the "mixed" late medieval Latin-English sermon.

PREACHING HANDBOOKS AND SERMON COLLECTIONS AS SOURCES OF IMAGERY

543. Amos, Thomas L., et al., eds. *De Ore Domini: Preacher and Word in the Middle Ages.* Kalamazoo, MI: Medieval Institute Publications, 1989.
Consists of an introduction and thirteen essays constituting a brief history of preaching. Ranges in date from the eighth century to the Reformation. Discusses how sermons were used at different periods and how they addressed their audiences. Subject index.

544. Avray, D. L. D.' *The Preaching of the Friars: Sermons Diffused from Paris before 1300.* Oxford: Clarendon, 1985.
Studies 'model' sermon collections written by friars based at the University of Paris, together with sermon collections diffused by the Paris University Stationers. Touches upon "The Background," "The Nature of the Medium," "Mendicant Preaching and the World of Learning," and "Social and Other Interpretations." Bibliography and indices.

545. Bataillon, L.- J. "Approaches to the Study of Medieval Sermons." *LSE*, n.s., 11 (1980): 19-35.
Offers a good English overview of the subject.

546. Bourgain, Louis. *La chaire française au XIIe siècle d'après les manuscrits.* Reprint. Geneva: Slatkine, 1973.
Covers medieval French preachers. Offers biographical discussion of their preaching, sermons, language, subjects, and composition to provide a view of twelfth-century society as depicted in sermon literature. Finishes with indices of preachers and of manuscripts for easy reference.

547. Caplan, Harry. "Classical Rhetoric and the Mediaeval Theory of Preaching." *CP* 28 (1933): 73-96.
Treats the iconographical depiction of the female figure Rhetoric in medieval art and literature and then goes on to treat the perception and use of rhetoric in medieval literature, focussing on preaching.

548. _____. *Mediaeval Artes Praedicandi: A Handlist* and *A Supplementary Handlist.* Cornell Studies in Classical Philology, nos. 24 and 25. Ithaca: Cornell Univ. Press; London: Humphrey Milford; Oxford: Oxford Univ. Press, 1934.
Studies manuscripts of the thirteenth-, fourteenth-, and fifteenth-century *Artes praedicandi,* or handbooks to help preachers construct and deliver their sermons. Organized according to *initia* and by names of authors divided by century.

549. Clark, David L. "Optics for Preachers: The *De oculo morali* by Peter of Limoges." *MAcad* 9, no. 3 (Winter 1977): 329-43.
Discusses this popular late thirteenth-century treatise organized on the visual metaphor of the eye and optics, its structure, arguments, dissemination, and relationship to the Franciscan revival of preaching.

550. Cole, Penny J. *The Preaching of the Crusades to the Holy Land, 1095-1270.* Medieval Academy Books, no. 98. Cambridge, MA: Medieval Academy, 1991.
Important for the study of Holy Land imagery in crusade and pilgrimage churches.

551. Davy, M. M. *Les sermons universitaires parisiens de 1230-1231.* Etudes de philosophie médiévale, no.15. Paris: Librairie Philosophique J. Vrin, 1931.

The first part of this volume discusses particular sermon collections, the practice and technique of the medieval university sermon generally, different topics of sermons, and the role of preachers. The second part consists of a list of published sermons from these years and the texts of a number of others. Bibliography and indices.

552. Heffernan, Thomas J. "Sermon Literature." *Middle English Prose: A Critical Guide to Major Authors and Genres.* Edited by A. S. G. Edwards. New Brunswick, NJ: Rutgers Univ. Press, 1984, pp. 177-207.
Surveys the large corpus of sermons in Middle English, with a generous bibliography of primary and secondary sources.

553. Kaeppeli, Thomas, O. P. *Scriptores Ordinis Praedicatorum Medii Aevi.* 3 vols. Rome: Istituto storico Dominicano, 1970-93.
Covers mendicant texts from 1221, the year of the death of St. Dominic, to about 1500.

554. Lecoy, A. de la Marche. *La chaire française au Moyen Age, specialement au XIIIe siècle.* Paris: Renouard, 1886.
A very thorough and detailed history—now much dated—discussing French preachers, their sermons, and society according to sermons, with this last area divided into the different topics treated in sermons. Lengthy bibliography of thirteenth-century sermons.

555. Lesnick, Daniel R. *Preaching in Medieval Florence: The Social World of Franciscan and Dominican Spirituality.* Athens and London: Univ. of Georgia Press, 1989.
Studies Dominican and Franciscan preaching in Florence. Appendices provide lists and discussions of Florentine friars active in various churches in the city. Bibliography and index.

556. Longère, Jean. *Oeuvres oratoires de maîtres parisiens au XIIe siècle: Etude historique et doctrinale.* 2 vols. Paris: Etudes augustiniennes, 1975.
An excellent introduction to the medieval sermon. Discusses the life and work of the preachers, with reference to passages from many works. Volume Two consists of extensive notes to Volume One, indices, and bibliography.

557. Machielsen, Johannis. *Clavis Patristica Pseudepigraphorum Medii Aevi IA-IB: Opera Homiletica.* 2 vols. Turnhout: Brepols, 1990.

This work is useful for identifying medieval sermons now believed anonymous, but which in the Middle Ages passed as the genuine works of patristic authors such as Saint Augustine or the Venerable Bede.

558. McLaughlin, R. Emmet. "The Word Eclipsed? Preaching in the Early Middle Ages." *Traditio* 46 (1991): 77-122.

A detailed historical account of preaching from the sixth to the twelfth century, discussing who did it, what rules guided it, how preachers were taught, surviving sermons, how much was oral or improvisational and how much written, what texts and collections were popular, how they were composed and from what authorities.

559. Morvay, Karin, and Dagmar Grube. *Bibliographie der deutschen Predigt des Mittelalters: Veröffentliche Predigten.* Munchener Texte und Untersuchungen, no. 47. Munich: C. H. Beck'sche, 1974.

Surveys the rich corpus of medieval German sermons from the Carolingian period through the early Franciscan sermon compilers and treats specific persons like Berthold von Regensburg and his period, then covers other well-known mystical and scholastic writers. Chapters on fifteenth-century German preachers also treat rimed sermons and even sermon parodies. This book provides a good overview of the subject.

560. Owst, G. R. *Literature and Pulpit in Medieval England: A Neglected Chapter in the History of English Letters & of the English People.* Oxford: Basil Blackwell, 1961.

A standard study of relations between medieval English literature, especially fourteenth-century vernacular, and contemporary sermons, according to various themes and types: allegory, the Virgin Mary, classical influences, animal fables, the Peasants' Revolt, the law, physicians, the drunkard and the tavern, gluttony and feasting, to name only a few of many subjects covered here. Index.

561. _____. *Preaching in Medieval England: An Introduction to Sermon Manuscripts of the Period c. 1350-1450.* New York: Russell and Russell, 1965.
Similar in emphasis to item 560.

562. Pfander, Homer G. *The Popular Sermon of the Medieval Friar in England.* New York: New York Univ. Press, 1937.
Studies "why [the sermons of medieval friars] were preached, why they took the form which they have, and what they contained." Presents many already-published, and two new, texts of sermons, "prefacing and accompanying them with considerable explanation of matters such as the conditions and manner of friar preaching, and the construction and contents of their sermons" (1). A number of useful excerpts from Middle English sermons containing animal and other conventional images are included.

563. Rico, Francisco. *Predicación y literatura en la espana medieval.* Cádiz, Spain: Instituto de Estudios Gaditanos. Centro Asociado Regional de UNED, 1977.
A twenty-three-page essay on the history of medieval Spanish sermons followed by an edition of a fifteenth century-Spanish sermon in an appendix.

564. Rouse, Richard, and Mary Rouse. *Preachers, Florilegia and Sermons: Studies on the Manipulus Florum of Thomas of Ireland.* Toronto: Pontifical Institute of Medieval Studies, 1979.
Detailed study of one of the most popular of medieval sermon aids.

565. Saperstein, Marc. *Jewish Preaching 1200-1800.* New Haven: Yale Univ. Press, 1991.
Studies Jewish sermons and their collections.

566. Schneyer, Johannes Baptiste. *Repertorium der lateinischen Sermonen des Mittelalters für die Zeit von 1150-1350.* 11 vols. Beiträge zur Geschichte der Philosophie und Theologie des Mittelalters, no. 43. Münster: Aschendorff, 1969-90.
Treats sermons and their authors from the twelfth through the fourteenth centuries.

567. _____. *Wegweiser zu lateinischen Predigtreihen des Mittelalters.*
Munich:Bayerischen Akademie der Wissenschaften,1965.
Continues his earlier work from the twelfth through the sixteenth
centuries.

568. Spencer, H. Leith. *English Preaching in the Late Middle Ages.*
Oxford: Clarendon, 1993.
Concerned chiefly with Middle English sermons in their learned
aspects, and their relation to the rise of Lollardy although there are
occasional comments on imagery. A very well written and
informative overview of what was a popular source of imagery in
England. Reviewed by A. S. G. Edwards in *Speculum* 71, no. 3 (July
1996): 764-6.

569. Swanson, Jenny. *John of Wales: A Study of the Works and Ideas
of a Thirteenth-Century Friar.* Cambridge Studies in Medieval
Life and Thought. Fourth Series. Cambridge: Cambridge Univ.
Press, 1989.
A detailed study of the life, works, and influence of this thirteenth-
century British Franciscan known for his numerous "encyclopaedic
preaching aids," with particular discussion of four of these works.
Including appendices providing lists of his works, surviving
manuscripts, and "individuals and institutions who owned copies"
(2).

570. Taylor, Larissa J. *Soldiers of Christ: Preaching in Late Medieval
and Reformation France.* Oxford: Oxford Univ. Press, 1992.
Covers later sermons and collections.

571. Zawart, Anscar. *The History of Franciscan Preaching and of
Franciscan Preachers (1209-1927): A Bibliographical Study.*
Franciscan Studies, no. 7. New York: Joseph Wagner, 1928.
The section on "Preaching before the Reformation(1209-1517)"
covers "Types of the Franciscan Sermon," "Saint Francis and His
Contemporaries," "The Scholastic Sermon," "Renaissance
Preachers," "Sacred Scripture and Homiletics," "The Sermon on the
Passion," "'Preaching the Cross,'" "Homiletic Aids and Materials,"
"Homiletics: The Theory," and "Bibliographical Statistics."
Bibliography and index.

572. Zink, Michel. *La prédication en langue Romane avant 1300.* Nouvelle Bibliothèque du Moyen Age, no. 4. Paris: Honoré Champion, 1976.

Discusses in detail the texts of sermons, their language, translations, the authors, their audiences, techniques of sermon writing and transmission, oratory art and allegorical expression, and topics commonly addressed. Bibliography and index.

PART TWO

Chapter Three: Learned Imagery

ALCHEMICAL IMAGES

573. Colnort-Bodet, Suzanne. *Le code alchimique dévoilé: Distillateurs, alchimistes et symbolistes.* Paris: Honoré Champion, 1989.
Studies one of the most important visual images in alchemical manuscripts, the alembic or distiller's vessal. An enthusiastic, though uncritical treatment of the subject, with an extensive bibliography. Many plates, but all from early printed books.

574. Gettings, Fred. *Dictionary of Occult, Hermetic and Alchemical Sigils.* London: Routledge and Kegan Paul, 1981.
Some 1500 different sigils or graphic symbols or signs associated with alchemy, astrology, geomancy, and related subjects and their processes. There is a graphic index by which the sigil can be identified. Bibliography.

575. Halleux, Robert. *Les textes alchimiques.* Typologie des sources du Moyen Age occidental, no. 32. Turnhout, Belgium: Brepols, 1979.
Begins with a bibliography and then covers such issues as the definition of alchemy; different approaches to it; origins, genres and their evolutions; problems in criticism; and alchemical texts as historical sources.

576. Kren, Claudia. *Alchemy in Europe: A Guide to Research.* Garland Reference Library of the Humanities, no. 692. New York: Garland, 1990.
A basic guide to the study of alchemy from its origins to the present.

577. Lennep, J. van. *Art & Alchimie: Etude de l'iconographie hermétique et ses influences.* Brussels: Meddens, 1966.
Examines the representation of various alchemical themes in manuscript illuminations, in engravings from alchemical tracts, and

in many other media, ranging from the Middle Ages up to the eighteenth century. Treats also alchemical images in church architecture, the transmutation of money and medallions, living quarters of alchemists, and particular alchemists and artists who depicted the subject, such as Nicolas Flamel, Albert Durer, Mantegna, Raphael, and Peter Breugel. Bibliography.

578. Newman, William R., ed. and trans. *The "Summa Perfectionis" of Pseudo-Geber: A Critical Edition, Translation and Study.* Leiden: Brill, 1991.
    Critical edition and translation of this alchemical treatise popular in the Middle Ages and attributed to 'Gerber,' a presumed Latinization of the name of one of the most famous Arabic alchemists, Jabir ibn Hayyan, who flourished about A.D. 800. Newman's text is based upon eight manuscript versions from the thirteenth and fourteenth centuries. Reviewed by Robert P. Multhauf in *Speculum* 69, no. 2 (April 1994): 540-42.

579. _____. " Technology and Alchemical Debate in the Late Middle Ages." *Isis* 80 (1989) : 423-45.
    Studies "the late medieval dispute over the importance of alchemy—whether it fit into the legitimate fields of knowledge and whether its claims were possible or even legal" (423), with the goal of showing that "in these obscure treatises of the thirteenth century, a propagandistic literature of technological development was born" (443). Includes as an appendix both the Latin text and an English translation of Paul of Taranto's discussion of the types of human technology.

580. Obrist, Barbara, ed. and trans. *Constantine of Pisa. The Book of the Secrets of Alchemy.* Collection de travaux de l'Académie Internationale d'Histoire des Sciences, no. 34. Leiden: Brill, 1990.
    Edition and translation of this thirteenth- century alchemical treatise in Latin, with extensive commentary on the place of the *Liber Secretorum Alchimie* in the context of medieval learning, with selected bibliography, figures from the manuscript, and index.

581. _____. *Les débuts de l'imagerie alchimique (XIVe-XVe siècles).*

Paris: Le Sycomore, 1982.

Reviews the state of research in the field, covers alchemical literature of the Middle Ages before it was illustrated and then investigates three of the oldest illustrated alchemical cycles: Constantine's *Secrets de ma Dame alchimie*, the anonymous Franciscan *Livre de la Sainte Trinité*, and the Swiss *Aurora consurgens*, analyzing numerous miniatures from the manuscripts to describe the iconography of alchemy and discuss the reasons for its development. Bibliography, plates, and index.

582. Patai, Raphael. *The Jewish Alchemists: A History and Source Book*. Princeton Univ. Press, 1994.

Looks at Jewish contributions to alchemy in the Bible and Talmud, the Hellenistic period, the early Arab world, and then by century from the eleventh onward, with discussion of particular philosophers and manuscripts. Some plates and an index.

583. Pereira, Michael. *The Alchemical Corpus Attributed to Raymond Lull*. Warburg Institute Surveys and Texts, no.18. London: The Warburg Institute, 1989.

According to the introduction, "this survey is not—nor can it be—a complete history of the origin and formation of the pseudo-Lullian alchemical corpus.... [The author has] assembled all available data concerning individual works, manuscript miscellanies, printed editions and historical testimonies in order to bring together and make available to scholars as much material as possible. [The author also] offers some tentative hypotheses about the formation of the corpus" (1). With chapters on the background, "The Spread of Pseudo-Lullian Alchemy," "The Legend of Lull the Alchemist," "Scholarly Disputes and Critical Assessment," and a "Catalogue of Alchemical Works Attributed to Raymond Lull" (with its own indices of manuscripts, titles, and incipits), along with a bibliography and index of names.

584. Pritchard, Alan. *Alchemy: A Bibliography of English-Language Writings*. London: Routledge and Kegan Paul: Library Association, 1980.

A basic guide to the study of alchemy from its origins to modern times, not focussing particularly on the medieval period. This bibliography covers alchemical texts arranged by country and works about alchemy arranged by country and then by subjects. Authors are listed alphabetically under each heading rather than by date or date of material covered, so the book is difficult to use for the medievalist but still a valuable resource. Somewhat more limited than item 576 [Kren] because it deals only with studies in English.

585. Roberts, Gareth. *The Mirror of Alchemy: Alchemical Ideas and Images in Manuscripts and Books from Antiquity to the Seventeenth Century.* London: The British Library, 1995.
Extremely useful study of alchemical iconography, with many pictures. Includes also a glossary of alchemical terms, bibliography, an appendix "Alchemical Texts and Writers: Manuscripts in the British Library," and an index.

ASTROLOGY, IMAGERY OF

General

586. Allen, Don Cameron. *The Star-Crossed Renaissance: The Quarrel about Astrology and Its Influence in England.* Reprint. New York: Octagon Books, 1966.
Covers "Ficino, Pico della Mirandola, Pontano, and the Astrologers' Doctrine," "Some Continental Attitudes," "Attack and Defense in Renaissance England," "Some Aspects of the Dispute about Astrology among Elizabethan and Jacobean Men of Letters," "Elizabethan and Jacobean Satires on the Almanack and Prognostication," and an appendix entitled, "Some Astrological Physicians and Their Works." A considerable amount of information about medieval medical astrology is provided. Bibliography and index.

587. Barkai, Ron. "L'astrologie juive médiévale: Aspects théoriques et pratiques." *LMA* 93 (1987): 323-48.

Examines the development of the distinction between magic and astrology and offers a chronology of Jewish astronomers of the Middle Ages and the reception or rejection of astrological ideas by Jewish thinkers.

588. Barton, Tamsyn. *Power and Knowledge: Astrology, Physiognomics, and Medicine under the Roman Empire*. Ann Arbor: Univ. of Michigan Press, 1994.
Studies late Roman astrology, physiognomics, and medical prognosis and shows how the modern distinction between science and pseudo-science was not one made in antiquity. Some plates.

589. Bober, Harry. "The Zodiacal Miniature of the Très Riches Heures of the Duc of Berry: Its Sources and Meaning." *JWCI* 11 (1948): 1-34.
Studies the significance of these well-known miniatures and their relation to the calendar tradition. Many plates.

590. Carey, Hilary M. *Courting Disaster: Astrology at the English Court and University in the Later Middle Ages*. New York: St. Martin's Press, 1992.
"[C]oncerns the social and intellectual context in which astrology operated and the people who found themselves attracted to it in the later Middle Ages" (1), covering astrology before 1376; books, libraries, and scholars; and astrology in the Merton Circle and in the courts of Edward III, Richard II, Charles V, Henry V, and Henry VI. Supplemented by some plates, lengthy bibliography, and index, and by the following useful appendices listing "Manuscripts of known provenance with texts concerning astrology, divination and some related matters, with their owners, donors, and readers"; "Books on astrology in the medieval libraries of the Universities of Oxford and Cambridge"; "Horoscopes in English manuscripts"; and "Bibliographical guide to the technical practice of medieval astrology." Reviewed by John B. Friedman in *Speculum* 69, no. 4 (October 1994): 1135-8.

591. Eamon, William. *Science and the Secrets of Nature: Books of Secrets in Medieval and Early Modern Culture*. Princeton Univ. Press, 1994.
A detailed, informative discussion of the genre with a lengthy

bibliography and index, some illustrations and tables, and an appendix reproducing an Italian booklet of secrets from the sixteenth or seventeenth century.

592. Fontaine, Jacques. "Isidore de Séville et l'astrologie." *Tradition et actualité chez Isidore de Séville*. London: Varorium Reprints, 1988, pp. 271-300.
A collection of articles on Isidore previously published by this author in other places concerning astrology, rhetoric, encyclopaediae, and the like. The item mentioned here discusses Isidore's key distinction between astrology and astronomy.

593. Gettings, Fred. *The Secret Zodiac: The Hidden Art in Mediaeval Astrology*. London and New York: Routledge and Kegan Paul, 1987.
According to the preface, "this book deals with the esoteric significance of a thirteenth-century zodiac in one of the most beautiful churches in Italy" The church treated is San Miniato al Monte, Florence (ix). Some plates.

594. Grant, Edward. "Medieval and Renaissance Scholastic Conceptions of the Influence of the Celestial Region on the Terrestrial." *JMRS* 17 (1987):1-23.
Examines the belief so central to astrology that "celestial bodies exerted a vital and even controlling influence over material things in the terrestrial region" (1), its sources in Aristotle and Ptolomy, and its permutations in various medieval writers.

595. _____. *Planets, Stars, and Orbs: The Medieval Cosmos, 1200-1687*. Cambridge: Cambridge Univ. Press, 1994.
Treating the clash between Aristotelian cosmology and Copernican, this work offers a detailed, scholarly investigation on the nature and sources of medieval cosmology. Index and bibliography and some illustrations.

596. Jervis, Jane L. *Cometary Theory in Fifteenth-Century Europe*. Polish Academy of Sciences. The Institute for the History of Science, Education and Technology Centre for Copernican Studies. Dordrecht: D. Reidel, 1985.

Looks at cometary theory in antiquity as well as in the early and later Middle Ages. Also considers individual Renaissance theorists such as Jacobus Angelus, Paolo Toscanelli, Georg Peurbach, and Johannes Regiomontanus. Appendices provide facsimile editions of Jacobus Angelus's "Tractatus de cometis" and Regiomontanus's "Sixteen Problems," as well as Toscanelli's mathematical computations and the Latin text of "De cometa," attributed to Regiomontanus. Includes indices of subjects and names.

597. Laistner, M. L. W. "The Western Church and Astrology during the Early Middle Ages." *HTR* 34 (1941): 251-75.
Examines the Church's opposition to astrology, with numerous quotations from patristic writers such as Ambrosiaster, Bede, and Gregory of Nazianzus, and the actions taken or not taken to suppress it in the early Middle Ages.

598. Matheson, Lister M., ed. *Popular and Practical Science of Medieval England.* Medieval Texts and Studies, no. 11. East Lansing, MI: Colleagues Press, 1994.
A collection of twelve edited Middle English texts in the areas of astrology, prognostication, medicine, horticulture, and navigation. According to the editor, "each text is prefaced by an introduction explaining the general scientific and cultural contexts of the text's field and a description of the manuscripts and early printed editions (if any) from which the text has been edited. Where appropriate, the significance of the text as background to Middle English literary works is noted" (xi). Glossary and several indices. Reviewed by John B. Friedman in forthcoming *JEGP.*

599. Means, Laurel. *Medieval Lunar Astrology: A Collection of Representative Middle English Texts.* Lewiston, NY: Edwin Mellen, 1993.
A critical edition of eighteen Middle English astrological texts in verse and prose and prognostica for all aspects of human life, and for medical, physiognomic, and astral influence. Includes a selected bibliography.

600. North, J. D. "Celestial Influence: The Major Premiss of Astrology." *'Astrologi Halucinati': Stars and the End of the World in Luther's Time. Papers Presented at the International Seminar*

at the Wissenschaftskolleg zu Berlin 28-29 May 1984. Edited by
Paola Zambelli. Berlin and New York: Walter de Gruyter,
1986, pp. 45-100.
North writes, "Here I want to consider the more general problem of
ways in which the celestial bodies were supposed to produce their
effects, whether by an influx of infusion, or by some other means yet
to be specified" (45). Covers a great many mostly medieval
astrological writers.

601. _____. *Horoscopes and History.* Warburg Institute Surveys and
        Texts, no. 13. London: The Warburg Institute, Univ. of
        London, 1986.
A technical book with many charts and graphs. Discusses
mathematical techniques employed in astrology. Index. Reviewed
by Richard Kremer in *Speculum* 65, no.1 (January 1990): 206-9.
According to Kremer, "North has written a narrow yet fascinating
study of the central feature of astrological grammar—the mundane
houses and the mathematical rules requires for their construction.
His is the first reliable and thorough treatment of 'domification'"
(207).

602. _____. "Medieval Concepts of Celestial Influence: A Survey."
        Astrology, Science and Society: Historical Essays. Edited by
        Patrick Curry. Woodbridge, Suffolk: Boydell, 1987, pp. 5-18.
An overview of the subject beginning with ideas from Aristotle and
Ptolemy. Short bibliography.

603. Poulle, Emmanuel. *Les sources astronomiques (textes, tables,
        instruments).* Typologie des sources du Moyen Age occidental,
        no. 39. Turnhout: Brepols,1981.
Begins with a bibliography, then covers cosmology, astronomy, the
"primum mobile," planetary astronomy, particular applications
(including the calendar, eclipses, and comets), and the historian and
astronomical sources. With a few illustrations and tables.

604. Smoller, Laura Ackerman. *History, Prophecy, and the Stars: The
        Christian Astrology of Pierre D'Ailly, 1350-1420.* Princeton
        Univ. Press,1994.
A detailed examination of the astrological theories in their historical

setting of D'Ailly, scholar and churchman who so influenced the beliefs of Christopher Columbus. Select bibliography and index.

605. Tester, S. J. *A History of Western Astrology.* Woodbridge, Suffolk and Wolfeboro, NH: Boydell, 1987.
Reviewed by Richard Kremer in *Speculum* 65, no.1 (January 1990): 206-9. According to Kremer, Tester "surveys not the language of astrology but rather the history of its use, defense, and defamation, from the second century B. C. through the eighteenth century" (208).

COMPLEXIONS AND PHYSIOGNOMY

606. Azouvi, F. "Remarques sur quelques traités de physiognomonique." *LEP* 48 (1978): 431-48.
General cultural study of medieval and Renaissance physiognomy.

607. Caputo, Cosimo. "La struttura del segno fisiognomico. (G.B. Della Porta e l'universo culturale del Cinquecento.") *Il Protagora,* 4th ser., 22 (June-July 1982): 63-102.
Studies syllogisms involving physignomic concepts by the sixteenth-century Neapolitan dramatist and logician, Giovambattista Della Porta. Towards the end of the article there is some general treatment of physiognomy.

608. Forster, Richard, ed. *Scriptores physiognomonici graeci et latini.* 2 vols. Stuttgart and Leipzig: B. G. Teubner, 1994.
Volume One includes Physiognomonica Pseudoaristotelis, Graece et Latine, Adamantii cum epitomis Graece, Polemonis e recensione Georgii Hoffmanni Arabice et Latine continens. Volume Two includes Physiognomonica anonymi, Pseudopolemonis, Rasis, Secreti Secretorum Latine, anonymi Graece, fragmenta, and indices. The standard edition of the late antique physiognomists.

609. Friedman, John B. "Another Look at Chaucer and the Physiognomists." *SP* 78 (1981): 138-52.

Examines the use of "affective" physiognomy in Chaucer's poetry, glances, blushing, and the like, with a general overview of medieval physiognomy.

610. _____, ed. *John de Foxton's Liber Cosmographiae (1408): An Edition and Codicological Study.* Leiden: Brill, 1988.
Provides in the introduction under the section "The Pictures" full-page miniatures of the four temperaments and discussion of these.

611. Jordan, Leo. "Physiognomische Abhandlungen." *RM* 29 (1911): 680-720.
Very valuable study of the theory of physiognomy in the Middle Ages. Numerous quotations in Old French from two unpublished physiognomic treatises illustrate both the theory of the subject and—body part by body part—the characters of men and women with the physical traits in question. Portions of a fourteenth or fifteenth-century French manuscript are also published containing a chiromantic treatise. Some attention is paid to physiognomic theory in the sixteenth century as well.

612. Neubert, Fritz. "Die volkstümlichen Anschauungen über Physiognomik in Frankreich bis zum Ausgang des Mittelalters." *RF* 29 (1911): 557-679.
Extremely useful overview of the pseudo-science of physiognomy, or how a person's moral disposition can be known from facial features. Develops not only working definitions of the subject from passages in Old and Middle French *chansons de geste* and romances, but also explains how various diabolical moral qualities are tied to specific features or nationalities as described in these poems. Among the features touched on are size (giants and dwarves), beards, and old age. Then, one by one, Neubert proceeds to consider head, hair, beard, eyes, nose, mouth, teeth, and ears, as well as more abstract elements of stature such as hunchbackedness, skinnyness, and manner or emotion such as melancholy, anger, and love.

613. Squatriti, Paolo. "Personal Appearance and Physiognomics in Early Medieval Italy." *JMH* 14 (1988): 191-202.
"Starting with an analysis of the physical description of bishops in the Italian episcopal *Gesta*, the paper proceeds to a consideration of

the importance of personal appearance for early medieval leaders. Light is cast on these issues thanks to the use of late antique physiognomic theory. Physiognomic thinking, it is demonstrated, was current at least at an informal level amongst many authors in Italy as well as being familiar even in non-literate social categories. The paper likewise uses physiognomics to explain the relationship between the literary physical descriptions and the paintings on which they were often based" (191). Bibliography.

614. Thorndike, Lynn. "De complexionibus." *Isis* 49 (1958): 398-408.
Discusses this theme as it appears in a number of medieval manuscripts, most unpublished, with passages quoted from these, considering different variations on the idea of complexions (here taken to mean "one's physical constitution or bodily makeup as a whole") associated with the four humors: sanguine, phlegmatic, choleric, and melancholic.

GEOGRAPHICAL IMAGERY

615. Andrews, M. C. "The Study and Classification of Medieval Mappae Mundi." *Archaeologia* 75 (1926): 61-76.
Useful for an illustration of the different forms of the T-O map.

616. Arentzen, J.-G. *Imago Mundi Cartographica. Studien zur Bildlichkeit mittelalterlicher Welt- und Ökumenekarten unter besonderer Berücksichtigung des Zusammenwirkens von Text und Bild.* Munich: Wilhelm Fink, 1984.
Outlines the history of medieval cartography and explains the great religious maps like that of Ebstorf in their teaching and pilgrimage contexts. Treats late developments like the portolani, and the highly idiosyncratic maps of Opicinis da Canistris. An excellent bibliography and a large collection of black-and-white illustrations of most of the major medieval world maps add to the volume's utility.

617. Betten, Francis S. "The Knowledge of the Sphericity of the Earth During the Earlier Middle Ages." *CHR* 9, n.s., 3 (1923): 74-90. Explodes the common belief that medieval people visualized the world as flat.

618. Brincken, A.-D. von den. *Kartographische Quellen: Welt-, See- und Regionalkarten.* Typologie des sources du Moyen Age occidental, no. 51. Turnhout: Bepols, 1988. Examines the Biblical, patristic, and classical thinking which lay behind the various world maps and nautical charts of the Middle Ages. Some plates and a useful list of medieval world and regional maps. A full bibliographical study. Reviewed by G. Kish in *Speculum* 64, no. 4 (1989): 1047-8.

619. _____. "Mappa mundi und Chronographia. Studien zur Imago Mundi des abenlaendischen Mittelalters." *DAEM* 24 (1968): 118-86. Further studies by this author on the world map with special reference to the concept in Honorius of Autun.

620. _____ "'. . .ut describeretur universus orbis.' Zur Universalkartographie des Mittelalters."*MM* 7 (1970): 249-78. Detailed account of the development of medieval cartography. With some plates.

621. Bologna, Corrado, ed. *Liber Monstrorum de diversis generibus/ Libro delle mirabili difformità.* Milan: Bompiani, 1977. Latin and Italian edition of one of the most fascinating of medieval monster books, composed probably in England or Ireland in the seventh to eighth centuries.The work has sometimes been associated with Aldhelm of Malmsbury. Places the work historically and gives a bibliography and explanatory notes.

622. Buridant, Claude, ed. *La traduction de l' "Historia Orientalis" de Jacques de Vitry.* Bibliothèque française et romane, ser. B: Editions critiques de textes, no. 19. Paris: Klincksieck, 1986. Provides a critical edition of the French text of this work. Reviewed by J. G. Rowe in *Speculum* 63, no. 1 (January 1988): 130. Rowe explains, "The *Historia Orientalis* is an important witness to what

the thirteenth century thought the early crusades were all about To the derivative historical narrative are added a short treatment of Islam and essays on the flora and fauna, the cities, and the indigenous populations of Syria-Palestine" (130).

623. Campbell, Mary B. *The Witness and the Other World: Exotic European Travel Writing, 400-1600.* Ithaca and London: Cornell Univ. Press, 1988.
"Part One: The East" discusses travel writing about the fabulous East, "The Utter East: Merchant and Missionary Travels during the 'Mongol Peace,'" and Mandeville. "Part Two: The West" looks at Columbus and Raleigh. With some plates and index.

624. Dainville, François de. *Le langage des géographes.* Paris: A. and J. Picard, 1964.
Though this book concerns maps from 1500 onward, it is extremely useful for a study of medieval cartography, especially from the iconographic point of view. It opens with general definitions of terms like cardinal points, cosmography, and zone, and others often extremely technical, giving these terms in several different languages. Numerous line drawings illustrate these often abstract ideas.Terms of measurement like league and mile are also given, and defined with both Latin and vernacular examples, as are place names like Bosphorus and architectural ones like mansus. A few plates of manuscript miniatures from Jean Corbechon's translation of Bartholomaeus Anglicus' *De Proprietatibus Rerum* showing geographical features preface a number of details from maps of the woodcut period. There is a very full index of terms and places referred to in the book.

625. Destombes, Marcel, ed. *Mappemondes AD 1200-1500: Catalogue preparé par pour la Commission des Cartes Anciennes de l'Union Geographiques Internationale.* Vol. I of *Monumenta Cartographica Vetustioris Aevi, AD 1200-1500.* Amsterdam: N. Israel, 1964.
Standard catalogue and discussion of the corpus of medieval world maps.

626. Flint, Valerie I. J. *The Imaginative Landscape of Christopher Columbus.* Princeton Univ. Press, 1992.

Attempts "to reconstruct, and understand, not the New World Columbus found, but the Old World which he carried with him in his head" and his "medieval cosmology" but to distinguish "fact" from "fantasy" in his voyage. Explains how "a surprising number of Columbus's descriptions were influenced by, and reflect, particular expectations; and that many of these expectations were, to us, extraordinary ones" (xi). Plates of maps, bibliography and index. Reviewed by Scott Westrem in *Speculum* 68, no. 3 (July 1993): 764-8.

627. _____. "Monsters and the Antipodes in the Early Middle Ages and Enlightenment." *Viator* 15 (1984): 65-80.
Examines the debates in the eighth century and then again in the seventeenth on the existence and nature of the other side of the world and the possible human inhabitants there, with numerous passages cited, especially from the earlier phase of this debate.

*   Friedman, John B. *The Monstrous Races.* Cited below as item 1337. Explores medieval attitudes towards, and iconographical depiction of, monstrous races believed to exist in far away places such as "India, Ethiopia, Albania, or Cathay," and later, as these regions began to be explored, in "the Far North and ultimately the New World" (1). Includes numerous plates of the monstrous races as presented in medieval art works, lengthy bibliography, and an index.

628. Gosman, Martin. *La lettre du Prêtre Jean: Les versions en ancien français et en ancien occitan. Textes et commentaires.* Groningen: Bouma's Boekhuis bv, 1982.
A critical edition of the surviving manuscript versions in Old French and Provençal of a twelfth century letter to Pope Alexander III written by the Christian emperor-priest of a fabulous land near India. This letter appears in a variety of medieval works on travel and was a very important sources of imagery. Gosman discusses manuscripts, dating, and authorship.

629. Gumilev, L. N. *Searches for an Imaginary Kingdom: The Legend of the Kingdom of Prester John.* Translated by R. E. F. Smith. Past and Present Publications. Cambridge: Cambridge Univ.

Press, 1987.
There is some material in this book on the medieval legend of Prester John, though its actual focus is on the history of the Great Steppe from the eighth century to the formation of the Mongol Empire in the first half of the thirteenth century. Index. Bibliography, chiefly in Russian.

630. Harley, J. B., and David Woodward, eds. *The History of Cartography.* Vol.1: *Cartography in Prehistoric, Ancient, and Medieval Europe and the Mediterranean.* Chicago and London: Univ. of Chicago Press, 1987.
The first place to turn to for any investigation into medieval maps. Part three, "Cartography in Medieval Europe and the Mediterranean," pp. 281-509, covers "Medieval Maps: An Introduction," "Medieval 'Mappemundi,'" "Portolan Charts from the Late Thirteenth Century to 1500," and "Local and Regional Cartography in Medieval Europe," with many plates, lists and descriptions of medieval maps of all sorts, general index, and bibliographical index.

631. Harvey, P. D. A. *Mappa Mundi. The Hereford World Map.* London: The British Library,1996.
Studies the Hereford map in some detail, making the early studies by Crone and Moir obsolete, and placing it in the context of other world maps of the twelfth through the fourteenth centuries. Color plates.

632. _____. *Medieval Maps.* London: The British Library, 1991.
An introduction to the subject containing numerous attractive color plates and covering "World maps before 1400," "Portolan charts before 1400," "The fifteenth century," "Maps of regions," and "Local maps."

633. Helleiner, Karl F. "Prester John's Letter: A Mediaeval Utopia." *The Phoenix* 13 (1959): 47-57.
Discusses the twelfth-century letter in which Prester John describes his encounters with pagans who are virtuous and idealized, the dissemination of this text, and the history and ideas of the East surrounding it.

634. Hyde, J. K. "Real and Imaginary Journeys in the Later Middle

Ages." *BJRL* 65 (1982-83): 125-47.
An historical exploration of the medieval interest in (and lack of interest in) accurate geography. Looks at many writers' geographical descriptions and where they get them.

635. Jaffe, Irma B., et al., eds. *Imagining the New World: Columbian Iconography.* Rome and New York: Istituto della Enciclopedia Italiana, 1991.
Gives a visual sense of the world as Columbus and his contemporaries would have seen it. With representations of many places and concepts mentioned by Columbus.

636. Kliege, Herma. *Weltbild und Darstellungspraxis hochmittelalterlicher Weltkarten.* Münster: Nodus, 1991.
This excellent book is a good overview and catalogue of most of the known medieval world maps, The author begins with a general essay on cartography from antiquity through the Middle Ages along with a discussion of zone and climate theory. The treatment of the techniques and conventions of maps, drawing them, placement and character of legends, and T-O map types is also valuable. Three longer essays on the Lambert of St. Omer maps, the Duchy of Cornwall fragments and the London Psalter map, add to the work's value. Chapter Five is a listing of major world maps up through about 1350, with location, secondary literature, and the like. The book is completed by several plates including some in color of the different map types and a thorough bibliography.

637. Kügler, Hartmut, et al., eds. *Ein Weltbild vor Columbus. Die Ebstorfer Weltkarte. Interdisziplinäres Colloquium 1988.* Weinheim: VCH Acta Humaniora, 1991.
Seventeen essays all in German, by scholars eminent in the field of medieval cartography on one of the most famous medieval world maps, the enomous map once in the Ebstorf cloister but destroyed in World War II. Many of the essays treat the imagery of the map in considerable detail. Numerous in-text black-and-white plates. No bibliography is provided but there are indices of places on the map and modern authors. Tends to focus only on German scholarship.

638. Miller, Konrad. *Mappaemundi: Die altesen Weltkarten.* 6 vols.

Stuttgart: J. Roth, 1895, 1898.
The standard corpus of maps and the only collection to give a large-scale reproduction of the now destroyed Ebstorf map.

639. Nowotny, Karl A. *Beiträge zur Geschichte des Weltsbildes, Farben und Weltrichtungen.* Wiener Beiträge zur Kulturgeschichte und Linguistik, no. 17. Horn and Vienna: Ferdinand Berger, 1970.
A study of the visual schemes by which both the old and new worlds were conceived from many nations and periods. Some plates of medieval representations and a bibliography.

640. Pelletier, Monique, ed. *Géographie du Monde au Moyen Age et à la Renaissance.* Mémoires de la section de géographie, no. 15. Paris: Comité des travaux historiques et scientifiques, 1989.
A collection of articles on the subject from a conference held in Paris in 1987, divided into the following sections: medieval "mappemondes," allegorical cartography of the Renaissance, cartographical methods of the great discoveries, and cartography of islands. With numerous plates throughout.

641. Phillips, J. R. S. *The Medieval Expansion of Europe.* Oxford and New York: Oxford Univ. Press, 1988.
This historical book has three goals: it "seeks to determine the extent and nature of the relations between western Europe and the three continents of Asia, Africa, and America between about 1000 and 1500;[secondly] to assess the degree to which new information gained about the other world was absorbed into scholarly theory and popular conceptions;[and thirdly] to discuss the relationship between the medieval expansion of Europe and the ideas about the world which were current in medieval Europe, and the better known and more thoroughly documented expansion of Europe which took place in the fifteenth century" (vi-vii).

642. Roncière, Monique de la, and Michel Mollat du Jourdin, et al. *Les portulans: Cartes marines du XIIIe au XVIIe siècle.* Fribourg: Office du Livre, 1984.
Portolani were practical sailing charts of coast lines, winds and distances for navigators. However, many of the more ornate examples had a great deal of interesting and exotic imagery which reflected the iconographic concerns of their age. This book offers a

quarto-sized collection of these maps drawn for ship navigation from the thirteenth- to seventeenth-century arranged by date, in color, and accompanied by descriptions. An introduction discusses the history of these charts. Bibliography and index.

643. Samarrai, Alauddin. "Beyond Belief and Reverence: Medieval Mythological Ethnography in the Near East and Europe." *JMRS* 23 (1993): 19-42.
Examines the similarity between medieval Latin and Arabic sources, and the long survival of the ideas contained in these texts, with many interesting examples such as descriptions of Gog and Magog and the Amazons.

644. Scheiwiller, Vanni, ed. *De Moribus Brachmanorum liber Sancto Ambrosio falso adscriptus.* Milan: Apo,1956.
Latin edition of this work with very brief Latin textual note.

645. Westrem, Scott D., ed. *Discovering New Worlds: Essays on Medieval Exploration and Imagination.* Garland Medieval Casebooks, no. 2. Garland Reference Library of the Humanities, no. 1436. New York and London: Garland, 1991.
A collection of essays concerning such subjects as descriptions of landscape in medieval pilgrimage, oriental monstrosities, Mongol cannibalism, Amazons, Mandeville, canon law on the question of the "humanity" of foreigners, and discovery in Dante. Bibliography and index.

646. Wittkower, Rudolf. "Marvels of the East: A Study in the History of Monsters." *Allegory and the Migration of Symbols* (item 272), pp. 45-74.
Studies the Plinean tradition of monstrous races of men living in Africa and India. Many plates.

647. Yankowski, S.V., trans. *The Brahman Episode*. Anspach: Ansbach: E. Kottmeier and E. G. Kostetzky, 1962.
Translation of the work.

MEDICAL ICONOGRAPHY

648. Biedermann, Hans. *Medicina Magica: Metaphysical Healing Methods in Late-antique and Medieval Manuscripts with Thirty Facsimile Plates.* Translated by Rosemarie Werba. The Classics of Medicine Library. Birmingham, AL: Gryphon, 1986.
An introduction discussing such topics as metaphysical healing theories, the Four Humours, and magical drugs, precedes the color plates, each with a full description of the medical healing method it depicts. **See also items 1537, 1544-7.**

649. Campbell, Sheila, et al., eds. *Health, Disease and Healing in Medieval Culture.* New York: St. Martin's, 1992.
A collection of essays on the subject discussing such topics as cancer, Anglo-Saxon views on the causes of disease, surgical anesthetics, and surgery in medieval Iceland. Plates.

650. Friedman, John B. "The Friar Portrait in Bodleian Library MS Douce 104: Contemporary Satire? " *YLS* 8 (1994): 177-84.
Treats satiric use of images of urinoscopy flasks being examined by friars in manuscript illustration of *Piers Plowman.*

651. Gottfried, Robert S. *Doctors and Medicine in Medieval England 1340-1530.* Princeton Univ. Press, 1986.
Presents "a study of English doctors and medicine from the Black Death to the foundations of the Royal College of Physicians" (3), looking at the rise of surgery especially for military and political reasons, the later return to physic, the position of doctors as "part of a bourgeois middle class," "quality of practice" (5), and sources of knowledge, among other topics. Plates from medieval art works, bibliography, and index.

652. Imbault-Huart, Marie-José. *La médecine au Moyen Age à travers les manuscrits de la Bibliothèque Nationale.* Paris: Porte Verte, 1983.
A diverse collection of color plates from medieval manuscripts in the Bibliothèque Nationale concerning medicine with introduction

and descriptions and divided up into the following categories: medicine, surgery and obstetrics, materia medica (herbs, beakers), and society and treatment (hospitals and the like).

653. Jacquart, Danielle, and Claude Thomasset. *Sexuality and Medicine in the Middle Ages.* Translated by Matthew Adamson. Princeton Univ. Press 1988.
Considers ideas of physiology, venereal disease, and the influence of anatomical treatises on popular views of the human body. Also considers medieval erotic art, questions of impotence and hysteria, and how female sexuality was perceived as corrupt. The original French text of this work first published in 1985 was reviewed by John M. Riddle in *Speculum* 65, no. 1 (January 1990): 178-80.

654. Jones, Peter Murray. *Medieval Medical Miniatures.* Austin: Univ. of Texas Press published in co-operation with The British Library, 1985.
As Jones explains in the introduction, "this book is intended to display some of the extraordinary wealth of medical illustration to be found in medieval manuscripts" (9). Jones provides discussion of the plates and background to medical practice in the period, divided up under the following sections: anatomy; diagnosis and prognosis; materia medica; cautery and surgery; and diet, regimen, and medication. Index.

655. Kurtz, Otto. "The Medical Illustrations of the Wellcome Manuscript" Appendix to "A Spiritual Encyclopaedia" (item 500), pp. 137-42.
Looks at the medical illustrations in this fifteenth-century manuscript in light of the tradition of medieval medical iconography, with plates from a number of different sources.

656. Kuss, René, and Willy Gregoir. *Histoire illustrée de l'urologie de l'antiquité à nos jours.* Paris: Les éditions Roger Dacosta,1988.
A large coffee-table book treating a variety of matters relating to the urinary tract. The first chapter is chiefly interesting for the medievalist, with many illustrations of uroscopy flasks drawn from medieval manuscripts. Many plates throughout and a select bibliography. Index.

657. MacKinney, Loren. *Medical Illustrations in Medieval Manuscripts.*
     Berkeley and Los Angeles: Univ. of California Press, 1965.
     Part one has sections on hospitals, diagnosis and prognosis by
     uroscopy, pulse-reading and astrology, pharmacy and medication,
     healing by cauterization and phlebotomy, surgery,
     orthopaedics,obstetrics, dentistry, the bath, and veterinary medicine.
     Each description relates to miniatures at the back of the book. Part
     two consists of a checklist of "medical miniatures in extant
     manuscripts," compiled with the assistance of Thomas Herndon.
     Select bibliography, and index.

658. Miller, Elaine. *Sources in Medieval Medicine: A Bibliography.* New
     York: Garland, 1982.
     A bibliography arranged by various types of medieval medical
     treatises.

659. Pouchelle, Marie-Christine. *The Body and Surgery in the Middle
     Ages.* New Brunswick, N.J: Rutgers Univ. Press, 1991.
     Focusses on the image of the body in fourteenth-century France and
     on the surgical treatise by Henri de Mondeville, the first physician
     to write on the subject.

660. Rawcliffe, Carole. *Sources for the History of Medicine in Late
     Medieval England.* Kalamzoo, MI: Medieval Institute
     Publications, 1995.
     Uses printed books and manuscript sources to give information on
     English medicine from the fourteenth through the sixteenth centuries.
     Good on the way Latin medical texts were translated into the
     vernaculars.

661. Robbins, Rossell Hope. "Medical Manuscripts in Middle English."
     Speculum 45, no. 2 (1970): 393-415.
     Robbins mentions over 350 Middle English medical manuscripts
     of prognosis, diagnosis, and treatment, mostly undiscussed and
     unpublished; classifies the type of materials contained in them, and
     draws conclusions about the lay practice of medicine in later
     medieval England.

662. Schleissner, Margaret R., ed. *Manuscript Sources of Medieval*

Medicine: A Book of Essays. New York and London: Garland, 1995.
Essays on particular medical manuscripts, authors, and topics such as a history of twelfth-century German medical manuscripts and manuscript sources on birth control. Index.

663. Schuler, Robert M. *English Magical and Scientific Poems to 1700: An Annotated Bibliography.* Garland Reference Library of the Humanities, no. 169. New York and London: Garland, 1979.
Arranged alphabetically and with an index of subjects and one of names.

664. Siraisi, Nancy. *Medieval & Early Renaissance Medicine: An Introduction to Knowledge and Practice.* Chicago and London: Univ. of Chicago Press, 1990.
Has as subject, "western European literate and technical medicine and its practitioners between about the mid-twelfth and the end of the fifteenth century," with chapters on "The Formation of Western European Medicine," "Practitioners and Conditions of Practice," "Medical Education," "Physiological and Anatomical Knowledge," "Disease and Treatment," and "Surgeons and Surgery." Includes plates, "Guide to Further Reading," list of "Selected Primary Sources Available in English Translation," bibliography, and index.

665. Wickersheimer, Ernest. *Les manuscrits latins de médecine du haut Moyen Age dans les bibliothèques de France.* Documents, études et répertoires publiés par l'Institut de Recherche et d'Histoire de Textes, no. 11. Paris: CNRS, 1966.
A catalogue of medieval Latin medical manuscripts in French libraries with descriptions and arranged alphabetically by region. Includes some plates and a number of indices for easy reference.

MYTHOLOGICAL IMAGERY

General

666. Rager, Catherine. *Dictionnaire des sujets mythologiques, bibliques, hagiographiques et historiques dans l'art.* Turnhout: Brepols, 1994.
    A useful single volume compendium with brief entries on a variety of topics relating to iconography, understood more in the sense of identifying personages and objects than in developing their symbolism. Thus, we are told who Orpheus or Absolom or Saint Barbara or Hannibal were, and what texts give the fullest accounts of them.

667. Reid, Davidson Jane. *The Oxford Guide to Classical Mythology in the Arts 1300-1990's.* 2 vols. Oxford: Oxford Univ. Press, 1993.
    Recounts the myth in question with general bibliography, then lists authors, artists, and composers who use it, with editions of their works. Breaks the myths down into major narrative components, such as the loss of Eurydice in the Orpheus and Eurydice story. Although visual treatments are not considered, the literary background for them is well handled.

Astrological treatments of myths

668. McGurk, Patrick, ed. *Catalogue of Astrological and Mythological Illuminated Manuscripts of the Latin Middle Ages IV: Astrological Manuscripts in Italian Libraries (Other than Rome).* London: Warburg Institute, 1966.
    The purpose of this series (which was never completed) was to provide a collection of pictures and texts pertaining to medieval astrological, rather than mythological, imagery. Includes some plates.

669. Saxl, Fritz, and Hans Meier, eds. *Catalogue of Astrological and Mythological Manuscripts of the Latin Middle Ages III: Manuscripts in English Libraries.* 2 vols. London: The Warburg Institute, 1953.
Provides a collection of pictures and texts on which to base a documented history of mediaeval astrological imagery. Volume Two consists of the plates.

Classical Myth Medievalized

670. Chance, Jane. *Medieval Mythography from Roman North Africa to the School of Chartres, AD 433-1177.* Gainesville: Univ. of Florida Press, 1994.
Studies the ways various authors interpreted classical figures as models of Christian virtue, treating not only major figures like Orpheus, Hercules, and Aeneas, but specific images, like Cupid's quiver and Bacchus's fan.

671. _____, ed. *The Mythographic Art: Classical Fable and the Rise of the Vernacular in Early France and England.* Gainesville: Univ. of Florida Press, 1990.
Treats Latin and Old French mythographers, especially in their allegorizations of myths, and considers how the poets who used them, such as Chaucer, reflected these allegories in their works.

672. Fyler, John M. *Chaucer and Ovid.* New Haven and London: Yale Univ. Press, 1979.
Explores Ovid's influence on Chaucer's poetry.

673. Heckscher, William S. "Relics of Pagan Antiquity in Mediaeval Settings." *JWCI* 1 (1937-38): 204-20.
Considers the way medieval Christians imagined their roles in relation to antiquity and how they regarded monuments and relics of antiquity, especially engraved amulets and gems. Includes plates.

674. Heinrichs, Katherine. *The Myths of Love: Classical Lovers in*

Medieval Literature. State College: Pennsylvania State Univ. Press, 1990.
Considers the conventions of mythological allusion in a variety of vernacular love poems. Reviewed by Karla Taylor in *Speculum* 68, no. 1 (January 1993): 130-32.

675. Kallendorf, Craig. *Latin Influences on English Literature from the Middle Ages to the Eighteenth Century: An Annotated Bibliography of Scholarship, 1945-1979.* New York and London: Garland, 1983.
Considers several Roman mythological poets, such as Ovid and Virgil, and their influence.

676. MacFarlane, Katherine Nell. *Isidore of Seville and the Pagan Gods (Origines VIII.11). TAPS* 70, no. 3 (1980).
Presents the text of *Origines* VIII.11, *De Dis Gentium,* describes sources and influences, and discusses Isidore's avenues to earlier materials. There is a critical introduction, bibliography, and indices of gods and other mythological figures discussed as well as of classical and patristic writers.

677. Mathews, Thomas F. *The Clash of Gods: A Reinterpretation of Early Christian Art.* Princeton, NJ: Princeton Univ. Press, 1993.
Deals with the replacement, between the third and sixth centuries AD, of the images of the pagan gods with the new imagery of Christ and the saints.

678. Müntz, M. E. "La tradition antique au Moyen Age." *JS* (1888): 162-77.
Discusses the appearance of mythological motifs in Romanesque and early Gothic sculpture.

679. Pfeiffer, Rudolf. *History of Classical Scholarship from 1300 to 1850.* Oxford: Clarendon, 1976.
Treats such subjects as the revival of classical scholarship in the Italian Renaissance, and humanism and scholarship in northern Europe.

680. Saxl, Fritz, and Erwin Panofsky. "Classical Mythology in Mediaeval Art." *MMS* 4 (1932-33): 228-80.

Looks at medieval adaptations and transformations of classical myths
in art. Includes many plates.

681. _____, et al. *A Bibliography of the Survival of the Classics.* 2
     vols. London: The Warburg Institute, 1934-38.
     An annotated German bibliography with an English introduction
     listing works concerning the survival of classical antiquity divided
     by time period and by subject, for instance, folklore, music, and the
     like.

682. _____. *Lectures.* 2 vols. London: The Warburg Institute, 1957.
     Consists of lectures focusing on iconography in the Middle Ages,
     and treating the persistence and transformation of a number of
     antique myths. With numerous plates.

683. Seznec, Jean, *The Survival of the Pagan Gods: The Mythological
     Tradition and Its Place in Renaissance Humanism and Art.*
     Translated by Barbara F. Sessions. Bollingen Series, vol. 38.
     New York: Pantheon Books, 1953.
     Examines how the ancient gods survived during the Middle Ages
     by virtue of Euhemeristic and allegorical interpretations of their
     origins and nature.

684. Smalley, Beryl. *English Friars and Antiquity in the 14th Century.*
     New York: Barnes and Noble, 1960.
     Explains how certain mendicant writers commented on classical
     myths of the gods, especially from a pictorial point of view. Among
     the authors studied are Robert Holkot, Thomas Waleys, John Ridwall
     and his *Fulgentius Metaforalis,* and John Lathbury.

Commentaries on Classical Texts as a Source of Imagery, by Author

[Anonymous]

685. Brown, Virginia. "An Edition of an Anonymous 12th-century *Liber de Natura Deorum.*" *MS* 34 (1972): 1-70.
An edition of the only extant manuscript, Oxford, Bodleian Library MS Digby 221, of an early fourteenth-century treatise on the pagan gods. Includes a critical apparatus identifying earlier sources of specific passages.

686. Jones, Julian Ward, Jr., ed. *An Aeneid Commentary of Mixed Type: The Glosses in MSS Harley 4946 and Ambrosianus G111 inf.* Pontifical Institute Studies and Texts, no. 126: Toronto: Pontifical Institute, 1996.
A commentary of the Servian type on Book Five and Six of the *Aeneid*, with a lengthy English introduction.

[Arnulphus of Orléans]

687. Holzworth, Jean. "Hugutio's *Derivationes* and Arnulfus' Commentary on Ovid's *Fasti.*" *TAPA* 73 (1942): 259-76.
Rehandles some of the author's 1940 Bryn Mawr dissertation material

[Bernard of Chartres]

688. Dutton, Paul Edward, ed. *Glossae super Platonem of Bernard of Chartres*. Toronto: Pontifical Institute of Medieval Studies, 1991.
An edition of Bernard of Conches's *Glosae* on the *Timaeus*. Done about 1000-1115, this was perhaps the most popular group of glosses on the *Timaeus* and an important source for the dissemination of Platonic images.

[Bernard Silvester]

689. Jones, Julian Ward, and Elisabeth Frances Jones, eds. *Bernard Silvestris. The Commentary on the First Six Books of the "Aeneid" Commonly Attributed to Bernardus Silvestris: A New Critical Edition.* Lincoln and London: Univ. of Nebraska Press, 1977.
A scholarly edition with introduction, selected bibliography, and indices of authors, names, and things.

690. Padoan, Giorgio. "Tradizione e fortuna del commento all' 'Eneide' di Bernardo Silvestre." *IMU* 3 (1960): 227-40.
Treats the manuscript history of the commentary with bibliography and some brief excerpts from Bernard's text.

691. Schreiber, Earl G., and Thomas Maresca, trans. *Bernardus Silvestris. Commentary on the First Six Books of Virgil's Aeneid*. Lincoln: Univ. of Nebraska Press, 1979.
Makes item 000 [Jones] a little more accessible for the non-Latinist. The authors note in the preface that Bernard's commentary "is one of the few sustained analyses of a major secular poem surviving from that period and it differs radically from most other medieval commentaries on classical literature by going far beyond their more pedestrian series of equations for fables" (ix).

692. Westra, Haijo Jan, ed. *The Commentary on Martianus Capella's 'De Nuptiis Philologiae et Mercurii' attributed to Bernardus Silvestris*. Studies and Texts, no. 80. Toronto: Pontifical Institute of Medieval Studies, 1986.
A critical edition of Cambridge University Library MS CUL Mm.1.18 with indices.

[Geoffrey de Vitry]

693. Clarke, A. K., and Phyllis M. Giles, eds. *The Commentary of Geoffrey of Vitry on Claudian "De Raptu Proserpinae."* Mittelateinische Studien und Texte. Leiden and Köln: Brill, 1973.
A critical edition of this twelfth-century work with an introduction treating the commentary's significance, date, influences, and manuscripts. There is also a bibliography, a general index, and an *index nominum*.

[Giovanni del Virgilio]

694. Ghisalberti, Fausto, ed. "Giovanni del Virgilio e espositore delle Metamorfosi." *GD* 34, n.s., 4 (1933).
An edition of an important early fourteenth-century text of the

Allegorie, an exposition of the major fables in Ovid's *Metamorphoses* and their allegorical significance, with an index of allegories and of manuscripts.

[John of Garland]

695. Born, Lester K. "The Manuscripts of the Integumenta on the Metamorphoses of Ovid by John of Garland." *TAPA* 60 (1929): 179-99.
A critical study of this popular and widely disseminated twelfth-century commentary on Ovid with a detailed exploration in the introduction of the interest in Ovid throughout the Middle Ages.

[John Ridwall]

696. Friedman, John B. "John de Foxton's Continuation of Ridwall's *Fulgentius Metaforalis.*" *SI* 7-8 (1981-82): 65-79.
Discusses the uses and transformations of Ridwall's moralizations of classical gods in John de Foxton's *Liber Cosmographiae* of 1408, focussing particularly upon iconography and including plates.

697. Liebeschütz, Hans, ed. *Fulgentius Metaforalis: Ein Beitrag zur Geschichte der antiken Mythologie im Mittelalter.* Studien der Bibliothek Warburg, vol. 4. Leipzig and Berlin: B. G. Teubner, 1926.
An edition of John Ridwall's Christian moralization of Fulgentius's *Mythologiae,* describing how the classical gods symbolize Christian virtues, with illustrations from MS Vaticanus Palatinus Latinus 1066.

[Pierre Bersuire]

698. Engels, Joseph, et al., eds. *Petrus Berchorius: Reductorium morale, Liber XV: cap I. De Formis Figurisque Deorum naar de Parijse druk van 1509.* Werkmaterial uitgegeven door het Instituut voor Laat Latijn der Rijksuniversiteit, no.1. Utrecht: Instituut voor Laat Latijn der Rijksuniversiteit, 1960.
One of the most important texts for a study of medieval mythography, this edition of Bersuire's oft-revised text consists of the first chapter of the fourteenth-century *Ovidus Moralizatus,* the

fifteenth book of the *Reductorium Morale* transcribed from the printed version of 1509. The author describes the gods one by one and offers a Christian moralization for each story.

699. _____"Berchoriana. Les pseudo-Bersuires." *Vivarium* 3 (1965): 128-48.
On works often confused with the mythographic writing of Bersuire.

700. _____. *Petrus Berchorius. Reductorium morale, Liber XV: Ovidus moralizatus, Cap I. De Formis Figurisque Deorum: Textus e codice Brussels, Bibl. Reg. 863-9 critice editus.* Werkmaterial uitgegeven door het Instituut voor Laat Latijn der Rijksuniversiteit, no. 3. Utrecht: Instituut voor Laat Latijn der Rijksuniversiteit, 1966.
A critical edition of Bersuire's oft-revised text, here as it appears in Brussels, Bibliothèque Royale MS 863-69.

701. _____. *Petrus Berchorius. Reductorium Morale, Liber XV, Cap. ii-xv: Ovidius moralizatus naar de Parijse druk van 1509.* Werkmaterial uitgegeven door het Instituut voor Laat Latijn der Rijksuniversiteit, no. 2. Utrecht: Instituut voor Laat Latijn der Rijksuniversiteit,1962.
As the text is transcribed from the 1509 printed version, it is not a critical edition.

702. Ghisalberti, Fausto. "L'Ovidius Moralizatus de P. Bersuire." *Studi Romanzi* 23 (1933): 102-32.
Contains large excerpts from Bersuire's moralizations of the first nine books of the *Metamorphoses.*

703. Gieben, S. "Berchoriana: Girardus Valete, O. Min., Source of the Repertorium morale." *Vivarium* 6 (1968): 62-64.
A new Franciscan source for the Repertorium.

704. Reynolds, William Donald. "The Ovidus moralizatus of Petrus Berchorius: An Introduction and Translation." Ph.D. diss., Univ. of Illinois at Urbana-Champaign, 1971.

Includes a translation of book fifteen of Berchorius's *Reductorium,* his "De Formis Figurisque Deorum," and his commentary on all fifteen books of the *Metamorphoses,* with introduction and notes indicating sources.

705. _____. "Sources, Nature and Influence of the 'Ovidius Moralizatus of Pierre Bersuire." *The Mythographic Art* (item 670), pp. 83-99.
    Attempts to establish the relationship of this fourteenth-century text to earlier Ovid commentaries.

706. Samaran, Charles, and Jacques Montfrin. *Pierre Bersuire, prieur de Saint-Eloi de Paris 1290-1360.* Paris: Klincksieck, 1964.
    The standard biographical and literary study of Pierre Bersuire and his work.

[Remigius of Auxerre]

707. Bolton, Diane K. "Remigian Commentaries on the *Consolation of Philosophy* and Their Sources." *Traditio* 33 (1977): 381-94.
    Gives the classical sources Remigius used, both cited and uncited.

[Servius]

708. Marshall, Peter K. *Servius and Commentary on Virgil.* New York: Pegasus, 1996.
    A general study of Servius, who produced the earliest major commentary on the *Aeneid.*

709. Taylor, John Prentice. *The Mythology of Virgil's Aeneid According to Servius.* New York: New York Univ. Press, 1917.
    Goes through the poem, indicating how various gods and subjects were treated by Servius in his commentary.

[William of Conches]

710. Dronke, Peter. "William of Conches's Commentary on Martianus Capella." *Etudes de civilisation médiévale (IXe-XIIe siècles): Mélanges offerts à Edmond-René Labande.* Edited by Bernadette Leplant. Poitiers: CESCM, 1974, pp. 223-35.

Attempts to envision this now-lost work by looking at two manuscripts which may have been influenced by William's commentary.

711. Wilson, Bradford, ed. William of Conches, *Glosae in Iuvenalem.* Textes philosophiques du Moyen Age, no. 18. Paris: J. Vrin, 1980.
Consists of a critical edition of William's glosses on Juvenal's *Satires*, chiefly on difficult grammatical constructions and unusual mythological allusions, and three critical essays with indices.

[Vatican Mythographers]

712. Burnett, Charles S. F. "A Note on the Origins of the Third Vatican Mythographer." *JWCI* 44 (1981): 160-63.
Examining the extant manuscripts closely, the author concludes that this text was a sourcebook for the myths of the Greek and Roman gods and their iconography throughout the Middle Ages and Renaissance, and, in fact, that it existed in fully developed form earlier than had been previously supposed.

713. Krill, Richard M. "The Vatican Mythographers: Their Place in Ancient Mythography." *Manuscripta* 23 (1979): 173-77.
Provides a brief account of these works and the current state of their scholarship.

714. Kulcár, Peter, ed. *Mythographi Vaticani I et II.* CCSL, vol. 91. Turnholti: Typographi Brepols Editores Pontificii, 1987.
The standard edition of these extremely important texts. The Vatican mythographers are the works most commonly cited by late medieval authors writing pictorialized descriptions of the pagan gods.

715. Sjöström, Henning."Magister Albericus Lundoniensis, Mythographus Tertius Vaticani: A Twelfth-Century Student of Classical Mythology." *C&M* 29 (1968): 249-64.
Looks at Albericus's sources and the dissemination of his work and establishes a relationship between this author and a number of illuminated manuscripts whose pictures seem modeled on his verbal descriptions.

716. Zorzetti, Nevio, and Jacques Berlioz, eds. and trans. *Le premier mythographe du Vatican.* Collections des Universités de France, Série Latine, no. 328. Paris: Les Belles Lettres, 1995.
A French translation of this extremely influential commentary on classical mythology and to our knowledge, the only vernacular translation ever made. Extensive introduction and textual notes. Index.

Commentaries on Specific Classical and Late Antique Authors by Name

[Boethius]

717. Courcelle, Pierre. *La Consolation de Philosophie dans la tradition littéraire: Antécédents et postérité de Boèce.* Paris: Etudes Augustiniennes, 1967.
Treats the *fortuna* and images of the *Consolation.* Contains many plates, a bibliography and a handlist of manuscripts.

718. Silk, Edmund T. *Saecvli noni avctoris in Boetii consolationem philosophiae commentarivs.* Papers and Monographs of the American Academy in Rome, vol. 9. Rome: American Academy, 1935.
An edition of one of the most elaborate of the early commentaries on the *Consolation of Philosophy.*

[Fulgentius]

719. Whitbread, Leslie George, ed. and trans. *Fulgentius the Mythographer.* Columbus: Ohio State Univ. Press, 1971.
A translation with commentary of the *Mythologiae* of Fulgentius as well as of his commentaries on Virgil and on the *Thebiad.*

[Juvenal]

720. Anderson, W. S. "The Marston Manuscript of Juvenal." *Traditio* 23 (1957): 407-14.

Publishes Carolingian glosses from this manuscript, some of which have mythographic content.

721. Sanford, Eva M. "Juvenalis." *Catalogus Translationum et Commentariorum.* Edited by Paul Oskar Kristeller. Vol. I. Washington, DC: Catholic Univ. of America Press, 1960, pp.176-7.
Discusses the early glosses to the work of this author.

722. Wessner, Paul, ed. *Scholia in Iuvenalem Vetustiora.* Leipzig: Teubner, 1931.
An edition of some of the early scholia, or brief commentaries on individual words or phrases.

[Martianus Capella]

723. Wirth, Karl-August. "Eine illustrierte Martianus-Capella-Handschrift aus dem 13. Jahrhundert." *SJ*, n.s., 2 (1969): 43-75.
Studies the illuminations in four ninth- through thirteenth-century manuscripts of Martianus (with a particular focus on Wölfenbuttel MS Hzg. August Bibl. 62 Gud. lat. 2) and presents many reproductions of the marriage and the seven liberal arts illuminations.

[Ovid]

724. Allen, Judson Boyce. "Eleven Unpublished Commentaries on Ovid's *Metamorphoses* and Two Other Texts of Mythographic Interest: Some Comments and a Bibliography." *The Mythographic Art* (item 670), pp. 281-89.
Useful bibliographical survey of some mythographic texts like John Ridwall's *Fulgentius Metaforalis.*

725. Alton, E. H. "The Mediaeval Commentators on Ovid's 'Fasti." *Hermathena* 44 (1926): 119-51.
Examines a number of medieval commentaries on this text.

726. Boer, C. de, ed. *"Ovide Moralizé: Poème du commencement du quatorzième siècle (publié d'après tous les manuscrits connus).* 5 vols. Verhandelingen der Koniklijke Akademie van

Wetenschappen te Amsterdam, Afdeeling Letterkunde N.R. 15, 21, 30, nos. 3, 37, 43. 5 vols. Reprint. Weisbaden: Sändig, 1966-68.
The most elaborate medieval attempt to allegorize every detail of Ovid's *Metamorphoses*.

727. Born, Lester K. "The Manuscripts of the Integumenta." Cited above as item 695.

728. Desmond, Marilynn R., ed. *Ovid in Medieval Culture: A Special Issue*. Binghamton, NY: Center for Medieval and Renaissance Studies, 1989.
Essays by various hands on reception of Ovid's poetry.

729. Engles, Joseph. *Etudes sur l'Ovide Moralizé*. Bij J. B. Wolters' Uitgevers-Maatschappij n.v., Groningen: Batavia, 1945.
Dates and establishes the author of the text and looks at which version of the *Metamorphoses* the author might have used, at other sources, at the changes he made to his sources, and offers corrections and interpretations of difficult passages.

730. Ghisalberti, Fausto. "Arnolfo d'Orleans, un cultore di Ovidio nel secolo XI." *MRIL* 24, no. 4 (1932): 157-234.
Contains sizable excerpts from the 'Allegorie' on the *Metamorphoses* with useful notes, an index of names and sources, and an excellent introduction touching on the tradition of annotations of Ovid's works in the Middle Ages.

731. _____. "Medieval Biographies of Ovid." *JWCI* 9 (1946): 10-59.
Examines *accessus ad auctores* and commentaries containing biographies of the poet from the twelfth to the fourteenth centuries, focussing on the views current in schools and learned circles.

732. Haureau, B. "Mémoire sur un commentaire des *Métamorphoses* d'Ovide." *MINF* 30, part 2 (1883): 45-55.
Looks at several manuscripts containing mis-attributed commentaries and concludes that they make up the fifteenth book of Pierre Bersuire's *Reductorium Morale*.

733. Hexter, Ralph. *Ovid and Medieval Schooling: Studies in Medieval*

School Commentaries on Ovid's "Ars amatoria," "Epistulae ex Ponto," and "Epistulae Herodium." Münchener Beiträge zur Mediävistik und Renaissance-Forschung, no. 38. Munich: Bei der Arbeo-Gesellschaft, 1986.
Provides information on medieval glosses on Ovid, work by work, with much information on current scholarship. There are appendices of texts and manuscripts and a full bibliography.

734. Jung, Marc René. "Ovide, texte, translateur et gloses dans les manuscrits de l'Ovide moralisé." *The Medieval Opus: Imitation, Rewriting, and Transmission in French Tradition.* Edited by Douglas Kelly. Amsterdam: Rodopi, 1996, p.75-98.
Good overview of this vast repository of individual allegories on stories from Ovid's *Metamorphoses.*

735. Levine, R. "Medieval Allegorization of the Metamorphoses." *MR* 14 (1989): 197-213.
Discusses practices of finding Christian and other forms of allegory in Ovid's poem.

736. Martindale, Charles, ed. *Ovid Renewed: Ovidian Influences on Literature and Art from the Middle Ages to the Twentieth Century.* Cambridge: Cambridge Univ. Press, 1988.
Essays by various hands, rather general, on Ovid's influence. A few pertain to the Middle Ages.

737. Robson, C. A. "Dante's Use in the Divina Commedia of the Medieval Allegories on Ovid." *Centenary Essays on Dante, by Members of the Oxford Dante Society.* Oxford: Clarendon Press, 1965, pp.1-38.
Discusses Dante's knowledge of the early allegories on Ovid's poetry, especially the *Metamorphoses.*

738. Roob, Helmut. "Unvollendete Miniaturen in einer Ovid-Handschrift der Gothaer Bibliothek." *FF* 38 (1964): 174-7.
A fourteenth-century Italian illustrated manuscript of Ovid's *Metamorphoses* with commentary of Thomas Walleys. Roob publishes several of the miniatures and discusses their style and character.

739. Sant, Jeannette Th. M. van't. *Le commentaire de Copenhague de l'Ovide moralisé avec l'édition critique du septième livre.* Amsterdam: H. J. Paris, 1929.
A critical edition of the commentary preceding this fifteenth-century French manuscript of the *Ovide moralisé* (the twentieth listed by De Boer). The commentary is not found in any other manuscript of the work, but it is similar to one in an early printed edition.

740. Stapleton, Michael L. *Harmful Eloquence: Ovid's* Amores *from Antiquity to Shakespeare.* Ann Arbor, MI: Univ. of Michigan Press, 1996.
Studies the artistry of the *Amores* themselves, then turns to their transmission and influence between the years 500 and 1600, treating the medieval Latin poets, the troubadours, Dante, Petrarch, and Shakespeare.

[Prudentius]

741. Stettiner, Richard. *Die Illustrierten Prudentiushandschriften.* 2 vols. Berlin: Grote, 1895-1905.
Standard collection of plates depicting the illustrations from a variety of Prudentius manuscripts, chiefly in German libraries.

742. Wieland, Gernot Rudolf. *The Latin Glosses on Arator and Prudentius in CUL Gg, 5.35.* Studies and Texts, no. 61. Toronto: Pontifical Institute of Medieval Studies, 1988.
Looks at glosses to Arator's *De Actibus Apostolum* and Prudentius's *Psychomachia* in this manuscript to see how Anglo-Saxon scholars could better understand texts through them and how they may have been used in Anglo-Saxon classrooms and literary criticism.

[Virgil]

743. Baswell, Christopher. *Virgil in Medieval England: Figuring the Aeneid from the Twelfth Century to Chaucer.* Cambridge: Cambridge Univ. Press, 1995.
Considers the *fortuna* of a group of Latin Virgil manuscripts as they made their way from the twelfth century to Chaucer. Examines how medieval vernacular poets responded to Virgil. Reviewed by John

B. Friedman in *AHR* 102 (April 1997): 438-9.

Classsical and Mythological Figures by Name

[Achilles]

744. King, Katherine Callen. *Achilles: Paradigms of the War Hero from Homer to the Middle Ages.* Berkeley: Univ. of California Press, 1987.
Chapters Three, "Lover of War: Classical Rome to Medieval Europe," and Four, "Soldier of Love: Archaic Greece to Medieval Europe," are particularly relevant here in King's investigation of the changing perception of Achilles.

[Apollo]

745. Barnard, Mary E. *The Myth of Apollo and Daphne from Ovid to Quevedo: Love Agon and the Grotesque.* Durham: Duke Univ. Press, 1987.
Considers among other things the Christianization of the story in Ovid's commentary and its appearance in Petrarch. Some plates.

[Cerberus]

746. Bloomfield, M. *Cerberus the Dog of Hades.* Chicago and London: The Open Court Publishing Company and K. Paul, Trench, Trübner, 1905.
Though he treats the tradition of Cerberus mainly before Virgil, it is the Virgilian context which is that chiefly known to medieval mythographers.

747. Friedman, John B. "Medieval Cartography and *Inferno* 34: Satan's Three Faces Reconsidered." *Traditio* 39 (1983): 447-56.
Offers a connection between the three faces of Lucifer in Dante's *Inferno* 34 with the three races of men found in the post-Noachic Continental divisions of medieval T-O world maps, where the world

is a disk surmounted by a T-shaped confluence of the rivers Don and Nile, and Mediterranean sea all surrounded by an O-like circle of ocean.

748. Savage, J. J. "Medieval Tradition of Cerberus." *Traditio* 7 (1949-51): 405-10.
Examines allusions to Cerberus and his associations in many medieval texts.

[Charon]

749. Terpening, Ronnie H. *Charon and the Crossing: Ancient, Medieval and Renaissance Transformations of a Myth*. Lewisburg, PA: Bucknell Univ. Press, 1985.
Chiefly considers works of Italian literature; Part Two: "Charon in Italy from Dante to Marino" is the most relevant for the iconographer.

[Circe]

750. Yarnall, Judith. *Transformations of Circe: The History of an Enchantress*. Urbana: Univ. of Illinois Press, 1994.
Does not treat Circe in the Middle Ages but does deal with her in antiquity and the Renaissance.

[Daphne]

751. Giraud, Yves F.-A. *La fable de Daphné: Essai sur un type de métamorphose végétale dans la littérature et dans les arts jusqu'à la fin du XVIIe siècle*. Histoire des idées et critique littéraire, no. 92. Geneva: Droz, 1968.
Examines the survival of this myth, and supplies copious quotations from art, music, and literature across many cultures. There is a large section on both the Middle Ages and the Renaissance. Many plates.

[Diana and Actaeon]

* See also item 1480.

[Ganymede]

752. Kempter, Gerda. *Ganymed: Studien zur Typologie, Ikonographie und Ikonologie.* Cologne and Vienna: Hermann Böhlau, 1980. The first three chapters treat the reception of the Ganymede legend by antique, medieval, and Renaissance artists. Considers both the rape of Ganymede and also his relation to the constellation of Aquarius in medieval manuscript painting and Romanesque sculpture. There is a handlist of Ganymede representations chiefly in emblems and Renaissance art, and a full bibliography, as well as a number of black-and-white plates of medieval manuscript miniatures.

[Lucretia]

753. Donaldson, Ian. *The Rapes of Lucretia: A Myth and Its Transformations.* Oxford: Clarendon, 1982. Looks at the transformation of this myth in painting, literature, and patristics, especially Augustine's view of the myth, throughout history, but focusses on Renaissance and later manifestations.

[Medea]

754. Morse, Ruth. *The Medieval Medea.* Woodbridge, Suffolk: Boydell and Brewer, 1996. Treats Jason and Medea in Dante, Chaucer, Boccaccio, Gower, and Christine de Pisan.

[Minerva]

755. Wittkower, Rudolf. "Transformations of Minerva in Renaissance Imagery." *Allegory and the Migration of Symbols* (item 272), pp. 129-42. In spite of its title, this study offers some information on late medieval views of Minerva.

[Narcissus]

756. Vinge, Louise. *The Narcissus Theme in Western European Literature up to the Early 19th Century.* Translated by Robert

Dewsnap. Lund: Gleerups Skänska Centraltryckeriet, 1967.
Includes chapters on the theme in antiquity and then treats Narcissus
from the twelfth century onward.

[Neptune]

757. Gerhardt, Mia L. *Old Men of the Sea: From Neptunus to Old French
Luiton: Ancestry and Character of a Water Spirit.* Utrecht:
Utrecht Univ. Press, 1967.
This work's title indicates its range and concerns.

[Orion]

758. Fontenrose, Joseph. *Orion: The Myth of the Hunter and the
Huntress.* University of California Classical Studies, vol. 23.
Berkeley: Univ. of California Press, 1981.
Although this study concerns the story of Orion and hunting in
antiquity, it will still be useful to medievalists.

[Orpheus]

759. Coulson, Frank T., ed. *The Vulgate Commentary on Ovid's
Metamorphoses: The Creation Myth and the Story of Orpheus.*
Toronto Medieval Latin Texts, no. 20. Toronto: Pontifical
Institute of Medieval Studies, 1991.
A critical edition with bibliography of Selestat Bibliothèque
Humaniste MS 92, a thirteenth-century editor, glossator, etymologist
and literary critic's attention to this part of the Ovid tradition.
Reviewed by Robert Levine in *Speculum* 68, no. 4 (October 1993):
738-9.

760. Friedman, John B. *Orpheus in the Middle Ages.* Cambridge:
Harvard Univ. Press, 1970. Reprint. Syracuse: Syracuse Univ.
Press, 1998.
Traces the adoption of the Orpheus legend by medieval Christian
poets and artists. Many plates.

761. Warden, John, ed. *Orpheus: The Metamorphosis of a Myth.* Toronto:
Univ. of Toronto Press, 1982.
A collection of essays considering the myth of Orpheus from

antiquity through the end of the Renaissance and tracing its growth and its reconstitution in successive ages. Reviewed by John B. Friedman in *Speculum* 59, no. 2 (April 1984): 213-14.

[Pandora]

762. Panofsky, Dora, and Erwin Panofsky. *Pandora's Box: The Changing Aspects of a Mythical Symbol.* Bollingen Series, vol. 52. New York: Pantheon, 1962.
Investigates the transformations of the Pandora myth and the representations of Pandora in art and literature from antiquity through the Middle Ages and up through the Victorian era.

[Paris]

763. Damisch, Hubert. *The Judgement of Paris.* Translated by John Goodman. Chicago and London: Univ. of Chicago Press, 1996.
An iconographic study of Paris's choice of Venus as more beautiful than Juno or Pallas with 116 black-and-white plates.

764. Ehrhart, Margaret J. *The Judgment of the Trojan Prince Paris in Medieval Literature.* Philadelphia: Univ. of Pennsylvania Press, 1987.
A study of the legend of Paris's choice of Venus as more beautiful than Juno or Pallas in medieval literature, with ten black-and-white plates.

[Polyphemus]

765. Thomas, Ruth Stanford. "Polyphemus in Art and Literature." Ph.D. diss., Tufts, 1970.
Traces the development of Polyphemus in classical literature and studies his iconography.

[Prometheus]

766. Trousson, Raymond. *Le thème de Promethée dans la littérature europeénne.* 2 vols. Genève: Droz, 1964.
Examines this theme from antiquity up to the present. Chapters Two

and Three of Volume One concern medieval and Renaissance syncretistic treatments of the myth, and the development of the story in mythographic manuals such as Boccaccio's *Geneology of the Pagan Gods*.

[Psyche]

767. Le Maitre, H. *Essai sur le mythe de Psyché, dans la littérature française des origines à 1890*. Paris: Boivion, n.d.
Only the first thirty-five pages of this book concern the story in the Middle Ages.

[Pygmalion]

768. Egbert, V. W. "Pygmalion as sculptor." *PLC* 28, no. 1 (1966): 20-23.
Provides plates and discusses depictions of Pygmalion as a sculptor in manuscripts of the *Roman de la Rose*.

[Pyramus and Thisbe]

769. Heinz, Peter Ubach. *Zwei mittellateinische Pyramus-und Thisbe-Dichtungen*. Lateinische Sprache und Literatur des Mittelalters, no. 3. Bern: Hubert Lang; Frankfort: Peter Lang , 1975.
Studies some medieval mythographic poems embodying the story.

770. Liver, Ricarda. "Mittelalterliche Gestaltung von antiken Erzählstoffen am Beispiel von Pyramus und Thisbe im lateinischen und romanischen Mittelalter." *Kontinuität und Transformation* (item 40), pp. 315-25.
Reception study of the myth.

771. Schmitt-von Mühlenfels, Franz. *Pyramus und Thisbe. Rezeptiontypen eines Ovidischen Stoffes in Literatur, Kunst und Musik*. Heidelberg: C. Winter, 1972.
More on antique than on medieval treatments. Includes 34 plates and a bibliography.

[Saturn]

772. Ciavolella, Massima, and Amilcare A. Ianucci, eds. *Saturn from Antiquity to the Renaissance.* University of Toronto Italian Studies, no. 8. O Haud: Dovehouse Editions, 1992.
Considers aspects of the Saturn myth unexamined in item 773. The focus of the essays is chiefly on Saturn in medieval literature, though one of the essays deals specifically with painting.

773. Klibansky, Raymond, et al. *Saturn and Melancholy: Studies in the History of Natural Philosophy, Religion, and Art.* New York: Basic Books, 1964.
Treats the development of the idea of melancholy from the ancient world to the present, as well as the iconography of Saturn in different cultures, particularly as he influenced melancholy. Contains many medieval miniatures and woodcuts.

774. Tinkle, Theresa. "Saturn of the Several Faces: A Survey of the Medieval Mythographic Tradition." *Viator* 18 (1987): 289-307.
Investigates the presentations of Saturn in the works of the major mythographers in order to explain Chaucer's portrayal of him in *The Knight's Tale.*

[Sibyl]

775. Kinter, William L., and Joseph R. Keller. *The Sibyl: Prophetess of Antiquity and Medieval Fay.* Philadelphia, PA: Dorrance, 1967.
Considers the medieval legends of Monte Della Sibilla, the three Sibyls and the faery Sibyl, and the Matter of Britain as well as the faery Sibyl's connection with Morgan. Includes an appendix of medieval romances whose heroines may be types of the faery Sibyl, as well as a bibliography.

[Venus]

776. Friedman, John B. "L'iconographie de Vénus et de son miroir à la fin du Moyen Age." *L'érotisme au Moyen Age.* Edited by Bruno Roy. Montreal: L'Aurore, 1977, pp. 53-82.

Examines the comb, mirror, and raised skirt of Venus as elements in her traditional iconography, as well as her connection with the siren. Many plates.

777. Hollander, Robert. *Boccaccio's Two Venuses.* New York: Columbia Univ. Press, 1977.
Looks at Boccaccio's presentations of Venus and Amor or Cupid and how he uses the story in an ironic attack on the religion of love.

778. Tinkle, Theresa. *Medieval Venuses and Cupids: Sexuality, Hermeneutics and English Poetry.* Stanford Univ. Press, 1996.
Examines transformations of the love deities Venus and Cupid in late Middle English and French poetry and their relation to the Ovidian arts of love.

EUHEMERISM

779. Cooke, J. D. "Euhemerism: A Mediaeval Interpretation of Classical Paganism." *Speculum* 2, no. 2 (April 1927): 396-410.
Traces the technique of making pagan mythology acceptable to Christian exegesis by claiming that the gods were actually gifted mortals deified by a grateful populace.

780. Menner, R. J. "Two Notes on Mediaeval Euhemerism." *Speculum* 3, no. 2 (April 1928): 246-8.
Comments on Alfred and Aelfric's use of Euhemeristic arguments and the substitution of Nimrod for Ninus in Peter Comestor's *Historia Scholastica* and the *Cursor Mundi.*

NUMBER SYMBOLISM IN ART AND LITERATURE

781. Callaghan, Mary. "Number and Numerical Composition: Tradition and Practice in *Sir Gawain and the Green Knight.*" DAI 1982

Sept. v.43(3) p.796-A.
Examines the "long-standing tradition in earlier literature and aesthetics" behind the *Gawain*-poet's use of numerical composition looking at "two distinct literary considerations . . . number as a symbolic, allusive, occult entity, and number as structural organizational principle"(*DAI* 796-A).

782. Eckhardt, Caroline D., ed. *Essays in the Numerical Criticism of Medieval Literature.* Lewisburg: Bucknell Univ. Press; London: Associated Press, 1980.
General studies of numerical structures in *Gawain, Chanson de Roland, The Consolation of Philosophy*, Chaucer, *Beowulf*, and the *Nibelungenlied*. Several plates and index.

783. Ernst, Ulrich. "Kontinuität und Transformation der mittelalterlichen Zahlensymbolik in der Renaissance: Die *Numerorum Mysteria* des Petrus Bungus." *Euphorion* 77 (1983): 247-325.
Studies the late antique and medieval background of this important sixteenth- century author of one of the most developed of number symbolism treatises. The Bongus text was edited by Ernst as *Pietro Bongo. Numerorum Mysteria*. Hildesheim and New York: G. Olms,1983.

784. Fleming, John V. "The Centuple Structure of the *Pearl.*" *The Alliterative Tradition in the Fourteenth Century.* Edited by Bernard S. Levy and Paul E. Szarmach. Kent, OH: Kent State Univ. Press, 1981. pp. 81-98.
Looks at the numerological implications of this poem's structure, which, as with *Sir Gawain* in the same manuscript, contains101 stanzas. Discusses its structure with reference to other significant medieval works with similar organizational patterns or in which this number also figures prominently.

785. Gilligan, Janet. "Numerical Composition in the Middle English *Patience.*" *SN* 61 (1989): 7-11.
A technical analysis of this poem, which Gilligan argues does pay attention to numerical symbolism in its structure as *Pearl* and *Gawain* from the same manuscript have been shown to do.

786. Hill, Thomas D. "Number and Pattern in *Lilja*." *JEGP* 69 (1970): 561-7.
    Studies the extremely complex numerical structure of this Old Icelandic poem "concerned with the sequence of Christian History and praise of the Virgin Mary," showing "that this structure is intrinsically related to the larger meaning of the poem" (561).

787. Hughes, B., ed. "*De Numeris Misticis* by John Pecham: A critical edition." *AFH* 78(1985): 3-28 and 333-83.
    An edition of a medieval treatise on numerology.

788. Jones, Karen Q. "Graphic and Numerical Analogues for Old English Poetry: A Consideration of the Historical and Literary Evidence Supporting their Existence. " DAI 1988, Oct. v.49(4) 814-A.
    Surveys the numerical tradition in classical works, the Bible, and exegesis as a background to the practice in Anglo-Saxon poetry and discusses when and how Old English poets may have used these complex patterns. Posits that, even while their audience may not have understood the patterns, they did consciously use them for "the Greater Glory of God."

789. Klemp, P. J. "Numerology and English Renaissance Literature: Twentieth-Century Studies." *BB* 40 (1983): 231-41.
    An annotated bibliography of the subject with brief introduction and discussion of general studies and collections of essays as well as works on individual authors.

790. Lange, Hanne, ed. *Traités du XIIe siècle sur la symbolique des nombres: Geoffroy d'Auxerre and Thibault de Langres.* Cahiers de l'Institut du Moyen Age Grec et Latin, no. 29. Copenhagen: Univ. of Copenhagen, 1978.

791. _____. *Traités du XIIe siècle sur la symbolique des nombres: Odon de Morimond, Analetica Numerorum et Rerum in Theographyam.* Cahiers de l'Institut du Moyen Age Grec et Latin, no. 40. Copenhagen: Univ. of Copenhagen, 1981.
    These two works by Lange offer critical editions of three twelfth-century Latin treatises on numerical symbolism.

792. Meyer, H., and R. Suntrup, eds. *Lexicon der mittelalterlichen*

Zahlenbedeutungen. Mittelalter-Schriften, no. 56. Munich: Münstersche, 1987.
A useful encyclopaedic work on medieval numerology.

793. Surles, Robert L., ed. *Medieval Numerology: A Book of Essays*. Garland Reference Library of the Humanities, no. 1640. Garland Medieval Casebooks, no. 7. New York and London: Garland, 1993.
A collection of essays on the topic, treating such subjects as God as monad; the specific numbers two, three, and eleven; and various works such as *The Phoenix, Erec and Enide*, Dante's *Commedia*, the *Grail* Family, and Hartmann's *Gregorius*.

794. Versluis, Arthur. "*Piers Plowman*, Numerical Composition, and the Prophecies." *CJCD* 1 (1991): 103-39.
A detailed analysis of the numerical symbolism of the prophecies in *Piers Plowman*, linking medieval gematria and symbolic alphanumeric patterns to the prophecies.

TOPOI AND SPECIFIC FIGURES

Ages of Man

795. Burrow, J. A. *The Ages of Man: A Study in Medieval Writing and Thought*. Oxford: Clarendon, 1986.
Looks at different beliefs "mainly from England, from the time of Bede to the end of the Fifteenth Century" (1) concerning "three, or four, or six, or seven *aetates hominum*" (2). With quotations from numerous different works and with sections on Nature, Time, Ideals of Transcendence, and Ideals of Nature. Includes an appendix of "Loci Classici" in translation, some plates, and an index. Reviewed by John B. Friedman in *YLS* 3 (1989): 137-52. According to Friedman, "Burrow's particular approach to the subject is through the idea . . . [of] changes in a man's appearance, behavior,

temperament, and the like, which are seasonable or appropriate to a given age. He examines this notion chiefly in English age lore, from the time of Bede through the end of the fifteenth century" (142).

796. Dal, Erik, and Povl Skaå. *The Ages of Man and the Months of the Year: Poetry, Prose and Pictures outlining the 'douze mois figurés' motif mainly found in Shepherds' Calendars and Livres d'Heures (14th-to 17th Century).* Det kongelige Vidensakbernes Selskab Historisk-filosofiske Skrifter, no. 9.3. Copenhagen: Munksgaard, 1980.
Numerous works of art and literature in which ages and months motifs are included and discussed.

797. Dove, Mary. *The Perfect Age of Man's Life.* Cambridge: Cambridge Univ. Press, 1986.
Reviewed by John B. Friedman in *YLS* 3 (1989): 137-52. Dove fastens "primarily on one of the four or five or six or seven or twelve ages, on what might be called the middle age or middle of man's life." (Friedman, 145). Some plates, bibliography, and index.

798. Sears, Elizabeth. *The Ages of Man: Medieval Interpretations of the Life Cycle.* Princeton Univ. Press, 1986.
This book's "subject is how medieval artists and writers, but fewer of the latter than the former, considered and portrayed the periodization of man's life from birth through childhood, adolescence, manhood, old age, and extreme senescence, that is, late antique and medieval views of aging. By looking at philosophical, exegetical, and in some cases literary texts as well as at schematic diagrams in manuscripts and their elaborations in wall paintings, the author shows the evolution of ideas of man's ages, imagined variously as three, four, five, six, seven, and twelve." (Friedman, 138). Includes a large number of plates.

Alexander the Great

799. Bieber, M. *Alexander the Great in Greek and Roman Art.* Chicago: Argonaut, 1964.

4Examines

Examines representations of Alexander and his adventures in vase painting and sculpture. Sixty-three plates and bibliographical footnotes.

800. Bunt, Gerrit H. V. *Alexander the Great in the Literature of Medieval Britain.* Mediaevalia Groningana, no. 14. Groningen: Engbert Forsten, 1994.
Surveys the reception of the Alexander legend in medieval England and Scotland. Considers Middle English Alexander romances, portrayals of his life in chronicles, works of moral instruction, and travel books. One chapter is devoted to Alexander as one of the Nine Worthies. Select bibliography and index. **See also Nine Worthies.**

801. Ehltert, Trude. "Alexander und die Frauen in spätantiken und mittelalterlichen Alexander-Erzählungen." *Kontinuität und Transformation* (item 40), pp. 81-103.
Studies the women, like Roxane, who appear in the medieval Alexander stories. Several other articles in the same collection (Sektion I) deal with the reception of the Alexander legend and are also useful to the student.

802. Ross, David J. A. *Alexander Historiatus: A Guide to Medieval Illustrated Alexander Literature.* 2nd ed. Athenaums Monografien, Altertumswissenschaft, no.186. Frankfurt am Main: Athenaum, 1988.
A revision of the first edition published in 1963 by the Warburg Institute. Lists briefly the illustrated manuscripts connected with the deeds of Alexander in antiquity and in the Middle Ages. Divided into various types and genres, Hebrew Alexander narratives for example, and chronicle-biographies and romances. Updated bibliography. Reviewed by Hoyt Duggan in *Speculum* 66, no.1 (January 1991): 233-4. According to Duggan, "not only did [Ross] attempt to delineate systematically the relations among the historiated versions of the numerous historical and romance accounts of Alexander, but he also 'tried to include every important version of the story whether or not it is found in an illustrated form' (p. 1)" (233). Covers modern editions and scholarship.

803. _____. *Illustrated Medieval Alexander-Books in Germany and the*

Netherlands. Cambridge: Modern Humanities Research Council, 1971.

A study of these books and the illustrations and iconographic programs for various manuscript versions of the Alexander legends. Many excellent black-and-white plates and bibliography. Reviewed by John B. Friedman in *JEGP* 72 (1973): 118-22.

804. Settis-Frugoni, Chiara. *Historia Alexandri elevati per Griphos ad Aerem. Origine, iconografia, e fortuna di'un tema.* Rome: Istituto Storico Italiano per il Medio Evo, 1973.

This thorough and learned book takes the ascent episode, a famous addition to the Greek Alexander romance, and traces its history. Considers the origins of the legend and offers a filiation for its appearance in various branches. Studies the development of the griffin as a fabulous creature in antiquity and the Middle Ages and its relation to late antique traditions of imperial apotheosis and to various "philosophical" ascents of the soul. Particularly interesting for the medievalist are Chapters Eight and Nine on text and illustration of the ascent story in the later Middle Ages, especially in manuscript illustration and in church mosaics and sculpture. Many black-and-white pictures in the text and a handlist of illuminated Alexander manuscripts.

805. Warburg, Aby. "Aeronave e sommergibile nella imagginazione medievale." *La Rinascita del Paganismo Antico.* Edited by Gertrude Bing. Florence: La Nuova Italia, 1966, pp. 275-82.

A brief early study (1913) by the great art historian. Two plates. See also **Flight and Griffin.**

Aristotle Ridden by Phyllis or Campaspe

806. Delbouille, Maurice. *Le lai d'Aristote de Henri d'Andeli publié d'après tous les manuscrits par Maurice Delbouille.* Bibliothèque de la Faculté de philosophie de lettres de l'université de Liège, no. 123. Paris: Société d'édition Les Belles Lettres, 1951.

An account of the story of Aristotle ridden by a woman, sometimes named Phyllis, Campaspe, or Candacis. Henri was probably indebted to an exemplum using the story in the *Sermones feriales et communes* of Jacques de Vitry.

807. Marsilli, Pietro. "Réception et diffusion iconographique du conte de *Aristote et Phillis* en Europe depuis le Moyen Age." *Amour, mariage et transgressions au Moyen Age, actes du Colloque des 24, 25, 26 et 27 mars 1983.* Edited by Danielle Buschinger and André Crépin. Göppingen: Kümmerle, 1984, pp. 239-69.
A general survey of the legend's history, especially in art, with a chronological list dating from 1280 up to 1784 of art works of all kinds reproducing this image. Each entry describes the work in question, its iconographical depiction of the subject, and its location. Does not include plates.

808. Springer, Otto. "A Philosopher in Distress: Apropos of a Newly Discovered Medieval German Version of Aristotle and Phyllis." *Germanic Studies in Honor of Edward Henry Sehrt.* Edited by Fritjof Andersen Raven, et al. Coral Gables, FL: Miami Univ. Press, 1968, pp. 203-18. Republished in Otto Springer. *Arbeiten zur Germanischen Philologie und zur Literatur des Mittelalters.* Munich: Fink, 1975, pp. 259-70.
Discusses the Aristotle and Phyllis myth in medieval German literature, with examples from various manuscripts and focusses particularly on its appearance in two Shrovetide plays.

809. Storost, Joachim. "Femme chevauchat Aristote." *ZFSL* 66 (1956): 186-201.
Of the two complementary pieces by this author cited, this is probably the more useful, as it has a very full collection of plates showing the theme in ivory carving, painting, church capital sculpture, wood cuts, and stained glass.

810. _____. "Zu Aristoteles-Sage im Mittelalter." *Monumentum Bambergense: Festgäbe für Benedikt Kraft.* Edited by Gerhard Eis, et al. Munich: Kösel, 1955, pp. 298-348.
Uses the story in a variety of medieval exempla, both Eastern and Western, warning against lust and the dangers of female domination. Among the Western exempla collections treated are those of Jacques

de Vitry and Etienne de Bourbon. Though visual treatments are not considered, the literary background for them is well handled.

Arthur, Legends of

811. Hindman, Sandra. *Sealed in Parchment: Rereadings of Knighthood in the Illuminated Manuscripts of Chrétien de Troyes*. Chicago and London: Univ. of Chicago Press, 1994.
   On the iconographical depictions of knights in nine illuminated manuscripts of Chrétien's works made between 1275 and 1325. Includes plates of miniatures from these manuscripts. Divided into chapters on *Li Clerc*, *Li Bacheler*, *Li Seignor*, *Li Combateor*, and *Li Roi*, each dealing with a specific social class treated in the romances. Written from the point of view of the "New Philology" in which each manuscript with all its variants, represents a valued text, rather than a misconception of the original by the scribe or illustrator. Reviewed by William J. Diebold in *Speculum* 71, no. 2 (April 1996): 430-3.

   * Lejeune, Rita. "La légende du roi Arthur." Cited above as item 182. [art]

812. Loomis, Roger Sherman. *Arthurian Legends in Medieval Art*. Reprint. New York: Kraus, 1975.
   A standard work, though now somewhat dated, on representations of Arthur in a variety of medieval art forms. Many plates.

813. Stones, Alison. "Arthurian Art since Loomis." *Arturus Rex, II. Acta Conventus Lovaniensia*. Edited by Willy van Hoecke, et al. Louvain: Louvain Univ. Press, 1991, pp. 21-78.
   An overview article on Arthurian art since the publication of item 812 [Loomis] and suggesting new directions for further study. Divided by region.

814. _____. "Illustrating Lancelot and Guinevere." *Lancelot and Guinevere: A Casebook*. Edited by Lori J. Walters. New York and London: Garland, 1966, pp. 125-57.
   An examination of the iconography of the lovers' first kiss and their

adultery (two of a number of crucial episodes Stones lists as commonly depicted in cycles of pictures representing this story) comprehensive up to the thirteenth century and with major examples from fourteenth- and fifteenth-century manuscripts. Numerous plates.

815. Whitaker, Muriel. *The Legends of King Arthur in Art*. Cambridge: D. S. Brewer, 1990.
Ranges from the medieval period up to the present, with a large number of plates from a variety of different works of art, such as manuscripts, and early printed books, sculpture, mosaic, tapestry, and glass, Of interest to the medievalist may be the chapters on images of Arthurian romances, illuminated Arthurian romances, painted chambers, and Arthur as one of the Nine Worthies. 35 color and 72 black-and-white illustrations. **See also Nine Worthies**

Bivium

816. Harms,Wolfgang. *Homo viator in bivio. Studien zur Bildlichkeit des Weges*. Munich: Wilhelm Fink, 1970.
Studies the allegorization of the letter Y in antiquity and the Middle Ages, the so-called Pythagorean letter whose branches represent good and bad choices of direction in man's life.

Canon and Roman Law Representations

817. Dolezalek, G. *Verzeichnis der Handschriften zum römischen Recht bis 1600*. 4 vols. Frankfurt-am-Main: Max-Planck Institut für europäische Rechtsgeschichte, 1972.
Monumental typescript listing of legal manuscripts in library collections arranged by city and country in the first two volumes. Scribes and owners are listed in the third, and *tituli* and *incipits* given in the fourth. Unfortunately for the iconographer, there is no

indication of illuminations.

818. Melnikas, Anthony. *The Corpus of Miniatures in the Manuscripts of Decretum Gratiani.* Vol. 1. Studia Gratiana Post Octava Decreti Saecularia. Collectanea Historiae Ivris Canonici, no. 16. Rome: Studia Gratiana, 1975.
Discussion of Gratian's twelfth-century legal work, *Decretum* and detailed, thorough analysis of the iconography of canon law, "interrelated functions of civil and ecclesiastical authority," and "Christ as grantor of ecclesiastical and civil authority" in the miniatures. Then Melnikas examines a number of different *causae,* providing throughout many color and black-and-white plates from a variety of different manuscripts.

819. Owen, Dorothy M. *The Medieval Canon Law: Teaching Literature and Transmission.* The Sandars Lectures in Bibliography. Cambridge: Cambridge Univ. Press, 1990.
"This study examines the provision for students [of canon law] (especially in Cambridge), the choice of available textbooks, and the collections of legal books made by the university and colleges and by private individuals" (i). Includes a bibliography of works quoted, manuscripts and works of canon lawyers pre-and post-Reformation, and an index. A useful overview for understanding the specific images often found in legal manuscripts of the period.

Compass

820. Friedman, John Block. "The Architect's Compass in the Creation Miniatures of the Later Middle Ages." *Traditio* 30 (1974): 419-29.
Examines the iconography of the image of "the creator marking out the universe with a compass" (419) with discussion of passages from various works of Jewish Biblical exegesis known to the Latin west, examination of sources, and a number of plates in which this image appears.

Fortune and the Wheel of Fortunne

821. Cioffari, Vincent. *Fortune and Fate from Democritus to St. Thomas Aquinas*. New York: Columbia Univ. Press, 1935.
Investigates ancient and medieval philosophers' and theologians' treatments of Fortune and Fate, excluding astrological views and pictorial representations.

823. Courcelle, Pierre. *La Consolation de Philosophie dans la tradition littéraire*. Paris: Etudes Augustiniens. 1967.
Offers an extensive study of *Fortuna* and her wheel within the larger treatment of Boethius. Many plates.

824. Doren, A. "Fortuna im Mittelalter und in der Renaissance." *VBW* 2, no. 1 (1924): 71-144.
General study of the topos of *Fortuna*'s mutability.

825. Frakes, Jerold C. *The Fate of Fortune in the Early Middle Ages: The Boethian Tradition*. Studien und Texte zur Geistesgeschichte des Mittelalters, no. 23. Leiden: Brill, 1988.
Frakes explains clearly the aim of his book: "the present study investigates the concept of *fortuna* in several distinct stages of its historical development up through the eleventh century: in its religious and literary significance in ancient Roman, especially Neo-platonic, and early Patristic thought; in Boethius's interpretation and adaptation of earlier tradition, which he incorporated into the system of cosmological order in his *De Consolatione Philosophiae*; in the further modifications of the Boethian concept in the early Latin commentaries on the Boethian text; and in the interpretations by Alfred the Great and Notker Labeo in their translations of the *Consolatio*" (vii). Bibliography and index.

826. Patch, Howard R. *The Goddess Fortuna in Mediaeval Literature*.

Reprint. Folcroft, PA: Folcroft Library Editions,1976.
A detailed study of the goddess *Fortuna* in medieval literature, including passages from Latin works and a number of plates. Covers "the philosophy of fortune," "traditional themes of fortune," "functions and cults," "the dwelling-place of fortune," and "fortune's wheel." Bibliography and index.

827. Robinson, David M. "The Wheel of Fortune." *CP* 41 (1946): 207-16.
Searches for the origin of the Wheel of Fortune, discussing many of the earliest references to this wheel and to the Ball of Fortune, looking at what it symbolized and its development through antique, medieval, and Renaissance writing.

828. Schilling, Michael. "Rota Fortunae. Beziehungen zwischen Bild und Text in mittelalterlichen Handschriften." *Deutsche Literatur des Späten Mittelalters. Hamburger Colloquium 1973.* Edited by Wolfgang Harms and L. Peter Johnson. Berlin: Erich Schmidt, 1975, pp. 293-313.
General study of Fortune's wheel in medieval manuscript illumination, with six in-text black-and-white plates.

829. Walther, Hans. "Rota Fortunae im lateinischen Verssprichwort des Mittelalters." *ML* 1 (1964): 48-58.
Study of Latin proverbial poetry on Fortune's wheel.

Fountain of Life

830. Underhill, Evelyn. "The Fountain of Life: An Iconographical Study." *BM* 17 (April-September 1910): 99-109.
Calls attention to a previously unnoticed picture in the Church of the Petit Beguinage at Ghent and then discusses generally the iconography of the group of fifteenth- and sixteenth-century "Fountain of Life" pictures, analyzing in detail a number of different artistic representation of this image.

Geometrical Shapes

831. Brendel, Otto J. *Symbolism of the Sphere: A Contribution to the History of Earlier Greek Philosophy.* Etudes préliminaires aux religions orientales dans l'empire Romain, no. 67. Leiden: Brill, 1977.

Beginning with a number of examples of globes and spherical shapes in Greek art (with plates), this article goes on to describe some of the philosophical ideas behind and the iconographical significance of various types of spheres. In passing also occasionally describes the survival into the Middle Ages of the ideas discussed, with some quotations.

Grammar as a Visual Symbol

832. Wittkower, Rudolf. "'Grammatica' from Martianus Capella to Hogarth." *Allegory and the Migration of Symbols* (item 272), pp. 167-72.

The earlier part of this article considers the common medieval personification of Grammatica.

Hieroglyphics

833. Iversen, Erik. *The Myth of Egypt and Its Hieroglyphs in European Tradition.* Copenhagen: Gec Gad Publishers, 1961.

Discusses the system of "hieroglyphic writing" from the classical tradition up through the nineteenth century. Chapter Three, pp. 57-87, concerns the persistence of the myth in the Middle Ages and Renaissance, although it focusses mostly on the Renaissance, with some plates.

Labyrinths

834. Doob, Penelope Reed. *The Idea of the Labyrinth from Classical Antiquity through the Middle Ages.* Ithaca: Cornell Univ. Press, 1990.
Surveys labyrinths in literature from antiquity through the Middle Ages and treats a number of labyrinth mosaics. Includes bibliographical references and index.

835. Matthews, W. H. *Mazes and Labyrinths: A General Account of Their History and Developments.* London: Longmans, Green, 1922.
Looks at a large number of labyrinths in art, gardens, and in literature from antiquity through the nineteenth century, with numerous plates and pictures. Including a Bibliography of Mazes and Labyrinths, covering general, classical, in ancient art, in churches (by country, many medieval), turf labyrinths (including Renaissance works on the subject), stone labyrinths, and the labyrinth in non-European countries. Index.

Man as an Upside-Down Tree

836. Edsman, Carl-Martin. "Arbor Inversa. Heiland, Welt und Mensch als Himmelspflanzen." *Festschrift Walter Baetke.* Edited by Kurt Rudoph, et al. Weimar: Hermann Böhlau, 1966, pp. 85-109.
This idea seems to derive from Aristotle's *De Anima* where "antropos quasi arbor inversa," and reappears in Alan of Lille, *Distinctiones, PL* 210.707 who says "proprie, dicitur homo, unde Graece anthropos dicitur, id est arbor conversa; quia sicut caput arboris terrae adhaeret, et membra superius, it a per contrarium homo habet caput superius et membra inferius." Popular treatments

include Innocent III, *De Miseria Condicionis Humane*, ed. and trans. R. E. Lewis, Athens, GA: Univ. of Georgia Press ,1978, p. 106: "For what is man in his shape but a tree trunk turned upside down? Its roots are the hair, its base is the head along with the neck, its trunk is the chest along with the belly, its branches are the arms along with the legs, its foliage is the fingers and toes along with the joints." Edsman traces such a tradition, chiefly in German texts.

Mirror

837. Grabes, Herbert. *The Mutable Glass: Mirror-Imagery in Titles and Texts of the Middle Ages and English Renaissance.* Translated by Gordon Collier. Cambridge: Cambridge Univ. Press, 1982. Examines the history and iconography of the mirror as title in literary passages and in art, including a large number of plates of medieval and Renaissance art works in which the mirror or title of mirror appears. Bibliography.

838. Hartlaub, G. F. *Zauber des Spiegels. Geschichte und Bedeutung des Spiegels in der Kunst.* Munich: R. Piper, 1951. Studies the mirror—chiefly in antiquity and the post-medieval period—from many points of view, as a symbol of vanity, of speech and art, and the like. Treats mirrors in the works of the fifteenth-century Flemish easel painters. Many color in-text plates and black-and-white plates at the end. A commentary on the pictures serves as a bibliography of secondary literature.

839. Jónnson, Einar Már. *Le miroir: Naissance d'un genre littéraire.* Paris: Les Belles Lettres, 1995. Really more concerned with the idea of a mirror as a type of didactic tract, such as the *Speculum Virginum* but does treat symbolic mirrors held by Luxuria and the like. Sixteen black-and-white plates. Reviewed by Renate Blumenfeld-Kosinski in *Speculum* 72, no.1 (January 1997): 181-3.

840. Nolan, Edward Peter. *Now Through a Glass Darkly, Specular*

Images of Being and Knowing from Virgil to Chaucer. Ann
Arbor: Univ. of Michigan Press, 1991.
This book treats the mirror as a metaphor in writers such as Ovid,
Virgil, St. Augustine, Dante, and Chaucer.

841. Schwarz, Heinrich. "The Mirror in Art." *AQ* 15 (1952): 97-118.
Starts with van Eyck's Arnolfini portrait, then proceeds to examine
at length the iconography of the mirror in medieval and Renaissance
art and literature, moving up to the present, but with a focus on the
medieval period. Many plates.

842. _____. "The Mirror of the Artist and the Mirror of the Devout:
Observations on Some Paintings, Drawings, and Prints of the
Fifteenth Century." *Studies in the History of Art Dedicated to
William E. Suida on His Eightieth Birthday.* London: Phaidon
for the Samuel H. Kress Foundation, 1959, pp. 90-105.
Discusses the use of perspective as it would be seen through circular
convex mirrors in various fifteenth-century works, why this was
done, what mirrors represented, and the iconographical depiction of
mirrors themselves in the period.

843. Torti, Anna. *The Glass of Form: Mirroring Structures from Chaucer
to Skelton.* Woodbridge, Suffolk and Rochester, NY: Boydell
and Brewer 1991.
Contains a lengthy chapter on the image of the mirror in medieval
thought. Reviewed by Charles Blythe in *Speculum* 68, no. 4
(October 1993): 1227-9.

844. Zucker, Wolfgang M. "Reflections on Reflections." *JAAC* 20, no.
2 (Winter 1961): 239-50.
Examines the mirror's function in van Eyck's Arnolfini portrait and
in medieval and Renaissance paintings especially as a representative
of the artists's perspective and of the Divine Cosmos. Several plates.

Nine Worthies

845. Dickins, Bruce. "The Nine Unworthies." *Medieval Literature and
Civilization: Studies in Memory of G. N. Garmonsway.* Edited

by D. A. Pearsall and R. A. Waldron. London: Athlone, 1969, pp. 228-32.

The Nine Worthies were famous figures from antiquity and the Middle Ages who signified a continuing tradition of martial and chivalric excellence. Usually arranged in groups of three (pagans, Jews, and Christians), they were common in medieval art, especially tapestries and manuscript illumination. The nine were, antique: Hector of Troy, Alexander the Great, and Julius Caesar; Biblical: Joshua, David, and Judas Maccabaeus; and later Christian: Charlemagne, Godfrey of Bouillon, and King Arthur of Britain. They were often contrasted with nine unworthy figures, the subject of the present article. These were Nero, Cain, and Pontius Pilate; Jehoram (an evil king of Israel) Jereboam, and Ahab; and Judas Iscariot, Julian the Apostate (Emperor from 361 to 363 and believed to have attempted to reestablish pagan worship), and Bernabo Visconti, 1323-1385 (a tyrant of Milan). A set of female worthies, Lucretia, Veturia, Virginia, Esther, Judith, Jael, and saints Helen, Bridget of Sweden, and Elizabeth of Hungary is somewhat less frequently encountered. In the course of discussing the development of the unworthies, Dickins surveys this tradition in medieval art and literature.

846. Loomis, Roger Sherman. "Verses on the Nine Worthies." *MP* 15, no. 4 (August 1917): 19-27.
Brings to the reader's attention and prints verses from the fourteenth and fifteenth centuries on the Nine Worthies.

847. _____. "The Heraldry of Hector or Confusion Worse Confounded." *Speculum* 42, no.1 (January 1967): 32-5.
Treats the occasional confusion of Hector and Alexander as worthies, with a good selection of plates depicting the worthies in art.

848. Russell, H. Diane, with Bernadine Barnes. *Eva/Ave:Woman in Renaissance and Baroque Prints.* Washington: National Gallery of Art; New York: The Feminist Press at the City Univ. of New York, 1990.
One section by Barnes, entitled "Heroines and Worthy Women" looks at the tradition of the nine female worthies.

849. Schroeder, Horst. *Der Topos der Nine Worthies in Literatur und bildender Kunst.* Göttingen: Vanderhoeck and Ruprecht, 1971. Traces the theme of the Nine Worthies, both male and female, in German, French, and Old English literature as well as early Welsh sources up through the late Renaissance. Studies its first full-scale appearance in the French Alexander poem, *Les Voeux du Paon.* Of particular interest is the discussion of the motif in the Gobelin tapestries, wall and glass painting, decorative arts like wood and metal work, and in heraldry. There are many plates and a full bibliography and index.

Psychomachia and Virtues and Vices Imagery

850. Houlet, Jacques. *Les combats des vertus et des vices: Les psychomachies dans l'art.* Paris: Nouvelles éditions latines, 1969.
A detailed investigation into how the theme of the combat between virtues and vices derived from the *Psychomachia* of Prudentius is represented in the Romanesque and Gothic church sculpture of Western France, with plates, descriptions of the sculptures, bibliographical references, and discussion of the origins of the iconography.

851. Katzenellenbogen, Adolf. *Allegories of the Virtues and Vices in Mediaeval Art.* New York: Norton, 1964.
Overview essay followed by a study of the *Psychomachia* and its illustrative cycle with a special focus on the carvings at Notre Dame Cathedral. Plates and indices of places, names, and subjects.

852. Labande-Mailfert, Y. "Pauvreté et paix dans l'iconographie romane (XIe-XIIe siècle)." *Etudes sur l'histoire de la pauvreté.* Edited by Michel Mollat. Paris: Publications de la Sorbonne, 1974, pp. 319-43.
Treats the iconographical depiction of poor people and the "virtue" of poverty in eleventh- and twelfth-century sculpture and manuscript illumination, those who were already poor as well as those who gave

up their money for the love of God, discovering in the process the link between poverty and peace. Various figures (Job, Lazarus, St. Martin) and themes (hermits, church benefactors, virtues and vices, and the evil knight who attacks the poor peasant) are discussed.

853. Newhauser, Richard. *The Treatise on Vices and Virtues in Latin and the Vernacular.* Typologie des sources du Moyen Age occidental, no. 68. Turnhout: Brepols, 1993.
Like others in this series, a standard bibliography of the development of the genre, with a number of color plates from illustrated medieval treatises at the back.

854. Norman, Joanne S. *Metamorphosis of an Allegory:The Iconography of the Psychomachia in Medieval Art.* New York and Berne: Peter Lang, 1988.
Treats the *fortuna* of the *Psychomachia* illustrative cycle in later medieval art and the rise of new *Psychomachia* allegories like the *Etymachia* in the fourteenth and fifteenth centuries. Also treats King David. Many black-and-white plates and a full bibliography.

855. O'Reilly, Jennifer. *Studies in the Iconography of the Virtues and Vices in the Middle Ages.* A Garland Series: Outstanding Theses in the Fine Arts from British Universities. New York and London: Garland, 1988.
Discusses the origins, context, and iconography of the *Psychomachia* in the Middle Ages; the didactic context of other systems of Virtues and Vices; the Cardinal Virtues; the Gift Virtues; "The Devotional and Penitential Context of the Later Middle Ages"; and "Trees of Virtues and Vices, Life and Death." Includes a bibliography and numerous plates.

856. Thérel, Marie-Louise. "'Caritas' et 'paupertas' dans l'iconographie médiévale inspirée de la *psychomachie*." *Etudes sur l'histoire de la pauvreté,* (item 852) pp. 295-317.
Examines the iconographical representation of the theme of the battle of virtue and vice, especially as linked with Prudentius, in medieval sculpture and manuscript illustration, with plates.

  *   Stettiner, Richard. *Die Illustrierten Prudentiushandschriften.* Cited

above as item 741.

857. Wenzel, Siegfried. "Vices, Virtues and Popular Preaching." *Proceedings of the Southeastern Medieval and Renaissance Studies,summer 1976*. Edited by Dale B. Randall. Durham: Duke Univ. Press, 1976, pp. 28-54.
Examines the treatment of the Seven Deadly Sins in preaching of the late Middle Ages.

858. Willard, Charity Cannon. "Christine de Pisan's 'Clock of Temperance.'" *L'Esprit créateur* 2 (1962): 149-54.
Looks at medieval treatments of the clock, particularly as a moral symbol or as connected with temperance, to explain a clock associated with temperance appearing in several manuscripts of Christine de Pisan.

Queenship

859. Huneycutt, Lois. "Medieval Queenship." *HT* 39 (June 1989): 16-22.
A historical look at the medieval perceptions of the queen, her role, and appropriate attributes, with a focus on iconographical depictions of queens in art as well as in literary descriptions. With plates.

Riding Backwards

860. Mellinkoff, Ruth. "Riding Backwards: Theme of Humiliation and Symbol of Evil." *Viator* 4 (1973): 153-76.
Explores the medieval folk roots of this theme which persists up tothe present, looking at literature and art with passages cited and plates mostly from the medieval period but also some from later ages.

Roland Iconography

861. Lejeune, Rita, and Jacques Stiennon. *The Legend of Roland in the
     Middle Ages.* Translated by Christine Trollope. London:
     Phaidon, 1971.
     These two large volumes provide a very thorough description of
     medieval art works depicting this legend—a crucial source for any
     iconographical investigation. Volume One covers artistic
     representations of the Roland legend during the Romanesque and
     Gothic periods in manuscript illustration, church sculpture, wall
     painting, and stained glass, and includes some color plates. Volume
     Two consists of the accompanying black-and-white plates,
     appendices indexing the plates according to "Episodes in the life of
     Roland," and "Episodes in the life of Ganelon," color plates, and
     black-and-white illustrations, as well as an index. Reviewed by D.
     J. A. Ross in *MA* 37 (1968): 46-65.

Skull as a symbol

862. Wittkower, Rudolf. "Death and Resurrection in a Picture by Marten
     de Vos." *Allegory and the Migration of Symbols* (item 272),
     pp. 159-66.
     Though chiefly about the Renaissance conflation of the skull and
     putti, or angelic children, this article does offer considerable
     information on earlier views of the skull as a visual symbol.

Time, Images of

863. Borst, Arno. *The Ordering of Time: From the Ancient Computus to
     the Modern Computer.* Translated by A. Winnard. Chicago:
     Univ. of Chicago Press, 1993.

The focus is on time-reckoning in the Middle Ages and its visual schemata, but Borst also briefly traces the connection between the words computus and computer (and digit, digital, datum, and data), and discusses early counting machines, both real and imagined.

Tristan Legend

* Eames, Elizabeth. "Inlaid Tile Mosaic." Cited above as item 189.

864. Fouquet, Doris. *Wort und Bild in der mittelalterlichen Tristantradition: der älteste Tristanteppich von Kloster Wienhausen und die textile Tristanüberlieferung des Mittelalters.* Berlin: E. Schmidt, 1971.
Studies the Tristan story in some medieval tapestries.

* Früehmorgen-Voss, Hella. *Text und Illustration im Mittelalter.* Cited above as item 339.

* Loomis, Roger Sherman. *Illustrations of Medieval Romance.* Cited above as item 183.

865. Walworth, Julia. *"Tristan in Medieval Art." Tristan and Isolde: A Casebook.* Edited by Joan Tasker Grimbert. Arthurian Characters and Themes, no. 2. New York and London: Garland, 1995, pp. 255-300.
Examines "both the narrative and the single-scene works" (261) depicting the Tristan story, with a number of plates, and discusses their presentations of this story, suggesting the great complexity and diversity of Tristan iconography. **See also Arthur**

Troy Matter

866. Borchardt, Frank L. *German Antiquity in Renaissance Myth.*

Baltimore and London: Johns Hopkins Univ. Press, 1971.
Examines Renaissance German interest in tracing the sources for its myths and legends and the values implied in them back to ancient and medieval times, especially to the myth of the dispersion of famous Trojan warriors after the fall of Troy. Arranged mostly by author or important figure of the legend. Includes a section onbibliography and status of the scholarship, a chronology of important ancient through Renaissance figures, and an index.

867. Graus, F. "Troja und trojanische Herkunftssage im Mittelalter." *Kontinuität und Transformation* (item 40), pp. 25-43.
An overview of the response to the Troy story in medieval writers chiefly German.

868. Jung, Marc-René. *La légende de Troie en France au Moyen Age: Analyse de versions françaises et bibliographie raisonée de manuscrits.* Romanica Helvetica, no.114. Basel and Tübingen: Francke, 1996.
Studies the Troy story in a vareity of French narrative poems. Especially useful for its forty-three black-and-white plates of scenes from the Troy legend in medieval manuscripts, tapestries, and the like.

869. MacDougall, Hugh A. *Racial Myth in English History: Trojans, Teutons, and Anglo-Saxons.* Montreal: Harvest House; Hanover and London: Univ. Press of New England, 1982.
Studies the origin, development, and effects of the two great racial myths in the English past, the one of Celtic Britain begun by Geoffrey of Monmouth's *History of the Kings of Britain*, and the other, arising predominantly in the sixteenth-century, "variously referred to as Anglo-Saxonism, Teutonism, Gothicism" (2). Some discussion of medieval but much more of Renaissance and modern racialism. Index.

Wisdom, figure of

870. Alverny, Marie-Thérèse d'. *Etudes sur le symbolisme de la Sagesse et sur l'iconographie*. Edited by Charles Burnett, with a Preface by Peter Dronke. Aldershot, England and Brookfield, VT: Variorum, 1993.
A collection of previously published essays on the figure of Wisdom and on cosmology from a visual point of view.

World Grown Old

871. Dean, James. "The World Grown Old and Genesis in Middle English Historical Writings." *Speculum* 57, no. 3 (July 1982): 548-68.
Argues that medieval theologians and historians envisioned mankind as in a "moral and physical decline" from Adam with each progressive generation, and supplements his argument with numerous quotations. As Dean explains, "specifically I find five stages of antediluvian and one stage of postdiluvian decline: Original Sin, fratricide, development of the city, technocracy, illicit sexuality and giants, and empire" (549).

872. _____. *The World Grown Old in Later Medieval Literature*. Cambridge, MA: The Medieval Academy of America, 1997.
Studies the popular topos of the world's supposed decline from the golden age of the ancients.

World Upside Down

873. Odenius, O. "Mundus Inversus: Några inledande bibliografiska anteckningar kring tre mellansvenska bildvarianter." *Arv* 10 (1954): 142-70.
Considers "three variants of 'Mundus Inversus' which are found in

paintings in churches in the Swedish midlands" (146). Includes an English summary and plates.

874. Randall, Lilian M. C. "A Medieval Slander." *AB* 42 (1960): 24-39. Traces the world upside topos in exempla, proverbs, and marginalia, where traditional roles and activities no longer pertain; for example, men hatch eggs.

875. Simpson, J. "The World Upside Down Shall Be." *JAF* 91 (1978): 559-67.
Treats doomsday imagery as a form of this topos.

Yvain Iconography

876. Rushing, James A., Jr. *Images of Adventure: Yvain in the Visual Arts*. Philadelphia: Univ. of Pennsylvania Press, 1995.
Studies representations of this romance hero in a variety of works of art. Numerous black-and-white plates. **See also Arthur**

Chapter Four: The Christian Tradition

BIBLE

General

877. Gameson, Richard. *The Early Medieval Bible: Its Production, Decoration and Use.* Cambridge Studies in Palaeography and Codicology, no. 2. Cambridge: Cambridge Univ. Press,1994.
Treats the significance of the Bible in early medieval culture in eleven linked studies on issues such as history, art history, and Bible manuscripts.

878. Gibson, Margaret T. *The Bible in the Latin West.* The Medieval Book, no.1. Notre Dame and London: Univ. of Notre Dame Press, 1993.
A study of the Latin Vulgate Bible, with accounts of vernacular versions and of Latin commentaries.

879. Hindman, Sandra. *Text and Image in Fifteenth-Century Illustrated Dutch Bibles.* Corpus Sacrae Scripturae Neerlandicae Medii Aevi Miscellanea, no. 1. Leiden: Brill, 1977.
Discusses Jacob van Maerlant's *Rijmbijbel,* a loose reworking and translation of Peter Comestor's *Historia Scholastica* as a source for important Genesis legends. Other parts of this fascinating book concern the role of the history Bible in Dutch Bible tradition, and narrative illustration and pictorial realism in their miniature cycles. There are many plates.

880. Smeets, Jean Robert. "Les traductions, adaptations, et paraphrases de la Bible en vers." *La Littérature didactique, allégorique et satirique.* Vol.1. Edited by Jürgen Beyer. Heidelberg: C. Winter, 1968-70, pp. 48-57 and 81-96.

Treats "adaptations" broadly understood, of the Bible, like that of Peter of Riga.

881. Vernet, André, and Anne-Marie Genevois. *La Bible au Moyen Age: Bibliographie.* Paris: CNRS, 1989.
Covers the role of the Bible in the Middle Ages. The authors offer current bibliographies, lists of periodicals, and dictionaries, then move on to the Greek, Hebrew, Latin, and vernacular versions used in the Middle Ages. Glosses, concordances, and, exegetical works of all kinds (the last named arranged according to the books of the Bible they comment on) are also surveyed. Particularly useful is the section "Histoire de l'art" which ends the work; it treats Biblical characters, situations, and images in the arts of the Middle Ages.

Apocrypha

882. Charlesworth, James H. *The New Testament Apocrypha and Pseudepigrapha: A Guide to Publications with an Excursus on Apocalypses.* Alta Bibliography Series, no. 17. Metuchen, NJ and London: The American Theological Library Association and the Scarecrow Press, 1987.
Concerns the Apocalypse of John and its influence on subsequent apocalypses in both the Jewish and Christian traditions. Includes texts with English translations. Extensive bibliography.

883. _____. *The Old Testament Pseudepigrapha.* 2 vols. Garden City, NY: Doubleday, 1983-85.
Surveys apocalyptic literature and "Testaments," expansions of the Old Testament and legends associated with it, "Wisdom" literature, prayers, Psalms and odes, and fragments of Jewish and Hellenistic works associated with the Old Testament. Provides English translations of these works.

884. _____. *The Old Testament Pseudepigrapha and the New Testament.* London and New York: Cambridge Univ. Press, 1985.
The most useful single work on Old and New Testament apocryphal texts. In the form of an annotated bibliography and guide to research.

885. _____. *The Pseudepigrapha and Modern Research with a Supplement.* Society of Biblical Literature Septuagint and Cognate Studies Series, no. 7S. Chico, CA: Scholars Press, 1981.
Provides bibliography on these "extra-Biblical" books pseudonymically attributed to an Old Testament figure. Gives brief introduction to the work and surveys the current scholarship.

886. _____. "Research on the New Testament Apocrypha and Pseudepigrapha." *Aufstieg und Niedergang der römischen Welt.* Edited by Wolfgang Haase. Berlin: Walter de Gruyter, 1988, pp. 3919-68.
Discusses critical interest in this group of texts, reviews scholarship, and gives extensive bibliography.

887. Elliott, J. K. *The Apocryphal New Testament: A Collection of Apocryphal Christian Literature in an English Translation Based on M. R. James.* Oxford: Clarendon Press, 1993.
A reworking of item 892. Includes medieval as well as late antique versions of apocryphal gospels, acts, epistles, and apocalypses. Each is accompanied by an introduction with bibliography.

888. Geerard, M. *Clavis Apocryphorvm Novi Testamenti.* Turnhout: Brepols, 1992.
Provides up to date scholarship, primarily textual, on the following categories of apocryphal works: apocrypha of Christ's public life, infancy gospels, gospels of Nicodemus and Bartholomew and related texts, apocrypha of the Virgin and John the Baptist, apocryphal acts of the Apostles and Sibylline Oracles.

889. Gero, Stephen. "Apocryphal Gospels: A Survey of Textual and Literary Problems." *Aufstieg* (item 886), pp. 3969-96.

Aims "to provide a survey of connected narrative accounts of Jesus found outside the canonical gospels" (3970), divided according to types of gospel, such as Infancy, Passion, and The Secret Gospel of Mark.

890. Himmelfarb, Martha. *Ascent to Heaven in Jewish and Christian Apocalypses.* New York and Oxford: Oxford Univ. Press, 1993.
Treats the Book of Enoch, the Testament of Levi, the Apocalypses of Zephaniah and of Abraham, and the Ascension of Isaiah. Contains an index and very full bibliography.

891. Izdorczyk, Zbigniew, ed. *The Medieval Gospel of Nicodemus: Text, Intertexts and Contexts in Western Europe.* Binghamton, NY: MRTS, 1996.
Essays on the Gospel of Nicodemus in various medieval literatures, with a thematic bibliography and an index of manuscripts.

892. James, M. R., ed. and trans. *The Apocryphal New Testament.* Oxford: Clarendon,1955.
See item 887, Elliott, above.

893. Lipscomb, William Lowndes, trans. *The Armenian Apocryphal Adam Literature.* Armenian Texts and Studies, no. 8. Philadelphia: Univ. of Pennsylvania Press,1990.
A critical edition with the original texts and translations of a group of brief Armenian Adam books which often incorporate folkloric elements into the Adam narratives.

894. McNamara, M. *The Apocrypha in the Irish Church.* Dublin: Institute for Advanced Studies, 1975.
This useful bibliographical work offers information on published editions and an annotated list of major studies. The introduction studies the significance and influence of Irish apocrypha.

895. Van Os, A. B. *Religious Visions: The Development of the Eschatological Elements in Mediaeval English Religious Literature.* Amsterdam: H. J. Paris, 1932.
Presents original texts, sometimes with translations, of a variety of Old and Middle English visions of the afterlife and of the underworld. An intoduction treats vision literature generally.

Bibles, Moralized

896. Behrends, R. *The Biblia Pauperum and Apocalypse. A Facsimile of Weimar MS Fol. max 4.* Leiden: Brill, 1978.
Facsimile edition of this important example of a moralized picture Bible.

897. Cornell, Henrik. *Biblia Pauperum.* Stockholm: Thule-Tryck,1925. This first serious study of the genre treats the way typological concepts from the Old and New Testaments are transferred to manuscript illuminations. Seventy-two black-and-white plates drawn from a great many manuscripts of this very important source of medieval imagery as well as thirty-seven in-text pictures add to the book's utility. An account of the manuscripts known of this work as of 1925 is combined with full discussions of the *Biblia Pauperum*'s relation to similar texts like the *Speculum Humanae Salvationis*.

898. Fawtier, Robert. *La Bible historiée toute figurée de la John Rylands Library: Reproduction intégrale du manuscrit French 5 accompagnée d'une étude.* Paris: Pour les trustees et gouverneurs de la John Rylands Library, 1924.
Describes and relates the history of this manuscript along with a discussion of sources, style, and a description of the plates. Accompanied by numerous reproductions from the manuscript in the form of detached black-and-white plates in an envelope.

899. Haussherr, Reiner. "Petrus Cantor, Stephan Langton, Hugo von St. Cher und Isaias-Prolog der Bible Moralisée." *Verbum et Signum* (item 908 below), vol. 1, pp. 347-64.
Studies the way these exegetes may have contributed to the glosses in the moralized Bibles.

900. Henry, Avril, ed. *Biblia Pauperum: A Facsimile Edition.* Ithaca: Cornell Univ. Press, 1987.
A facsimile of the manuscript of this work now in the Sachsische Landesbibliothek

901. Laborde, Alexandre De, ed. *La Bible moralisée conservée à Oxford, Paris, et Londres. Société de reproductions de manuscrits à peintures.* Paris: SFRMP, 1911-27.
Facsimile of a thirteenth-century manuscript of the *Bible Moralisée* accompanied by plates from similar Bibles and a discussion of background and sources.

Distinctiones and Etymologies

902. Amsler, Mark. *Etymology and Grammatical Discourse in Late Antiquity and the Early Middle Ages from 200-1000 AD.* Amsterdam Studies in the Theory and History of Linguistic Science, 3rd ser., vol. 44. Amsterdam/Philadelphia: John Benjamins, 1989.
From the perspective of recent linguistic developments, Amsler looks back at ideas about etymology in the Middle Ages, with treatments of technical and exegetical grammar before and after Isidore of Seville.

903. Bloch, R. Howard. *Etymologies and Genealogies: A Literary Anthropology of the French Middle Ages.* Chicago: Univ. of Chicago Press, 1983.
Chapter One treats the evolution of the idea of etymology from the antique through the early medieval periods.

904. Curtius, Ernst Robert. "Etymology as a Category of Thought." *European Literature and the Latin Middle Ages.* Bollingen ser. no. 36. Translated by Williard Trask. Princeton Univ. Press, 1953, pp. 495-500.
An excellent introduction to the ideas behind etymology in classical and medieval Christian writing, with many quotations from medieval authors.

905. _____. "Nomina Christi. "*Mélanges de Joseph de Ghellinck.* Vol. 2: *Moyen Age. Epoques moderne et contemporaine.* Gembloux: Éditions J. Duculot, S.A., 1951, pp.1029-32.

Brief treatment of various medieval names and epithets for Christ, often with unusual etymologies.

906. Engles, Joseph. "La portée de l'etymologie isidorienne." *SM,* 3rd ser., 3, no.1 (1962): 99-128.
   Provides the text of Isidore of Seville's major statement on etymology, with French translation, and offers a helpful account of Isidore's practices in etymologizing words.

907. Fontaine, Jacques. *Isidore de Seville et la culture classique dans l'Espagne wisigothique.* 2 vols. Paris: Etudes Augustiniennes, 1959.
   The standard work situating Isidore in his period.

908. Fromm, Hans, et al., eds. *Verbum et Signum: Beiträge zur mediävistischen Bedeutungsforschung.* 2 vols. Munich: Wilhelm Fink, 1975.
   This festschrift for Friedrich Ohly contains several studies of medieval etymological practice; in particular those of Gudrun Schleusener-Eicholz, Uwe Ruberg, and Willy Sanders in Volume One are especially relevant here.

909. Hillgarth, J. N. "The Position of Isidorian Studies: A Critical Review of the Literature 1936-1975." *SM,* 3d ser., 24, no. 2 (1983): 817-905.
   Very useful annotated bibliography with full indices.

910. Klinck, Roswitha *Die lateinische Etymologie des Mittelalters.* Medium Ævum, no.17. Berlin: Wilhelm Fink, 1970.
   Treats the concept of etymology in the Middle Ages, and its relation to, and use by, Christian exegetes, and gives a number of examples of words etymologized in Christian contexts.

911. Laurant, Jean-Pierre. *Symbolisme et écriture. Le cardinal Pitra et la 'Clef' de Méliton de Sardes.* Paris: Les Éditions du Cerf, 1988.
   One example of the *distinctio* genre or terms taken from scripture with allegorical or symbolic significance appended, is the *Clavis* of Melito of Sardis. It is especially useful for the iconographer. Long accessible only in a rather rare edition by Pitra, much of it is now

available in French. This work gives the Latin text of Pitra and a French translation.

912. Lindsay, W. M., ed. *Isidori. . . Etymologiarum sive originum libri XX.* 2 vols. Oxford: Clarendon, 1911.
An edition of Isidore's best -known encyclopaedic and etymological work.

913. Maltby, Robert. *A Lexicon of Ancient Latin Etymologies* Leeds: Cairns, 1991.
This is a handlist of etymologies given to various words by Latin grammarians from Varro to Isidore of Seville.

914. Poerck, Guy de. "Etymologia et origo: A travers la tradition latine." ANAMNHΣΙΣ: *Gedenkboek Prof. Dr. E. A. Leemans.* Edited by I. Strubbe. Bruges: De Tempel, 1970, pp. 191-228.
Considers the origins of etymology among the Roman grammarians, with many passages cited and a particularly important section on Isidore of Seville.

915. Reta, Jose Oroz, and Manuel-A. Marcos Casquero, eds. *San Isidro de Sevilla, Etimologias.* Biblioteca de autores christianos, no. 433. Madrid: BAC, 1982-83.
A modern standard edition of Isidore of Seville with Spanish translation.

916. Schweickard, Wolfgang. "Etymologia est origo vocabulorum. . .' Zum Verständnis der Etymologie definition Isidors von Sevilla." *HL* 121, no. 2 (1985): 1-25.
This article considers the key phrase in Isidore which appears in the title. Not historically based, the article is chiefly valuable for the examples of etymological technique it offers from late antique writers.

917. Weijers, Olga. *Dictionnaires et répertoires au Moyen Age.* Item 501.
Treats Isidore's etymology among other lexicographical works.

Glosses and Exegesis

918. Gibson, Margaret, and Karlfrid Froehlich, eds. *Glossa ordinaria.* 4 vols. Turnhout: Brepols, 1992.
This is a facsimile of the first printed edition, that by Adolph Rusch, Strassburg, 1480, of one of the most important medieval commentaries on the Bible. The introduction to the *Glossa* by Gibson outlines the manuscript history of the work, and the edition is more convenient to use than that printed in the *Patrologia Latina.*

919. Ginzberg, Louis. *The Legends of the Jews.* 4 vols. New York: Simon and Schuster, 1961.
Jewish folkloristic or midrashic additions to the account of the Creation and Fall in Genesis were an important source of imagery and were known to the Latin West through the *Historia Scholastica* of Peter Comestor among other avenues. Rashi (see items 928,930 below) is the name most often cited in connection with this material. Ginzberg's work is a standard and accessible collection of such material in English.

920. Hamel, Christopher De. *Glossed Books of the Bible and the Origins of the Paris Book Trade.* Woodbridge, Suffolk, Great Britain: D. S. Brewer, 1984.
Looks at the creation, transmission, and dissemination of the glossed Latin Bible, which developed in the twelfth century and remained popular until the close of the Middle Ages. Offers an index of manuscripts cited and detailed information on which books of the Bible are glossed.

921. Hull. P. and R. Sharpe."Peter of Cornwall and Launceston." *CS* 13 (1986): 5-53.
Though the focus of the article is on Cornish history, it contains a considerable amount of information about Peter of Cornwall, 1140-1221, Augustinian Canon and prior of Holy Trinity, Aldgate, London. Peter's enormous *Pantheologus,* a preachers' handbook, which has never been edited, is discussed in some detail, and a list of manuscripts is provided.

922. Keenan, Hugh T., ed., *Typology and English Medieval Literature.* New York: AMS, 1992.
Essays on the influence of typological imagery in works such as *Piers Plowman, Sir Gawain and the Green Knight,* and *The Canterbury Tales.* The book has an extensive annotated bibliography and forms a concise introduction to this vast subject.

923. Luscombe, David. "Peter Comestor." *The Bible in the Medieval World: Essays in Memory of Beryl Smalley.* Edited by Katherine Walsh and Diana Wood. Studies in Church History. Subsidia, no. 4. Oxford: B. H. Blackwell, 1985, pp. 109-29.
Important for the transmission of midrashic ideas to the Latin West was the *Historia Scholastica,* about 1170, a Bible abridgement and gloss whose chapters on Genesis especially, were full of midrashic echoes. Widely translated, it served as a popular Bible while at the same time its Latin text formed a part of university study. It is believed that Peter, dean of the Cathedral of Troyes, had contact in that city with the rabbinical school of Rashi and that such was the manner in which he acquired his Hebrew learning. In addition to these contacts, Peter was acquainted with Josephus, and Jerome's introductions to the Vulgate Bible for other Jewish materials. This article is a general study of what is known about Peter's life, work, sources, and influence.

924. Morey, James H. "Peter Comester, Biblical Paraphrase and the Medieval Popular Bible." *Speculum* 68, no. 1 (January 1993): 6-35 and 109-29.
This is a thorough study of Peter as a source of Bible imagery.

925. Nordström, Carl-Otto. "Rabbinic Features in Byzantine and Catalan Art." *CA* 15 (1965): 179-205.
General discussion of how rabbinic exegesis adds a very concrete visual dimension to illustrative programs. Deals specifically with scriptural episodes such as "Jacob's Dream at Bethel," "Joseph and Judah," "The Anointing of David," "Eliezer and Rebecca," and "The Feasts of Belshazzar and Ahasuerus," supplemented with a number of plates.

926. _____"Rabbinica in früchristlichen und byzantinischen Illustrationen zum 4. Buch Moses." *Idea and Form: Studies in the History of Art*. Edited by Teddy Brunius, et al. Uppsala: Almqvist and Wiksells, 1959, pp. 24-47.
Considers how the illustration of a number of legends to do with Moses in the book of Numbers are governed by midrashic information available to the painter. Among these legends are the stoning of Moses and the stories of Balaam and Phineas. Numerous black-and-white photographs in the text.

927. Porton, Gary G. *Understanding Rabbinic Midrash: Texts and Commentary*. The Library of Judaic Learning, no. 5. Hoboken, NJ: KTAV, 1985.
Explains the influence of midrash, a body of late antique rabbinic folklore and commentary. Provides numerous examples in English translation, with an especially important section on the midrashic commentary which developed around the book of Genesis.

928. Sed-Rajna, Gabrielle, ed. *Rashi, 1040-1990: Hommages à Ephraim E. Urbach*. Paris: Cerf, 1993.
A festschrift containing a large number of articles on Rashi and his importance for the later Middle Ages. Many plates. Analyzed in *Speculum* 70, no. 1 (January 1995): 238-9.

929. Shereshevsky, Esra. "Hebrew Traditions in Peter Comestor's *Historia Scholastica*." *JQR* 59 (1968-69): 268-89.
Argues for Rashi as a source for Peter Comester's midrashic knowledge and imagery.

930. _____. *Rashi, The Man and His World.* New York: Sepher-Hermon Press, 1982.
Treats the important medieval commentator on the Bible, Rabbi Shlomo Yitzhaki Solomon ben Isaac, or from the initial letters of these words, Rashi. Offering biographical and historical material, the author discusses at length many of Rashi's interpretations of scripture and includes a bibliography and indices of Biblical and midrashic sources.

NEW TESTAMENT FIGURES AND IMAGES

Antichrist

931. Bender, Margaret, ed. *Le Torneiment Anticrist by Huon de Méri: A Critical Edition.* University of Mississippi Romance Monographs, no. 17. Jackson, MS: Univ. of Mississippi Press, 1976.
A critical edition of this thirteenth-century French text, a highly imaginative allegory of a great tournament between Antichrist and his minions and the forces of Rightousness.

932. Emmerson, Richard Kenneth. *Antichrist in the Middle Ages: A Study of Medieval Apocalypticism, Art, and Literature.* Seattle: Univ. of Washington Press, 1981.
Outlines traditional depictions of Antichrist as complex and divergent but with a certain unity about who he is, when he will appear, what he will do, and what will become of him. Thorough treatment of the relationship of Antichrist to such topics as apocalypticism, scriptural exegesis, and literary and artistic depictions. Plates and an index of Biblical passages dealing with Antichrist.

933. Evelyn, Charlotte d'. "The Middle English Metrical Version of the 'Revelationes' of Methodius; With a Study of the Influence of Methodius in Middle English Writings." *PMLA* 33 (1918): 135-203.
Gives a Middle English text of the work with notes and prints the short Latin text.

934. Prinz, Otto. "Eine frühe abendländische Aktualisierung der lateinischen Übersetzung des Pseudo-Methodios." *DAEM* 41, no. 1 (1985): 1-23.
Provides a modern scholarly edition of the short version.

935. Rauh, Horst Dieter. *Das Bild des Antichrist im Mittelalter: Von Tychonius zum Deutschen Symbolismus.* Beiträge zur Geschichte der Philosophie und Theologie des Mittelalters, n.f. 9. Münster: Aschendorff, 1973.
Traces the antichrist motif from Isaiah and Ezechiel through Hildegard of Bingen. No plates but an extensive bibliography.

936. Wright, Rosemary Muir. *Art and Antichrist in Medieval Europe.* Manchester and New York: Manchester Univ. Press, 1995.
Considers a variety of Antichrist representations in medieval art and their intellectual backgrounds. 65 black- and- white plates. Reviewed by Suzanne Lewis in *Speculum* 72, no. 3 (July 1997): 902-7.

Apocalypse Illustrations

937. Behrends, Rayner, et al., eds. *Biblia Pauperum Apocalypses: The Weimar MS.* New York: Hacker, 1978.
A facsimile edition.

938. Bing, Gertrude. "The Apocalypse Block-Books and Their Manuscript Models." *JWCI* 5 (1942): 143-58.
Examines the Wellcome Apocalypse in order to establish the tradition out of which come the popular block books of the early fifteenth century. Includes many plates and a fold-out chart that compares how specific images are depicted by the Wellcome designer with how they appear in Oxford University Library MS Bodley Auct. D.4.17 and three early blockbooks.

939. Brieger, Peter H., ed. *The Trinity College Apocalypse.* 2 vols. London: Eugrammia Press, 1967.
This is a facsimile of the manuscript with transcription and English translation.

940. Coxe, H. O., ed. *The Apocalypse of St. John the Divine (Bodleian MS. Auct.D.4.17).* Roxburghe Club. London: Nichols and Sons, 1876.

A facsimile of this thirteenth-century illuminated manuscript with a preface discussing the illuminations.

941. Delisle, Léopold and Paul Meyer. *L'apocalypse en français au XIIIe siècle.* SATF. Reprint. New York: Johnson, 1965.
This volume reproduces the text of a French Apocalypse in the Bibliothèque Nationale, MS fr. 403, but its utility is far greater, as the author comments on a group of thirteenth-century apocalypses from England and northern France and indeed has provided the basis for the investigation of English illustrated apocalypse manuscripts. Though there are no plates, the author describes in great detail the pictures in the various manuscripts and compares the cycles. He also introduces the Angers tapestries into the comparison.

942. Deuchler, Florens, et al., eds., *The Cloisters Apocalypse: An Early Fourteenth-Century Manuscript in Facsimile.* 2 vols. New York: Metropolitan Museum of Art, 1971.
A handsome facsimile of this famous manuscript.

943. Emmerson, Richard K., and Suzanne Lewis. "Census and Bibliography of Medieval Manuscripts Containing Apocalypse Illustrations, *ca.* 800-1500." *Traditio* 60 (1984): 337-79; 61 (1985): 367-409; 62 (1986): 443-72.
This work's interest was to expand on M.R. James's *The Apocalypse in Art* item 949 and provide more current bibliographies.

944. Hassall, A. G. and W. O., eds. *The Douce Apocalypse.* Faber Library of Illuminated Manuscripts. London: Faber, 1961.
A facsimile edition. See item 945 below.

945. Henderson, George. "An Apocalypse Manuscript in Paris: BN, MS Lat. 10474." *AB* 52 (1970): 22-31.
A detailed examination of the iconography in this codex, comparing it with that of the Cambridge, Trinity College MS R.16.2 Apocalypse and the Bodleian Library MS Douce 180 Apocalypse, so as to place them within an illustrated English Apocalypse tradition. Some plates.

946. _____. "Studies in English Manuscript Illumination. Part I: Stylistic Sequence and Stylistic Overlap in Thirteenth-Century English Manuscripts." *JWCI* 30 (1967): 71-104.

In these two studies, Henderson questions the division Delisle and Meyer make in their book on English Apocalypse manuscripts (item 941) into two distinct "families," and then looks at a number of these codices to show the more complex relationship between the iconography of the different cycles. Some plates in each article.

947. _____."Studies in English Manuscript Illumination. Part II. The English Apocalypse 1." *JWCI* 30 (1967): 104-37.
See item 941 above.

948. _____. "Studies in English Manuscript Illumination. Part III. The English Apocalypse 2." *JWCI* 31 (1968): 104-47.
A careful treatment of the iconography in the Dyson Perrins, Douce, Lambeth, and Abingdon manuscripts or cycles, drawing comparisons between them and discussing influence. Some plates.

949. James, Montague Rhodes. *The Apocalypse in Art.* The Schweich Lectures of the British Academy, 1927. London: Oxford Univ. Press, 1931.
Offers a list of apocalypse manuscripts and treats them in three groups: up to the beginning of the thirteenth century, then from the thirteenth through the fifteenth centuries, and finally from the end of the fifteenth century to the present day. Though there are specific descriptions of cycles, there are no plates.

950. _____. *The Apocalypse in Latin: MS 10 in the Collection of Dyson Perrins.* Introduction by M. R. James. Oxford: Oxford Univ. Press, 1927.
James's lengthy introduction provides a list of illustrated apocalypse manuscripts of the thirteenth and later centuries, information on apocalypse cycles in general, and commentary on the plates.

951. _____, ed. *The Dublin Apocalypse.* Roxburghe Club.Cambridge: Cambridge Univ. Press, 1932.
A facsimile edition of this magnificent manuscript, which discusses the cycle of illustrations and the provenance of the codex.

952. Lejard, André. *Les tapisseries de l'apocalypse de la cathédral d'Angers: Accompagnés du texte de "L'Apocalypse de St Jean"*

dans la traduction de Le Maistre de Sacy. Paris: Albin Michel, 1942.
Presents plates from this tapestry accompanied by the relevant Biblical passages in French and a brief introduction on the presentation of the Apocalypse in medieval Christian art.

953. Lurçat, Jean, and Jacques Levron. *L'Apocalypse d'Angers.* Angers: Au Masque d'Or, 1955.
Presents plates of this fourteenth- or fifteenth-century tapestry comissioned by Louis, duke of Anjou, each accompanied by the relevant Biblical passages. A French introduction treats the history of tapestry generally and of this one in particular.

954. Morgan, Nigel, ed. *The Lambeth Apocalypse: Manuscript 209 in Lambeth Palace Library: A Critical Study.* 2 vols. London: Harvey Miller, 1990.
Superb facsimile of this manuscript with a detailed discussion of the illustrations.

955. Musper, H. Th., ed. *Die Urausgaben der holländischen Apokalypse und Biblia-Pauperum.* Munich: Prestel, 1961.
A fine facsimile of an Apocalypse blockbook.

956. Noppen, J. G. "The Westminster Apocalypse and Its Source." *BM* 61 (July-December 1934): 146-59.
Describes in detail the various parts of this famous wall-painting in the Chapter-House of Westminster Abbey, with references to the Apocalypse scenes they represent. With plates.

957. Planchenault, René. *L'Apocalypse d'Angers.* Paris: Caises nationale des monuments historiques et des sites, 1966.
Studies the great fourteenth-century tapestry now in Angers Cathedral. Facsimiles of the different parts of the tapestry are accompanied by commentary and the verses from the Apocalypse to which the various scenes refer. An introduction explains the history, production, and restoration of this tapestry.

958. Wardrop, James. "The Dublin Apocalypse." *BM* 57 (July-December 1930): 154-60.

Briefly describes the illustrated Apocalypse manuscript of Trinity College, Dublin, K. 4. 34 (old numbering), and offers an East Anglian provenance of circa 1300. Four plates.

Apocalypse Imagery

959. Alexander, Paul J. *The Byzantine Apocalyptic Tradition.* Edited by Dorothy Abrahams. Berkeley: Univ. of California Press, 1985.
    Treats such Eastern versions as the Syriac Pseudo-Methodius and various Byzantine visions of Daniel, with information on manuscripts, sources, and similar texts in other cultures. Especially valuable are the author's thematic treatments of the Last Roman Emperor, Gog and Magog, and the legend of Antichrist.

960. _____. "Medieval Apocalypses as Historical Sources." *AHR* 73, no. 4 (April 1968): 997-1018.
    Suggests that late antique and early medieval apocalypses may offer actual historical information. Gives examples from sixth- to ninth-century pseudonymous Byzantine apocalypses.

961. Barral i Altet, Xavier. " L'iconographie de caractère sythétique et monumental inspirée de l'apocalpyse dans l'art médiéval d'occident (IXe-XIIIe siècles)." *L'Apocalypse de Jean: Traditions exégètique et iconographiques, IIIe-XIIIe siècles, Actes du Colloque de la Fondation Hardt, 29 fevrier-3 mars, 1976.* Edited by Y. Christe. Études et documents, Section d'Histoire de la faculté des lettres de l'université de Genève. Geneva: Droz, 1979, pp.187-216.
    A detailed study of visual responses to the story of St. John's Apocalypse.

962. Bett, Henry. *Joachim of Flora.* Reprint. Merrick, NY: Richwood, 1976.
    This reprint of a 1931 study treats the subject generally with chapters on the life, work, doctrines, relations to the University of Paris, and the Spiritual Franciscan movement of this important writer on the

Apocalypse. It is chiefly useful for the iconographer to place Joachim historically before coming to his *figurae*.

963. Burger, Edward K., ed. Joachim of Fiore, *Enchiridion super Apocalypsim*. Pontifical Institute Texts and Studies, no. 78. Toronto: Pontifical Institute, 1986.
A modern scholarly edition of this important commentary.

964. Christe, Y. "Traditions littéraires et iconographiques dans l'interprétation des images apocalyptiques." *L'Apocalypse* (item 961), pp. 109-134.
This is perhaps the most generally useful essay in the collection mentioned above, treating images from the Apocalypse in various forms of medieval art.

965. Costa, Dennis J. *Irenic Apocalypse: Some Literary Uses of Apocalyptic in Dante, Petrarch and Rabelais.* Stanford French and Latin Studies, no. 31. Saratoga, CA: Anima Libri, 1981.
Looks at the "irenic" images of apocalypse in these authors. especially images of dreaming or reposing, reading, keeping vigil, and eating.

966. Daniel, E. Randolph. *Abbot Joachim of Fiore Liber de Concordia Noui ac Veteris Testamenti. TAPS* 73, no. 8 (1983).
A modern scholarly edition.

967. Emmerson, Richard Kenneth. "The Prophetic, the Apocalyptic, and the Study of Medieval Literature." *Poetic Prophecy in Western Literature.* Edited by Jan Wojcik and Raymond-Jean Frontain. London: Associated Univ. Presses, 1984, pp. 40-54.
Investigates how the Middle Ages viewed the prophetic and the apocalyptic and turns to *Piers Plowman* to show how an awareness of Langland's use of prophetic and apocalyptic matter will help us better to understand the poem and its attitudes to contemporary social and religious problems.

968. _____, and Bernard McGinn, eds. *The Apocalypse in the Middle Ages.* Ithaca, NY: Cornell Univ. Press, 1993.

This collection of essays examines the heritage of Tyconius and St. Augustine in sections on the Apocalypse in medieval thought, art, and culture. Many plates.

969. Freyhan, R. "Joachism and the English Apocalypse." *JWCI* 18 (1955): 211-44.
Investigates Joachist influence on English illustrated Apocalypse cycles. Numerous plates from medieval manuscripts.

970. Joachim. *Vaticinia.* Berlin: Zentralantiquariat, 1972.
A reprint of the 1559 edition.

971. Klein, P. K. "Les cycles de l'apocalypse du haut Moyen Age." *L'Apocalypse* (item 961), pp. 135-86.
Studies programs of illustration.

972. Krey, Philip D. W., ed. and trans. *Nicholas of Lyra's Apocalypse Commentary.* TEAMS Commentary Series. Binghamton: State Univ. of NY Press, 1996.
Makes available to the non-specialist one of the most important commentaries on the Book of Revelation, that of Nicholas of Lyra, the great French thirteenth-century Fransciscan exegete,who used the work of Rashi among other sources.

973. Lewis, Suzanne. *Reading Images: Narrative Discourse and Reception in the Thirteenth-Century Illuminated Apocalypse.* Cambridge: Cambridge Univ. Press, 1995.
Considers the place of ideologies such as anti-Jewish sentiment, the crusade ideal, and expectation of the world's end in some English illuminated apocalypses. 252 plates.

974. McGinn,Bernard."Apocalypticism in the Middle Ages:An Historiographical Sketch." *MS* 37 (1975): 252-86.
An overview of scholarship on this subject up through 1973.

975. _____. "Awaiting an End: Research in Medieval Apocalypticism, 1974-1981." *M&H* 11 (1982): 263-89.
Picks up where item 974 left off, although McGinn explains in an addendum that he was not able to include a section on medieval

apocalyptic art that he had originally intended, so the bibliography does not cover this topic.

976. _____. *Visions of the End: Apocalyptic Traditions in the Middle Ages.* Records of Civilization: Sources and Studies, no. 96. New York: Columbia Univ. Press, 1979.
An anthology of translations from a variety of apocalyptic writings organized chronologically from 400 through 1500 AD. There are introductions to each text.

977. Meer, Frederick Vander. *Apocalypse: Visions from the Book of Revelation in Western Art.* New York: Alpine Fine Arts Collection, 1978.
Examines works of art, chiefly manuscript miniatures, stained glass, tapestry, and sculpture depicting scenes from the Book of Revelation from the medieval through the Renaissance periods. Divided into chapters, each section treating one artist, like Durer, or one topic, such as the lamb, in various works of art. Especially useful is a checklist of works of art inspired by the Apocalpyse. Numerous color plates.

978. Patrides, C. A., and Joseph Wittreich, eds. *The Apocalypse in English Renaissance Thought and Literature: Patterns, Antecedents and Repercussions.* Manchester: Manchester Univ. Press, 1984.
Essays on various aspects of the Apocalypse, chiefly in Renaissance Europe and England. Ends with a bibliography of studies on the Apocalypse.

979. Potestà, Gian Luca. *Storia ed escatologia in Ubertino da Casale.* Vita e Pensiero. Milan: Università Cattolica del Sacro Cuore, 1980.
A basic study of Ubertino, an important writer on millennialism, Antichrist, and Apocalypse prophecies. Most useful are the section on Antichrist and the appendices on tree imagery and symbols. There is an excellent bibliography.

980. Reeves, Marjorie. *The Figurae of Joachim of Fiore.* Oxford-Warburg Studies. Oxford: Clarendon, 1972.

Studies Joachim's system of thought through his *figurae*, and in particular through the *Liber Figurarum*. Focuses on the visual images in his work, studying them as a whole and then going over them image by image. Plates and indices.

981. _____. "Joachimist Influences on the Idea of a Last World Emperor." *Traditio* 17 (1961): 323-70.
Details contending beliefs on the identity and nationality of the evil tyrant (manifestation of Antichrist) and the last world emperor, two players in the final drama of the Apocalypse, in literature and history from the Middle Ages through the seventeenth century.

982. Vicaire, M.-H., ed. *Fin du monde et signes des temps: Visionnaires et prophètes en France méridionale (fin XIIIe-début XVe siècle)*. Cahiers de Fanjeaux: Collection d'histoire religieuse du Languedoc aux XIIIe et XIVe siècles, no. 27. Toulouse: Privat, 1992.
Essays on the topic of visions of the end of the world in France from the late thirteenth to the early fifteenth century, most focusing on an individual author or very specific time and place.

983. West, Delno C., ed., *Joachim of Fiore in Christian Thought*. 2 vols. New York: Burt Franklin, 1975.
This collection of photographically reproduced older essays is chiefly useful for its introduction and bibliography from 1954-75, though the focus is not iconographic.

984. _____, and Sandra Zimdars Swartz. *Joachim of Fiore, A Study in Spiritual Perceptions and History*. Bloomington: Indiana Univ. Press, 1983.
Chapters on the life, relation to the Latin Fathers, works, and influence of this important twelfth-century figure. Sees him as the founder of a whole new form of apocalyptic interpretation, especially in regards to how historical inquiry could lead the believer closer to God. Five plates. Reviewed by Richard K. Emmerson in *Speculum* 59, no. 4 (October 1984): 964-7.

985. Williams, Ann, ed. *Prophecy and Millenarianism: Essays in Honour of Marjorie Reeves*. Essex, England: Longman Group, 1980.
Essays treating chiefly Joachim of Fiore.

986. Zambelli, Paola, ed."*Astrologi hallucinati*": *Stars and the End of the World in Luther's Time.* Item 600.
Though not focused on visual representations of Apocalypse imagery, the essays contained in this book deal with philosophical, religious, and political backgrounds for Apocalypse and millennial themes.

Beatus of Liebana's Commentary on the Apocalypse

987. Williams, John. *The Illustrated Beatus: A Corpus of the Illustrations of the Commentary on the Apocalypse. 1: Introduction:2: The Ninth and Tenth Centuries.* London: Harvey Miller, 1994.
The first volumes of a five-volume publication treating the whole body of Beatus' commentary on the Apocalypse. The introduction in volume One treats the meaning and purpose of Beatus' imagery. 41 color and many black-and-white plates. Reviewed by Walter Cahn in *Speculum* 72, no.3 (July 1997): 900-2.

Christ, Images of, by Type

[Body as bait]

988. Koppenfels, Werner von. *Esca et Hamus: Beitrag zu einer historischen Liebesmetaphorik.* Munich: Bayerischen Akademie der Wissenschaften,1973.
Originating as a gloss on Job 40.20 "'Numquid poteris capere Leviathan hamo?" the idea developed that Christ fishes for Satan in the sea of this world with the hook of the cross and the bait of his humanity. It is elaborated in Jacob of Voragine's *Legenda Aurea* and appears in many places such as a Marian homily by Amadeus of Lausanne, G. Bavaud, et al., eds. and trans. *Huit homélies mariales.* SC 72. Paris: Les Éditions du Cerf, 1960 ,p. 144: "O praestantissima eius vulnera quibus mundi vulnera sanata sunt! O victoriosissima

eius vulnera quibus mortem occidit et inferna momordit! Mors, inquit, ero mors tua, morsus tuus ero, inferne. Captus est Leviathan hamo, et dum hiat ad escam vermis clamantis in Psalmo: Ego sum vermis et non homo, horum vulnerum ferro sauciatus inhaesit. His ergo tam pretiosis vulneribus irretitus est diabolus et homo liberatus." Koppenfels' short monograph examines such metaphors of the hook and bait.

989. Marchand, James W. "Leviathan and the Mousetrap in the Niørstigningarsaga." *SS* 47, no. 3 (Summer 1975): 328-38.
    Detailed discussion of the provenance and dissemination of different iconographical presentations of Satan as a serpent or whale caught by the hook of Christ's divinity or oddly, caught in a mousetrap, with citations from many different sources.

[Cross Legends]

990. Baert, Barbara. "Aspects of the Invention of the Cross Iconography around 1400 and Its Relationship with the Genre of the Classes and the Adamite Peasant." Item 399, pp. 309-25.
    A full treatment of the Finding of the Cross legend with many plates reproducing illustrations from various manuscripts.

991. Borgehammer, Stephan. *How the Holy Cross was Found: From Event to Medieval Legend.* Biblioteca Theologiae Practicae Kyrkovetenskapliga Studier, no. 47. Stockholm: Almqvist and Wiksell International, 1991.
    Studies the many versions of this legend and their development. Includes an Appendix of "Inventio Crucis" texts and a very lengthy bibliography. Reviewed by Kenneth G. Hoilum in *Speculum* 69, no. 2 (April 1994): 425-6.

992. Ladner, Gerhart. "St. Gregory of Nyssa and St. Augustine on the Symbolism of the Cross." *Late Classical and Mediaeval Studies in Honor of Albert Mathias Friend.* Edited by Kurt Weitzmann. Princeton Univ. Press, 1955, pp. 88-95.
    Discusses the similarities and differences in these two authorities' views on the symbolism of the cross.

993. Overgäard, Mariane, ed. *The History of the Cross-Tree down to Christ's Passion. Icelandic Legend Versions.* Editiones Arnamagnæanæ, Ser. B, vol. 26. Copenhagen: Munksgaard, 1968.
An edition of a number of Icelandic texts containing the history of the cross-tree legends down through the Passion, chiefly medieval in origin.

994. Rahner, Hugo. *Greek Myths and Christian Mystery.* London: Burns and Oates, 1963.
Traces the influence of Greek mythology in the earlier Christian church with many quotations in translation from the Greek and Latin fathers and also with some illustrations. Chapter Two treats the cross in detail.

995. Schönbach, Anton E. *Altdeutsche Predigten.* Reprint. Darmstadt: Wissenschaftliche Buchgesellschaft, 1964.
Though a general study of medieval German preaching, this book lists various theological writers through the twelfth century who deal with the popular iconography of the four spiritual dimensions of the cross, *latitudo, longitudo, sublimitas,* and *profundium.*

[Incarnation as a unicorn hunt]

996. Albert, L. "Die Einhorn-Jagd in der Literatur und Kunst der Mittelalters." *Schauinsland* 25 (1898): 68-91.
Studies the idea that Christ in the guise of a unicorn was "hunted" out of heaven by the angel Gabriel, who then placed his "head" in the lap of a virgin as the Incarnation.

997. Graus, J. "Das Einhorn und seine Jagd in der mittelalterlichen Kunst." *Kirschensmuck* 25 (1894): 73-81.
Similar in content to the entry above.

998. Kuntze, F. "Die Jagd des Einhorns in Wort und Bild." *AKG* 5 (1907): 273-310.
Considers the theme in medieval art, chiefly German. Some plates.

[Passion]

999. Frank, Grace. "Popular Iconography of the Passion." *PMLA* 46 (1931): 333-40.
Presents plates from a late fourteenth- or early fifteenth-century copy of *Le Livre de la Passion* in the Vatican library, *Codex Reginensis* 473, and briefly discusses the iconography of their depiction of Christ's Passion.

1000. Friedman, John B. *Northern English Books, Owners, and Makers in the Late Middle Ages.* Syracuse Univ. Press, 1995.
Chapters treat iconographic motifs of the passion such as the *arma Christi*, Veronica, and side wound in late medieval English manuscripts. Plates and bibliography.

1001. Gurewich, Vladimir. "Observations on the Iconography of the Wound in Christ's Side, with Special Reference to Its Position." *JWCI* 20 (1957): 358-62.
Treats the subject from the early medieval period to this century. Plates.

Last Judgment

1002. Davidson, Clifford, and Thomas H. Seiler, eds. *Homo, Memento Finis: The Iconography of Just Judgment in Early Drama, Art and Music.* Monographs Series, no. 6. Kalamazoo, MI: Medieval Institute Publications, 1985.
Five essays study dramatic and iconographical representations of the Just Judgment. Of particular relevance to the iconographer is Pamela Sheingorn, "'For God Is Such a Doomsman': Origins and Development of the Theme of Last Judgment"; Richard Emmerson, " 'Nowe ys Common this Daye': Enoch and Elias, Antichrist and the Structure of the Chester Cycle"; and Pamela Sheingorn and David Bevington, "'All this was Token Domysday to Drede'": Visual Signs of Last Judgment in the Corpus Christi Cycles and Late Gothic Art."

1003. Grodecki, Louis. "Les quinze signes précurseurs de la fin du monde dans les vitraux allemand, français et alsaciens." *Kunst des Mittelalters in Sachsen: Festschrift Wolf Schubert dargebracht zum sechzigsten Geburtstag AM 28. Januar 1963.* Edited by Elizabeth Hutter, et al. Weimar: Herman Böhlau, 1967, pp. 292-99.
      Treats this popular motif in German, French, and Alsatian glass. Many plates.

1004. Heist, William W. *The Fifteen Signs before Doomsday.* East Lansing, MI: Michigan State College Press, 1952.
      Studies this legend, its origin, development, and transmission. Includes an *en-face* passage concerning this legend in the Old Irish *Saltair na Rann.* Annotated handlist of the many versions of the fifteen signs, bibliography, and index.

Magi

1005. Kaplan, Paul H. D. *The Rise of the Black Magus in Western Art.* Ann Arbor, MI: Univ. of Michigan Press, 1985.
      Looks at the development of the iconography of the Black African Magus (one of the three kings present at the birth of the Christ child, though not described as African in the Gospels) from the early Christian period up until the end of the fifteeenth century. With many illustrations, a bibliography, and an index. Reviewed by Jeffrey Chipps Smith in *Speculum* 63, no. 1 (January 1988): 181-3.

Mary Magdalen

1006. Malvern, Majorie M. *Venus in Sackcloth: The Magdalen's Origins and Metamorphoses.* Carbondale and Edwardsville, IL: Southern Illinois Univ. Press, 1975.
      A study of the changing iconography of Mary Magdalene in medieval art and literature.

Pilate

1007. Longland, Sabrina. "Pilate Answered: What I Have Written I Have
Written."*BMMA* 26 (1967-68): 410-27.
Treats medieval artists' and commentators' interest in Pilate's
writing of the title, "Jesus of Nazareth, The King of the Jews" on a
plaque above the cross on which Christ was crucified. Looks at art
works depicting the crucifixion and this plaque, as well as medieval
interest in the inscription generally, with plates.

Presentation in the Temple

1008. Schorr, Dorothy C. "The Iconographic Development of the
Presentation in the Temple." *AB* 28 (1946): 17-32.
Examines specifics concerning the iconography in different forms of
medieval Renaissance art of the scene in which, after Mary's
purification, the Christ child is presented to God in a temple in
Jerusalem. Plates.

Virgin Mary

1009. Ancona, Mirella Levi d'. *The Iconography of the Immaculate
Conception*. Monographs on Archaeology and Fine Arts
sponsored by the Archaeological Institute of America and the
College Art Association of America, no. 7. New York: The
College Art Association of America in conjunction with the *Art
Bulletin*, 1957.
Investigates which images were used to depict the Immaculate
Conception and why some rather than others were popular at
different times. Usefully organized by subject such as "Triumph over

Death Depicted as a Skeleton" or "Mary in the Womb of Anne."
Contains a number of plates with differing depictions of Mary.

1010. Bergamini, Laurie J. "From Narrative to Icon: The Virgin Mary and
the Woman of the Apocalypse in Thirteenth-Century English Art
and Devotion." *SI* 13 (1989-90): 80-112.
Examines the similarities in iconography of the Virgin Mary and of
the "star-crowned woman" of Revelations and how the one became
identified with the other. Many plates of this motif in art works from
the thirteenth through the fifteenth centuries.

1011. Boitani, Piero. "'His desir wol fle withouten wynges': Mary and
Love in Fourteenth-Century Poetry." *The Tragic and the
Sublime in Medieval Literature*. Edited by Piero Boitani.
Cambridge: Cambridge Univ. Press, 1989, pp. 177-222.
Considers versions of Marian prayers containing strongly visual
imagery surviving in lyric and narrative poetry by Dante, Guillaume
Deguilleville, Petrarch, and Chaucer.

1012. Coletti, Teresa. "Devotional Iconography in the N-Town Marian
Plays." *CD* 2 (1977): 22-44.
Argues that the N-Town drama shows an extreme awareness of the
characteristic motifs of devotion to the Virgin. Studies the N-Town
cycle as a form of devotional art. Plates.

1013. Forsyth, Ilene H. *The Throne of Wisdom.* Cited above as item 454.
Considers wooden sculpture of the Virgin holding the Christ
child in her lap. Contains numerous plates each described in a
register of principal examples of such sculptures up through the
twelfth century.

1014. Newlyn, Evelyn S. "Between the Pit and the Pedestal: Images of Eve
and Mary in Medieval Cornish Drama." *New Images of
Medieval Women: Essays Toward a Cultural Anthropology.*
Mediaeval Studies, vol. 1. Edited by Edelgard E. DuBruck.
Lewiston, NY: Edward Mellen Press, 1989, pp.121-64.
Examines the "bipolar" characterization of women in four plays from
the Cornish Ordinalia cycle.

OLD TESTAMENT

General

1015. Cockerell, Sydney C. *Old Testament Miniatures: A Medieval Picture Book with 283 Paintings from the Creation to the Story of David.* New York: George Braziller, 1969.
Very useful for an idea of how various medieval illuminators conceived of the major Old Testament scenes.

1016. Ehrenstein, Theodor. *Das Alte Testament im Bild.* Vienna: Albert Kende, 1923.
A study of virtually all the major stories of the Old Testament, Adam and Eve, Cain and Abel, Susanna, and the like, with black-and-white illustrations drawn from a variety of periods, early Christian through the nineteenth century, in which the scene is depicted. A handlist at the back locates the work of art. There is no commentary or bibliography.

1017. Erffa, Hans Martin von. *Ikonologie der Genesis: Die Christlichen Bildthemen Aus dem Alten Testament und ihre quellen.* 2 vols. Munich: Deutscher Kunstverlag, 1989.
This invaluable book is organized in Volume One around the major themes of Genesis, for example the creation of heavens, and Adam and the animals, as well as the Fall of Man with types and anti-types such as Adam-Christ and Eve-Mary. Sections on Cain, Abel, Lamech, the Flood, Noah's Ark, and the Tower of Babel are all useful. Each entry is accompanied by appropriate citations to the *PL* followed by a bibliography of recent scholarship, chiefly German, and the whole is geared to the plates in Volume Two.

1018. Harrison, Frederick. *Treasures of Illumination: English Manuscripts of the Fourteenth Century (c. 1250-1400).* London and New York: The Studio Ltd and The Studio Publications, 1937.

The work collects important miniatures from various fourteenth-century manuscripts with a general introduction giving information on the different manuscripts by type such as Bibles and psalters. For example, a scene of Lamech's accidental killing of Cain from the St. Omer Psalter occurs on Plate nine.

1019. Hassall, W. O. *The Holkham Bible Picture Book.* London: The Dropmore Press,1954.
A facsimile of this important manuscript with a useful assortment of Genesis miniatures.

1020. James, Montague Rhodes. *Illustrations of the Book of Genesis.* Oxford: Oxford Univ. Press, 1921.
Extremely useful treatment of various cycles of illustration in manuscripts, chiefly English or in English collections. Many plates.

Adam and Eve Iconography

1021. Bergouignan, Paul, and André. *Le pèche originel. Quelques images de l'art ancien non conformés au texte biblique.* Paris: Vigot, 1952.
Treats some midrash-based elaborations of the Fall story in Genesis. Plates.

1022. Esche, Sigrid. *Adam und Eva. Sündenfall und Erlösung.* Düsseldorf: L. Schwann, 1957.
An extremely useful book focussing on Adam and Eve compositions in art, such as discussions of Adam-Christ and Eve-Maria typologies. The plates are numerous, full page, spendidly clear, and range from depictions on sarcophagi and in catacomb painting to Romanesque Bible painting and some of the great sculptures of Eve, such as at Bamberg and Autun Cathedrals. Gothic manuscript illlustrations containing Adam and Eve are not represented.

1023. Green, Rosalie B. "The Adam and Eve Cycle in the 'Hortus Deliciarum.'" *Late Classical* (item 992), pp. 340-47.

Discusses the Adam and Eve cycle in the Strasbourg codex of this work, dating from the second half of the twelfth century. Though destroyed in the war of 1870, the manuscript exists in a nineteenth-century copy. Green relates the cycle to that in British Library MS Cotton Ortho B.vi. Includes illustrations.

1024. Guldan, Ernst. *Eva und Maria: Eine Antithese als Bildmotiv.* Graz-Cologne: Hermann Böhlau, 1966.
Contrasts Eve and Maria, with Mary as a "second," "thornless," Eve in the art of the Middle Ages and Renaissance. This idea is largely derived from a pseudo-Bernardine homily, *PL* 184, 1020; it also occurs in the Roman breviary. In essence the homily notes that because of the destruction of human wisdom at the Fall, God took on flesh from a woman to return like for like. This topos is called "pia fraus," where contrary is cured by contrary. Thus, Eve was the wounding thorn, Mary the healing rose. Eve the thorn, brought death to all; Mary the rose brought salvation. Many plates, mostly drawn from works like the *Biblia Pauperum,* and a bibliography.

*   Hoffeld, Jeffrey M. "Adam's Two Wives." Cited below as item 1383.
In the process of explaining the iconography of "a hexagonal boxwood statue base at the Cloisters" (430), the writer studies the medieval iconography of Lilith, first wife of Adam, especially as a woman-headed snake. He looks also at some features of the iconography of Adam and Eve. Plates.

1025. Mazure, André. *Le thème d'Adam et Eve dans l'art.* Paris: Editions d'art Lucien Mazenod, 1967.
Presents several large color plates depicting Adam and Eve from various works of art, with a commentary on the plates. Divided into sections such as Terrestrial Paradise, Original Sin, and the like. Many black-and-white plates.

1026. Mély, F. de. "Nos premiers parents dans l'art: Adam, Eve, Lileth." *Mélanges Hulin de Loo.* Edited by Paul Bergmans. Brussels and Paris: Librairie nationale d'art et d'histoire, 1931, pp. 116-22.
A brief look at these three figures in art and at their descriptions in texts from the third century AD up to the end of the fifteenth.

1027. Östling, Christine. "The Ploughing Adam in Medieval Church-Paintings." *Man and Picture: Papers from the First International Symposium for Ethnological Picture Research in Lund 1984.* Edited by Nils-Arvid Bringéus. Stockholm: Almqvist and Wiksell International, 1986, pp. 13-19.
    Studies medieval church-paintings representing the first labor with Adam ploughing, discusses the iconography of ploughing generally, and compares these representations to later ones in which he is shown performing other tasks such as digging, chopping wood, and hoeing. Plates.

1028. Phillips, John A. *Eve, the History of an Idea.* San Francisco: Harper and Row, 1984.
    Investigates different perceptions of Eve up until the present time in Western culture, with numerous quotations from contemporary texts. Although the book is not organized chronologically but rather according to the way Eve is presented, many of the examples are drawn from medieval art.

Babel, Tower of

1029. Borst, Arno. *Der Turmbau von Babel.* 6 vols. Stuttgart: Anton Hiersemann, 1956-63.
    A magisterial study of the Tower of Babel motif in scripture. Volume Two concerns the Middle Ages and treats the image from the Fathers of the Church through the end of the fourteenth century with discussions of the theme in Peter Comestor and in Dante among others.

1030. Céard, Jean. "De Babel à la Pentecôte: La transformation du mythe de la confusion des langues au XVIe siècle." *BHR* 42 (1980): 577-94.
    Deals with Renaissance interest in languages and the idea of a first or primary language, with the value of Latin as opposed to the vernaculars, and with the interpretation of the stories of the Tower of Babel and of the miracle of Pentecost.

1031. Minkoski, Helmut. *Vernutungen über den Turm zu Babel*. Freren: Lucca,1991.
This work collects a number of manuscript miniatures showing the Tower of Babel.

Cain

1032. Aptowitzer,V. *Kain und Abel in der Agada, den Apokryphen, der hellenistischen, christlichen und muhammedanischen Literatur*. Vienna and Leipzig: R. Löwitt, 1922.
A study of the major elements of the Cain and Abel story with many references to midrashic texts in German translation. Especially useful are the sections on the murder weapon, mentioned as the jawbone of an ass or even the horn of a unicorn, and the death of Cain at the hands of the blind archer, Lamech.

1033. Barb, A. A. "Cain's Murder Weapon and Sampson's Jaw Bone of an Ass." *JWCI* 35 (1972): 386-9.
Most commonly Cain is shown killing Abel with an animal jaw bone, but he sometimes uses stones, the coulter of Abel's plough, a sword or a scythe or even the horn of a unicorn. Sometimes he employs no weapon and is shown biting Abel, beating, or strangling him. Traces the development of the different weapons Cain used and how they are simplified in time to the jaw bone of an ass.

1034. Braude, Pearl F. "'Cokkel in oure Clene Corn': Some Implications of Cain's Sacrifice." *No Graven Images: Studies in Art and the Hebrew Bible*. Edited by Joseph Gutmann. New York: KTAV, 1971, pp. 559-99.
Studies the exegesis of Cain's rejected offering of a sheaf of grain to God. With many plates.

1035. Dahan, Gilbert. "L'exégèse de l'histoire de Caïn et Abel du XIIe au XIVe siècle en occident: Notes et textes." *BTAM* 49 (1982): 21-89 and 50 (1983): 5-68.

Provides examples of exegetical treatments of the brothers from medieval commentators. The author discusses the glosses, dividing them into literal and tropological ones, and then gives a bibliographic overview, listing scholarly editions of many of these commentaries. Dahan's work is basic for a study of the brothers, especially of Cain as the first serf or slave.

1036. Henderson, G. "Cain's Jaw-Bone." *JWCI* 24 (1961): 108-14.
Notes the earliest depiction of the weapon as a jaw bone in an eleventh-century Anglo-Saxon manuscript. He thinks that the connection of Sampson and Cain was made through the medium of book illustration, where the jaw bone is confused with the earlier and fairly common plow coulter as Cain's weapon.

1037. Kronholm,Tryggve. *Motifs from Genesis 1-11 in the Genuine Hymns of Ephrem the Syrian with Particular Reference to the Influence of Jewish Exegesis.* Coniectanea Biblica. Old Testament Series, no. 11. Lund, Sweden: C. W. K. Gleerup, 1978.
Focusses on the influences of Jewish writers on Ephraim (b. Nisibis *ca.* 306) in his Nisibene hymns. Among the topics covered are images of the Creation of the World and of man, the Fall, and the stories of Cain and Abel, and Noah and the flood.

1038. Mellinkoff, Ruth. *The Mark of Cain.* Berkeley: Univ. of California Press, 1981.
Surveys early exegesis on the mark of Cain, dividing the major interpretations into those treating a mark on his body, movement of his body, and blemishes associated with his body. There is an index, bibliography, and many plates.

1039. Michel, Paul Henri. "L'iconographie de Caïn et Abel." *CCM* (1958): 194-99.
Among the interesting topics treated is the identity and depiction of Cain's wife, usually in Adam apocrypha Lebuda, Lusia, or more commonly Chalmana. She was Cain's twin sister. One tradition, perhaps midrashic, for Abel's murder by Cain was through sexual jealousy over her. Michel treats such themes as Cain's mark and murder weapon. Plates.

1040. Sanoner, G. "L'iconographie de la Bible d'après les artistes de l'antiquité et du Moyen Age." *BMon* 80 (1921): 212-38.
Examines the iconographical depiction of the sacrifices of Cain and Abel, discussing many specific art works, with plates of a number of them, especially sculpture.

1041. Schapiro, Meyer. "Cain's Jawbone That Did the First Murder." *AB* 24 (1942): 205-12.
Looks at representations of Cain's use of the jaw bone of an ass to kill Abel in art and how this tradition came to displace the idea of Cain's using a club or agricultural implement. Some plates.

1042. Ulrich, Anna. *Kain und Abel in der Kunst: Untersuchungen zur Ikonographie und Auslegungs Geschichte.* Bamberg: Kurt Urlaub, 1981.
Deals with sarcophagus carving and early Bible illustration, as well as specific motifs such as Cain's murder weapon and death and Abel's blood. Extensive bibliography, chiefly German, and many plates, mostly from the earlier Middle Ages.

David

1043. Frontain, Raymond-Jean, and Jan Wojckik, eds. *The David Myth in Western Literature.* West Lafayette, IN: Purdue Univ. Press, 1981.
Essays, arranged chronologically, on different representations of David. The first three will be of particular use to the medievalist.

1044. Gosselin, Edward A. *The King's Progress to Jerusalem: Some Interpretations of David during the Reformation Period and Their Patristic and Medieval Background.* Humana Civilitas. Sources and Studies Relating to the Middle Ages and the Renaissance, no. 2. Malibu, CA: Undena, 1972.
Examines the commentaries of St. Augustine and Nicholas of Lyra on David, and then contrasts them to sixteenth-century Protestant commentaries and their very different treatments of this Biblical figure.

*   Norman, Joanne S. *Metamorphosis of an Allegory*. Cited above as item 854.

1045.   Steger, Hugo. *David Rex et Propheta. König David als vorbildliche Verköperung des Herrschers und Dichters im Mittelalter.* Nurnberg: H. Carl,1961.
Early treatments by painters of the David story in the Bible. Plates.

Decalogue in Art

1046.   Abrahams, Israel. "The Decalogue in Art." *No Graven Images* (item 1034), pp. 19-35.
Examines medieval and Renaissance representations of the bestowing of the Decalogue, mostly in Hebrew art, where God is not depicted. Very detailed with many quotations and specific descriptions but no plates.

1047.   Weitzmann, Kurt. "The Question of the Influence of Jewish Pictorial Sources on Old Testament Illustration." *No Graven Images* (item 1034), pp. 309-28.
Studies Jewish influence on early Bibles. Many plates.

Isaac

1048.   Smith, Alison M. "The Iconography of the Sacrifice of Isaac in Early Christian Art." *AJA* 26 (1922): 159-73.
Examines different programs used in illustrating this key story. Plates.

Jesse

* Kirby, H. T. "The Jesse Tree Motif in Stained Glass." Cited below as item 1578.
  Compares the iconographical portrayals of this tree showing "the descent of Christ from Jesse through a line of kings" in fourteenth-century English stained glass.

* Watson, Arthur. *The Early Iconography of the Tree of Jesse.* Cited below as item 1579.
  Dated but still very useful on the motif in the later Middle Ages.

Job

1049. Besserman, Lawrence L. *The Legend of Job in the Middle Ages.* Cambridge, MA and London, England: Harvard Univ. Press, 1979.
  Studies the Biblical origins of Job, apocryphal and ecclesiastical traditions about him, and the medieval literary heritage of the Job story accompanied by many quotations from authors mentioning Job. A lengthy bibliography, an index, and plates from works of art featuring Job.

1050. Terrien, Samuel. *The Iconography of Job through the Centuries: Artists as Biblical Interpreters.* State College: Pennsylvania State Univ. Press, 1996.
  Treats the Job tradition from Hebrew and early patristic texts onward. 142 black-and-white plates.

Jonah

1051. Allenbach, Jean. "La figure de Jonas dans les textes préconstantiniens ou l'histoire de l'exégèse au secours de l'iconographie." *La Bible et les pères. Colloque de Strasbourg*

(1er-3 octobre 1969). Bibliothèque des centres d'études supérieures spécialisés. Paris: Presses Universitaires de France, 1971, pp. 97-112.
Covers Jonah's depiction in scripture, in Judaism, and in patristic texts, his iconographical representations, and the history of his exegesis and iconography. No plates but the author does describe how Jonah appears in some art works.

1052. Bowers, R. H. *The Legend of Jonah.* The Hague, Netherlands: Martinus Nijhoff, 1971.
Examines the legend of Jonah in five chapters covering Hebraic and patristic literature, and Jonah's role in medieval allegory.

1053. Duval, Yves-Marie *Le livre de Jonas dans la littérature chrétienne grecque et latine: Sources et influences du commentaire sur Jonas de saint Jerome.* 2 vols. Paris: Etudes Augustiniennes, 1973.
Though this book does not deal with visual representations of Jonah, it is useful for understanding the allegorizing which took place, especially in visual representations. Volume One treats various patristic commentaries on Jonah while Volume Two treats the Jonah story in sermon material and considers how preachers made Jonah a figure foreshadowing Christ.

1054. Friedman, John B. "Bald Jonah and the Exegesis of 4 Kings 2.23." *Traditio* 44 (for 1988) (1990): 125-44.
Considers the typological association of Jonah with Christ through the plucking of beard and hair and with the "ascende calve" passage in Isaiah. Many plates.

1055. _____. "Figural Typology and the Middle English *Patience*." *The Alliterative Tradition in the 14th-Century.* Item 784, pp. 99-129.
Considers the way the *Patience* poet may have known Leviathan iconography (see item 988 above) and typological treatments of Jonah and Christ. Some plates.

Lamech

1056. *De Rijmbijbel van Jacob van Maerlant: een in 1332 voltooid handschrift uit het Rijksmuseum Meermanno-Westreenianum.* 's-Gravenhage: Staatsuitgeverij, in samenwerking met het Rijksmuseum Meermann Westreenianum/Museum van het Boek, 1985.
     Shows this elaboration among other midrash additions to Genesis. Jacob van Maerlant expanded on his source in Peter Comester for an account of Lamech's bigamy. Some colored plates.

  * Hindman, Sandra. *Text and Image.* Cited above as item 369.
     Pages 17-21 discusse Jacob van Maerlant's *Rijmbijbel* as a source for important legends about Lamech .

1057. Reiss, Edmund. "The Story of Lamech and Its Place in Medieval Drama." *JMRS* 2 (1972): 35-48.
     Studies the function of the scene occuring in some cycle plays in which Lamech, known as the first adulterer and bigamist because of his two wives, kills Cain with a misdirected arrow.

Moses

1058. Mellinkoff, Ruth. *The Horned Moses in Medieval Art and Thought.* Berkeley: Univ. of California Press, 1970.
     A thorough investigation of the iconography of Moses appearing with horns, with numerous plates, bibliography, and index. As Mellinkoff explains, "this book is an interdisciplinary study touching not only upon medieval art, but also upon such disciplines as medieval history, history of the Church, Latin and vernacular literature, both religious and secular, medieval drama, mythology and folklore" (vii).

Noah

1059. Allen, D. C. *The Legend of Noah.* Urbana, IL: Univ. of Illinois Press, 1963.
Though these linked essays chiefly concern rationalism in Renaissance approaches to the Creation story, there is much useful information on the medieval Noah here. Full bibliography and some plates.

1060. Cohn, Norman. *Noah's Flood. The Genesis Story in Western Thought.* New Haven, CT:Yale Univ. Press, 1996.
This eminent scholar traces the reception of the flood legend over the centuries. 20 color and 55 black-and-white pictures.

1061. Crick-Kuntzinger, Marthe. "Une tapisserie bruxelloise de l'histoire de Noé." *BMRAH,* 4th ser., 19 (1947): 20-25.
This short article describes a seventeenth-century tapestry acquired by the Museum and compares it to two contemporary tapestries also depicting the story of Noah. With plates showing all three.

1062. DiMarco,Vincent. "Uxor Noah Rediviva: Some Comments on Her Creation and Development." *LJ,* n. s., 21 (1980): 21-37.
Studies possible sources and reasons for the presentation of Noah's wife in the Chester, York, and Wakefield cycles as initially refusing to board the ark.

1063. Unger, Richard W. *The Art of Medieval Technology: Images of Noah the Shipbuilder.* New Brunswick, NJ: Rutgers Univ. Press, 1991.
Both a work on art history and the history of technology with many plates of Noah shipbuilding from the third century AD up through the seventeenth century. Examines the changes in the technology of shipbuilding and the manner of depicting it. Bibliographical references, index, and forty-seven pages of plates.

Seth

1064. Klijn, A. F. J. *Seth in Jewish, Christian and Gnostic Literature.* Leiden: Brill, 1977.
Focuses on Seth as a very important figure in Gnostic literature, and traces his development in Jewish and Christian tradition. Provides a list of medieval writings mentioning Seth, but the work is more on antiquity than on the Middle Ages.

1065. Quinn, Esther Casier. *The Quest of Seth for the Oil of Life.* Chicago: Univ. of Chicago Press, 1962.
Important study of an apocryphal tradition, often depicted in art, concerning Seth, Adam's son.

Solomon

1066. Gutmann, Joseph, ed. *The Temple of Solomon: Archaeological Fact and Medieval Tradition in Christian, Islamic and Jewish Art.* American Academy of Religion, Society of Biblical Literature, Religion, and the Arts, no. 3. Missoula, MT: Scholars Press, 1976.
Contains essays on Solomon's temple in Hebrew, Islamic, early Christian, Byzantine, and Romanesque art. A bibliography, indices, and numerous plates complete the book.

WORSHIP AND THEOLOGY BY CONCEPT

Fertility Topos

1067. Cohen, Jeremy. *"Be Fertile and Increase, Fill the Earth and Master It": The Ancient and Medieval Career of a Biblical Text.* Ithaca and London: Cornell Univ. Press, 1989.
According to the dust-jacket, "this innovative, interdisciplinary book reconstructs the career of Genesis 1:28 ("Be fertile and increase, fill the earth and master it . . .") in Judaism and Christianity, from antiquity through the Reformation. Cohen tracks the text through all the Jewish and Christian sources in which it figures significantly, such as law, exegesis, theology, philosophy, and even vernacular poetry. In his view, the verse situates mankind on a cosmic frontier, midway between the angelic and the bestial, charging it with singular responsibilities that bear directly on Jewish and Christian ideas of God's chosen people.

God as a Circle

1068. Harries, Karsten. "The Infinite Sphere: Comments on the History of a Metaphor." *JHP* 13 (1975): 5-15.
God as a circle whose center is everywhere and whose circumference is nowhere is a common topos, occurring in the Hermetica, in the work of Alan of Lille, and elsewhere. Develops the tradition with a focus on the transference of the metaphor of the sphere as God to its representing the universe by the fifteenth-century cardinal, Nicolas of Cusa.

Heaven and Heavenly Otherworlds

1069. Cavendish, Richard. *Visions of Heaven and Hell.* New York: Harmony Books, 1977.
Really more a coffee-table book ranging widely from antiquity to the present with many illustrations, a number from the medieval period, divided according to the following subjects: Life After Death, Paradise and Heaven, The Perfect Existence, The Underworld, and The Abyss of Hell. Bibliography and index.

1070. Cerulli, Enrico. *Il "Libro della scala" e la questione delle fonti Arabo-spagnole della Divina Commedia.* Rome: Vatican City, 1949.
Publishes Latin and Old French translations of the *Liber Scalae*—an important treatise on the concept and imagery of heaven and the afterlife—and discusses not only Dante's but other authors' like Bacon's use of the book. Cerulli treats the *fortuna* of the *Liber Scalae* among a variety of anti-Islamic polemicists and offers copious excerpts from translations of the work. The *Liber* was very important for making available to the Latin West a variety of visual images of the Islamic paradise, heavens made of different gem stones, Adam crowned among the saints, the four rivers of Paradise, and the like.

1071. _____. *Nuove richerche sul Libro della scala e la conoscenza dell'Islam in occidente.* Rome: Vatican City, 1972.
Gathers additional material on the theme mentioned.

1072. Davidson, Clifford, ed. *The Iconography of Heaven.* EDAM Monographs Series, no. 21. Kalamazoo, MI: The Medieval Institute, 1994.
Essays dealing with saints and angels, the bread of heaven, Paradise, the smell and light of heaven, and heavenly music. Thirty-one illustrations.

1073. Dinzelbacher, P. *Revelationes.* Typologie des sources du Moyen Age occidental, no. 57. Turnhout: Brepols, 1991.
A German bibliographical study of "revelations" or vision literature. Such works, like the vision of Tundale, were often important sources of iconographic motifs. Provides a handy chart at the end listing writers of visions from Eugenus in the sixth century to Camilla Battista in 1527 and mentioning editions.

1074. Gardiner, Eileen, ed. *Medieval Visions of Heaven and Hell: A Sourcebook.* Garland Medieval Bibliographies, no. 11. New York: Garland, 1993.
This annotated bibliography covers general vision literature and then treats specific medieval visions giving history, dating, and the like. Index.

1075. _____. *Visions of Heaven & Hell Before Dante.* New York:
      Italica, 1989.
      According to the Preface, "the following volume presents in
      translation a collection of twelve of the most important, best known,
      and most influential medieval visions of heaven and hell written
      before Dante's *Divine Comedy.* They are arranged chronologically
      from the apocalyptic books of the second through fourth centuries to
      the literary visions of northern Europe dating from the late thirteenth
      century" (ix). With information on primary sources, a bibliography
      of secondary sources, and an index.

1076. Grabar, André. "L'iconographie du ciel dans l'art chrétien de
      l'antiquité et du haut Moyen Age." *CA* 30 (1982): 5-24.
      Looks at iconographical portrayals of the sky, or heavens, in ancient
      and medieval Christian art, with plates.

1077. Grimm, Reinhold R. *Paradis coelestis Paradisus terrestris.* Medium
      Aevum, Philologische Studien, no. 33. Munich: Wilhelm Fink,
      1977.
      Surveys treatments of paradise in Hellenistic, geographical and
      patristic writers from Philo through Origen, Augustine, Cyprian,
      Ambrose, Gregory, Isidore, Bede, Aethicus and the Brendan legend
      and among the twelfth-century exegetes like Bruno, Peter Lombard,
      and Neckam. No plates or specific iconographic focus but does treat
      the four rivers tradition. Brief bibliography and index.

1078. Hughes, Robert. *Heaven and Hell in Western Art.* New York: Stein
      and Day, 1968.
      Five chapters treat the images of "The Mansion and the Dungeon,"
      "A Garden Enclosed," "The Heavenly Mansions," "The Map of the
      Pit," and "The Shapes of Satan." Each chapter then is subdivided
      into categories, such as "The Garden of Love." Chiefly a collection
      of plates depicting these images, the majority drawn from medieval
      and Renaissance art, accompanied by commentary tracing the ideas
      behind the iconography in the Bible and in the patristic period.
      Including many plates representing their iconography in sculpture,
      painting, manuscript illumination, and mosaic, ranging "from the
      dawn of Christianity to the middle of the nineteenth century" (7).
      Hughes explains, "my intent is limited to noting certain recurrent

images and themes in paintings and carvings of Heaven and Hell, showing (in the broadest of outlines) how and why they changed their *basic features,* and thus constructing an elementary outline of the iconography of Heaven and Hell in the art of the Christian west."

1079. Loffler, Christa Maria. *The Voyage to the Otherworld Island in Early Irish Literature.* Salzburg Studies in English Literature. Elizabethan and Renaissance Studies, no. 103. 2 vols. Salzburg: Institut für Anglistik und Amerikanistik Universität Salzburg, 1983.
Explores such subjects as Ireland as an other world realm, other worlds across the sea, and the symbolic significance of the voyage to the other world.

1080. McDannell, Colleen, and Bernhard Lang. *Heaven, A History.* New Haven and London: Yale Univ. Press,1988.
Considers chronologically how Biblical exegetes, mystical writers and others have imagined heaven in art and literature. The chapter on the Medieval Period, pp. 69-110, touches on the topics of the Paradise Garden and the medieval view of heaven.

1081. Morgan, Alison. *Dante and the Medieval Other World.* Cambridge: Cambridge Univ. Press, 1990.
Treats the *Divine Comedy* in the light of "the visions of the other world found in popular writings, painting and sculpture from the centuries leading up to its composition" (i), with numerous quotations from literature and plates from medieval art works. Sections treat "Topographical motifs of the other world," "The inhabitants of the other world," "The guide," "The classification of sin," "The mountain of Purgatory," and "The representation of Paradise." Bibliography and indices.

1082. Smith, Forrest S. *Secular and Sacred Visionaries in the Late Middle Ages.* Garland Publications in Comparative Literature. New York and London: Garland, 1986.
As Smith explains, "this study considers one type of vision, the imaginative journey to heaven and hell, a mode common in ancient sacred texts, in both Testaments of the Bible, in Classical literature, and abundantly in early and late medieval lore and literature" (ix-x).

1083. Tristram, Hildegard L. C. "Stock Descriptions of Heaven and Hell in Old and Middle English Prose and Poetry." *NM* 79 (1978): 102-113.
Closely examines the formulae or phrasing commonly used to describe heaven and hell.

Hell and the Devil

1084. Bartelink, G. J. M. "Les demons comme brigands." *VC* 21(1967): 12-24.
Examines the presentation in Early Christian literature of the Christian's battle against devils, particularly with the devil as robber, with quotations and citations from a variety of ecclesiastical writers.

1085. Bernstein, Alan E. *The Formation of Hell: Death and Retribution in the Ancient and Early Christian Worlds*. Ithaca and London: Cornell Univ. Press,1993.
Treats Greek and Roman underworlds, the idea of an afterlife in Judaism, and the New Testament development of Hell as a place. An index and an extensive bibliography for each chapter make this volume particularly useful.

1086. Bilson, John. "Notes on a Remarkable Sculptured Representation of Hell Cauldron, lately found at York." *PSAL* 21 (1906): 248-60.
A detailed description of this interesting late twelfth-century hell cauldron (stone carving with hell-mouths full of souls among other figures such as devils, snakes, and lizards) and its iconography, with accompanying plate.

1087. Creasy, William C. "The Shifting Landscape of Hell." *Comitatus* 11 (1980): 40-65.
Charts the change in art and literature from a hell full of "physical torment" in the Middle Ages to one full of the more spiritual torture of "isolation and despair" (40) in the seventeenth century, with numerous quotations from different works and some plates.

1088. Davidson, Clifford. "The Fate of the Damned in English Art and Drama." *The Iconography of Hell* (item 1089 below), pp. 41-66

Studies punishments for the damned in hell, touching on flesh hooks, cauldrons, and the like. Some plates.

1089. _____, and Thomas H. Seiler, eds. *The Iconography of Hell.* EDAM Monograph, no. 17. Kalamazoo, MI: Medieval Institute Publications, 1992.

A companion volume to item 1072 above, this work contains nine essays, about half on hell representations in drama. Contains items 1089, 1098, and 1103-04.

1090. Don, Gerard Le. "Structures et significations de l'imagerie médiévale de l'enfer." *CCM* 22 (1979): 363-72.

Looks at some typical iconographical portrayals of the space of hell, such as the mouth of hell, in art and literature. With plates.

1091. Erich, Oswald Adolf, *Die Darstellung des Teufels in der christlichen Kunst.* Berlin: Deutscher Kunstverlag, 1931.

Studies the representation in drawing and painting of the devil in medieval art. Many plates.

1092. Guldan, Ernst. "Das Monster Portal an Palazzi Zuccari in Rom. Wandlungen eines Motius vom Mittelalter zur Manierismus." *ZFK* 32 (1969): 229-261.

Examines the tradition of the medieval hell-mouth in various art forms. Many plates.

1093. Himmelfarb, Martha. *Tours of Hell: An Apocalyptic Form in Jewish and Christian Literature.* Philadelphia: Univ. of Pennsylvania Press, 1983.

Treats various forms of infernal voyage and types of sins and punishments.

1094. *Le Diable au Moyen Age (doctrine, problèmes moraux, représentations).* Senefiance, no. 6. Aix-en-Provence: Publications de CUER MA. Paris: Champion, 1979.

A collection of essays dealing with such subjects as hell and the devil's representation in Romanesque sculpture, the devil and Jews, and his representation in a large number of texts from the Middle Ages.

1095. McAlindon, T. "The Emergence of a Comic Type in Middle-English Narrative: The Devil and Giant as Buffoon." *Anglia* 81 (1963): 365-71.
    With passages demonstrating this portrayal of devil and giant.

1096. Ott, Norbert H. *Rechtpraxis und Heilgeschichte zu Überlieferung. Ikonographie und Gebrauchssituation des deutschen "Belial."* Munich: Artemis, 1983.
    The portion of this work of interest here deals with the illustrations for Jacob of Theramo's *Belial*, recounting a supposed legal trial involving Christ and Satan. The work has a good collection of color and black-and-white manuscript illuminations showing devils and hell mouth scenes.

1097. Owen, D. D. R. *The Vision of Hell: Infernal Journeys in Medieval French Literature.* New York: Barnes and Noble, 1971.
    Owen explains, "it is not my intention merely to present in these pages a descriptive catalogue of medieval French accounts of Hell and its visitors. I shall try as well to suggest how in their treatments the authors disclose something of their own attitudes towards the Christian Otherworld, and in doing so give us a curious insight into the general medieval consciousness" (xi). Goes through the Latin accounts, Ireland, the Anglo-Normans, the French, Antiquity and Islam, Allegory and Satire, Kings and Heroes, Parody and Burlesque, Travelers' Tales, Hell on Stage, and Historian of Hell, Regnauld le Queux. Only six plates. Three appendices: *La Vision de saint Paul*, The Descent Episode from the *Histoire de Charles Martel et de ses successeurs,* and Table of Contents of Regnauld le Queux's *Baratre infernal*. Bibliography and index.

1098. Palmer, Barbara. "The Inhabitants of Hell: Devils." *The Iconography of Hell* (item 1089), pp.20-40.
    Traces representations of devils in harrowing of Hell and other scenes from medieval art. Some plates.

1099. Rodari, Florian, et al., eds. *Diables et Diableries: La représentation du diable dans la gravure des XVe et XVIe siècles.* Geneva: Cabinet des Estampes du Musée d'art et d'histoire, 1977.
A series of short essays on devils in engravings, investigating how they were iconographically portrayed in the fifteenth and sixteenth centuries. In the introduction (pp. 9-11), Jean Wirth discusses generally the medieval typology of the devil and the proliferations of his representation. The volume contains numerous plates and a catalogue of engravings from the period in which the devil appears. Among the most useful essays are Didier Helg, "La fonction du diable dans les textes hagiographiques," pp.13-17; Barbara Obrist, "Les deux visages du diable," pp. 19-29, which traces the development of a devil type first appearing in twelfth-century English art with two faces, one in its stomach, which later moves to other parts of the body; Rosanna Brusegan, "Femmes au miroir," pp. 31-37, which examines the iconography of the devil when he is seen in a woman's mirror; Gisela Bucher, "Le diable dans les polemiques confessionnelles," pp. 39-53; and Viviane Minne, "L'enfer," pp. 55-69, which looks at the different iconographical representations of hell and the devils in it in medieval woodcuts.

1100. Rudwin, Maximilian. *The Devil in Legend and Literature.* Chicago and London: The Open Court Publishing Co., 1931.
Ranges all the way up to the twentieth century and includes no reproductions of medieval works of art, but does include information and quotations from a variety of sources on the devil and his portrayal. With index.

1101. Russell, Jeffrey Burton. *Lucifer: The Devil in the Middle Ages.* Ithaca and London: Cornell Univ. Press, 1984.
Concerns "ideas about the Devil that were prevalent in the Middle Ages. It includes Eastern Orthodox and Islamic views but emphasizes Western Christian thought, which gives the Devil most due. . . . The primary components of Christian diabology in the medieval period are patristic, scholastic, and mystical theology; art, literature, and drama; popular religion, homiletics, and saints' lives; and folklore" (11). With plates, an essay on the sources, bibliography, and index.

1102. Schmidt, Gary. *The Iconography of the Mouth of Hell: Eighth-Century Britain to the Fifteenth Century.* Selisgrove: Susquehanna Univ. Press, 1995.
Traces the hell-mouth image from several sources such as the scriptural mouth of the lion, and the Anglo-Saxon dragon, as well as the idea of being swallowed into hell from the Psalms. Many plates.

1103. Seiler, Thomas H. "Filth and Stench as Aspects of the Iconography of Hell." *The Iconography of Hell* (item 1089), pp. 132-40.
Seiler thinks hell stinks not only because of various associations with tanners' yards and the like but also from a long scatological tradition.

1104. Sheingorn, Pamela. "'Who Can Open the Doors of His Face?': The Iconography of Hell Mouth." *The Iconography of Hell* (item 1089), pp. 1-19.
Describes various ways in which the mouth of hell was visualized in medieval manuscript art. Some plates.

1105. Stuart, Donald Clive. "The Stage Setting of Hell and the Iconography of the Middle Ages." *RR* 4 (1913): 330-42.
To discuss the reason for the iconographic portrayal and positioning of heaven and hell on stage sets of the fifteenth century, the author turns back to study how heaven and hell were iconographically depicted in the art of the Middle Ages.

1106. Villeneuve, Roland. *Le diable dans l'art: Essai d'iconographie comparée apropos des rapports entre l'art et le satanisme.* Paris: Denöel, 1957.
Discusses the origins of representations of the devil, how he is portrayed, and how his domain is depicted, providing plates ranging up at least to the nineteenth century, but with a number of examples from the Middle Ages discussed. Although the plates and discussion may be useful to scholarly investigation, the book is undocumented.

1107. Woolf, R. E. "The Devil in Old English Poetry." *RES,* n.s., 4 (1953): 1-12.
Looks at words or phrases conventionally associated with Satan in Old English poetry and their possible provenance in the Norse Loki and other "characters native to Germanic literature" (1).

Liturgy and Church Feasts

1108. Gueranger, Prosper. *The Liturgical Year.* Translated by Laurence Shepherd. 12 vols. London: Burns and Oates, 1911—.
Divided according to different feasts of the liturgical cycle of the year like a breviary. Each section provides an explanation of the liturgy for each day of the feast.

1109. James, E. O. *Seasonal Feasts and Festivals.* London: Thames and Hudson, 1961.
Describes the development of seasonal festivals in a variety of cultures as a background to those of the Christian liturgy. Treats medieval Christian drama and folk drama and dances, like Morris dances.

1110. Kellner, K. A. Heinrich. *Heortology: A History of the Christian Festivals from Their Origin to the Present.* London: Kegan Paul, Trench, Trübner, 1908.
Introduces the beginner to the festivals of the Catholic church. Lists each festival and explains in detail its history, provenance, and forms of celebration in different countries and eras.

1111. Lechner, Joseph, and Ludwig Eisenhofer. *The Liturgy of the Roman Rite.* Translated by A. J. and E. F. Peeler. Edited by H. E. Winstone. Freiburg: Herder and Herder, 1961.
Offers a comprehensive survey of liturgical history and practice, vessals, furnishings, settings and vestments, and insignia for the Easter, Christmas, and immovable feasts, sacraments and the divine office.

Sacraments

1112. Nichols, Ann Eljenholm. *Seeable Signs: The Iconography of the Seven Sacraments 1350-1544*. Woodbridge, Suffolk: Boydell and Brewer, 1994.
Especially useful for imagery on baptismal fonts in wood and stone.

Saints

1113. Abt-Baechi, Regina. *Der Heilige und das Schwein. Ein psychologischer Beitrag*. Zurich: Daimon,1983.
A study of Saint Antony from a Jungian perspective. No plates. The discussion of Saint Antony's pig is also based chiefly on the writings of Jung.

1114. André, Lewis J. "Saint George the Martyr, in Legend, Ceremonial, Art, Etc." *AJ* 57 (1900): 204-23.
Examines the development of the legend of this Christian soldier and martyr, its popularity in literature and society, and in various art works, English and Continental, from the Middle Ages onward.

1115. _____. "Saint John the Baptist in Art, Legend, and Ritual." *AJ* 50 (1893): 1-19.
A detailed investigation of this saint's iconographical representation in all types of medieval European art. Also discusses the history of devotion to him in the Middle Ages, treating the celebration of his various feasts, among other topics.

1116. Baring-Gould, S. *The Lives of the Saints*. 16 vols. Edinburgh: John Grant, 1914.
Proposes to supplement Butler's work by adding detail to the stories, filling in with anecdotes on each saint. The work is organized according to the dates of the saints' feasts, with Volume Sixteen containing an appendix and indices to the entire collection.

1117. Blumenfeld-Kosinski, Renate and Timea Szell, eds., *Images of Sainthood in Medieval Europe*. Ithaca and London: Cornell Univ. Press, 1991.
This collection of fourteen essays treats the issue of how sainthood was regarded in the Middle Ages and the role representations played in culture and politics. The essays are not specifically devoted to visual depictions, but some do have plates. It is analyzed in an unsigned notice in *Speculum* 68, no. 4 (October 1993): 1242.

* Boglioni, Pierre. "Il Santo e gli Animali." Cited below as item 1250. Treats a number of saints, like Antony, and the animals which represent them in art. Contains a very useful bibliographical handlist of such saints.

1118. Butkovich, Anthony. *Iconography: St. Birgitta of Sweden*. NP: Rosan, Inc. Ecumenical Foundation of America, 1969.
An informative discussion of the iconography up until the present with much discussion of the medieval period and many plates.

1119. *Butler's Lives of the Saints*. Edited by Michael Walsh. San Francisco: Harper and Row, 1985.
An edition of Butler's lives of the saints originally published 1756-59, listing saints (and patron saints) by the dates of their feasts. With an index of saints.

1120. Chastel, André. "La Véronique." *Revue de l'art* 40-41 (1978): 71-82.
A detailed investigation of the 'vernical' or cloth held by saint Veronica on which the image of Christ's face was imprinted miraculously in medieval and Renaissance art, with plates and illustrative quotations from various medieval sources.

1121. Drake, Maurice, and Wilfred Drake. *Saints and Their Emblems*. London: T. Werner Laurie, 1916.
A dictionary of saints providing their emblems in different traditions and then often also describing how each saint was depicted with information about the legend. Includes appendices on the emblems of patriarchs, prophets, and sibyls, and on the patron saints of the arts, trades, and professions.

1122. Duchet-Suchaux, Gaston, and Michel Pastoureau. *The Bible and the Saints*. Translated by D. R. Howell. Flammarion Iconographic Guides. Paris and New York: Flammarion, 1994.
An iconographic encyclopedia, with each item listed alphabetically and discussed with particular reference to its representation and iconography. Many entries are accompanied by plates of representations mostly from the medieval and Renaissance periods. In addition to listing saints and Biblical figures, the guide covers real and imaginary animals, plants, objects, allegorical personifications, and the insignia of office of religious dignitaries when these items are in compositions containing saints.

1123. Dunn-Lardeau, Brenda, ed., *Legenda aurea*. Cited below as item 1251.

1124. Husenbeth, F. C. *Emblems of Saints: By Which They Are Distinguished in Works of Art*. Edited by Augustus Jessops. Norwich, England: A. H. Goose, 1882.
A useful reference tool. Alphabetically lists each saint and provides the emblem associated with this saint as well as those for prophets and patriarchs. Similarly lists emblems and keys them to their saints. Treats saints which are patrons of countries, cities, and trades as well. Appendices on sibyls and saints in heraldry complete the volume.

1125. Kieckhefer, R. *Unquiet Souls: Fourteenth-Century Saints and Their Religious Milieu*. Chicago and London: Univ. of Chicago Press, 1984.
As Kieckhefer explains, "in setting forth the theological vision of fourteenth-century hagiography, this book will—after introductory sketches of three representative saints—explore. . . the virtues of the saints, with special reference to the virtue of patience; their private devotions, specifically their devotion to the passion of Christ; their participation in the sacramental life of the Church, with the focus on penance; and their inner spirituality, as seen in their experiences of rapture and revelation" (15-16). Index, but no plates.

1126. Korte, Gandulf. *Antonius der Einsiedler in Kult, Kunst und Brauchtum*. Werl, Westfalen: D. Coelde, 1952.

This study of the St. Antony legend in art has thirty-two pages of plates and includes indices and bibliography.

1127. Lewis, Flora. "The Veronica: Image, Legend and Viewer." *England in the Thirteenth Century: Proceedings of the 1984 Harlaxton Symposium.* Edited by W. M. Ormrod. Woodbridge, Suffolk and Dover, NH: Boydell, 1986, pp.100-7.
Studies devotional images of Christ's face inspired by the Veronica, in particular, the iconography of those depicting "a very dark face of Christ: deep brown, grey or even black" (101), and discusses medieval commentaries upon these Veronicas. Plates.

1128. Maguire, Henry. "Disembodiment and Corporality in Byzantine Images of Saints." *Iconography at the Crossroads* (item 243), pp. 75-90.
While attempting to show how "modes" function in iconography, this article examines "the formal means by which different classes of saints, such as monks, soldiers, bishops, and apostles, were distinguished from each other . . . the iconographic significance of these variations, and . . . their relevance to social history" (75), with plates.

1129. Milburn, R. L. P. *Saints and Their Emblems in English Churches.* Oxford: Blackwells, 1957.
Looks at the emblems that typically distinguish one saint from another, such as the pig of Antony or the wheel of Katherine, in ecclesiastical art. These emblems serve clearly to identify the saint even when, as is often the case, the figure lacks any identifying inscription or title. Provides brief biographies along with each saint's emblem in the form of a handbook. An appendix on angels, prophets, and sibyls; an alphabetical list of emblems; and a note on ecclesiastical vestments complete this indispensable volume.

1130. Nordenfalk, Carl. "Saint Bridget of Sweden as Represented in Illuminated Manuscripts." *De Artibus Opuscula XL: Essays in Honor of Erwin Panofsky.* Edited by Millard Meiss. New York: New York Univ. Press, 1961, pp. 371-93.
Contains thirty-eight illustrations of this important northern European saint.

1131. Perdrizet, Paul. "De la véronique et de sainte Véronique."
      Seminarium Kondakovianum 5 (1932):1-15.
      Examines the great difference between Orthodox and Roman
      Catholic iconographical depictions of the holy face. The orthodox
      tradition attempted to recreate the true image whereas the Roman
      Catholic allowed more artistic license. Includes plates.

1132. Pieper, Paul. "Zum Werk des Meisters der Heiligen Veronika."
      Festschrift für Gert von der Osten. Edited by Rudolf Hillebrecht.
      Cologne: M. DuMont Schauberg, 1970, pp. 85-99.
      This important study, though chiefly devoted to the work of the so-
      called Master of St. Veronica, also offers a good deal of information
      about *Arma Christi* iconography and has a number of valuable plates.

1133. Reames, Sherry L. *The Legenda Aurea, a Reexamination of Its
      Paradoxical History.* Madison,WI: Univ. of Wisconsin Press,
      1985.
      Treats the importance and cultural centrality of the thirteenth-
      century *Aurea Legenda* from the point of view of dissemination and
      reception in different eras.

1134. Rhodes, James F. "The Pardoner's *Vernycle* and his *Vera Icon.*"
      MLS 13, no. 2 (Spring 1983): 34-40.
      Looks at the medieval tradition behind the vernicle as pilgrim badge
      as a guide to understanding why Chaucer's Pardoner wears one.

1135. Rochelle, Mercedes. *Post-Biblical Saints Art Index: A Locator of
      Paintings, Sculptures, Mosaics, Icons, Frescoes, Manuscript
      Illuminations, Sketches, Woodcuts, and Engravings Created
      from the 4th Century to 1950.* Jefferson, NC: McFarland, 1994.
      An index of places to find saints depicted in works of art. Some
      attention is paid to the Middle Ages.

1136. Wormald, Francis. "Some Illustrated Manuscripts of the Lives of the
      Saints." *BJRL* 35, no. 1 (1952): 248-56.
      Treats in detail the development of lives of saints during the Middle
      Ages, describing the different manuscripts, how they were illustrated
      and decorated, and how they influenced each other.

1137. Zender, Frank Gunther. "Salve sancta facies. Zu Christusbildern in der Kölner gotischen Malerei." *Museen der Stadt Köln Bulletin* 3 (1986): 41-44.

Studies various images of the holy face chiefly in early panel painting from Cologne. Several excellent plates.

Chapter Five: The Natural World

GENERAL

1138. Ashworth, William B., Jr. "Natural History and the Emblematic World View." *Reappraisals of the Scientific Revolution*. Edited by David C. Lindberg and Robert S. Westman. Cambridge: Cambridge Univ. Press, 1990, pp. 303-33.
Focuses on the zoological side of natural history, chiefly during the Renaissance, where animals were widely used by the compilers of emblem books and the engravers of the plates.

1139. Bianciotto, Gabriel, and Michel Salvat, eds. *Epopée animale fable fabliau: Actes du IVe colloque de la Société Internationale Renardienne Evreux, 7-11 septembre 1981*. Paris: Presses Universitaires de France, 1984.
A large collection of articles on animals. Contains items 1170, 1254, and 1267.

1140. Clébert, Jean-Paul. *Bestiaire Fabuleux*. Paris: Albin Michel, 1971.
Has an encyclopaedic format, with animals listed alphabetically. Focusses on the folklore and symbolism of each animal. Includes plates and illustrations.

1141. Gerhardt, Mia L. "Zoologie médiévale: Préoccupations et procédés." *MM* 7 (1970): 231-48.
Treats the supposed nineteenth-century academic dismissal of the medieval *Physiologus* as naive and superstitious and then goes on to discuss the function medieval animal lore had for its contemporary audience and their conceptions of zoology, truth, and authority.

1142. Gransden, Antonia. "Realistic Observation in Twelfth-Century England." *Speculum* 47, no. 1 (January 1972): 29-51.
Includes observation of small objects such as jewelry and books, of physiognomy and human character, and of the appearance and behavior of animals and birds. Offers many citations from twelfth-century English writers and some plates of manuscript miniatures illustrating a realistic rather than a fanciful view of animals.

1143. Hutchinson, G. Evelyn. "Attitudes towards Nature in Medieval England: The Alphonso and Bird Psalters." *Isis* 65 (1974): 5-37.
    Examines illuminated manuscripts from the end of the thirteenth and the beginning of the fourteenth centuries and traces the rise of a concern for naturalism in illustration (especially in depictions of birds) which reflects a changing human outlook on nature.

1144. Langlois, Charles. *La connaissance de la nature et du monde au Moyen Age d'après quelques écrits français à l'usage des laïcs.* Paris: Hachette, 1927.
    Focusses mainly on French works or French translations of Latin originals: Philippe de Thaün; Gossuin's *L'image du monde*; the *Letter of Prester John*; the *Secreta Secretorum*; *Sidrach and Bokkus;* Brunetto Latini's *Trésor,* and Corbechon's Bartholomaeus Anglicus' *De Proprietatibus Rerum* to arrive at popular beliefs concerning nature.

1145. Raven, Charles E. *English Naturalists from Neckam to Ray.* Cambridge: Cambridge Univ. Press, 1947.
    Traces the evolution of the scientific process as it concerns the study of the natural world. Focusses chiefly on the Renaissance through the seventeenth century and offers detailed accounts of discoveries by various naturalists. Includes an index of flora at the end.

1146. Roberts, Lawrence D., ed. *Approaches to Nature in the Middle Ages: Papers of the Tenth Annual Conference of the Center for Medieval and Early Renaissance Studies.* Binghamton, NY: Center for Medieval and Early Renaissance Studies, 1982.
    Six papers with responses on various philosophic aspects of nature in the Middle Ages.

1147. Salisbury, Joyce E. *Animals in the Middle Ages.* New York and London: Routledge, 1994.
    Treats animals as property, food, and sexual objects, and considers their economic, legal, theological, literary, and artistic status.

1148. _____, ed. *The Medieval World of Nature: A Book of Essays.*
New York and London: Garland, 1993.
Concerns specific animals, insects, animals and people, and people
and the land. Contains items 1215,1244,1248,1285,1330,1382,
1398,1449, and 1499.

1149. White, Lynn, Jr. "Natural Science and Naturalistic Art in the Middle
Ages." *AHR* 52 (1947): 421-35.
Explains the general medieval view of the universe and its impact
upon the development of science and shows how changing
perceptions of the universe are reflected in works of art.

ANIMALS IN BESTIARIES AND THE *PHYSIOLOGUS* AS SOURCES OF IMAGERY

General

1150. Cahier, Charles, and Arthur Martin. "Le physiologus ou bestiaire."
MAHL 1 (1851): 85-232; 2 (1852): 106-232; 3 (1853): 203-88;
4 (1854): 55-87.
Studies a large number of animals (including an entry on the
Barnacle Goose which grows on trees and the so-called "Fire
Stones") and provides, for each, French and Latin prose texts, as
well as the French verse bestiary texts from various manuscripts.
Plates are included at the ends of the volumes.

1151. Carmody, Francis M. "Le diable des bestiaires." *CAIEF* 3, no. 5 (July
1953): 79-85.
Looks at animals symbolizing the devil in various bestiaries. **See
also items 1094,1096,1098,1099,1100, and 1106.**

1152. Clark, Willene B., and Meradith T. McMunn, eds. *Beasts and Birds
of the Middle Ages: The Bestiary and Its Legacy.* Philadelphia:
Univ. of Pennsylvania Press, 1989.

A collection of useful essays on bestiaries, their imagery, and composition. The volume contains an excellent and lengthy bibliography.

1153. Cogliati, Luisa Arano . "Approccio metodologico al Bestiario medioevale." *Atti del I Congresso Nazionale di Storia dell' Arte, Roma, 11-24 settembre 1978.* Vol. 1. Edited by Corrado Maltese. Rome: Consiglio nazionale delle ricerche, 1980, pp. 137-50.
Considers numerous programs of illustration in several thirteenth- and fourteenth-century bestiaries, with many black-and-white plates.

1154. Cook, Albert Stanburrough, and James Hall Pitman, eds. and trans. *The Old English Physiologus.* New York: Folcroft Library edition, 1973.
An edition with translation of the stories of the panther, whale, asp, turtle-dove, and partridge.

1155. Del Zotto Tozzoli, Carla, ed. *Il "Physiologus" in Islanda.* Biblioteca Scandinavia de Studi, Richerche e Testi. Collana diretta Jørgen Stender Clausen, no. 7. Pisa: Giardini Editori e Stampatori, 1992.
A critical edition with *en-face* Italian translation, including a photographic facsimile of the two manuscript fragments.

1156. Diekstra, F. N. M. "The Physiologus, the Bestiaries, and Medieval Animal Lore." *NM* 69 (1985): 142-55.
A general introduction to the *Physiologus*, and its transmission and influence.

1157. Druce, George Claridge. "The Medieval Bestiaries and Their Influence on Ecclesiastical Decorative Art." *JBA,* n.s., 25 (1919): 41-82, and 26 (1920): 35-79.
This extremely useful pair of articles treats a great many animals, examining a large number of sculptures and manuscripts, with detailed information and quotations from the latter, showing the correspondences between texts and carven images. Many plates.

1158. _____ . "Queen Camel Church: Bosses on the Chancel Roof." *PSAHNS* 83 (1937): 89-107.
Looks at the thirty-five roof bosses of the fifteenth-century Queen Camel church (Somersetshire) with special emphasis on the animals and how they reflect twelfth- and thirteenth-century bestiary models. Includes plates.

1159. Eden, P. T., ed. *Theobaldi Physiologus*. Mittellateinische Studien und Texte, no. 6. Leiden: Brill, 1972.
A critical edition with text and translation.

1160. George, Wilma, and Brunsdon Yapp. *The Naming of the Beasts: Natural History in the Medieval Bestiary*. London: Duckworth, 1991.
Studies the relationship of actual animals to those depicted in bestiaries. Reviewed by John B. Friedman in *MH* 36 (1992): 340-41.

1161. Harthan, John P. "Animals in Art: Medieval Bestiaries." *GM* 22 (1949): 182-220.
A popular treatment of bestiary material from the Middle Ages to the present day, with a number of excellent plates.

1162. Hassig, Debra. *Medieval Bestiaries: Text, Image, Ideology*. Cambridge, Cambridge Univ. Press, 1995.
Studies twenty-eight twelfth-, thirteenth-, and fourteenth-century bestiaries and their illustrations. Especially useful for the way certain animals take on a symbolic role and for the way women and Jews were portrayed in these manuscripts. 176 plates.

1163. Henkel, Nikolaus. *Studien zum Physiologus in Mittelalter*. Tübingen: Max Niemeyer, 1976.
Though much of this work is concerned with the various versions of the *Physiologus* and their textual relation to each other, the author does give in Chapter 7 a most useful handlist of animals in the *Physiologus* and indicates where they appear in patristic and didactic works, in medieval encyclopaediae, and in vernacular literature, chiefly German. There is a bibliography, again chiefly German.

1164. Ives, Samuel A., and Hellmut Lehmann-Haupt. *An English 13th-Century Bestiary: A New Discovery in the Technique of Medieval Illumination.* New York: H. P. Kraus, 1942.
Analyzes the text and miniatures of one manuscript. Some plates.

1165. Lantschoot, A. van. "A-propos du Physiologus." *Coptic Studies in Honor of W. E. Crum.* Edited by Thomas Wittemore. Boston: The Byzantine Institute, 1950, pp. 339-63.
This work offers fragments of the Coptic *Physiologus* gathered from various manuscripts and discusses the tradition of the *Physiologus* generally in light of these discoveries.

1166. McCulloch, Florence. *Mediaeval Latin and French Bestiaries.* University of North Carolina Studies in the Romance Languages and Literatures, no. 33. Chapel Hill: Univ. of North Carolina Press, 1962.
The place to start an investigation of a particular animal or of bestiaries in general, with chapters on the Greek and Latin *Physiologus*, and bestiaries, both plain and illustrated. The book's core is "General Analysis of the Principal Subjects Treated in Latin and French Bestiaries," in which the author describes how each animal appears in the different bestiary traditions, with examples from specific manuscripts. In an appendix, there are descriptions of the alerion, argus, barnacle goose, basilisk, cricket, echeneis, elements and senses, harpy, orphan bird, titmouse, and wild man.

1167. Millet, J. *L'Animal dans l'art:symbolique et iconographique.* Paris:Odéon,1984.
General survey, often fanciful, of animal and bestiary imagery. Plates.

1168. Muratova Xenia. "Bestiaries: An Aspect of Medieval Patronage." *Art and Patronage in the English Romanesque.* Edited by Sarah Macready and F. H. Thompson. The Society of Antiquaries of London Occasional Papers, n.s., 8. London: Burlington House/ Thames and Hudson, 1986, pp. 118-44.
Surveys the popularity, transmission, influence, and ownership of a variety of twelfth- and thirteenth-century bestiaries.

1169. _____. "I Manoscritti miniati del bestiario medievale: origine, formazione e sviluppo dei cicli di illustrazioni. I bestiari miniati in Inghilterra nei secoli XII-XIV." (item 1250 below), *L'Uomo de fronte al mondo animale.* Vol. 2, pp. 1319-62].
Surveys the illustrative traditions of a number of bestiary manuscripts. Contains fifty black-and-white plates, not all of which are from bestiaries or the *Physiologus*, and of which one shows the animals on the Alne church archivolt.

1170. _____. "Problèmes de l'origine et des sources des cycles d'illustrations des manuscrits des bestiaires." Item 1139, *Epopée*, pp. 383-408.
Considers the ways in which the English illustrated bestiaries of the twelfth and thirteenth centuries influenced more than 500 illustrated similar but slightly later works. Many plates.

1171. Orbán, Arpád, ed. *Novus Phisiologus, MS Darmstadt 2780.* Leiden: Brill, 1989.
Scholarly edition of the work.

1172. Orlandi, Giovanni. "La Tradizione del 'Physiologus' e i prodromi del Bestiario Latino." Item 1250 below, *L'Uomo di fronte al Mondo Animale.* Vol. 2, pp. 1057-06.
A learned general treatment of the various versions of the *Physiologus* and their patristic sources.

1173. Ringger, Kurt. "Bestiaires et lapidaires: Un genre littéraire?" *Actes du XVIIIe Congrès International de Linguistique et de Philologie Romanes, Université de Trèves 1986.* Edited by Dieter Kremer. Tübingen: Max Niemeyer, 1988, pp. 136-48.
Sees the two genres as "anagogic fables" and looks more at their allegorical importance than at their place in the transmission of natural history.

1174. Sbordone, Francesco, ed. *Physiologus.* Milan: In Aedibus Societatis Dante Alighieri-Albrighi, Segati, 1936.
Contains the Greek text.

1175. Schrader, J. L. *A Medieval Bestiary.* New York: Metropolitan
       Museum of Art, 1986.
       Appends translations from T. H. White's *Book of Beasts* (item 1190
       below) to numerous plates of art works from the Metropolitan
       Museum of Art.

1176. Seel, Otto, ed. *Der Physiologus.* Zurich-Stuttgart: Artemis, 1960.
       Edition of the Greek text.

1177. Solms, Elisabeth de, and Jean Claude Nesmy. *Bestiaire roman:
       Textes médiévaux.* Yonne: Zodiaque, 1977.
       A coffee-table book with many excellent plates depicting animals
       in manuscripts and in capital and tympanna sculpture. In contrast to
       many works of its type, the plates are actually identified by the
       author.

1178. Squires, Ann, ed. *The Old English Physiologus.* Durham Medieval
       Texts, no. 5. New Elvet, Durham, England: Durham Medieval
       Texts, 1988.
       A scholarly edition with introduction and notes. Texts in Old English
       with translation. Appendices contain Latin and Greek versions. No
       plates.

1179. Treu, Ursula. *Physiologus: Frühchristliche tiersymbolik.* Berlin:
       Union, 1981.
       A study of this work's influence on early Christian animal
       symbolism.

                     Bestiaries and *Physiologus* by Name

[Alnewick Bestiary (MS 447)]

1180.   Millar, Eric G. *A Thirteenth-Century Bestiary in the Library of
        Alnewick Castle.* Oxford: Roxburghe Club, 1958.

A facsimile edition. Included are plates from British Library MS Royal 12 C. xix for comparison.

[Arundel Bestiary (British Library MS Arundel 292)]

1181. Faraci, Dora. *Il Bestiario Medio Inglese (MS Arundel 292 della British Library).* L'Aquila-Roma: Japadre Editore, 1990.
This edition has an excellent bibliography and thirteen colored miniatures drawn from other English and Latin bestiary manuscripts.

[Ashmole Bestiaries (Oxford, Bodleian Library MSS Ashmole 1504 and 1511)]

1182. Barker, Nicholas, ed. *Two East Anglian Picture Books: A Facsimile of the Helmingham Herbal and Bestiary, and Bodleian MS. Ashmole 1504.* Oxford and London: Roxburghe Club, 1988.
Includes a detailed commentary on the manuscripts and on their illuminations and the context in which they were created. Contains a great many useful plates of animals and plants.

1183. Unterkircher, Franz. *Bestiarium: Die Texte der Handschrift MS. Ashmole 1511 der Bodleian Library Oxford in lateinischer und deutscher Sprache 3.* Interpretationes ad Codices. Graz, Austria: Akademische Drück-und Verlagsanstalt, 1986.
Presents the complete Latin text of one Ashmole bestiary with a modern German facing translation. There is a German index of plants and animals, but no illuminations from the codex are provided; however a German index of pictures folio by folio offers fairly complete descriptions of the miniatures.

1184. *Vollstandige Faksimile-Ausgäbe im Originalformat der Handschrift MS Ashmole 1511: Bestiarum aus der Besitz der Bodleian Library, Oxford der Reihe Codices Selecti.* Graz, Austria: Akademische Drück-und Verlagsanstalt, 1982.
Facsimile of the entire manuscript.

[Bern *Physiologus* (Codex Bongarsianus 318)]

1185. Steiger, Christoph von, and Otto Homburger, eds. *Physiologus Bernensis: Völl-Faksimile ausgäbe des Codex Bongarsianus 318 der Burgerbibliothek Bern.* Basel: Alkuin,1964.
A facsimile edition of this magnificent manuscript, with an introduction, a commentary on the plates, and a transcription of the text with a German translation of the Latin. There are brief bibliographies of works on the Bern codex and on the *Physiologus* generally.

1186. Woodruff, Helen. "The *Physiologus* of Bern: A Survival of Alexandrian Style in a Ninth-Century Manuscript." *AB* 12 (1930): 226-53.
Looks at possible sources for images in this manuscript and discusses the tradition of the *Physiologus* generally.

[Bestiary of Brunetto Latini]

1187. Baldwin, Spurgeon P., ed. *The Medieval Castilian Bestiary from Brunetto Latini's Tesoro.* Exeter Hispanic Texts, no. 31. Exeter: Univ. of Exeter, 1982.
Contains an introduction to the text and an index of creatures and plants.

[Cambridge Bestiary (CUL MS Ii. 4. 26)]

1188. James, M. R., ed. *The Bestiary, Being a Reproduction in Full of the Manuscript Ii. 4. 26 in the University Library, Cambridge.* Oxford: Roxburghe Club, 1928.
Facsimile of this twelfth-century illustrated Latin bestiary with an introduction discussing the text and comparing it to other manuscript versions of the work.

1189. _____, ed. *A Peterborough Psalter and Bestiary of the Fourteenth Century.* Oxford: Roxburghe Club, 1921.
Facsimiles of many of the illustrations from both manuscripts along with codicological descriptions.

1190. White, T. H., ed. and trans. *The Book of Beasts: Being a Translation from a Latin Bestiary of the Twelfth Century.* New York: Dover, 1984.
A popular account of bestiaries with a translation and reproductions of miniatures from several.

[Bestiary of Guillaume le Clerc]

1191. Druce, George Claridge, trans. *The Bestiary of Guillaume LeClerc (Originally written in 1210-1211).* Ashford, Kent: Headley Brothers Invicta Press, 1936.
A popularizing English translation of the Anglo-Norman rhyming bestiary. Some plates.

1192. Hippeau, C., ed. *Le bestiaire divin de Guillaume Clerc de Normandie, trouvère du XIIIe siècle.* Collections de poètes français du Moyen Age, no. 1. Geneva: Slatkine, 1970.
Contains a substantial, though now dated, introduction on the background of the work.

1193. Reinsch, Robert. *Le Bestiaire. Das tierbuch des normannischen dichters Guillaume le Clerc.* Weisbaden: Martin Sändig, 1967.
An edition with German glossary of the Anglo-Norman text.

[Leningrad Bestiary (Saltykov-Schedrin Library MS Q.v.V.I)]

1194. Konstantinowa, Alexandra. *Ein Englisches Bestiar des zwölften jahrhunderts in der Staatsbibliothek zu Leningrad.* Berlin: Deutscher Kunstverlag, 1929.
Chiefly a descriptive study, with many excellent plates from the manuscript. A facsimile of this bestiary, now Saltykov-Schedrin Library MS Q.v.V.I, can be ordered from Victor Kamkin Bookstore, 4950-56 Boiling Brook Parkway, Rockville, MD, 20852.

1195. Muratova, Xenia. *The Medieval Bestiary.* Translated by Inna Kitrosskaya. Moscow: Iskusstvo Art Publishers, 1984.
A dual-language edition (Russian and English) of an illuminated English bestiary in Latin of the end of the twelfth century now preserved in the Leningrad Public Library. Facsimiles of the

manuscript pages are accompanied by Russian and English text explaining the legend of the particular animal there presented and the relation of this description to the bestiary tradition.

[Lulle Bestiary]

1196. Liniares, Armand, ed. and trans. *Raymond Lulle. Le Livre des Bêtes.*
Bibliothèque française et romane, serie B: Textes et documents, no. 3. Paris: Librairie C. Klincksieck, 1964.
An edition of a fifteenth-century French version of a bestiary by Lulle with an *en-face* modern French translation. There are plates reproduced from the manuscript, an introduction, an appendix of probable sources, and a bibliography.

[Middle English *Physiologus*]

1197. Wirtjes, Hanneke, ed. *The Middle English Physiologus.* EETS: OS, 299. Oxford: Oxford Univ. Press, 1991.
An edition with introduction discussing animals, bestiaries and sources.

[Millstadt *Physiologus*]

1198. Wilhelm, Friedrich. *Milstaetter Genesis und Physiologus Handschrift.* Codices Selecti Phototypice Impressi, no. 10. Graz, Austria: Akademische Drück-und Verlagsanstalt, 1967.
A complete facsimile of the Millstadt Genesis and *Physiologus* manuscripts.

[Mondovi bestiary]

1199. Davis, J. I., ed. *Libellus de Natura Animalium: A Fifteenth-Century Bestiary.* London: Dawson's of Pall Mall, 1958.
This is a facsimile of an early woodcut bestiary describing fifty-two animals including man. It is accompanied by high-quality woodcuts.

[Monza Bestiary]

1200. Barbier de Montault, Xavier. "Fragments d'un physiologus du XIIe siècle, à Monza." *Le Manuscrit* 2 (1894): 181-84.
Provides the text of an unpublished twelfth-century bestiary in Latin entitled "Liber scintillarum."

[Oxford Bestiaries]

1201. Hassall, William O. "Bestiaires d'Oxford." *DA* 16 (May-June 1976): 71-81.
This article is a general or non-specialist introduction to bestiaries and their study. Offers detailed descriptions and quite a few plates from Oxford manuscripts, with discussion of what is traditional or unique about these particular works.

[Bestiary of Phillipe de Thaün]

1202. Muratova, Xenia. "The Decorated Manuscripts of the Bestiary of Philippe de Thaon (The MS. 3466 from the Royal Library in Copenhagen and the MS. 249 in the Merton College Library, Oxford) and the Problem of the Illustrations of the Medieval Poetical Bestiary." Item 1224, *Third International*, pp. 217-46.
A good account of three illuminated manuscripts of this important vernacular bestiary and how they were intended to include illustrations, with a study of the sources and the style of the miniatures. Speaks more of the lion and the goat than of most of the other animals.

1203. Phillipe de Thaün. *Le bestiaire.* Edited by Emmanuel Walberg. Geneva: Slatkine, 1970.
A critical edition with introduction and glossary. No plates.

[Bestiary of Pierre de Beauvais (Oxford, Bodleian Library MS Bodley 764)]

1204. Barber, Richard, trans. *Bestiary: Being An English Version of the Bodleian Library, Oxford, M.S. Bodley 764.* Cambridge: Boydell and Brewer, 1993.

Primarily a coffee-table book, with an introduction, translation, and reproductions of the original miniatures but no notes or bibliography.

1205. Bianciotto, Gabriel, trans. *Pierre de Beauvais, Guillaume le Clerc, Richard de Fournival, Brunetto Latini, Jean Corbechon: Bestiaires du Moyen Age.* Paris: Stock, 1980.
A modern French translation of six bestiaries.

1206. Mermier, Guy R., trans. *A Medieval Book of Beasts—Pierre de Beauvais' Bestiary.* Lewiston, ME: Edwin Mellen, 1992.
Offers a diplomatic transcription of the Malines manuscript and also an English translation of the Cambrai Bestiary.

[Bestiary of Richard de Fournival]

1207. Beer, Jeanette. *Master Richard's Bestiary of Love and Response.* Berkeley: Penny Royal Press, 1985.
A limited edition of a translation.

1208. Segre, Cesare, ed. *Li bestiaires d'amours di maistre Richart de Fornival e li response du bestiaire.* Milan and Naples: Riccardo Ricciardi, 1957.
A critical edition with a study of the manuscripts.

1209. Thordstein, Arvid, ed. *Bestiaire d'amour rimé.* Etudes romanes de Lund, no. 2. Lund: W. K. Gleerup and Copenhagen: Ejnar Munksgaard, 1941.
A scholarly edition with introduction, notes, and glossary of this thirteenth-century bestiary.

ANIMALS IN GENERAL

The following works of Ulisse Aldrovandus, standard early studies on animals, plants, and trees incorporating considerable classical and patristic lore, are available on Microcard. All the works include woodcuts and engravings. See the Readex Microprint in the Landmarks of Science series edited by Harold Hartley and Duane H. D. Roller.

1210. Aldrovandi, Ulisse. *De animalibvs insectis libri septem cvm singvlorvm iconibvs adviuum expressis.* Bononiae: N. Tebaldinum, 1602.
Includes as "insects" many members of other families.

1211. _____. *De quadrupedibus digitatis viviparis.* Bononiae: N. Tebaldinum, 1637.
Treats clawed or toed mammals.

1212. _____. *Quadrvpedvm omnivm bisvlcorvum historia.* Bononiae: N. Tebaldinum, 1621.
Treats animals with a cloven hoof.

1213. _____. *De reliquis animalibvs.* Bononiae: N. Tebaldinum, 1606.
Treats animals not easily categorized.

1214. Anon. *The Animal Kingdom: Illustrated Catalogue of an Exhibition of Manuscript Illuminations, Book Illustrations, Drawings, Cylinder Seals and Bindings.* New York: Pierpont Morgan Library, 1940.
Shows animal imagery as it occurs in the manuscripts collected in the Pierpont Morgan Library. Arranged by such categories as labors of the months, fables, and the like.

1215. Benton, Janetta Rebold. "Gargoyles: Animal Imagery and Artistic Individuality in Medieval Art." *The Medieval World of Nature* (item 1148), pp. 147-65.
A general overview of the function and makeup of gargoyles with plates and discussion of their role in medieval life.

1216. Best, M. R., and F. H. Brightman, eds. *The Book of Secrets of Albertus Magnus of the Virtues of Herbs, Stones and Certain Beasts; Also a Book of the Marvels of the World.* Oxford: Clarendon, 1973.

Offers English translations of parts of a medieval *florilegium* made from the scientific works of Albertus Magnus dealing with animals, stones, the influence of the planets, and geographical wonders.

1217. Blankenburg, Wera von. *Heilige und dämonische Tiere: Die Symbolsprache der Deutschen Ornamentik in frühen Mittelalter.* Leipzig: Koehler and Amelang, 1943.
Studies polymorphic animal carvings and narratives on archivolts, capitals, baptismal fonts, and other sculptural forms, chiefly German Romanesque. Many excellent photographs from German churches and a bibliography now somewhat outdated. The text draws chiefly on the *Physiologus* and is anthropological in focus.

1218. Carrol, William Meridith. *Animal Conventions in English Renaissance Non-Religious Prose (1550-1600).* New York: Bookman Associates, 1954.
Particularly useful for the medievalist will be the introductory chapter of this work: it traces the channels by which animal imagery came to English literature and includes a very useful alphabetical list of animals, giving for each the conventions associated with it. The work draws chiefly on the natural history writing of Aristotle, Pliny, and Edward Topsell.

1219. Cohen, I. B., and Giuseppe Olmi. " Ulisse Aldrovandi." *FMR* 12 (1985): 61-92.
This work gives an overview of Aldrovandus's work, his sources and influences and contains a number of excellent color plates taken from his works on animals. Latin passages from his writings are given in Italian translation.

1220. Druce, George Claridge. "Animals in English Wood Carvings." *WS* 3 (1913-14): 57-73.
Surveys a variety of animals and birds, some fabulous, in wood carvings and discusses their symbolism as recounted in the bestiaries. Includes many plates.

1221. Fischer, Nancy. "Handlist of Animal References in Middle English Religious Prose." *LSE* 4 (1970): 49-110.

Examines a large number of manuscripts, listing animals alphabetically and indicating what is said about each one from the viewpoint of scripture, natural history, and fables.

1222. Flores, Nona C., ed. *Animals in the Middle Ages: A Book of Essays.* New York: Garland, 1995.
Deals with a variety of animal topics, treats the *Physiologus*, and also considers imaginary beasts such as werewolves and the woman-headed serpent.

1223. Gesner, Conrad. *Historia Animalium.* Tiguri: C. Froschoverum, 1551.
Like the volumes of Aldrovandus mentioned above, this Latin work is an excellent source for medieval beliefs about animals. Organized by animal rather like an encyclopaedia, it is very detailed and contains many engravings. Sir Harold Hartley and Duane H. D. Roller, eds. *Landmarks of Science,* Readex Microprint, 1972 provide a more accessible microfiche edition.

1224. Goossens, Jan, and Timothy Sodmann, eds. *Third International Beast Epic, Fable and Fabliau Colloquium Münster 1979 Proceedings.* Cologne-Vienna: Böhlau, 1981.
The articles in this collection of use to the iconographer are itemized under the specific animal. Contains items 1202, 1276, and 1440.

1225. Hicks, Carola. *Animals in Early Medieval Art.* Edinburgh: Edinburgh Univ. Press, 1993.
Examines animals in Anglo-Saxon art. Many black-and-white plates.

1226. Holbrook, R. T. *Dante and the Animal Kingdom.* New York: Columbia Univ. Press, 1902.
Treats the allusions to animals in Dante's works, chiefly the *Divine Comedy*, giving historical contexts, and general beliefs about animals in the Middle Ages, and then the poet's own view. Some of Holbrook's intepretations are now quite dated.

1227. Jones, Malcolm. "Folklore Motifs in Late Medieval Art III: Erotic Animal Imagery." *Folklore* 102, no. 2 (1991): 192-219.

Explores the erotic associations of the cockerel, the rabbit, the squirrel, the foxtail, and the ass, as well as of cockles and mussels.

1228. Klingender, Francis D. *Animals in Art and Thought to the End of the Middle Ages.* Edited by Evelyn Antal and John Harthan. Cambridge, MA: MIT Press, 1971.
A well-illustrated historical study of the relationships between man and animal from antiquity through the late Middle Ages.

1229. Michel, Paul. *Tiere als Symbol und Ornament.* Weisbaden: Ludwig Reichert, 1979.
Considers the use of animals and polymorphic beings in allegory and patristic exegesis, with many citations from works of the Latin Fathers. One chapter is devoted to such material represented on the capitals in the choir of Zurich Cathedral. There are some illustrations of these capitals.

1230. Polome, Edgar C. "The Vision of India in Medieval Encyclopedias." *Interpreting Texts from the Middle Ages: The Ring of Words in Medieval Literature.* Edited by Ulrich Goebel and David Lee. Lewiston, ME: Edwin Mellen, 1994, pp. 257-79.
Treats among other things dragons, wondrous stones, and polymorphic creatures believed to live in India.

1231. Robin, P. Ansell. *Animal Lore in English Literature.* London: John Murray, 1932.
Considers animal allusions in earlier English literature. Provides chiefly a general overview of beliefs about animals.

1232. Rowland, Beryl. *Animals with Human Faces: A Guide to Animal Symbolism.* Knoxville: Univ. of Tennessee Press, 1973.
Treats alphabetically various symbolic animals from antiquity to the present in art, literature, and folklore. Accompanying plates, drawn from medieval manuscript illustrations, vary widely in place and date.

1233. _____. *Blind Beasts: Chaucer's Animal World.* Kent, OH : Kent State Univ. Press, 1971.

A detailed study of Chaucer's use of animals, especially the boar, the hare, the wolf, the horse, the sheep, and the dog.

1234. Schmidtke, Dietrich. *Geistliche Tierinterpretation in der deutschsprachigen Literatur des Mittelalters (1100-1500).* 2 vols. Berlin: Freie Universität, 1968.
Considers the *Physiologus* and bestiaries; animals in patristic and medieval exegesis and homilies; animals in encyclopaediae and exempla collections; and other works dealing with animal interpretation. Chiefly concerned with animal symbolism in German-speaking lands during the Middle Ages.

1235. Szovérffy, Josef. "'Et Conculcabis Leonem et Draconem.' Embellishments of Medieval Latin Hymns: Beasts in Typology, Symbolism and Simile." *CF* 17 (1963): 1-4.
Gives examples of animal images in Latin hymns composed between the fourth and the sixteenth centuries.

1236. Toynbee, J. M. C. *Animals in Roman Life and Art.* Ithaca: Cornell Univ. Press, 1973.
Organized by animal, this book provides a detailed account of the history and function of animals in Roman life, along with stories about them in various Roman authors. Many illustrations.

1237. Tugnoli Pattaro, Sandra. *Metodo e sistema delle scienze nel pensiero di Ulisse Aldrovandi.* Bologna: Clueb, 1981.
Useful guide to the thought and reception of this important naturalist.

1238. Weimann, Klaus, ed. *Middle English Animal Literature.* Exeter Medieval Texts. Exeter: Univ. of Exeter Press, 1975.
A collection of well-known Middle English texts treating the lion, panther, whale, fox, eagle, and hart, with notes and glossary.

1239. Wolff, Phillipe, ed. *Le monde animal et ses représentations au Moyen Age (XIe-XVe siècles). Actes du XVème congrès de la Société des historiens médiévistes de l'enseignement supérieur public, Toulouse, 25-26 mai 1984.* Toulouse: Université de Toulouse-le-Mirail, 1985.
This collection contains item 1252.

1240. Wright, Thomas. *A History of Caricature and Grotesque in Literature and Art.* Reprint. New York: Ungar, 1968.
Covering the grotesque from its beginnings in antiquity through the early ninteenth century, this book treats the ass, ape, goose, and fox in Chapters V and VI. There are numerous drawings made from such medieval art forms as misericords and manuscript illumination.

1241. Ziolkowski, Jan. *Talking Animals, Medieval Latin Beast Poetry 750-1150.* Philadelphia: Univ. of Pennsylvania Press, 1993.
Explores at length the poems in this genre and contains translations of thirty-two texts, as well as an extensive bibliography. Reviewed by Marc Wolterbeek in *Speculum* 69, no. 2 (April 1994): 589-91.

Fables of Animals

1242. Henderson, Arnold Clayton. "Medieval Beasts and Modern Cages: The Making of Meaning in Fables and Bestiaries." *PMLA* 97 (1982): 40-49.
Shows how English and French fabulists adapted traditional patristic interpretations of animals to the purposes of the social criticism of an emerging bourgeoisie.

1243. _____. "'Of heigh or lough estat': Medieval Fabulists as Social Critics." *Viator* 9 (1978): 265-90.
Studies fabulists' use of various animals as vehicles for social criticism.

1244. Salisbury, Joyce E. "Human Animals of Medieval Fables." *The Medieval World of Nature* (item 1148), pp. 49-65.
Looks at how, in fables of Marie de France and Odo, animals with human attributes function to teach lessons on how to preserve social order. No plates.

Heraldic Uses of Animals

1245. Baxter, Ronald. "A Baronial Bestiary: Heraldic Evidence for the Patronage of Manuscript Bodley 764." *JWCI* 50 (1987): 196-200.
Discusses the elephant in this manuscript.

1246. Pastoureau, Michel. "Le bestiare héraldique au Moyen Age." *RFHS* 42 (1972): 3-17.
Considers the development of animal images in coats of arms from simple dragons on shields in the Bayeaux tapestries to the common heraldic use of some fifty animals by the mid-fifteenth century. Treats the lion, leopard, eagle, dog, fish, and monstrous forms such as the griffon. Like most of this author's work, the piece is slight and undocumented.

Medicine Employing Animals

1247. Forbes, Thomas, R. "Medical Lore in the Bestiaries." *Med. H* 12 (1968): 245-53.
Considers the caladrius, beaver, stag, dog, elephant, and mandrake, as well as curative stones and their roles in medieval veterinary science.

1248. Sprunger, David A. "Parodic Animal Physicians from the Margins of Medieval Manuscripts." *The Medieval World of Nature* (item 1148), pp. 67-81.
Looks at the iconography of these images as a reflection of social anxiety over human physicians, with plates.

Naming of the Animals

1249. Muratova, Xenia. "Adam donne leur noms aux animaux: L'iconographie de la scène dans l'art du Moyen Age et ses traits particuliers dans les manuscrits des bestiaires enluminés du XIIe et du XIIIe siècles." *SM* 18 (1977): 367-94.
Discusses in detail the iconography of Adam naming the animals in Genesis. Does not focus on particular animals but more on the relationship shown between them and Adam, the portrayal of Adam, which animals are included, sources for the depiction, and the function of this Biblical scene in bestiaries. Some plates.

Saints with Animal Attributes

1250. Boglioni, Pierre. "Il Santo e gli Animali nell'alto Medioevo." *Settimani di studio del centro italiano di studi sull' alto medioevo*, no. 31. Vol. 2: *L'Uomo de fronte al mondo animale nell' alto medioevo 7-13 aprile 1983.* Edited by Tullio Gregory, Spoleto: Panetto and Petrelli, 1985, pp. 936-93.
Treats a number of saints, like Antony, and the animals which represent them in art. Contains a very useful bibliographical handlist of such saints.

1251. Dunn-Lardeau, Brenda, ed., *Legenda aurea: Sept Siècles de diffusion: Actes du Colloque International sur la "Legenda aurea:"Texte Latin et branches vernaculaires, à l'Université du Québec é Montréal 11-12 mai 1983.* Montreal: Bellarmin; Paris J. Vrin, 1986.
L. Guilbert's article, "L'animal dans la *Legende Dorée*," pp. 77-94, treats animals' associations with saints in Jacob of Voragine's great collection of saints' legends, the *Aurea legenda.*

Seven Deadly Sins Personified by Animals

*. Norman, Joanne S. *Metamorphosis of an Allegory*. Cited above as
    item 854.
    Studies the way in which animals were associated with the sins and
    vices in medieval art. Richly illustrated with 112 pictures drawn
    from sculpture and manuscript illumination.

1252. Vincent-Cassy, Mireille. "Les animaux et les péchés capitaux de la
    symbolique à l'emblématique." *Le monde animal* (item 1239),
    pp. 121-32.
    By the fifteenth century, seven specific animals represented the sins,
    but in the earlier Middle Ages many different ones were used, and
    the author examines the historical development of the seven specific
    animals.

Trials of Animals

1253. Agnel, Emile. *Curiositiés judiciaires et historiques du Moyen Age:
    Procès contre les animaux*. Paris: Dumoulin, 1858.
    Describes various trials in both ecclesiastical and civil courts against
    offending animals during the Middle Ages. Treats punishments
    inflicted on the animals and collects extracts from various
    manuscripts and published sources concerning such trials.

Tropical Animals

1254. DuFeil, Michel-Marie. "Animaux de tropiques réel (en Europe vers
    1325)." *Epopée animale fable fabliau* (item 1139), pp. 169-
    78.

Examines Jordan of Severac's treatise on tropical animals as a source for exotic animal lore.

Wind, Animals Impregnated by

1255. Zircle, Conway. "Animals Impregnated by the Wind." *Isis* 25 (1936): 95-130.
Collects and comments on antique and medieval stories in which mares, vultures, and hens, as well as women, are fertilized by the wind.

Wood and Stone Carvings of Animals

1256. Allen, J. Romilly. *Early Christian Symbolism in Great Britain and Ireland before the Thirteenth Century: Norman Sculpture and the Medieval Bestiaries.* Rhind Lectures for 1885, nos. 5 and 6. Reprint. Felinfach: Llanerch, 1992.
The second lecture, entitled "The Medieval Bestiaries," attempts to explain the apparently incongruous association of all kinds of animal forms with sacred Christian symbols in pre-Norman capitals and tympanna. In-text illustrations but no plates.

1257. Anderson, Mary D. *Animal Carvings in British Churches.* Cambridge: Cambridge Univ. Press, 1938.
Surveys the animal symbolism represented in the carvings of tympanna, capitals, fonts, and bosses, drawing on the bestiary, romances like the *Roman de Renart,* heraldry, and the like as sources of imagery. Includes many plates and a useful list of animals arranged alphabetically, each followed by a list of cathedrals in which they are depicted.

1258. _____. *The Medieval Carver.* Cambridge: Cambridge Univ. Press, 1935.
Focussing on the iconography of medieval wood and stone sculpture in English Gothic architecture, this work treats masons and their imagery. Looks to standard sources such as scripture; lives of the Virgin and the saints; and images from allegorical and satiric works, romances, and bestiaries.

1259. Collins, Arthur H. *Symbolism of Animals and Birds Represented in English Church Architecture.* New York: McBride, Nast, 1914.
Itemizes much fauna, real and imaginary, appearing on capitals, archivolts, and tympanna and offers some photographs of them.

1260. Debidour, V.-H. *Le bestiaire sculpté en France.* Grenoble: Arthaud, 1961.
An excellent collection of photographs, with running commentary, of carvings from French churches containing animals and zoomorphic forms, ranging in date from the early Christian period through the sixteenth century. Includes a geographical handlist.

1261. Dubourg-Noves, Pierre. "Les animaux dans la sculpture médiévale." *Médecine de France*, 3e trimestre (1969): N. P.
Excellent close-up photographs of animals on Romanesque capitals, archivolts, and the like from French churches.

1262. Evans, E. P. *Animal Symbolism in Ecclesiastical Architecture.* New York: Henry Holt, 1896.
Covers a wide range of animals and other symbols in bestiaries and in ecclesiastical architecture. Miscellaneous but informative. Includes an index.

ANIMALS, LAND

By Specific Type

[Ape]

1263. Bernabò, M. "Adamo, gli animali, le sue vesti e la sfida di Satana. Un complesso rapporto testo-immagine nella illustrazione bizantina dei settanta." *Miniatura* 2 (1989): 11-33.
Treats the ape's symbolism as a diabolical parody of divine goodness.

1264. Janson, Horst W. *Apes and Ape Lore in the Middle Ages and the Renaissance.* London: Warburg Institute, 1952.
Investigates beliefs related to the ape and includes many plates from manuscript illustrations and from church sculpture containing apes.

1265. McDermott, William Coffman. *The Ape in Antiquity.* Johns Hopkins University Studies in Archaeology, no. 27. Baltimore: Johns Hopkins Univ. Press, 1938.
Describes the iconographical depictions of all "infra-human primates" mainly in works of classsical literature and art. This includes a catalogue of apes depicted on figurine sculpture, vases, paintings, mosaics, and architectural reliefs.

[Asp]

1266. McCulloch, Florence. "The Metamorphoses of the Asp in Latin and French Bestiaries." *SP* 56 (1959): 7-14.
Starting with the oldest account, probably second century AD, the author discusses depictions of the asp in various bestiaries.

1267. Schwab, Ute. "Die Bedeutungen der Aspis und die Verwandlungen des Marsus." *Epopée animale fable fabliau* (item 1139), pp. 549-64.
Gathers much patristic literature about the asp.

[Ass]

1268. Adolf, Helen. "The Ass and the Harp." *Speculum* 25, no. 1 (January 1950): 49-57.

Discusses the symbolism of the ass with the harp in the Middle Ages, drawing on classical and patristic sources.

1269. Clément, Félix. "Drame liturgique. L'âne au Moyen Age." Parts 1, 2. *AA* 15 (1855): 373-86; 16 (1856): 26-38.
Considers the ass as a symbol of Christ and his doctrine. Provides numerous patristic quotations, often with French translation, that concern the ass. Also describes how this animal appears in some church sculpture.

1270. Stauder, W. "Asinus ad lyram." *Frankfurter Musikhistorische Studien. Helmuth Osthoff zu seinem siebzigsten Geburtstag.* Überreicht von Kollegen, Mitarbeiten und Schulern. Edited by Wilhelm Stauder, et al. Tutzing: H. Schneider, 1969, 25-32.
Traces the motif of the ass playing a lyre popular on Romanesque capitals. Many black-and-white plates.

1271. Wireker, Nigel. *A Mirror for Fools.* Translated by J. H. Mozley. Notre Dame: Univ. of Notre Dame Press, 1963.
A convenient edition of *Speculum Stultorum,* a twelfth-century satire by Nigel Longchamp, or Wireker, which uses the ass as a persona, in the manner of Apuleius.

[Beaver]

1272. Malaxecheverria, Ignacia. "Castor et lynx médiévaux: Leur senefiance." *Florilegium* 3 (1981): 228-38.
Applying some modern theoretical constructs from the works of Jung, Bachelard, and Gilbert Durand to the medieval accounts of these beasts, the author cites numerous passages concerning them, comparing the medieval interpretations with contemporary theoretical ones.

[Boar]

1273. Thiébaux, Marcelle. "The Mouth of the Boar as a Symbol in Medieval Literature." *RP* 22 (1968-69): 281-99.
This very useful and extremely detailed article looks at both literal hunting accounts and allegorical treatments of the boar and studies the animal's symbolism in western European literature.

[Cat]

1274. Sillar, Frederick Cameron, and Ruth Mary Meyler. *Cats, Ancient and Modern.* London: Studio Vista, 1966.
An eclectic collection of information on cats crossculturally and throughout history, consisting mainly of translated passages from works about cats and plates of representations in art. Some of the texts are medieval.

[Deer or Stag]

1275. Bath, Michael. "The Serpent-Eating Stag in the Renaissance." *Épopée animale fable fabliau* (item 1139), pp. 55-64.
Provides some information on the image of the stag at the stream and on the belief that it ate serpents.

1276. _____ "The White Hart, the 'cerf volant,' and the Wilton Diptych." *Third International Beast Epic (* item 1224), pp. 25-42.
Dealing mainly with the heraldic sense of the hart as a royal badge, the author provides some good reproductions of manuscript miniatures and wall paintings of the hart.

1277. Gandilhon, René. "Symbolisme du cerf: Les deux cerfs de Reims." *MSM* 99 (1984): 17-46.
Studies the stag motif in seals and in civic heraldry, with plates.

[Dog]

1278. Friedman, John B. "The Dreamer, the Whelp, and Consolation in the *Book of the Duchess.*" *CR* 3 (1969): 145-62.
Discusses the healing power of the dog's tongue in Thomas of Cantimpré as well as other favorable and unfavorable connotations of the dog.

1279. Huhn, Vital. "Löwe und Hund als Symbole des Rechts." *MJGK* 7 (1955): 1-63.

Studies the symbolism of these two animals as meaning rightousness and law in funerary art, heraldry, and family names in German-speaking lands during the later Middle Ages.

1280. Leach, Maria. *God Had a Dog: Folklore of the Dog.* New Brunswick, NJ: Rutgers Univ. Press, 1961.
A discussion, ranging in time and place, of the folklore of the dog.

1281. London, H. Stanford. "The Greyhound as a Royal Beast." *Archaeologia* 97 (1959): 139-63.
Examines the genealogical use of this animal in Tudor heraldry. While the focus is neither strictly medieval nor iconographic, there are numerous interesting illustrations of the greyhound in heraldry.

1282. Schmitt, Jean-Claude. *The Holy Greyhound: Guinefort, Healer of Children since the Thirteenth Century.* Translated by Martin Thorn. Cambridge: Cambridge Univ. Press, 1983.
Discusses the popularity in the Middle Ages of an exemplum on the healing power of a dead greyhound and how the animal became the center of a folk "cult."

[Elephant]

* Baxter, Ronald. "A Baronial Bestiary." Cited above as item 1245. Discusses the elephant

1283. Cross, J. E ."The Elephant to Alfred, Ælfric, Aldhelm, and Others." *SN* 37 (1965): 367-73.
Traces the possible sources for various beliefs about the elephant among Anglo-Saxon authors, in particular, its supposed vulnerability at the navel.

1284. Druce, George Claridge. "The Elephant in Medieval Legend and Art." *AJ* 76 (1919): 1-73.
Covers all aspects of medieval thought about the elephant, with a wealth of illustrations drawn from medieval manuscripts, wall paintings, and sculpture.

1285. Flores, Nona C. "The Mirror of Nature Distorted: The Medieval Artist's Dilemma in Depicting Animals." *The Medieval World of Nature* (item 1148), pp. 3-45.
    Discusses medieval artists' depictions of animals either with photographic realism or in a symbolic manner. Dwells at length on the elephant and includes numerous plates.

1286. Hatto A.T. "The Elephant in the Strassburg *Alexander*." *LMS* 1 (1937-39): 399-429.
    Studies the elephant in Alexander romances, especially their manuscript illuminations, and in textiles and chessmen. Considers "The Elephant of the Book of the Maccabees: Its Vulnerable Spot, Its Mahout, Castle and Bellicosity"; "The Elephant's Solid Bones"; "The Elephant and Its Castle"; "The Elephant's Unbending Legs"; "Saint Thomas's Identification of Behemoth with the Elephant"; and "Non-Literary Evidence of the Elephant."

1287. Hecksher, William S. "Bernini's Elephant and Obelisk." *AB* 29 (1947): 155-82.
    In attempting to explain Bernini's seventeenth-century statue of an elephant with an Egyptian obelisk on its back, the author provides much lore and iconographical history for the animal in the Middle Ages. There are many illustrations. Also reprinted in [Hecksher]*Art and Literature* (item 250), pp. 65-96.

1288. Lloyd, Joan Barclay. *African Animals in Renaissance Art and Literature*. Oxford: Clarendon, 1971.
    This still remains the authoritative study of knowledge and depictions of African animals in the Middle Ages and Renaissance. Numerous plates.

1289. Romm, James. "Aristotle's Elephant and the Myth of Alexander's Scientific Patronage." *AJP* 110 (1983): 566-75.
    Discusses specific beliefs about the elephant while also examining *Alexander's Letter to Aristotle on the Wonders of India*.

1290. Sillar, Frederick Cameron, and Ruth M. Meyler. *Elephants, Ancient and Modern*. New York: Viking, 1968.

An eclectic collection of stories in translation and reproductions of art works concerning the elephant throughout history.

1291. Thibout. M. "L'éléphant dans la sculpture romane française." *B Mon* 105 (1947): 183-95.
Focusses on the various ways this exotic animal was represented, especially in eleventh- and twelfth-century Romanesque sculpture. Includes plates.

[Fox]

1292. Collins, A. H. "Some Twelfth-Century Animal Carvings and Their Sources in the Bestiaries." *Connoisseur* 106 (1940): 238-43.
Studies the animal carvings on Norman church portals, looking at the fox, the panther, the hyena, the manticore, the unicorn, the eagle, and the caladrius.

1293. Levy, Brian, and Paul Wackers, eds. *Reinardus: Yearbook of the International Reynard Society. Special Volume: The Fox and Other Animals (Selected Proceedings of the Spa Colloquium).* Amsterdam and Philadelphia: John Benjamins, 1993.
Contains a number of articles by different authors focussing on depictions of animals, and particularly of the fox, in the Middle Ages. Especially useful to the iconographer are Wilfried Schouwink, "The Fox's Funeral in European Art," and Paul Wackers, "The Image of the Fox in Middle Dutch Literature."

1294. Mossé, Ferdinand. "Le Roman de Renart dans l'Angleterre du Moyen Age." *LLM* 45 (1951): 70-84.
Treats Latin and Anglo-Norman versions of the Reynard legend in medieval England.

1295. Rombauts, E., and A. Welkenhuysen, eds. *Aspects of the Medieval Animal Epic. Proceedings of the International Conference, Louvain May 15-17.* The Hague: Louvain Univ. Press, 1975.
Most of the articles in this collection deal with the *Roman de Renart*, as for example, Norman F. Blake, "Reynard the Fox in England," pp. 53-65.

1296. Scheve, D. A. "Jonson's *Volpone* and Traditional Fox Lore." *RES*, n.s., 1 (1950): 242-44.
Draws upon Conrad Gesner and other early naturalists.

1297. Varty, Kenneth. *Reynard the Fox*. Leicester: Leicester Univ. Press, 1967.
Still the best treatment of the subject, tracing the iconographical history of depictions of Reynard. The book includes many plates, a general list of fox drawings and carvings, and a select bibliography.

[Giraffe]

1298. Boltz, Wiliam G. "Leonardo Olschki and Marco Polo's Asia (with an Etymological Excursus on *giraffe*)." *RP* 23, no. 1 (1969): 1-16.
Shows how the giraffe, which was not mentioned in medieval bestiaries, was often identified with the Biblical *cameleopard* or *camelion* by writers like John Wycliff and given an arabic name "Zarafa" by Albertus Magnus.

1299. Laufer, Berthold. "The Giraffe in History and Art." Field Museum of Natural History, Anthropology Leaflet, no. 27. Chicago: Field Museum, 1928.
Only a portion of this study treats the medieval giraffe, but there is some account of drawings of the animal by pilgrim writers like Bernard von Breydenbach and Arnold von Harff. A giraffe (a gift from the Mameluke sultan of Egypt) was actually owned by Lorenzo di Medici in the fifteenth century.

[Goat]

1300. Druce, George Claridge. "The Symbolism of the Goat on the Norman Font at Thames Ditton." *SAC* 21 (1908): 109-12.
Discusses the different ways the goat is used symbolically in bestiaries (for example to represent Lust) in order to indicate its significance in church sculpture.

[Hare]

1301. Bauer, J. B. "Lepusculus Domini: Zum altchristlichen Hasensymbol." *ZDK* 79 (1957): 457-66.
Suggests that the hare or rabbit can stand for Moses.

[Horse]

1302. Davies, Sioned, and Nerys Ann Jones, ed. *The Horse in Celtic Culture. Medieval Welsh Perspectives.*Cardiff: Univ. of Wales Press, 1997.
Mainly sociological and economic in emphasis, but twelve illustrations show something of the Welsh horse's iconographic interest.

1303. Dubost, Francis. "De quelques chevaux extraordinaires dans le récit médiéval: Esquisse d'une configuration imaginaire." *Le cheval dans le monde médiéval.* Edited by Margaret Betrand. Senefiance, no. 32. Aix: Centre Universitaire d'Etudes et de Recherches Médiévales d'Aix, 1992, pp. 189-208.
This essay is generally the most useful of the volume's twenty-eight brief pieces, some illustrated in color, from the seventeenth meeting of the Centre Universitaire d'Etudes et de Recherches Médiévales d'Aix. The topics covered range from the literary horses of romances to farm horses and veterinary and magical concerns, such as prayers for a sick horse.

1304. Fisher, John Hurt. "Chaucer's Horses." *SAQ* 60 (1961): 71-79.
Focusses on the appropriateness of their horses to the Canterbury pilgrims who ride them. While it does not deal specifically with the iconography of the horse, it does indicate what different colors and sizes of horses signified in the Middle Ages.

1305. Friedman, John B. "A Reading of Chaucer's *Reeve's Tale.*" *CR* 2 (1967): 9-18.
Examines traditional horse and rider lore as symbolizing reason and passion in Chaucer's poetry to show how he relied on it as a verbal shorthand, especially in *The Reeve's Tale.* This topos starts with Plato's allegory of the horses and Jeremiah 5:8: "They were as fed horses in the morning: every one neighed after his neighbour's wife"

as well as the Epistle to James 3:3. Later accounts of the idea can be found in the mid-fourteenth-century *Ayenbite of Inwyt,* where the senses, unconstrained by the bridle of reason, are like a horse without a bridle.

1306. Haines, Francis. *Appaloosa: The Spotted Horse in Art and History.* Austin: Univ. of Texas Press, 1962.

The chapter, "Spotted Horse in Europe," pp. 45-62, contains information on the representation of these horses in the art of the Middle Ages and Renaissance.

1307. Howey, Oldfield M. *The Horse in Magic and Myth.* London: William Rider, 1923.

Contains a good deal of folklore about horses through the ages. It is organized by types of horse, such as ghostly horses, sea horses, and the like. Brief bibliography.

1308. Rowland, Beryl. "The Horse and Rider Figure in Chaucer's Works." *UTQ* 35 (1966): 246-59.

Traces the history of horse and rider symbolism as body/woman and soul/man in the Middle Ages and Chaucer's use of the topos.

1309. Seidel, Linda."Early Medieval Images of the Horseman Re-Viewed." *The Study of Chivalry* (item 1657), pp. 373-400.

Focusses on a select number of iconographical associations of the horseman in the Middle Ages, with detailed discussion of specific art works for which plates are provided.

1310. Vogel, Mary Ursula. *Some Aspects of the Horse and Rider Analogy in "The Debate Between the Body and Soul."* Washington, D.C.: Catholic Univ. of America Press, 1948.

Studies how this commonplace expressed the relationship between an individual's body and soul and how the soul, the seat of the intellect and the will, should control man's actions. Examines how "The Debate between the Body and the Soul" fits into this tradition. The text of "The Debate" appears in an appendix and the introduction includes information on the text, manuscripts, and the use of the horse and rider motif in Chaucer.

[Lamb]

1311. Nikolasch, Franz. *Das Lamm als Christussymbol in den Schriften der Väter*. Vienna: Herder, 1963.
Traces the symbolic use of this animal from rabbinic exegesis through exegesis of the New and Old Testaments, especially of the lamb as a symbol of Christ. No plates.

[Lion]

1312. Bretèque, François de la. "Image d'un animal: Le lion, sa définition et ses 'limites' dans les textes et l'iconographie (XIe-XIVe siècles)." *Le monde animal* (item 1239), pp.143-54.
Examines the different forms of lion iconography and what are the limits within which the animal's form may vary and still be considered a lion.

1313. Bunt, Cyril G. E. "The Lion and the Unicorn." *Antiquity* 4 (1930): 425-37.
Studies antique, medieval, and Renaissance depictions in art and literature of a number of different cultures concerning the relationship between these two animals.

1314. Druce, George Claridge. "The Lion and the Cubs in the Cloister." *CCC* 23 (1936): 18-22.
Looks at the depiction in bestiaries, manuscript illustration, and architecture of the lioness who gives birth to dead cubs, lamenting over them for three days before the lion comes and restores them either with his breath or his roar.

1315. Friedmann, Herbert. *A Bestiary for Saint Jerome: Animal Symbolism in European Religious Art*. Washington, DC: Smithsonian Institution Press, 1980.
Considers, among other animals, the lion often found at the feet of St. Jerome in medieval manuscript illustrations and panel paintings. Contains many excellent plates, some in color, and a full bibliography.

1316. Igarashi-Takeshita, Midori. "Les lions dans la sculpture romane en
      Poitou." *Cahiers CM* 23, no. 1 (1980): 37-54.
      Studies this popular motif in Poitvin capitals, with plates and
      illustrations.

1317. Pastoureau, Michel. "Quel est le roi des animaux? " *Le monde
      animal* (item 1239), pp. 133-42.
      Examines the iconography of the lion, the bear, and the eagle, as
      well as the development of the idea that each animal dominates its
      specific group as a "king."

[Lynx]

1318. Malaxecheverria, Ignacia. "Castor et lynx médiévaux:" Cited above
      as item 1272.

[Ox]

1319. Taylor, Archer. "The Proverb 'The Black Ox Has not Trod on His
      Foot.'" *PQ* 20 (1941): 266-78.
      Studies the background of the proverb and some of its variants.

[Pig]

1320. Druce, George Claridge. "The Sow and Pigs: A Study in Metaphor."
      AC 46, n.d.: 1-6.
      Identifies the sow playing a musical instrument to her dancing piglets
      as a common iconographical image in medieval ecclesiastical
      sculpture and discusses its implications, looking at bestiary
      manuscripts and misericords containing similar images. Some plates.

1321. Kearney, Milo. *The Role of Swine Symbolism in Medieval Culture.*
      Lewiston, ME: Edward Mellen, 1991.
      Though not specifically iconographical in focus, this book offers
      wide-ranging information on pigs in the Middle Ages and their
      traditional associations with St. Antony.

1322. Pastoureau. Michel. *Le Cochon: Histoire symbolique et cuisine du porc.* Paris: Sang de la Terre, 1987.
Recycled material, as is often the case with this author, of miscellaneous pieces dealing with the pig. Some material on pig symbolism in virtues and vices literature. Plates.

1323. Silar, Frederick Cameron, and Ruth Mary Meyler. *The Symbolic Pig: An Anthology of Pigs in Literature.* Edinburgh and London: Oliver and Boyd, 1961.
Covers the symbolism of the pig from antiquity to the present in several cultures and in both art and literature. The book offers many examples of medieval and Renaissance pigs and has numerous plates. There is an Appendix entitled: "Where to Find Examples of Church Pigs in Britain."

[Rabbit]

1324. Abraham, Claude K. "Myth and Symbol: The Rabbit in Medieval France." *SP* 60 (1963): 589-97.
Traces the symbolism of the rabbit from antiquity through the Middle Ages and warns against viewing allegories of the rabbit too simplistically. Chiefly concerned with the different associations of this animal in medieval French literature.

[Rhinoceros]

1325. Alès, Adhémar d'. "Tertullianea: Le rhinocéros et le symbolisme de la croix." *RSL* 26, no. 1 (1936): 99-100.
Looks at Tertullian's discussion of the rhinoceros and his source in the work of Justin Martyr.

1326. Clarke, T. H. *The Rhinoceros from Durer to Stubbs (1515-1799).* New York: Sothebys,' 1986.
Treats the single horned rhinoceros as shown in the arts of Europe, with numerous color and black-and-white illustrations.

[Salamander]

1327. Koch, Robert A. "The Salamander in Van der Goes' Garden of Eden." *JWCI* 28 (1965): 323-26.

Discusses the painter's innovative substitution of a female-faced salamander for the traditional woman-headed snake in the Temptation scene in Eden. Koch explores the provenance of this idea and its later influence. There are several plates containing reproductions of medieval manuscript miniatures.

[Snake]

1328. Knortz, Karl. *Reptilien und Amphibien in Sage, Sitte, und Literatur.* Annaberg: Grasers, 1911.
A very general study which incidentally refers to some medieval discussions of snakes.

[Tiger]

1329. McCulloch, Florence. "Le tigre et le miroir: La vie d'une image de Pline à Pierre Gringore." *RSH* 130 (1968): 149-60.
Looks specifically at the development of the image of the tigress chasing hunters away from her cubs.

[Toad]

1330. Robbins, Mary E. "The Truculent Toad in the Middle Ages." *The Medieval World of Nature* (item 1148), p. 25-47.
Explores the iconography of the toad "as a symbol of either death or the pain of divine punishment in the literature and visual art of the Middle Ages" (25). Plates.

[Weasel]

1331. Duncan, T. "The Weasel in Religion, Myth, and Superstition." *WSU*, Humanistic Series, 12, no. 1 (1924): 33-66.
Treats antique beliefs about the weasel. However, the article has some information drawn from the Middle Ages.

1332. Treu, Ursula. "Das Wiesel im Physiologus." *WZR* 12, no. 2 (1963): 275-6.
Treats Christian symbolism associated with this animal.

ANIMALS, LAND, IMAGINARY

General

1333. Barber, Richard, and Anne Riches. *A Dictionary of Fabulous Beasts*. New York: Walker, 1972.
Lists some six hundred fabulous beasts alphabetically and gives a general description of each and of the provenance of its legend. Includes a bibliography.

1334. Caprotti, Erminio. "Animali Fantastici in Plinio." *Plinio e La Natura. Atti del Ciclo di Conferenze sugli aspetti naturalistici del' opera Pliniana Como 1979*. Edited by Angelo Roncoroni. Como: Camera di Commercio Industria Artigiano e Agricoltura di Como, 1982, pp. 39-61.
General article with some plates and bibliography on fantastic mammals in Pliny's encylopaedia.

1335. Clark, Anne. *Beasts and Bawdy*. London: J. M. Dent, 1975.
Considers fabulous beasts and various monstrous transformations of men into animals and animals into men, animal medicines, charms and animal parts used as aphrodisiacs. Includes a bibliography.

1336. Costello, Peter. *The Magic Zoo: The Natural History of Fabulous Animals*. London: Sphere Books, 1979.
Lists many fabulous animals from the Western tradition and gives an account of their history. Although the work is intended for a popular audience, it contains a detailed bibliography, beast by beast, which is useful for further study.

1337. Friedman, John B. *The Monstrous Races in Medieval Art and Thought*. Cambridge: Harvard Univ. Press, 1981.

Considers some chiefly animal monsters in medieval art and culture, though the focus of the book is on aberrant human forms.

1338. Holmes, Urban Tigner. "The Monster in Mediaeval Literature." *Studies in Honor of Alfred G. Engstrom.* Edited by R. T. Cargo and E. J. Mickel, Jr. Chapel Hill: Univ. of North Carolina Press, 1972, pp. 53-62.
Offers a definition and explanation of monstrous forms in the Middle Ages, with an account of some medieval theories of polymorphism.

1339. Mode, Heinz. *Fabulous Beasts and Demons.* London: Phaidon, 1975.
Focusses on the artistic representation of monsters in many cultures throughout history, with monsters understood as new shapes resulting from recombinations of the components or properties of living things. There are many plates and illustrations and an alphabetically arranged glossary of such creatures.

1340. Robinson, Margaret W. *Fictitious Beasts: A Bibliography.* London: Library Association, 1961.
Covers only European beliefs about animals and is confined to printed books containing the English view of the subject from antiquity to the present day. Touches on classical, medieval, Renaissance, and modern views of such creatures as the barnacle goose, basilisk, dragon, griffin, phoenix, unicorn, mermaid, and sea serpent.

1341. South, Malcolm, ed. *Mythical and Fabulous Creatures: A Source Book and Research Guide.* New York: Greenwood Press, 1987.
Contains essays on twenty fabulous beasts, describing in general terms their role in history and folklore crossculturally, including mention of the important works and scholarship on each. The last entry, "a Miscellany" by the editor, goes briefly over many animals not covered and offers some information about them. Contains items 1343,1346-47,1352,1357-8,1361-63,1375,1412,1474,1477 and 1829.

* Wittkower, Rudolf. "Marvels of the East." Cited above as item 272.

Looks at the transmission of Greek conceptions of ethnographical monsters, chiefly human but some animal, as depicted in Marvels of the East literature all the way up through the eighteenth century. Contains many plates.

By Specific Type

[Amphisbaena]

1342. Druce, George Claridge. "The Amphisbaena and Its Connexions in Ecclesiastical Art and Architecture." *AJ,* 2d ser., 67 (1910): 285-317.
Looks at the iconographical tradition of this creature from the twelfth through the sixteenth centuries in sculpture and manuscript illumination. Many plates.

[Basilisk]

1343. Breiner, Laurence A. "The Basilisk." *Mythical and Fabulous Creatures* (item 1341), pp. 113-22.
A general introduction to the iconography of the basilisk.

1344. Lecouteux, Claude. "Des Königs Ortnit Schlaf." *Euphorion* 73 (1979): 347-55.
Considers the basilisk in Old High German works such as *Ortnit.*

[Centaur]

1345. Dumezil, Georges. *Le problème des centaures: Etude de mythologie comparée Indo-Européenne.* Paris: Librairie Orientaliste Paul Geuthner, 1929.
Examines centaur myths in a variety of Indo-European languages and discusses their function in festivals and celebrations.

1346. Kollmann, Judith J. "The Centaur." *Mythical and Fabulous Creatures* (item 1341), pp. 225-39.
A general introduction to the iconography of the centaur.

[Chimera]

1347. Leeming, David Adams. "The Chimeras." *Mythical and Fabulous Creatures* (item 1341), pp 103-11.
Deals only tangentially with the Middle Ages.

[Cynocephalus or Dog- Headed People]

* Friedman, John B. *The Monstrous Races.* Cited above as item 1337.
Discusses the Cynocephali and offers numerous representations in medieval manuscripts.

1348. Lecouteux, Claude. "Les Cynocéphales: Etude d'une tradition tératologique de l'antiquité au XIIe siècles." *CCM* 24 (1981): 117-28.
Traces the classical analogues for this creature in the medieval period and discusses what the Cynocephali come to represent for the Middle Ages.

1349. White, David Gordon. *The Myths of the Dog-Man.* Chicago and London: Univ. of Chicago Press, 1991.
Traces the tradition in literature and the visual arts of the dog-man crossculturally and diachronically. Includes a selective but lengthy bibliography.

[Draconopede]

1350. Friedman, John B. "Antichrist and the Iconography of Dante's Geryon." *JWCI* 35 (1972): 108-22.
Argues that Dante's Geryon in *The Inferno* is in fact an "Antichristus mysticus" or hidden Antichrist from the Franciscan spiritual tradition in which two antichrists, one hidden and one open, would be vanquished at the Apocalyse. Discusses in passing the draconopede and serpent with a human face. Includes plates.

[Dragon]

1351. Dauphiné, J. "Le dragon dans la littérature et les miniatures arabo-persanes du Moyen Age." *La chasse au Moyen Age: Actes du colloque de Nice (22-24 juin 1979).* Edited by M. Martin. Publications de la faculté des lettres et des sciences humaines de Nice, no. 20. Paris: Les Belles Lettres, 1980, pp. 481-92.
Discusses the various legends and depictions of dragon encounters and combats from ancient and medieval Persian and Arab sources. Two plates.

1352. Evans, Jonathan D. "The Dragon." *Mythical and Fabulous Creatures* (item 1341), pp. 27-58.
A general introduction to the iconography of the dragon.

1353. Giet, S. "La bête et la dragon de l'Apocalpyse d'après des images anciennes." *RMAL* 21 (1965): 5-20.
Treats the dragon in apocalyptic imagery.

1354. Quaquarelli, Antonio. *Il Leone e il Drago nella Simbolica della 'Età Patristica. Quaderni di Vetera Christianorum,* no. 11. Bari: Istituto di letteratura cristiana antica, 1975.
Studies these two creatures in the works of the fathers, chiefly St. Augustine, and in the liturgy. Some plates.

1355. Wild, F. *Drachen im Beowulf und andere Drachen. Sitzungsberichte der Österreichische Akademie der Wissenschaft.* Philosophisch-Historische Klasse, vol. 238, no. 5. Vienna: H. Böhlau, 1962.
This monograph traces the history of the word dragon in classical literature and in the Bible, treats its connection with Saint George, and examines its role in Old English poetry. Some plates.

[Fairies]

1356. Harf-Lancner, L. *Les fées au Moyen Age. Morgue et Mélusine. La naissance des fées.* Paris: Librairie Honoré Champion, 1985.
Shows how classical fauns and nymphs join with folkloric images to make fairies.

[Gorgon Medusa]

1357. Suther, Judith D. "The Gorgon Medusa." *Mythical and Fabulous Creatures*, (item 1341), pp 163-78.
A general introduction to the iconography of the gorgon medusa.

[Griffin]

1358. Bartscht, Waltraud. "The Griffin." *Mythical and Fabulous Creatures* (item 1341), pp 85-101.
A general introduction to the iconography of the griffin.

1359. Bisi, Anna Maria. *Il grifone: Storia di un motivo iconografico nell'antico Oriente Mediterraneo.* Centro di Studi Università de Roma—Semitici. Studi Semitici, no. 13. Rome, Centro di studi semitici, Istituto di studi del Vicino Orienta, 1965.
Discusses the iconography of the griffin in antiquity throughout the Mediterranean world. Contains plates.

1360. Goldmann, B. "The Development of the Lion-Griffin." *AJA* 64 (1960): 319-28.
On the evolution of this creature in eastern antiquity.

   * Settis-Frugoni, Chiara. *Historia Alexandri elevati per Griphos ad Aerem.* Cited above as item 804.

[Manticore]

1361. Cheyney, David R. "The Manticora." *Mythical and Fabulous Creatures*, (item 1341), pp 125-31.
A general introduction to the iconography of the manticore.

[Mermicoleon] **See Oyster**

[Minotaur]

1362. Curley, Michael J. "The Minotaur." *Mythical and Fabulous Creatures* (item 1341), pp. 193-205.
A general introduction to the iconography of the minotaur.

[Satyr]

1363. Grootkerk, Paul. "The Satyr." *Mythical and Fabulous Creatures* (item 1341), pp. 207-23.
A general introduction to the iconography of the satyr.

1364. Kaufmann, Lynn Frier. *The Noble Savage: Satyrs and Satyr Families in Renaissance Art.* Epping: Bowker, 1984.
Focusses on the image of the lustful satyr as presented in Renaissance art paradoxically as "proud father and affectionate husband, head of a small household" (xix) and looks back also at his representation in ancient and medieval art for the development of this presentation. Though this study deals with the woodcut tradition, there is some material on the earlier conception and treatment of the satyr in the opening chapters. Numerous plates, bibliography, and index.

[Sphinx]

1365. Baer, Eva. *Sphinxes and Harpies in Medieval Islamic Art: An Iconographical Study.* Oriental Notes and Studies, no. 9. Jerusalem: The Israel Oriental Society, 1965.
A scholarly investigation of the human-headed quadruped or sphinx and the human-headed bird in medieval Islamic art. Numerous plates.

[Unicorn]

1366. Albert, P. *Die Einhornjagd in der Literatur und Kunst des Mittelalters vornehmlich am Oberrhein.* Freiburg im Breisgau: Schau-ins-Land, 1898.
Rather outdated general study of the motif of Christ as a unicorn hunted from heaven, with many in-text black-and-white plates of the motif drawn from medieval manuscripts and sculpture. See also Hunt.

1367. Beer, Robert Rüdiger. *Unicorn: Myth and Reality.* Translated by
       Charles M. Stern. New York: James J. Kery, 1975.
       Contains a wealth of information on the unicorn throughout history,
       with numerous plates. Treats its appearance in the *Physiologus* and
       considers the Virgin and unicorn hunt motif as well as the creature
       as a symbol of Christ.

1368. Brown, Robert, Jr. *The Unicorn: A Mythological Investigation.*
       London: Longmans, Green, 1881.
       Contains some specific discussion, particularly in the chapter on
       heraldry but ranges widely in time and place. The most useful
       chapters are "The Heraldic Unicorn," and "Opinions Respecting the
       Terrestrial Existence of the Unicorn."

1369. Einhorn, Jürgen W. *Spiritualis Unicornis. Das Einhorn als
       Bedeutungsträger in Literatur und Kunst des Mittelalters.*
       Munich: Wilhelm Fink, 1976.
       Surveys the spriritual background of the unicorn and then considers
       unicorn types in the Septuagint, patristic writing, and the
       Physiologus, as well as in travel writers like Marco Polo and the
       author of the Prester John letters. There is a thorough discussion of
       the unicorn in the encyclopaedists and moralizers, like John of San
       Gemigniano. Its associations with the Virgin and Mariology
       generally, as well as heraldry, complete the first part of the book.
       The second part is devoted to the animal in art: tapestries like those
       at the Cloisters, mosaics, wood and ivory carvings, and metal work.
       There is a list of early authors who cite the unicorn, a very extensive
       bibliography, chiefly German, and 174 black-and-white plates.

1370. Freeman, Margaret B. *The Unicorn Tapestries.* New York: E.P.
       Dutton, 1983.
       This book, in the process of publishing plates of the "Unicorn
       Tapestries" in the Cloisters, offers an account of the creature in
       ancient and medieval texts, as well as in medieval and early
       Renaissance art. It contains considerable material of interest on
       gardens and medieval hunting as well.

1371. Humphreys, H. H. "The Horn of the Unicorn." *ARCSE* 8 (1951): 377-83.
Traces the development of the word unicorn, as a mistranslation of the original Hebrew term for wild ox, and offers much information about unicorns in art and in particular the medieval medical and pharmacological beliefs about its horn and the tusk of the narwhal (thought to be a unicorn's horn) as items of trade in the Middle Ages.

1372. Jossua, Jean-Pierre. *La licorne: Images d'un couple.* Paris: Les Editions du Cerf, 1985.
Focusses specifically on artistic representation of the young girl capturing the unicorn in a wood.

1373. Planche, Aline. "La double licorne ou le chasseur chassé." *MR* 30 3-4 (1980): 237-46.
Looks at the alternate characterizations of the unicorn as terrifying and docile. Also covers the sex of unicorns.

1374. Shepard, Odell. *The Lore of the Unicorn.* New York: Harper and Row, 1979.
Historically reviews the lore of the unicorn from the earliest extant records in the east. Contains only a few illustrations.

1375. South, Malcolm. "The Unicorn." *Mythical and Fabulous Creatures* (item 1341), pp. 5-26.
A general introduction to the iconography of the unicorn.

1376. Verlet, Pierre, and Francis Salet. *The Lady and the Unicorn.* London: Thames and Hudson, 1961.
This is a coffee-table book with color reproductions and descriptions of the Unicorn Tapestries of the Musée Cluny.

[Werewolf]

1377. Ménard, Phillipe. "Les histoires de loup-garou au Moyen Age." *Symposium in honorem Prof. M. de Riquer.* Edited by Carlos Alvar, et al. Barcelona: Universitat de Barcelona: Quaderns Crema, 1984, pp. 209-38.
Collects medieval stories of werewolves or of human-wolf transformations and studies their similiarities and differences.

1378. Otten, Charlotte F., ed. *Werewolves in Western Culture: A Lycanthropy Reader*. Syracuse: Syracuse Univ. Press, 1986. Essays on werewolves, which survey the tradition.

1379. Quénet, Sophie. "Mises en récit d'une métamorphose: Le loup-garou." (item 1377), pp. 137-63.
Studies pagan and Christian writers' descriptions of the werewolf and its transformation from antiquity through the Middle Ages and Renaissance, with citations from a variety of different texts commenting upon this beast.

[Woman-Headed Snake]

1380. Bonnell, John K. "The Serpent with the Human Head in Art and in Mystery Play." *AJA*, n.s., 21 (1917): 255-91.
Discusses literary sources for this common image, its first appearances in the art of the thirteenth and fourteenth centuries, and its transmission through the mystery plays. Examines specific texts and art works up through the seventeenth century. **See also item 1327.**

1381. Courcelle, Pierre. "Le serpent à face humaine dans la numismatique impériale du Ve siècle." *Mélanges d'archéologie et d'histoire offerts à André Piganiol*. Edited by Raymond Chevallier. Vol. 1. Paris: S.E.V.P.E.N., 1964, pp. 343-53.
Examines coins bearing the image of a human-faced serpent from the fourth and fifth centuries and discusses this image's symbolism.

1382. Flores, Nona C. "'Effigies amicitiae. . .veritas inimicitiae': Antifeminism in the Iconography of the Woman-Headed Serpent in Medieval and Renaissance Art and Literature." *The Medieval World of Nature* (item 1148), pp. 167-95.
Focusses on the iconographic representation of the woman-headed serpent in art and literature from the thirteenth to the seventeenth centuries, looking only at "the dracontopede of Genesis 3 and analogous biform creatures associated with this figure" (not including folklore or romance) and at "examples in which the

depiction of the woman-headed snake underlines the sins ascribed to Eve at the Fall—primarily lust, pride, and fraud—all of which provided a basis for centuries of antifeminist moralizing" (169).

1383. Hoffeld, Jeffrey M. "Adam's Two Wives." *BMMA* 26 (1967-68): 430-40.
In the process of explaining the iconography of "a hexagonal boxwood statue base at the Cloisters" (430), the writer studies the medieval iconography of Lilith, first wife of Adam, especially as a woman-headed snake. Plates.

1384. Kelly, Henry Ansgar. "The Metamorphoses of the Eden Serpent during the Middle Ages and the Renaissance." *Viator* 2 (1971): 301-28.
Looks at the traditions and reasons behind the different depictions of the serpent with a woman's head. With plates.

[Yale]

1385. Druce, George Claridge. "Notes on the History of the Heraldic Jall or Yale." *AJ* 68 (1911): 173-99.
A history of the yale as it appears in art and literature throughout the Middle Ages. Many plates.

1386. George, Wilma. "The Yale." *JWCI* 31 (1968): 423-28.
Examines descriptions and illustrations of the yale from Pliny through the medieval encyclopaedists, and concludes that this animal is the Indian water buffalo.

1387. McCulloch, Florence. "L'éale et la centicore—deux bêtes fabuleuses." *Mélanges offerts à Rene Crozet à l'occasion de son soixante-dixième annivérsaire.* Edited by Pierre Gallais. Vol. 2. Poitiers: Centre d'études supérieures de civilisation médiéval, 1966, pp. 1167-72.
Looks at the descriptions of these two beasts as well as the basilisk and the confusion between them in texts and manuscript miniatures, especially in the illustrated *L'Image de Monde* of Gossuin de Metz and the manuscripts of Pierre de Beauvais' bestiary.

ANIMALS, MARINE

General

1388. Aldrovandi, Ulisse. *De piscibvs libri V et de cetis liber vnvs.*
      Bononiae: N. Tebaldinum, 1613.
      An important Renaissance source for medieval lore about fish and
      whales.

1389. Tucci, Hannelore Zug. "Il Mondo medievali dei pesci tra realtà e
      immaginazione," (item 1250), pp. 291-360.
      This learned and wide-ranging article is firmly based on patristic
      sources. It considers the various ways that fish were seen in religion,
      folklore, and literature during the Middle Ages and includes
      discussions of fish as food and of the whale and dolphin.

By Specific Type

[Barnacle]

1390. Heron-Allen, Edward. *Barnacles in Nature and Myth.* London:
      Oxford Univ. Press, 1928.
      Examines texts on, and iconographical depictions of, barnacles
      crossculturally and throughout history. Offers numerous examples
      from the medieval period.

[Conch]

1391. Barb, A. A. "Diva Matrix: A Faked Gnostic Intaglio in the
      Possession of P. P. Rubens and the Iconography of a Symbol."
      JWCI 16 (1953): 193-238.

Considers the symbolism of snail, conch, cockle, and shell as well as the iconography of the uterus.

[Crab]

1392. Deonna, W. "The Crab and the Butterfly: A Study in Animal Symbolism." *JWCI* 17 (1954): 47-86.
Considers the crab especially when it appears with the butterfly, particularly on Roman coins and in Renaissance emblem representations derived from them.

[Crocodile]

1393. Burton, T. L. "The Crocodile as the Symbol of an Evil Woman: A Medieval Interpretation of the Crocodile-Trochilus Relationship." *Parergon* 20 (1978): 25-33.
Focusses on the exemplum of the crocodile in the Middle English *Sidrak and Bocchus.*

1394. Druce, George Claridge. "The Symbolism of the Crocodile in the Middle Ages." *AJ* 66 (1909): 311-38.
A thorough study, with many illustrations from medieval art works.

[Cuttlefish]

1395. Gerhardt, Mia L. "Knowledge in Decline: Ancient and Medieval Information on 'Ink Fishes' and Their Habits." *Vivarium* 4 (1966): 144-75.
Cites numerous passages from antique and medieval writers on this creature and comments on their accuracy and their differing responses.

[Oyster]

1396. Donavan, Mortimer J. "Three Notes on Chaucerian Marine Life." *PQ* 31 (1952): 439-41.
Considers eels, oysters, and pickerel.

1397. McCulloch, Florence. "Mermecolion—A Mediaeval Latin word for 'Pearl Oyster.'" *MS* 27(1965): 331-34.

Studies the literary and iconographic treatment of the pearl oyster in various manuscripts.

[Pike]

1398. Hoffman, Richard C. "The Protohistory of the Pike in Western Culture." *The Medieval World of Nature* (item 1148), pp. 61-76..
Examines the history of this fish and its representation in medieval and Renaissance literature.

[Pilot Fish]

1399. Copenhaver, Brian P. "A Tale of Two Fishes: Magical Objects in Natural History from Antiquity through the Scientific Revolution." *JHI* 52 (1991): 373-98.
Examines the initial development of interest in the magical qualities of the pilot fish and electric ray (mainly attributed to etymological error concerning the meaning of their names) in antiquity and traces the beliefs about these fish (including their medieval Christian allegorical value) in detail as they develop up into the eighteenth century.

[Scallop]

1400. Bellew, G. "Escallops in Armory." *The Scallop: Studies of a Shell and Its Influence on Human Kind.* Edited by Ian Cox. London: The Shell Transport and Trading Company, 1957, pp. 89-104.
A detailed examination of the scallop in medieval heraldry, with plates.

1401. Bratschkova, Maria. "Die Muschel in der Antiken Kunst." *BIAB* 12 (1938): 1-131.
This is the definitive study of the scallop shell as a resurrection image. Tracing the motif from its connection with Aphrodite in antiquity through its development as a resurrection symbol in early Christian and Byzantine art, the author provides a lengthy catalogue

of depictions of scallop shells in various late antique and early
medieval art works.

1402. Hohler, Christopher. "The Badge of St. James," (item 1400), pp. 49-
70.
Examines the legend of the Apostle James, his shrine at
Compostella, and how the scallop became his "badge." Plates of
sculpture and paintings containing scallop shell motifs.

1403. Köster, Kurt. *Pilgerzeichen und Pilgermuscheln vom
Mittelalterlichen Santiagostrassen: Saint Leonard, Rocamadour,
Saint-Gilles, Santiago de Compostela.* Schleswiger Funde und
Gesamtüberlieferung. Neumünster: K. Wachholtz, 1983, pp.
119-55.
Studies the scallop shell as a symbol of pilgrimage especially in
relation to St. James of Compostella's shrine.

1404. _____. "Pilgrimsschelpen en -tekens van Santiago de Compostela
en de Europese bedevaartwegen naar Sint-Jacob in Galicie."
Santiago de Compostela. 1000 Jaar Europese Bedevaart.
Centrum vor Kunst en Cultuur Sint-Pieters abdij-Gent. Edited
by P. Caucci von Sauclen, et al. Ghent: Gemeen Tekridiet,
1985, pp. 85-95.
Studies the distribution of scallop shells found in recent times and
carried by pilgrims from Compostella as signs of pilgrimage routes.

1405. Steppe, J. K. "De iconografie van de Heilige Jacobus de Meersdere
(Santiago)." (See item 1404 above), pp. 129-52.
Studies the scallop shell along with other aspects of St. James's
iconography.

[Serra or Sawfish]

1406. Druce, George Claridge. "Legend of the Serra or Saw-Fish." *PSAL,*
2d ser., 31 (1918-19): 20-35.
Traces the diverse iconographic treatments of this beast, with plates.

[Whale] (considered a fish in the Middle Ages)

1407. Coulter, Cornelia Catlin. "The Great Fish in Ancient and Medieval
        Story." *TAPA* 57 (1926): 32-50.
        Looks chiefly at Eastern and Greco-Roman legends of whales with
        a few medieval accounts.

1408. Runeberg, J. "Le conte d' île-poisson.'" *MSNH* 3 (1902): 345-95.
        Provides relevant passages in French translation concerning the
        whale as an island from many literatures crossculturally. Then
        proceeds to compare the different ways the theme is handled.

1409. Ziolkowski, Jan. "Folklore and Learned Lore in Letaldus' Whale
        Poem." *Viator* 15 (1984): 107-18.
        Treats the whale among some patristic writers.

                Animals, Marine, Imaginary, by Specific Type

[Sea serpent]

1410. Heuvelmans, Bernard. "The Age of Terror, from Antiquity to the
        Middle Ages." *In the Wake of the Sea-Serpents.* New York: Hill
        and Wang, 1968, pp. 80-90.
        Offers descriptions of sea serpents in literature and art with a
        discussion of their sources.

[Sirens and Related Types]

1411. Barb, A. A. "Antaura. The Mermaid and the Devil's Grandmother."
        JWCI 29 (1966): 1-23.
        Covers many different forms of the female siren in antiquity and
        the Middle Ages crossculturally, and relates them to Christianity and
        other competing religions. Includes head-ache-causing demons that
        come from the sea and varieties that steal children.

1412. Berman, Ruth. "Mermaids" and "Sirens." *Mythical and Fabulous Creatures* (item 1341), pp.133-45 and pp. 147-53.
Distinguishes the mermaid from the siren and gives the history of each. Explains why and how they are so often confused.

1413. Cella, Mariaserena. "Le fonti letterarie della simbologia medieval: i bestiari." *Il Romanico, Atti del seminario di studi diretto da Piero Sanpaolesi. . .1973.* Edited by Maria Laurea Tomea. Milan: Istituto per la Storia dell' Arte Lombarda, 1975, pp. 181-90.
This article is rather misleadingly titled since it is actually about the siren in Romanesque sculpture in Lombardy rather than the bestiary. It offers a useful list of Italian representations and some plates.

1414. Clier-Colombani, Françoise. *Le fée mélusine au Moyen Age: Images, mythes, et symboles.* Paris: Le Léopard d'Or, 1991.
Focusses on iconographical images in nine illuminated manuscripts and seven incunables with wood cuts of the fifteenth century. Contains many plates.

1415. Courcelle, Pierre. "L'interpretation évhémériste des sirènes-courtisanes jusqu'au XIIe siècle." *Gesellschaft, Kultur, Literatur Rezeption und Originalität im Wachsen Einer Europäischen Literatur und Geistigkeit Beiträge Luitpold Wallach Gewidmet.* Edited by Karl Bosl. Stuttgart: Anton Hiersemann, 1975, pp. 33-48.
Surveys the tradition of siren as courtesan from antiquity through the Middle Ages.

1416. Deonna, W. "La sirène femme-poisson." *RA*, 5th ser., 27 (1928): 18-25.
Briefly considers the change from the twelfth century onward, in depictions of the siren, who first appears with a bird's body and then acquires a fish's tail in Christian iconography.

1417. Faral, Edmond. "La queue de poisson des sirènes." *Romania* 74 (1952): 433-506.
Looks historically at the changing description of sirens in texts, focussing specifically on the change from a half-woman half-bird to a half-woman half-fish.

1418. Jalabert, Denise. "De l'art oriental antique à l'art roman: Recherches sur la faune et la flore romanes. II: Les Sirènes." *BMon* 95 (1936): 433-71.
       Investigates in detail from antiquity through the Middle Ages two types of sirens, one with fish body and one with bird body, and their eventual appearance in Romanesque capital sculpture. Considers related iconographic features such as diadems and feathers. Plates and line drawings.

BIRDS

General

1419. Aldrovandi, Ulisse. *Ornithologiae hoc est de avibvs historiae libri XII.* Bononiae: N. Tebaldinum, 1599.
       Contains a great deal of medieval bestiary lore on various birds.

1420. Armstrong, Edward A. *The Folklore of Birds: An Enquiry into the Origin & Distribution of Some Magico-Religious Traditions.* New York: Dover, 1970.
       Organized by types of birds, some mythical or supernatural. The range is great, from antiquity through the Middle Ages and into the modern period. The work is accompanied by numerous photographs.

1421. Belon, Pierre. *L'histoire de la nature des oyseaux avec leur descriptions & naïfs portraicts retirez du naturel.* Paris: Cauellat,1555.
       Book one deals with birds generally, covering such subjects as conception, the nature of eggs, birds as food and as objects of study for past generations. In the following six books, Belon goes through each bird in turn, providing an illustration, and offering the natural history of each from a late medieval and early Renaissance perspective.

1422. Bombardier. "Chaucer Ornithologist." *Blackwood's Magazine* 256 (1944): 120-25.
Discusses the sources for Chaucer's beliefs about birds in the *Parlement of Foules* and situates them in their medieval contexts.

1423. Clark, Willene B., ed. and trans. *The Medieval Book of Birds: Hugh of Fouilloy's Aviarium.* Binghamton, NY: Medieval and Renaissance Texts and Studies, 1992.
A popular work, existing in ninety-six manuscripts, Hugh of Fouilloy's *Aviarium* is the only moralized nature treatise devoted entirely to birds. Clark provides a pictorial background for her many illustrations, a bibliography, and a catalogue of illuminated aviary manuscripts as well.

1424. Druce, George Claridge. "Notes on Birds in Mediaeval Church Architecture." *The Antiquary* 50 (1914): 248-53, 298-301, and 381-85.
Compares the depiction of various birds in ecclesiastical architecture to that in bestiaries, discussing their symbolism and how birds in architecture can be identified through the bestiaries. Contains detailed information on various birds and many plates.

1425. Harrison, Thomas P. *They Tell of Birds: Chaucer, Spenser, Milton, Drayton.* Austin: Univ. of Texas Press, 1956.
Provides for each of the authors discussed a list of allusions to birds in their works, as well as some of the traditions on which the allusions were based. In the case of Chaucer, there are plates from medieval manuscripts, and an index for each bird, showing where it appears in the poet's work.

1426. _____, and F. David Hoeniger, eds. *The Fowles of Heauen: History of Birdes by Edward Topsell.* Austin: Univ. of Texas Press, 1972.
This modern edition of Topsell's famous early seventeenth-century work listing birds alphabetically offers illustrations and very detailed information in an easily available form.

1427. Hinckley, Henry Barrett. "Science and Folk-lore in *The Owl and Nightingale*." *PMLA* 47 (1932): 303-14.

In discussing how the poem reflects various medieval scientific ideas of its time, Hinckley treats many beliefs about different birds from naturalist and exegetical sources.

1428. Ingersoll, Ernest. *Birds in Legend, Fable, and Folklore.* Detroit: Singing Tree Press, 1968.
This reprint of a 1923 study does not specifically concern medieval Europe. The author ranges widely across cultures, times, and places and organizes the book by uses of birds, such as messenger birds in the story of Noah's Ark. The sections on Tradition and Festival may be the most useful for the medievalist. Index of birds.

1429. Klingender, Francis. "St. Francis and the Birds of the Apocalypse." *JWCI* 16 (1953): 13-23.
Traces the iconographical tradition of St. Francis's Sermon to the Birds and how it was linked to depictions of the angel in Revelations calling down the birds of prey on human beings. There are plates of miniatures from medieval manuscripts.

1430. Martin, Ernest W. *The Birds of the Latin Poets.* Stanford: Stanford Univ. Press, 1914.
Though the focus of this book is on Roman attitudes to birds, it provides the non-specialist a good starting point for the medieval response to the birds of antiquity.

1431. Parmelee, Alice. *All the Birds of the Bible: Their Stories, Identifications and Meaning.* New York: Harper Brothers, 1959.
Chiefly a coffee-table book for religious bird lovers. The author looks at all the places that birds appear in the Bible and discusses the historicity of the descriptions. There are a number of illustrations from different sources, but the pictures are not identified specifically enough for the student to find them.

1432. Rowland, Beryl. *Birds with Human Souls.* Knoxville: Univ. of Tennessee Press, 1978.
Although many of the allusions and plates here pertain to medieval symbolism of birds, the information ranges so widely in date and

place as to provide chiefly an overview of the subject. There is a full index and a select bibliography. Reviewed by John B. Friedman in *JEGP* 79 (1980): 102-5.

1433. Stuart, Dorothy M. *A Book of Birds and Beasts: Legendary, Literary, and Historical.* London: Methuen, 1957.
Examines the interest in three specific animal types, (birds, dogs, and horses), from antiquity through the late nineteenth century, providing examples from texts and works of art in which the animals appear. The focus is not on medieval animals, though medieval treatments are discussed.

1434. Wittkower, Rudolf. "Miraculous Birds." *JWCI* 1 (1937-38): 253-57.
Looks at depictions of various birds (among them the Ichneumon, eagle, and the roc), either fighting snakes or carrying elephants. Especially useful sections are those on the *Physiologus* in Beatus manuscripts and on the Roc.

1435. Yapp, Brunsdon. *Birds in Medieval Manuscripts.* London: The British Library, 1981.
Organized by bird, the book provides many color plates taken from forty-one manuscripts, chiefly bestiaries, ranging in date from the seventh to the fifteenth centuries.

Birds by Specific Type

[Cock]

1436. Allen, Don Cameron. "Vaughan's 'Cock-Crowing' and the Tradition." *ELH* 21 (1954): 94-106.
Considers the symbolism of the cock in antiquity and the Middle Ages.

1437. Baird-Lange, Lorrayne. "Priapus Gallinaceous: The Role of the Cock in Fertility and Eroticism in Classical Antiquity and the Middle Ages." *SI* 7-8 (1981-82): 81-111.
Provides a great deal of lore on the cock as an erotic symbol, though it focusses much more on antiquity than on the Middle Ages.

1438. Callisen, S. A. "The Iconography of the Cock on the Column." *AB* 21 (1939): 160-78.
Examines the iconography of this symbol in late antique and early Christian art. Concludes that the cock on a column as it appears in Early Christian iconography is of Gallic origin and is taken over by Byzantine art at a later period. Some plates.

1439. Forsyth, Ilene H. "The Theme of Cockfighting in Burgundian Romanesque Sculpture." *Speculum* 53, no. 2 (April 1978): 252-82.
Offers a wealth of ancient and patristic lore on the cock, showing that this bird was a symbol of immortality in Roman and early Christian art. The cock in Romanesque art comes to represent the priest in his battle with sin and Satan. Numerous illustrations complement the article.

1440. Rowland, Beryl. "The Wisdom of the Cock." *Third International Beast Epic, Fable and Fabliau Colloquium Munster 1979 Proceedings* (item 1224), pp. 340-55.
Treats the cock's patristic and folkloric associations with wisdom.

[Crow]

1441. Ruberg, Uwe. "Signifikative Vogelrufe: Ain rapp singt all zeit 'cras cras cras.'" *Natura Loquax: Naturkunde und allegorische Naturdeutung vom Mittelalter bis zur frühen Neuzeit.* Edited by Wolfgang Harms and Heimo Reinitzer. Frankfort-Berne-Circencester: Peter Lang, 1981, pp. 183-204.
Considers the folklore and prophetic significance of the crow and its utterance.

[Dove]

1442. Shoaf, R. A. "Dante's 'columbi' and the Figuralism of Hope in the *Divine Comedy.*" *DS* 93 (1975): 27-59.
Contains much exegetical lore on doves.

[Eagle]

1443. Ameisenowa, Zofja. "Animal-Headed Gods, Evangelists, Saints and Righteous Men." *JWCI* 12 (1949): 21-45.
Studies human-animal conflations with attention to the eagle-headed evangelist. Some plates.

1444. Sheldon, Susan Eastman. "The Eagle: Bird of Magic and Medicine in a Middle English Translation of *Kyranides.*" *TSE* 22 (1977): 1-31.
Provides much medieval lore on the eagle and also on the vulture, with which it was often confused. Includes a section on the eagle from the Middle English *Kyranides* and a Latin "Letter of the Vulture."

1445. Wittkower, Rudolf. "Eagle and Serpent." *Allegory and the Migration of Symbols* (item 272), pp. 15-44.
Studies the diffusion of the motif of a combat between eagle and serpent in several cultures. Especially useful on the appearance of the motif in Romanesque church capital carving. Many plates.

[Falcon]

1446. Abeele, Baudouin van den. *La fauconnerie dans les lettres françaises du XIIe au XIVe siècle.* Louvain: Louvain Univ. Press, 1990.
Considers references to falconry in medieval French literature drawing on 153 different texts. There are indices of authors and of motifs as well. Reviewed by Larry Crist in *Speculum* 67, no. 3 (July 1992): 752-4.

1447. _____. *La fauconnerie au Moyen Age.* Paris: Editions Klincksieck, 1994.

This book treats acquisition, training, and veterinary care of falcons in four chapters, drawing information from vernacular falconry handbooks, encyclopaediae and compendiae like that of Albert the Great, imaginative literature, and iconographic representations. A large part deals with the medical care of falcons. There is an extensive bibliography.

1448. Braekman, W. L., ed. *Of Hawks and Horses: Four Late Middle English Prose Treatises.* Scripta: Medieval and Renaissance Texts and Studies, no. 16. Brussels: Omirel, 1986.
Detailed information, chiefly of a veterinary nature, on the care of both hawks and horses.

1449. Oggins, Robin S. "Falconry and Medieval Views of Nature." *The Medieval World of Nature* (item 1148), pp. 47-60.
Traces views about birds of prey in medieval writing from about the fifth through the fifteenth centuries and connects these with changing concepts of the natural world. Considers among other topics, hawk medicine and training and the growing realism both in treatises on falconry themselves and in their actual depictions of the birds in manuscript painting.

1450. Wood, Casey A., and Marjorie F. Fyfe. *The Art of Falconry Being the 'De arte Venandi cum Avibus' of Frederick II of Hohenstaufen.* Stanford: Stanford Univ. Press, 1943.
Contains many plates, some from medieval manuscripts, a comprehensive glossary of falconry terms, and an extensive annotated bibliography of ancient, medieval, and modern falconry.

[Goldfinch]

1451. Friedmann, Herbert. *The Symbolic Goldfinch: Its History and Significance in European Devotional Art.* Bollingen Series, no. 7. New York: Pantheon Books, 1946.
Studies, in an easy-to-use format, the goldfinch, especially in enthroned-madonna paintings, in many regions, and periods of European art. The emphasis is more on easel than on manuscript

painting. Accompanied by very full bibliographies, an index, and plates.

[Hoopoe]

1452. Dawson, Warren R. "The Lore of the Hoopoe." *The Bridle of Pegasus: Studies in Magic, Mythology and Folklore.* London: Methuen, 1930, pp.126-42 .
Deals chiefly with the bird in antiquity, though there is some discussion of it in the Middle Ages.

[Lark]

1453. Bawcutt, Priscilla. "The Lark in Chaucer and Some Later Poets." *YWES* 2 (1972): 5-12.
Explores the symbolism associated with this bird.

[Nightingale]

1454. Baird, Joseph L., and John R. Kane, eds. and trans. *Rossignol: An Edition and Translation with an Introductory Essay on the Nightingale Tradition by J. L. Baird.* Kent, OH: Kent State Univ. Press, 1978.
The introduction to the text and translation of John Peacham's Old French poem "Rossignol" provide a detailed description of the function and symbolism of this bird in Western literature.

1455. Chandler, Albert R. "The Nightingale in Greek and Latin Poetry." *CJ* 30 (1934): 78-84.
Traces the various traditions of the bird linked with the myth of a mother who murdered her son, symbolizing the poet, singing spring love songs, or singing God's praises.

1456. Pfeffer, Wendy. *The Change of Philomel: The Nightingale in Medieval Literature.* New York: Peter Lang, 1985.
Treats the nightingale in allegorical and debate poetry, religious literature, the *Carmina Burana*, and the troubadors, trouveres, and minnesingers.

1457. _____. "Spring, Love, Birdsong: The Nightingale in Two
      Cultures." *Beasts and Birds of the Middle Ages* (item 1152), pp.
      88-95.
      Discusses briefly the symbolism of the nightingale's song.

[Paradise, Bird of]

1458. Fisher, A . S . T. "Birds of Paradise." *N&Q* 188 (1945): 95-98.
      Treats the early Renaissance poet John Skelton's confusion of a
      ringed parakeet and a bird of paradise.

[Partridge]

1459. Friedmann, Herbert. "A Painting by Pantoja and the Legend of the
      Partridge of St. Nicolas of Tolentino." *AQ* 22 (1959): 45-55.
      Looks at this Spanish painter (1551-1608) and his depiction of the
      legend. In discussing the iconographic portrayal of the partridge,
      the author provides a good deal of information about the bird in the
      Middle Ages. Some plates.

[Peacock]

1460. Löther, Helmut. *Der Pfau in der Altchristlichen Kunst.* Leipzig:
      Dieterich, 1929.
      Studies the peacock in catacomb painting and other early Christian
      monuments as a symbol of immortality.

[Pelican]

1461. Druce, George Claridge. "The Pelican in the Black Prince's
      Chantry." *CCC* 18 (1934): 10-14.
      Describes the iconography of the pelican in sculpture and bestiaries
      made between the tenth and the fourteenth centuries.

1462. Gerhardt, Cristoph. "Arznei und Symbol. Bemerkungen zum
      Altdeutschen Geiertraktat mit einem Ausblick auf das
      Pelikanexempel." *Natura Loquax* (item 1441), pp. 109-82.

This study of the well-known allegory of the Pelican in its piety, feeding its young with flesh from its own breast as a symbol of Christ, is illustrated with a group of reproductions from manuscripts and wall paintings.

1463. _____. *Die Metamorphosen des Pelikans. Exempel und Auslegung in Mittelalterlicher Literatur. Mit Beispielen aus der Bildenden Kunst und einem Bildenhang.* Frankfurt and Bern: Peter Lang, 1979.

This "book" is actually a brief essay on the background and development of the allegory of the pelican described in item 1462, accompanied by an excellent collection of plates showing the allegory of the pelican in German manuscript illumination and church sculpture.

1464. Graham, Victor E. "The Pelican as Image and Symbol." *RLC* 36 (1962): 235-43.

Ranges widely from antiquity to the present and considers the bird in several cultures.

[Raven]

1465. Messelken, Hans. *Die Signifikanz von Rabe und Taube in der Mittelalterlichen Deutschen Literatur.* Inaugural diss., Univ. of Cologne, 1965.

This work's discussion of the raven and dove in Middle-High-German literature is illustrated by numerous passages of poetry. It also covers the classical and Biblical background in its brief introduction to each animal's literary history.

[Robin]

1466. Lack, David. *Robin Redbreast.* Oxford: Clarendon, 1950.

Surveys this bird's tradition in the art and literature of England. Though the book concentrates on the Neo-classic and Romantic periods, there is some material relating to the Middle Ages as well.

[Thrush]

1467. Donovan, Mortimer J. "*Sir Thopas,* 772-774." *NM* 57 (1956): 237-46.
   Beginning with this passage from Chaucer, Donovan discusses the various associations thrushes had in the Middle Ages.

Birds, Imaginary, by Specific Type

[Caladrius]

1468. Druce, George Claridge. "The Caladrius and Its Legend Sculptured upon the Twelfth-Century Doorway of Alne Church, Yorkshire." *AJ* 69 (1912): 381-416.
   Provides a detailed account of antique and medieval lore on this bird.

[Phoenix]

1469. Broek, R. van den. *The Myth of the Phoenix According to Classical and Early Christian Traditions.* Translated by I. Seger. Leiden: Brill, 1972.
   Detailed descriptions of the phoenix myth in illuminated manuscripts and other works of art in different cultures with an account of earlier scholarship on the subject.

1470. Gerhardt, Cristoph. "Der Phoenix auf dem dürren Baum." *Natura Loquax* (item 1441), pp. 73-108.
   Provides considerable background on the phoenix in the context of Wonders of the East literature.

1471. Heffernan, Carol Falvo. *The Phoenix at the Fountain: Images of Women and Eternity in Lactantius' 'Carmen de Ave Phoenice' and the Old English 'Phoenix.'* Newark: Univ. of Delaware Press, 1988.

Considers these two works in the context of the history of phoenix symbolism, especially with regard to female gestation and menstruation.

1472. Hubaux, Jean, and Maxime Leroy. *Le mythe du phénix dans les littératures grecque et latine.* Liège: Faculté de Philosophie et Lettres, 1939.
Provides the texts with French translations and with commentaries of the four longest sources on the phoenix legend.

1473. McDonald, Sister Mary Francis. "Phoenix Redivivus." *The Phoenix* 14 (1960): 187-206.
Traces the bird from Herodotus and Hesiod to the Middle Ages and touches on "The Phoenix in Hebrew Literature," "The Phoenix of the Physiologus," "The Phoenix of the Christian Fathers," and "The Phoenix in the Tradition of Christian Art." Includes numerous quotations from authors about this bird.

1474. McMilan, Douglas J. "The Phoenix." *Mythical and Fabulous Creatures* (item 1341), pp. 59-74.
A general introduction to the iconography of the phoenix.

1475. Mermier, Guy. "The Phoenix: Its Nature and Its Place in the Tradition of the *Physiologus*." *Beasts and Birds of the Middle Ages: The Bestiary and Its Legacy* (item 1152), pp. 69-87.
Describes the symbolism of the phoenix specifically in French bestiaries of the late Middle Ages.

1476. Reinitzer, Heimo. "Vom Vogel Phenix: Über Naturbetractung und Naturdeutung." *Natura Loquax* (item 1441), pp. 17-72.
Patristic and later medieval discussion of the phoenix.

[Roc]

1477. McMilan, Douglas J. "The Roc." *Mythical and Fabulous Creatures* (item 1341), pp. 75-83.
A general introduction to the iconography of the roc.

1478. Wittkower, Rudolf. "'Roc': An Eastern Prodigy in a Dutch Engraving." *Allegory and the Migration of Symbols* (item 272), pp. 94-96.
Offers a few accounts among early Eastern travelers, like Benjamin of Tudela and Marco Polo, of this creature.

HUNTING, IMAGES OF

1479. Abeele, Baudouin van den. *La littérature cynégétique.* Typologie des sources du Moyen Age, no. 75. Turnhout: Brepols, 1996.
A bibliographical study on the didactic texts relating to falcony and hunting, first in Latin and then from the thirteenth century onward in the vernacular. Surveys this literature, indicating directions of future research. Stongly grounded in the material culture of the Middle Ages. Seven miniatures make up an appendix.

1480. Barkan, Leonard. "Diana and Actaeon: The Myth as Synthesis." *ELR* 10 (1980): 317-59.
Investigates the changing significance and iconography of this Ovidian myth from the Middle Ages through the Renaissance.

1481. Ceresoli, A. *Bibliografia della opere Italiane Latine e Greche su la Caccia, la Pesca e la Cinologia.* Bologna: Forni, 1969.
Includes much Italian medieval material.

1482. Cómez, R. "La chasse dans la miniature gothique Castillane du XIIIe siècle." *La Chasse au Moyen Age* (item 1351), pp. 527-33.
Chiefly a collection of hunting miniatures drawn from Castillian manuscripts.

1483. Cummins, John. *The Hound and the Hawk: The Art of Medieval Hunting.* London: Weidenfeld and Nicolson, 1988.
A good introduction to hunting in the Middle Ages, including chapters on dogs and the different types of prey such as deer and

boar and even the unicorn. Many plates and appendices of falcons and hunting dogs.

1484. Fébus or Phébus, Gaston. *Livre de la chasse.* Edited by G. Tilander. Karlshamm: Cynegetica,1971.
This treatise exists in several illustrated manuscripts of which the most famous is Paris, Bibliothèque Nationale MS fr. 616. The preface contains a very unusual defence of hunting and the miniatures offer a great deal of information on medieval animal iconography.

1485. Helsinger, Howard. "Images on the Beatus Page of Some Medieval Psalters." *AB* 53 (1971): 161-76.
Studies the way hunting images are often incorporated into the decoration for the very important psalm "Beatus Vir."

1486. Lindner, Kurt. *Bibliographie der deutschen und der niederlandischen Jagdliteratur von 1480 bis 1850.* Berlin and New York: De Gruyter, 1976.
Annotated bibliography of German and Netherlandish sources on the hunt.

1487. Madden, Dodgson Hamilton. *A Chapter of Mediaeval History: The Fathers of the Literature of Field Sport and Horses.* Port Washington, NY, and London: Kennikat, 1969.
Investigates medieval and Renaissance beliefs about field sports and horses by looking at texts of the period. Treats Albertus Magnus's views of the horse, and various authors on, and works about, hunting, fishing, and falconry such as *Le Livre du Roy Modus,* Peter Crescentiis, Gaston Phébus, Froissart, the Book of St. Albans, and the *Ars Venandi* of Frederick II.

1488. Ménard, P. "Littérature et iconographie: Les pièges dans les traités de chasse d'Henri de Ferrières et de Gaston Phébus." *La chasse au Moyen Age* (item 1351), pp. 159-88.
Studies different methods of trapping birds and animals in hunting treatises. Has a great many plates from illuminated manuscripts.

1489. Núñez Rodríguez, M. "Scènes de chasse dans la peinture de l'Espagne chrétienne." *La Chasse au Moyen Age* (item 1351) , pp. 535- 47.
Offers miniatures of hunting scenes from Spanish Romanesque manuscripts.

1490. Pearsall, Derek. "Hunting Scenes in Mediaeval Illuminated Manuscripts." *Connoisseur* 196 (1977): 170-81.
Briefly discusses the conventions and iconography of the medieval hunt, with numerous plates.

1491. Rooney, Anne. *Hunting in Middle English Literature.* Cambridge, England: Boydell and Brewer, 1993.
Concerns aristocratic views of hunting in medieval England and uses hunting manuals as guides to literary texts such as *Gawain and the Green Knight.* Aside from much material on the actual practice of hunting, the author considers allegories and topoi associated with the hunt, such as the Hunt of the World and the Hunt for Christ as a unicorn.

1492. _____, ed. *The Tretyse off Huntyng.* Scripta: Medieval and Renaissance Texts and Studies, no. 19. Brussels: Omirel, 1987.
An edition of the only known manuscript of this fifteenth-century work. Rooney's introduction also lists and describes all other known classical and medieval hunting manuals.

1493. Schwenk, Sigrid, et al., eds. *Et Multum et Multa: Beiträge zur Literatur, Geschichte und Kultur der Jagd: Festgäbe für Kurt Lindner zum 27. November 1971.* Berlin and New York: De Gruyter, 1971.
Contains various essays on medieval hunting.

1494. Strubel, Armand, and Chantal de Saulnier. *La poétique de la chasse au Moyen Age. Les livres de chasse du XIVe siècle.* Paris: Presses Universitiares de France, 1994.
Six chapters outline the tradition from antiquity, the didactic purpose, the types, the esthetic intent and the symbolic value of medieval hunting treatises. No plates but a good brief bibliography

1495. Thiébaud, J. *Bibliographie des ouvrages français sur la chasse.*
Paris: Librairie Cynégétique, 1934.
A dated but valuable bibliography of French hunting treatises, many
from the late Middle Ages.

1496. Thiébaux, Marcelle. *The Stag of Love: The Chase in Medieval
Literature.* Ithaca: Cornell Univ. Press, 1974.
Focusses on metaphors of the stag chase in medieval literature, for
example, the pursuit of love, among others, drawing from handbooks
on hunting and hunt iconography in art.

1497. Tilander, Gunnar. *Essais d'etymologie cynégétique.* Cynegetica, no.
1. Lund: Hakan Ohlssons Boktryckeri,1954; *Nouveaux essais
d'etymologie cynégétique.* Cynegetica, no. 4. Lund: Hakan
Ohlssons Boktryckeri, 1957; Mélanges d'etymologie
cynégétique. Cynegetica, no. 5. Lund: Hakan Ohlssons
Boktryckeri, 1958; *Nouveaux mélanges d'etymologie
cynégétique.* Cynegetica, no. 8. Lund: Hakan Ohlssons
Boktryckeri, 1961; *Littré et remigereau comme lexicographes
et miscellanea cynegetica.* Cynegetica, no. 17. Lund: Hakan
Ohlssons Boktryckeri, 1968.
Offers a variety of highly specialized terms from the hunt, chiefly
Old and Middle French, helpful in understanding the iconography of
the hunt in manuscript illumination and in literary works like *Sir
Gawain and the Green Knight.*

INSECTS

General

* Aldrovandus, Ulisse. *De animalibvs insectis.* Cited above as item
1210.
Includes as "insects" many members of other families.

1498. Knortz, Karl. *Die Insekten in Sage, Sitte und Literatur.* Annaberg: Grasers, 1910.
This is a very general study which incidentally refers to some medieval discussions of insects in writers like Mandeville.

1499. Tilley, Maureen A. "Martyrs, Monks, Insects, and Animals." *The Medieval World of Nature* (item 1148), pp. 93-107.
A rather impressionistic survey of animal appearances in Greco-Roman and early Jewish literature, New Testament Apocrypha, saints' lives, and the works of the Desert Fathers.

Insects by Specific Types

[Bee]

1500. Misch, Manfred. *Apis est Animal—Apis est Ecclesia. Ein Beitrag zum Verhaltnis von Naturkunde und Theologie in spätmittelalter und mittelalterlichen Literatur.* Bern and Frankfurt: Herbert Lang and Peter Lang, 1974.
Traces the image of the social life of bees as a figure for the Catholic church in St. Ambrose and in Thomas of Cantimpré's *De Apibus*.

1501. Robert-Tornow, Walter. *De Apivm mellisqve apvd veteres: significatione et symbolica et mythologica.* Berlin: Weidmann, 1893.
This Latin work collects citations on the bee in classical literature. These are arranged in an index under such topic headings as bee as a symbol of chastity or of mortality, and the like.

[Fly]

1502. Chastel, André. "A Fly in the Pigment." *FMR* 19 (1986): 61-84.

Studies the appearance of this insect as a "trade mark" in a number of Flemish realist easel painters of the fifteenth and sixteenth centuries.

1503. Pigler, André. "La mouche peinte: Un talisman." *BMHBA* 24 (1964): 47-64.

Looks at the iconographical representation of one or two flies appearing always in a particular spot on Netherlandish, Italian, and German paintings dating from the middle of the fifteenth century to 1515. Provides plates of the paintings and discusses the painted fly's representation and especially its function as a sort of magical talisman to ward off bothersome living flies.

[Scorpion]

1504. Aurigemma, Luigi. *Le signe zodiacale du scorpion dans les traditions occidentales de l'antiquité greco-latine à la Renaissance.* Civilisations et sociétés, no. 54. Paris and the Hague: Mouton, 1976.

Discusses this symbol in detail from antiquity through the Middle Ages and the Renaissance with information about literary views of scorpions. There are many plates and an extensive bibliography.

1505. Deonna, W. "Mercure et le scorpion." *Latomus* 17 (1958): 614-58.

Concerned with ancient representations of scorpions in art and their connection with Mercury.

[Snail] (not an insect but considered one)

1506. Randall, Lilian M. C. "Pea-pods and Molluscs from the Master of Catherine of Cleves Workshop." *Apollo* 100 (November 1974): 372-9.

Although it focusses on border decorations, comparing two Dutch horae of *ca.* 1440, this article does discuss in passing the iconography of pea-pods and molluscs and provides some plates including them from the two manuscripts.

1507. _____. "The Snail in Gothic Marginal Warfare." *Speculum* 37, no. 3 (July 1962): 358-67.

Investigates variations on the motif of a man and a snail fighting with chivalric weapons and armor in Flemish, French, and English thirteenth- and fourteenth-century manuscript marginalia, with some account of snail symbolism drawn from medieval writers. Many plates.

Insects, Imaginary

[Ant Lion]

1508. Druce, George Claridge. "An Account of μυρμηκολεων or the Ant Lion." *AJ* 3 (1923): 347-64.
Discusses the various legends concerning this insect or animal and its symbolism. Some plates.

1509. Gerhardt, Mia L. "The Ant-Lion. Nature Study and Interpretation of a Biblical Text, from the *Physiologus* to Albert the Great." *Vivarium* 3 (1965): 1-23.
Examines different interpretations of this animal or insect.

LANDSCAPE AND SEASONS

General

1510. Pearsall, Derek, and Elizabeth Salter. *Landscapes and Seasons of the Medieval World.* Toronto: Univ. of Toronto Press, 1973.
A good introduction to this topic. This book includes chapters on classical and medieval landcape, the landscape of Paradise, the motif

of the *Hortus Conclusus,* and the labors of the months tradition. It has plates drawn from many illuminated manuscripts.

Cliffs

1511. Mirimonde, A. P. "Le symbolisme du rocher et de la source." *JKMA* 9 (1974): 73-100.
This is a survey of natural formations, such as cliffs and springs, in Flemish painting.

Deserts

1512. Bratton, Susan Power. "The Original Desert Solitaire: Early Christian Monasticism and Wilderness." *EE* 10 (1988): 31-53.
Treats the relation of the Desert Fathers to nature and to animals.

Earth Personified

1513. Leclercq-Kadaner, J. "De la terre-mère à la luxure: A propos de la migration des symboles." *CCM* 18 (1975): 17-41.
The earth personified as "Terra" suckling serpents or humans occurs in cosmological programs of manuscript illustration, and from the Ottonian period onward, the earth was often personified as a woman embracing a tree. The image was also common in Romanesque capital sculpture. Some plates.

Labors of the Months

*   Dal, Erik, and Povl Skaå. *The Ages of Man and the Months of the Year.* Cited above as item 796.

1514. Fowler, James. "On Mediaeval Representations of the Months and Seasons." *Archaeologia* 44 (1873): 137-224.
Chiefly a collection of tables showing how the seasons are represented in manuscripts, incunabula, almanacs, and various decorative art forms such as church wood carving, stained glass, and wall paintings.

1515. Specht, Henrik. *Poetry and the Iconography of the Peasant: The Attitude to the Peasant in Late Medieval English Literature and in Contemporary Calendar Illustration.* Anglica et Americana, no. 19. Copenhagen: Univ. of Copenhagen Department of English, 1983.
In the course of discussing the peasant in Middle English literature, Specht offers a useful treatment of landscape and labors of the months iconography with numerous plates from medieval manuscripts.

1516. Tuve, Rosemond. *Seasons and Months: Studies in a Tradition of Middle English Poetry.* Reprint. Totowa, NJ and Cambridge: Brewer, 1974.
Considers different strands in the literary and artistic representation of the labors of the months. Though there are no plates, the book is very detailed, with chapters on the *Georgics* and the labors tradition, the *Secretum Secretorum*, Goliardic songs, the encyclopaedic, and artistic traditions.

1517. Webster, James Carson. *The Labours of the Months in Antique and Medieval Art to the End of the Twelfth Century.* Northwestern University Studies in the Humanities, no. 4. Evanston and Chicago: Northwestern Univ. Press, 1938.
Examines the variations in the labors tradition through time and how it reflected the customs of different localities. Webster offers a

descriptive handlist of medieval manuscripts containing depictions of labors of the months. Has numerous plates.

Mountains

1518. Lecouteux, Claude. "Aspects mythiques de la montagne au Moyen-Age." *LMAR* (1982): 43-54.
Looks at the mountain as sacred, as place for feats of heroism and of initiation, as refuge, as place of perdition and reconciliation, and as paradise or hell throughout medieval literature.

1519. Nicholson, Marjorie Hope. *Mountain Gloom, Mountain Glory.* Reprint. Baltimore: Harvester Press, 1984.
Treats the paradoxical literary representation of mountains as either hideous or beautiful and sublime, focussing mainly on the seventeenth and eighteenth centuries, but with some references back to the Bible and to classical and medieval literature, with quotations from various works throughout. Index.

Winds, Iconography of

1520. Brown, A. K. "The English Compass Points." *MA* 47, no. 2 (1978): 221-46.
Offers information on the classical and Continental backgrounds of the wind names and portraits.

1521. Obrist, Barbara. "Wind Diagrams and Medieval Cosmology." *Speculum* 72, no. 1 (January 1997): 33-84.
An in-depth discussion of the iconography of all sorts of wind diagrams, showing how "wind diagrams of the seventh to early thirteenth centuries, and the texts associated with them, reveal manifold facets of medieval ideas about the nature of the universe" (84). Plates.

1522. _____. "Les vents dans l'astronomie de Nemrot." *Astronomie et sciences humaines. Publications de l'Observatoire astronomique de Strasbourg* 6, no. 2 (1994): 57-76.
Treats the tradition which made the Biblical Nimrod an astronomer and sometime meteorologist. Some plates.

1523. Pulsiano, Phillip. "Old English Nomina Ventorum." *SN* 66 (1994): 15-26.
Studies wind names in four Old English manuscripts.

1524. Raff, Thomas. "Die ikonographie der mittelalterlichen Windpersonifikationen." *AKB* 48 (1978-79): 71-218.
A long two-part article treating the winds, the faces used to represent them, and the personified cardinal directions associated with them. The first part examines the development of the classical names for the winds and their role in cosmological symbolism. The second part deals with the winds in Christian art, looking at various wind representations in the Old (especially the book of Jonah) and New Testaments. Subsections treat windroses and other schematics of the *ara ventorum*. The work has a register of wind personfications in medieval psalter illustration and a rich bibliography and index of motifs. There are numerous black-and-white in-text illustrations.

PLANTS, GARDENS, AND TREES

Gardens

1525. Ancona, Mirella Levi d'. *The Garden of the Renaissance: Botanical Symbolism in Italian Painting.* Arte Archeologia Studi e Documenti, no. 10. Venice: Leo S. Olschki, 1977.
The author best describes this invaluable book in her foreword: "The most common plants depicted in Italian Renaissance paintings are recorded . . . . About 160 plants are systematically explained,

over 1000 publications have been consulted for the meanings and sources of plant symbolism here included and over 25,000 paintings have been examined for the tabulation of plant motifs" (7). Plants are listed alphabetically according to their English names and are accompanied by illustrations from one sixteenth-century work, symbolism and sources (often including quotations from Antiquity, and the medieval, and Renaissance periods), a list of art works depicting the plant with the different plates of paintings including the plant. At the end, in addition to a lengthy bibliography, there are indices of artists, of iconography, of paintings by places, and of "symbols, attributes, meanings and legends."

1526. Carroll-Spillecke, M., ed. *Der Gärten von der Antike bis zum Mittelalter.* Mainz am Rhein: Philipp von Zabern, 1992.
A collection of essays on gardens with that of U. Willerding, "Gärten und Pflanzen des Mittelalters," pp. 249-84 the most useful. Many high-quality color plates and bibliographies are included with each entry.

1527. Harvey, John. *Mediaeval Gardens.* London: B. T. Batsford, 1990.
Investigates medieval gardens, touching on such subjects as garden aesthetics, why they were planted, what plants were popular, and the like. The book has many plates, a bibliography, and a dated list of plants showing when different species were first mentioned as being used in gardens.

1528. MacDougall, Elisabeth Blair, ed. *Medieval Gardens.* Washington, DC.: Dumbarton Oaks, 1986.
Essays by various hands provide an excellent introduction to the iconography of medieval gardens.

1529. McLean, Teresa. *Medieval English Gardens.* New York: Viking, 1980.
Considers English gardens between the Norman Conquest and the Renaissance. Touches on monastic, urban and rural, castle and manor gardens, practical vegetable gardens, and vineyards. Includes a bibliography.

1530. Stokstad, Marilyn, and Jerry Stannard. *Gardens of the Middle Ages.* Lawrence, KS: Spencer Museum of Art, 1983.

Contains the essays "Gardens in Medieval Art," and "Medieval Gardens and Their Plants" by the editors and then offers plates from an exhibition of garden art from castle, manor, house, and town in the later Middle Ages.

Herbals

1531. Blunt, Wilfrid, and Sandra Raphael. *The Illustrated Herbal.* New York: Thames and Hudson, 1994.
        Ranging through examples from antiquity to the eighteenth century, this work considers herbals in manuscript illumination as well as in wood cut and metal engraving formats. There is a full description of various herbals and their artists, accompanied by magnificent plates.

1532. Hassall, W. O., ed. *Bodleian Library, MS. Bodley 130. Illuminated Medieval Manuscripts in Microform Ser.1.* The Bodleian Library, no. 8. Oxford: Oxford Microform Publications, 1978. 6 microfiches.
        A microfiche facsimile of the herbal and bestiary in this manuscript.

1533. Opsomer, C., and Robert Halleux. *Les herbiers, bestiaires et lapidaires.* Typologie des sources du Moyen Age occidental, no. 32. Turnhout: Brepols, 1997.
        Identical to other works in this series, which survey the subject and offer an extensive bibliography.

1534. Stannard, Jerry. "Medieval Herbals and Their Development." *Clio Medica* 9 (1974): 23-33.
        Studies the herbal from Apuleius through medieval simple collections.

Plants, Flowers, and Fruits, General

1535. Behling, Lottlisa. *Die Pflanze in der mittelalterliche Tafelmalerei.*
Weimar and Cologne: Hermann Böhlau, 1967.
A very important study of medieval plant symbolism, offering many
examples drawn from manuscript and early panel painting.

1536. _____. *Die Pflanzenwelt in der mittelalterlichen Kathedralen.*
Cologne: Hermann Böhlau, 1964.
Studies plant representations on church capitals.

1537. Cogliati, Luisa Arano, ed. *A Medieval Health Handbook. Tacuinum
Sanitatis.* New York: Braziller, 1992.
A translation of the original Italian edition.

1538. Dierbach, Johann Heinrich. *Flora Mythologica oder Pflanzenkunde
in Bezug auf Mythologie und Symbolik.* Reprint. Weisbaden:
Martin Sändig, 1970.
This reprint of an 1833 volume treats chiefly the association of
flowers and classical personages, like Narcissus.

1539. Falkenburg, Reindert L. *The Fruit of Devotion: Mysticism and the
Imagery of Love in Flemish Paintings of the Virgin and Child,
1450-1550.* Translated by Sammy Herman. Amsterdam and
Philadelphia: John Benjamin, 1994.
Treats the iconography of the tasting of fruit and the smelling of
flowers in this group of paintings, tracing its origin and turning to
devotional tracts and medieval religious experience to elaborate upon
its development. Numerous plates, bibliography, and index.

1540. Jalabert, Denise. "La flore gothique: Ses origines, son évolution du
XIIe au XVe siècles." *BMon* 91 (1932): 181-246.
Considers the way artistic developments on the Ile-de-France in the
twelfth century transformed monumental sculpture and particularly
that representing floral themes. The author studies floral depictions
from the twelfth through the sixteenth centuries.

1541. _____. *La flore sculpté des monuments du Moyen Age en France. Recherches sur les origines de l'art français*. Paris: A. and J. Picard, 1965.
An extremely detailed and descriptive book on this art in France and its origins, including numerous plates and illustrations, arranged by region.

1542. Koch, Robert A. "Flower Symbolism in the Portinari Altar." *AB* 46 (1964): 70-77.
In the course of his discussion of the fresh-cut flowers in front of the Christ-Child in Hugo van der Goes' altar piece, Koch examines the symbolism of a large number of specific flowers in the Middle Ages. He provides quotations about them from a variety of texts and offers references to depictions of flowers in other works of art.

1543. Oldenburger-Ebbers, C. S. "The Scientific Study of Nature Reflected in the Composition of the Vegetation in Late-Medieval Paintings." *Janus* 60 (1974): 59-73.
Studies fifteenth- and sixteenth-century herbals and how flowers and herbs were used in panel paintings.

1544. Opsomer-Halleux, Carmelia. *L'art de vivre en santé. Images et recettes du Moyen Age: Le Tacuinum Sanitatis (manuscrit 1041 de la Bibliothèque de L'Université de Liège)*. Alleur: Editions du Perron, 1991.
Numerous illustrations from this fascinating manuscript and an excellent bibliography.

1545. Poirion, Daniel, and Claude Thomasset, eds. *L'art de vivre au Moyen Age*. Paris: P. Lebaud, 1995.
A facsimile of the Austrian National Library manuscript Nova 2644, a magnificently illustrated copy of the *Tacuinum Sanitatis,* originally an Arabic work by Ibn Butlan on medical plants, but acquiring many additional pictures in the Middle Ages.

1546. *Tacuinum Sanitatis: Buch der Gesundheit*. Munich: Heimeran, 1976.
Facsimiles of *Tacuinum* manuscripts, with plates in color.

1547. *Western Manuscripts and Miniatures Including the Tacuinum Sanitatis.* London: Sotheby's, 1991.
A sale catalogue containing a manuscript of this fascinating text relating to gardening and the cultivation of herbs and medical plants. Presents, as well, scenes of a variety of trades, like tailoring, in medieval life. Numerous color plates.

Plants, Flowers, and Fruits, Real, by Name

[Fleur-de-Lis]

1548. Koch, Robert A. "The Origin of the Fleur-de-lis and the 'Lilium Candidum' in Art." *Approaches to Nature in the Middle Ages.* Edited by Lawrence D. Roberts. Medieval & Renaissance Texts & Studies, no. 16. Binghamton: New York: State Univ. of New York Press, 1982, pp. 109-30.
Argues learnedly that the *Lilium Candidum* of antiquity becomes the Fleur-de-lis of late medieval heraldry.

[Pansy]

1549. Behling, Lottlisa. "Viola Tricolor." *Festschrift für Heinz Ladendorf.* Edited by Peter Bloch and Gisela Zick. Cologne and Vienna: Hermann Böhlau, 1970, pp. 137-43.
Discusses the symbolism of the pansy and its relationship through its tricolored petals to the Trinity. Some plates.

[Pea]

* Randall, Lilian M. C. "Pea-pods and Molluscs." Cited above as item 1506.

[Pear]

1550. Everest, Carol A. "Pears and Pregnancy in Chaucer's *Merchant's Tale.*" *Food in the Middle Ages: A Book of Essays.* (Item 1704), pp. 161-75.

Shows how pears were considered to have medical value in the Middle Ages for morning sickness and how thus the fruit became representative of pregnancy as well as of genitalia, with discussion of how this iconography functions in *The Merchant's Tale.*

[Rose]

1551. Joret, Charles. *La rose dans l'antiquité et au Moyen Age: Histoire, legendes et symbolisme.* Reprint. Geneva: Slatkine, 1970. Originally published in 1892, this study treats the rose, especially in "Carpe Diem" and Marian contexts.

[Strawberry]

1552. Ross, Lawrence J. "The Meaning of Strawberries in Shakespeare." *SR* 7 (1960): 225-40. Though really concerned with Renaissance strawberry symbolism, this study traces the iconographic history of this plant and its fruit back into the Middle Ages.

Plants, Imaginary

1553. Emboden, William A. *Bizarre Plants: Magical, Monstrous, Mythical.* New York: Macmillan, 1974. Discusses the legends behind plants such as orchids in witchcraft and medicine, herbs of black magic, herbs of grace, dragon's blood, plants that eat animals, mandragora, fungus, and others throughout the centuries and in different countries but with much material on the medieval period and with pictures of the plants and plates of their representation in various art works.

Plants, Imaginary by Name

[Mandrake]

1554. Menhardt, Hermann. "Die Mandragora im Millstätter Physiologus, bei Honorius Augustodunensis und im St. Trudperter Hohenliede." *Festschrift für Ludwig Wolff.* Edited by Werner Schröder. Neumünster: Karl Wachholtz, 1962, pp.173-94.
Traces the allegorical association of the mandrake with the bride and groom of the Song of Songs and offers a collection of passages from medieval authors illustrating this allegory, as well as pictures of the mandrake from several medieval manuscripts.

  * Rahner, Hugo. *Greek Myths.* Cited above as item 994.
Pages 223-77 offer background on the mandrake.

1555. Randolph, Charles Brewster. "The Mandragora of the Ancients in Folk Lore and Medicine." *PAAAS* 40 (1905): 487-537.
Offers chiefly Greek and Roman accounts of the mandrake.

1556. Rouge, Gustave Le. *La Mandragore Magique, Teraphim, Golem, Androides, Homoncules.* Paris: Pierre Belfond, 1967.
Studies the myth of the mandrake and how this plant was depicted or described, with emphasis upon how it appears in literature from antiquity up to the eighteenth century.

1557. Thompson, Charles J. S. *The Mystic Mandrake.* New Hyde Park, NY: University Books, 1968.
Studies the plant as an aphrodisiac and fertility symbol in several cultures. Has extensive bibliographical footnotes.

[Moly]

  * Rahner, Hugo. *Greek Myths.* Cited above as item 994.
Pages 179-222 offer discussion of the antique and medieval conceptions of the "plant."

Trees and Forests, General

1558. Aldrovandi, Ulisse. *Dendrologiae natvralis scilicet arborvm historiae.* Bononiæ: N. Tebaldinum, 1668.
Collects lore on trees and vines.

1559. Bechmann, Roland. *Trees and Man: The Forest in the Middle Ages.* New York: Paragon House, 1990.
Focussing on western Europe, the author gives a factual, historical study of the forest and its natural resources, including such topics as farmers in the forests and fuel and lumber as well as the legislative and administrative questions raised by forests.

1560. Bratton, Susan Power. "Oaks, Wolves and Love: Celtic Monks and Northern Forests." *JFH* 33 (1989): 4-20.
Demonstrates how medieval Christians had a far greater appreciation for the environment and environmental management than had formerly been thought. Looks at the control, protection, and appreciation of the landscape in particular texts, especially in saints lives and among the Celts, with sections on wolves and oaks.

1561. Harrison, Robert Pogue. *Forests: The Shadow of Civilization.* Chicago and London: Univ. of Chicago Press, 1992.
Though the work considers forests from antiquity to the present, only chapter Two concerns the changing depictions and symbolism of the forest in the Middle Ages and Renaissance.

1562. Lewes, Ulle Erika. *The Life in the Forest*: *The Influence of the St. Giles Legend on the Courtly Tristan Story.* Chattanooga, TN: Tristania Monograph Series, 1978.
Investigates why courtly versions of the Tristan legend idealize the lovers' stay in the forest of Morois, as opposed to the other versions' depiction of this stay as one of hardship. Lewes concludes that the courtly versions are influenced by the hagiographic tradition of the Desert Fathers and especially of the Life of St. Giles.

1563. O'Reilley, Jennifer. "The Trees of Eden in Mediaeval Iconography."
*A Walk in the Garden: Biblical, Iconographical and Literary
Images of Eden* . Edited by Paul Morris and Deborah Sawyer.
Journal for the Study of the Old Testament, Supplement Series,
no. 136. Sheffield: Sheffield Academic Press, 1992, pp.167-
204.
Describes the iconographical tradition in medieval manuscripts
treating the story of the Garden of Eden and focussing on trees.
Includes plates.

1564. Pastoureau, Michel. *L'arbre: Histoire naturelle et symbolique du
bois et du fruit au Moyen Age.* Les Cahiers du Léopard d'Or,
no. 2. Paris: Léopard d'Or, 1993.
Touches on fruit trees like the apple, pear, and cherry, in the Middle
Ages with an emphasis on heraldic uses.

1565. Saunders, Corrine J. *The Forest of Medieval Romance: Avernus,
Broceliande, Arden.* Cambridge: Boydell and Brewer, 1993.
Traces the development of the forest into an archetypal motif in
medieval romances. The author studies the origins of the romance
forest from the Avernus of antiquity through the Middle Ages and
Renaissance.

1566. Stauffer, Marianne. *Der Wald: zur Darstellung und Deutung der
Natur im Mittelalter.* Bern: Francke, 1959.
Treats the "forêt aventureuse" in various literary works from
romances through the *Divine Comedy,* as well as magic forests like
Brocéliande and forest magicians like Merlin.

Trees and Branches as Visual Organizing Metaphors

1567. Bruning, E. "Het *Lignum Vitae* van den H. Bonaventura in de
Ikonografie der Veertiende Eeuw." *Het Gildeboek* 11 (1928):
15-41.
Though focussed on Bonaventure's *Lignum Vitae* treatise, this article
examines devotional tree schemata with a variety of in-text plates of
miniatures showing trees as organizing designs.

1568. Dronke, Peter. *"Arbor Caritatis." Medieval Studies for J. A. W. Bennett: Aetatis suae LXX.* Edited by P. L. Heyworth. Oxford: Clarendon, 1981, pp. 207-43.
Examines the "fluidity and unpredictability" of the visual image of the allegorical tree of charity, starting with *Piers Plowman* and proceeding through works from the close of the Middle Ages.

1569. Evans, Michael. "The Geometry of the Mind." *AAQ* 12 (1980): 33-55.
Looks at "the use of diagrammatic illustrations—especially tree diagrams—to expound theoretical ideas as well as scientific facts" (32) in the Middle Ages, with sections as follows: geometry, art and argument, "figurae," "divisio scientiae," "arbor scientiae," the schematic tree, "arbor bitutum," tabulation, "scala virtutis," "turris sapientiae," text and image, "rotae," astronomy, "ars demonstrativa," "ennuntiatio" and "interrogatio," square of opposition, "scutum fidei," visions, and the five sevens. Each section includes plates from manuscripts in illustration.

1570. Friedman, John B . "Les images mnémotechniques dans les manuscrits de l'époque gothique." *Jeux de mémoire: Aspects de la mnémotechnie médiévale.* Edited by Bruno Roy and Paul Zumthor. Montreal and Paris: Presses de l'Université de Montréal et Vrin, 1985, pp. 169-84.
Studies trees and branches as organizing metaphors in various literary works. Plates.

1571. Greenhill, Eleanor Simmons. "Die geistigen Voraussetzungen der Bilderreihe des *Speculum Virginum.*" *BGPTM* 39, no. 2 (1962): 1-170.
This edition and study of the *Speculum Virginum,* a book intended for reflection and memorization by a nun, Theodora, contains a number of miniatures from different manuscripts of the work. These depict the typical use of vines and trees of virtues and vices as organizing devices for personified ideas in the work's twelve chapters.

1572. _____. *Die Stellung der Handschrift British Museum Arundel 44 in der Überlieferung des "Speculum Virginum."* Mitteilungen der Grabmann Institut der Universität München, no. 10. Munich: Max Hueber, 1966.
Contains two reproductions of trees of vices and virtues not from the Arundel manuscript but from one in Leipzig.

1573. Langosch, Karl. "Arbores Virtutum et Viciorum." *Studien zur lateinischen Dichtung des Mittlelalters. Ehrengäbe für Karl Strecker.* Edited by W. Stach and H. Walther. Dresden: Buchdruckerei der Wilhelm und Bertha von Baensch Stiftung, 1931, pp.117-31.
Publishes the Latin rubrics from some Trees of Virtues and Vices in several manuscripts in German libraries. Each vice rubric is then paralleled with one from a corresponding virtue.

1574. Lurker, Manfred. *Der Baum in Glauben und Kunst.* Baden-Baden: Valentin Koerner, 1976.
Approaches tree motifs from a Jungian point of view. Many plates and a large bibliography.

1575. Schrade, H. *Baum und Wald in Bildern deutschen Maler.* Munich, 1937.
Largely anthropological in focus.

1576. Sicard, Patrice. *Diagrammes médiévaux et exégèse visuelle: Le 'Libellus de formatione arche' de Hugues de Saint-Victor.* Bibliotheca Victorina, no. 4. Paris and Turnhout: Brepols, 1993.
Though devoted to the exegesis of the ark of Noah, there is interesting material here on other forms of medieval diagrammatic thinking. Reviewed by Stephen Chase in *Speculum* 71, no. 3 (July 1996): 761-2.

Trees, by Name or Type

[Hawthorn]

1577. Eberly, Susan S., and David Chamberlain. "'Under the Schaddow of Ane Hawethorne Grene': The Hawthorn in Medieval Love Literature." *New Readings of Late Medieval Love Poems.* Edited by David Chamberlain. Lanham, MD: Univ. Press of America, 1993, pp. 15-39.
Considers and documents the hawthorn's long association with eroticism and sexual excess.

[Jesse Tree]

1578. Kirby, H. T. "The Jesse Tree Motif in Stained Glass. A Comparative Study of some English Examples." *Connoisseur* 141 (April 1958): 77-82.
Examines the important motif of the line of Christ and the patriarchs coming from the chest of the sleeping Jesse in church windows.

1579. Watson, Arthur. *The Early Iconography of the Tree of Jesse.* Ann Arbor, MI: University Microfilms International, 1981.
Dated, but still very useful on the motif in the later Middle Ages.

[Tree of Life]

1580. Ameisenowa, Zofja. "The Tree of Life in Jewish Iconography." *JWCI* 2 (1938-39): 326-45.
Shows how the symbolism of the tree of life was passed on to early Christianity through Jewish sepulchral art of the Late Hellenistic period. Many plates.

[Palm]

1581. Danthine, Hélène. *Le palm-dattier et les arbres sacrés dans l'iconographie de l'Asie occidentale ancienne.* Paris: Geuthner, 1937.
Background source for the late antique and early medieval palm.

1582. Mayo, Penelope C. "The Crusaders under the Palm: Allegorical Plants and Cosmic Kinship in the *Liber floridus.*" *DOP* 27(1973): 29-67.
A discussion of allegorical plants (especially those providing allegories of genealogies) in Lambert's early twelfth-century encyclopaedia, with numerous plates and sections discussing specifically "*Arbor palmarum,*" "*Lylium inter spinas,*" "*Arbor bona* and *arbor mala,*" and the "Second Dream of Nebuchadnezzar." **See also items 518-22.**

[Willow]

* Rahner, Hugo. *Greek Myths.* Cited above as item 994.
Chapter six, pp. 286-327, studies the significance of the willow in antiquity and the Middle Ages.

STONES

1583. Baisier, Léon. *The Lapidaire Chrétien: Its Composition, Its Influence, Its Sources.* Washington, DC: Catholic Univ. Press of America, 1936.
Although this work focusses on a particular lapidary, it contains much information about them in general.

1584. Ernault, Emile. *Marbode, Evêque de Rennes: Sa vie et ses oeuvres (1035-1123).* Rennes: Société archéologique d'Ille-et-Vilaine,1889.
Studies the lapidary written by Marbode of Rennes.

1585. Evans, Joan, and Mary S. Serjeantson, eds. *English Mediaeval Lapidaries.* EETS: OS, 190. London: Humphrey Milford, Oxford Univ. Press, 1933.
Includes the Old English Lapidary, the earliest known vernacular example in western Europe. There are also six other Middle English

lapidiaries with introductions and notes. Each is accompanied by a
short introduction focussing chiefly on dating and sources.

1586. Evans, Joan. *Magical Jewels of the Middle Ages and the
Renaissance.* Oxford: Clarendon, 1922.
Contains some selections from medieval texts about stones and gives
beliefs and traditions about gems and the theory of their generation.

1587. Friedman, John B. "The Prioress' Beads 'Of Smal Coral.'" *MA* 39
(1970): 301-5.
Studies the symbolism of coral, believed to be a mineral in the
Middle Ages, and coral beads in rosaries as having apotropaic or
averting powers from its original unworked branched or tree-like
shape. Because of its cruciform character, coral was believed
especially efficacious for pilgrim travellers.

1588. Halleux, Robert. "Damigéron, Evax et Marbode: L'héritage
alexandrin dans les lapidaires médiévaux." *SM*, 3d ser., 15, no.1
(1974): 327-47.
A detailed investigation of three Latin lapidaries and their influence.

1589. Keiser, George R., ed. *The Middle English "Boke of Stones": The
Southern Version.* Scripta: Medieval and Renaissance Texts
and Studies, no. 13. Brussels: Omirel, 1984.
An edition of the earliest Middle English lapidary. The author also
treats the work's importance for the Middle English romance and
provides notes showing the relationship of this text to five French
lapidaries. Reviewed by Thomas Heffernan in *Speculum* 62, no. 3
(July 1987): 769-70.

1590. Klein-Franke, F. "The Knowledge of Aristotle's Lapidary during the
Latin Middle Ages." *Ambix* 17 (1970): 137-42.
Explores evidence for the knowledge and use of this text in the
Middle Ages.

1591. Mély, Fernand de, ed. *Les lapidaires de l'antiquité et du Moyen
Age.* 3 vols. Histoire des Sciences. Paris: E. Leroux, 1896-
1902.

Volumes Two and Three treat some of the Greek lapidaries, with Greek texts, translations and discussion of different traditions.

1592. Meyer, Paul. "Les plus anciennes lapidaires français." *Romania* 38 (1909): 481-552.
Reprints a number of texts with notes on sources.

1593. Pannier, Léopold. *Les lapidaires français du Moyen Age des XIIe, XIIIe, et XIVe siècles.* Paris: F. Vieweg, 1882.
This work deals with lapidaries derived from both Christian and oriental sources. Each text is accompanied by a discussion of its sources.

1594. Studer, Paul, and Joan Evans. *Anglo Norman Lapidaries.* Paris: P. Champion, 1924.
An edition of several Anglo-Norman lapidaries with analysis and discussion of sources.

1595. Tescione, G. *Il Corallo nella storia e nell'arte.* Naples: Arte,1965.
Considers coral in the literature and art of the Middle Ages and Renaissance.

Chapter Six: Medieval Daily Life

THE BODY

Beauty and Ugliness of Body

1596. Bambeck, Manfred. "'Malin comme un singe' oder Physiognomik und Sprache." *AK* 62 (1979): 292-316.
 Examines a popular saying that the ape's ugliness reveals its ugly moral nature and ties this to physiognomic treatments of people. Relies heavily on the early Greek and Latin physiognomies published by Forster.

1597. Brewer, D. S. "The Ideal of Feminine Beauty in Medieval Literature, Especially 'Harley Lyrics,' Chaucer, and Some Elizabethans." *MLR* 50 (1955): 257-69.
 Discusses with numerous quotations and examples the device generally, each of the specific topics in the title, and then the survival of the tradition. Shows how the first brief descriptions of female beauty were Darius Phygius's portraits of Helen in *De Excidio Troiae* and of ideal beauty in Maximianus, *Elegies* I.93, which offered late classical views of feminine loveliness. Medieval

rhetorical *descriptiones* of an ideal beautiful woman appear most importantly in Matthew of Vendôme.

1598. Houdoy, Jules. *La beauté des femmes dans la littérature et dans l'art, du XIIe au XIVe siècle; Analyse du livre de A. Niphus Du Beau et L'amour.* Paris: A. Aubry, 1876.
This text is available on microfilm in "History of Women." New Haven, CT: Research Publications, 1975, Reel 388, no. 2759. Examines considerations of beauty and ugliness throughout medieval literature and art chronologically, gathering citations from numerous authors although it does not include plates. Also covers specific topics like the beauty of different body parts and hair color. Eleven appendices provide short texts important for their descriptions of beauty or ugliness from such authors as Saint Jerome, Alan of Lille, and Vincent of Beauvais. The long sixteenth-century text by Niphus with introduction completes the volume.

1599. Köhn, Anna. *Das weibliche Schönheitsideal in der ritterlichen Dichtung.* Form und Geist, no. 14. Leipzig: Hermann Eichblatt, 1930.
Treats the ideal of aristocratic female beauty, mostly in the form of quotations from the texts of German romances by such writers as Hartmann, Gottfried, and Wolfram. No plates.

1600. Ott, André G. *Etude sur les couleurs en vieux français.* Paris: Emile Bouillon, 1899.
Includes appendices on Old French words for beautiful and ugly, especially as they are derived from colors.

1601. Renier, Rodolfo, *Il tipo estetico della donna nel medioevo.* Ancona: A. G. Morelli, 1885.
Rather dated treatment of medieval female beauty based on secondary sources.

1602. Schmolke-Hasselmann, Beate. "'Camuse chose': das Hässlichkeit als ästhetisches und menschliches Problem in der altfranzösischen Literatur." *Die Mächte des Guten und Bösen.* Edited by Albert Zimmermann. Berlin and New York: De Gruyter, 1976, pp. 442-52.

Examines depictions of beauty and ugliness in Old French chansons de geste and in some romances.

1603. Wisbey, Roy A. "Die Darstellung des Hässlichen im Hoch-und Spätmittelalter." *Deutsche Literatur* (item 828 above), pp. 9-34.

Discusses the importance of the literary tradition of ugliness chiefly in Middle High German texts. The ideal ugly woman, common in some German texts, derives from the portrait of Beroe by Matthew of Vendôme. For example, the mid thirteenth-century Ulrich de Turheim in his *Rennewart* describes a marvellously ugly woman called Guote. "Would you like to know what she looked like? Huge in stature, her skin was grass green and her head was huge, with coal black hair. She had a great forehead with bristling eyebrows, moon-like eyes, ears dangling like doorjams, and her long tongue lolled outside her mouth. Her breasts were like wooded cliffs. Her skin was dull, her neck and her nose were long, and her cheeks dry; her chin curved up like a bullhorn. Her hands and arms were ugly, with griffon-like nails. Her back was huge and her belly, her bottom and her feet agreed in size. And her sex was as huge and rough-furred as a bearskin." Also treats the hideously ugly shepherd in the woods of *Yvain* and similar grotesque male figures.

1604. Ziolkowski, Jan. "Avatars of Ugliness in Medieval Literature." *MLR* 79 (1984): 1-20.

Looks at conventional descriptions of ugliness throughout medieval European literature with numerous passages cited. Also a good source on beauty since it discusses this to clarify its opposite.

Body by Parts

[Beards and Hair]

1605. French, Katherine L. "The Legend of Lady Godiva and the Image of the Female Body." *JMH* 18 (1992): 1-19.

Examines the presentation of Godiva in different versions of the legend and her iconographical similarities to Eve, the Virgin Mary, and Mary Magdalene, exploring also contemporary views of, and laws concerning, women. Her long hair is one of the particular features discussed, along with her nudity.

1606. Jochens, Jenny. "Before the Male Gaze: The Absence of the Female Body in Old Norse." *Sex in the Middle Ages: A Book of Essays.* Edited by Joyce E. Salisbury. New York and London: Garland, 1991, pp. 3-29.
Besides discussing hair, this essay also treats beauty, clothing, clothes as gender markers, the head-dress, cross-gender dressing, and ugliness. The book includes essays on such subjects as erotic magic, sex and confession, sexual practices, boy love, bestiality, physician's guides to virginity and sexuality, and the like. Focused on texts, with no plates.

   *   Ménard, Philippe. "Les emblemes de la folie dans la littérature et dans l'art." Cited below as item 1769.

1607. Reynolds, Reginald. *Beards: Their Social Standing, Religious Involvements, Decorative Possibilities, and Value in Offense and Defence though the Ages.* New York and London: Harcourt Brace Jovanovich, 1949.
Early portion treats the medieval period. According to the back cover, "Among the countless aspects of beards investigated here are the taboos and dangers of barbering; insult and punishment through the cutting of beards; the linking of hair with sin and of beards with radical politics; the mystical significance of beards; the beard as a mask; prayers for shaving; false beards; and the legend of Bluebeard." No plates, but the medievalist will find here quotations and citations from various contemporary sources.

[Brain]

1608. O'Neill, Ynez Violé. "Diagrams of the Medieval Brain: A Study in Cerebral Localization." *Iconography at the Crossroads* (item 243), pp. 91-105.
Studies the iconography of medieval medical drawings of the brain,with plates, examining how scientific thought on the division and diagramming of the brain evolved from ancient through medieval times.

[Breasts]

1609. Levy, Mervyn. *The Moons of Paradise: Some Reflections on the Appearance of the Female Breasts in Art.* New York: The Citadel Press, 1965.
Examines the iconography of female breasts in ancient and Hindu art, moving on through the Renaissance. Many plates, mostly of sculpture and painting, but only a few from the early medieval period.

1610. Miles, Margaret R. "The Virgin's One Bare Breast: Female Nudity and Religious Meaning in Tuscan Early Renaissance Culture." *The Female Body in Western Culture: Contemporary Perspectives.* Edited by Susan Rubin Suleiman. Cambridge, MA: Harvard Univ. Press, 1986, pp. 193-208.
Examines the Virgin's typical depiction with one bare breast in fourteenth-century Tuscan painting and explains why this element became so popular.

1611. Romi. *Mythologie du Sein.* Bibliothèque internationale d'érotologie, no. 16. Paris: Jean-Jacques Pauvert, 1965.
A coffee-table book on the iconographical history of male obsession with breasts in art and literature but with examples from the medieval and Renaissance periods.

[Face]

1612. Evans, Elizabeth Cornelia. "Descriptions of Personal Appearance in Roman History and Biography." *HSCP* 46 (1935): 43-84.
Treats different Roman conventions for describing physical appearance with their sources and reference to numerous Roman writers for examples. Useful to the student looking for sources for medieval descriptions of personal appearance.

1613. Ménard, Philippe. *Le rire et le sourire dans le roman courtois en France au Moyen Age (1150-1250).* Geneva: Droz, 1969.
Covers smiles and laughing in all their manifestations in the courtly romance: comedy, burlesque, satire, parody, irony, and humor. Looks at how these expressions function in all aspects of life, such

as, for instance, in scenes of love and of battle, with such specific topics as the wink and the conniving grin and with passages quoted from many works, but no plates. Bibliography and indices.

1614. Tomlinson, Amanda. *The Mediaeval Face.* London: National Portrait Gallery, 1974.
A collection of plates from sculpture (many on tombs), manuscript illumination, panel painting, and stained glass from an exhibition shown at the Gallery in 1974, with a short introduction on the depiction of faces in medieval art.

[Genitalia]

* Anderson, Jørgen. *The Witch on the Wall.* Cited above as item 438.

1615. Gaignebet, Claude, and J[ean]-Dominique Lajoux. *Art profane et religion populaire au Moyen Age.* Paris: Presses Universitaires de France, 1985.
This book contains a large collection of plates and discusssion of vulgar, obscene, and grotesque art from the Middle Ages, covering many subjects such as genitalia, sexual acts, defecation, and various parts of the body often appearing in the form of church sculpture, stained glass, wood carving, and wall painting.

* Weir, Anthony, and James Jerman. *Images of Lust.* Cited above as item 442. **See also item 1617**

[Hands]

1616. Acker, Paul. "The Book of Palmistry." *Popular and Practical Science* (item 598), pp. 141-83.
Offers a brief "History of Chiromancy," "Palmistry as a Popular Science," and "Middle English Palmistries" in the introduction to this scholarly edition from an early fifteenth-century English manuscript. Two plates. **See also item 1781.**

[Senses, five]

1617. O'Connor, Eugene. "Hell's Pit and Heaven's Rose: The Typology of Female Sights and Smells in Panormita's *Hermaphroditus."* *M&H 23* (1996): 25-51.
Discusses medieval thoughts on women as either stinking cesspools, vessels of iniquity, or, on the other hand, as blessed beings without bodily orifices or bodily functions, who emit sweet scents, looking particularly at this fifteenth-century Italian work.

1618. Nordenfalk, Carl. "The Five Senses in Late Medieval and Rennaissance Art." *JWCI* 48 (1985): 1-22.
Treats visual representations or personifications of the senses, with plates.

CITY, IMAGES OF

1619. Frugoni, Chiara. *A Distant City: Images of Urban Experience in the Medieval World.* Translated by William McCuaig. Princeton Univ. Press, 1991.
Reviewed by Thomas F. Mayer in *Speculum* 68, no. 4 (October 1993): 1121-3. Mayer explains, "Frugoni argues that medieval Western Europeans—she usually means Italians—gradually brought images and experiences closer to one another in a progressive movement 'toward the truth'" (Mayer 1121) from the early Middle Ages through the Renaissance in their iconographical representations of cities. With special focus on the frescoes of Ambrogio Lorenzetti and including many plates.

COLOR SYMBOLISM

General

1620. Allen, Don Cameron. "Symbolic Color in the Literature of the English Renaissance." *PQ* 15 (1936): 81-92.
Allen demonstrates "that the symbolic interpretation of color which was adapted from the culture of the folk to the uses of art, blazonry, and the church ritual by the men of the Middle Ages, became an intrinsic form of symbolism in the English literature of the sixteenth century" (81). With short sections on black, blue, green, yellow, less mentioned colors, mixed colors, and the complete spectrum, including quotations from various works. No plates.

1621. Alexander, J. J. G. "Some Aesthetic Principles in the Use of Colour in Anglo-Saxon Art." *ASE* 4 (1975): 145-54.
Discusses how Anglo-Saxons made use of color in their art, as in how it was distributed, materials used, types of hues, and the like.

1622. Barley, Nigel F. "Old English Colour Classification: Where Do Matters Stand?" *ASE* 3 (1974): 15-28.
A technical look at the differences in the Anglo-Saxon vocabulary of color and our modern one, in terms of what was considered important. Emphasis on the Old English interest in light/dark opposition, discussing specific words and passages. The focus is on why they chose to name or discuss frequently certain colors. Includes comparison with terms in other older Germanic languages.

1623. Blanch, Robert J. "The Origins and Use of Color Symbolism." *IJS* 3, no. 3 (December 1972): 1-5.
Briefly discusses why color symbolism would have been considered important in the Middle Ages and some of its rules.

1624. Brusatin, Manlio. *Storia dei Colori.* Turin: Piccola Biblioteca Einaudi, 1983.
Treats color in the Middle Ages briefly.

1625. *Les couleurs au Moyen Age.* Senefiance, no. 24. Aix-en-Provence: Université de Provence, 1988.
A collaborative volume whose title is promising for the iconographer, but most of the articles in it simply collect references to colors in various literary works, and try to determine from within

the works, rather than from theoretical treatments of color in medieval encyclopaedists and elsewhere, what these colors might have signified. One article, by Michel Salvat on Bartholomeus Anglicus, prints passages on colors from his encyclopaedia, but does not add any extended commentary. Perhaps the most interesting piece in the collection is that by Christiane Deluz, who speaks of how infrequently the medieval pilgrim travellers mentioned colors in their travel narratives.

1626. Doak, Robert. "Color and Light Imagery: An Annotated Bibliography." *Style* 8 (1974): 208-59.
An index in the back arranged by time period makes this work a useful reference tool for the medievalist interested in color.

1627. Dronke, Peter. "Tradition and Innovation in Medieval Western Colour-Imagery." *The Realms of Colour: Die Welt der Farben: Le monde des couleurs.* Edited by Adolf Portmann and Rudolf Ritsma. Eranos Jahrbuch, no. 41. Leiden: Brill, 1972, pp. 51-107.
A lengthy treatment of medieval colors with a full bibliography.

1628. Indergrand, Michel. *Bibliographie de la couleur.* Paris: Société des amis de la Bibliothèque Forney, 1984.
Some works touching on medieval iconography can be found here.

1629. Meier, Christel. "Die Bedeutung der Farben im Werk Hildegards von Bingen." *FS* 6 (1972): 245-355.
This long article considers the symbolic senses in which colors—particularly black, white, grey, blue, green, red, and metallic gold—are used in the work of Hildegard of Bingen. There is one color plate containing images from three different manuscripts. Most of the discussion centers on references to colors in her works, especially colors associated with God's creative acts. There are copious quotations from the Latin works of Hildegard to support the interpretations.

1630. Ott, André G. *Etude sur les couleurs.* See item 1600.
This semantic or lexicographic study looks at the different words for various colors and their meanings in Old French, organized by color and with quotations from different Old French texts. With

appendices on words for beautiful and ugly, especially as they are derived from colors, and an index of all the different words studied.

1631. Parkhurst, Charles. "Roger Bacon on Color: Sources, Theories & Influence." *The Verbal and the Visual: Essays in Honor of William Sebastian Heckscher.* Edited by Karl-Ludwig Selig and Elizabeth Sears. New York: Italica, 1990, pp. 151-201.
Discusses Bacon's thirteenth-century tract on the senses, *De sensu et sensato*, and his theory of color, showing how it was influenced by, and fits in with, earlier and contemporary color theory. Treats how he viewed particular colors and hues, the mixing of colors, nomenclature, and his influence on artists. With some plates of Bacon's diagrams.

1632. Pastoureau, Michel. *Figures et couleurs: Etudes sur la symbolique et la sensibilité médiévales.* Paris: Léopard d'Or, 1986.
Contains a number of essays on various colors and their appearance in heraldry. This book, like other works of this author, consists of recycled pieces whose documentation is to works by Pastoureau rather than to medieval sources. Thus, this book is representative of most of the author's other studies of color, since the same essays occur under different titles in those places. Numerous plates from the Manesse manuscript and from heraldic manuscripts.

Colors by Specific Hues

[Black]

1633. Norden, Linda van. Compiled and edited by John Pollock. *The Black Feet of the Peacock: The Color-Concept 'Black' from the Greeks through the Renaissance.* Lanham, MD: Univ. Press of America, 1985.
Covers definitions of the color black and its symbolic nature in philosophy, alchemy, astrology, cabalism, and heraldry; uses of the peacock emblem; and how theories of color became fused with moral considerations in the Renaissance. With two appendices, "The

Importance of Color in Alchemy" and "Theories Explaining the Negro's Blackness" and an index.

[Blue]

1634. Pastoureau, Michel. "Et puis vint le bleu." *LMAM* 61 (October 1983): 43-50.
Traces blues chiefly in heraldry.

[Red]

1635. Munro, John H. "The Medieval Scarlet and the Economics of the Sartorial Splendour." *Cloth and Clothing in Medieval Europe* (item 1683), pp. 13-70.
Red costume is often associated with devils, as in the fall of the angels representation in the Besserar Chapel, *ca.* 1420, in Würtemberg Cathedral, Ulm, where Satan as a winged man in a bright red gown falls into a hellmouth. Satan wears red in a vernacular Bible illustration, *ca.* 1410, in Brussels, Bibliothèque Royale MS 9001 on the opening folio of Genesis. Munro's article looks at etymologies for medieval words for scarlets and purples and what they signify, along with a thorough discussion of the production, diffusion, and significance of scarlet cloths in medieval Europe.

1636. Pastoureau, Michel. "Rouge, jaune et gaucher: Note sur l'iconographie médiévale de Judas." *Couleurs, images, symboles: Etudes d'histoire et d'anthropologie.* Paris: Le Léopard d'Or, 1988, pp. 69-83.
Studies red and yellow as colors with a bad significance associated chiefly with betrayal.

[Yellow] **See items 298 and 1636.**

CRAFTS AND TRADES

1637. Basing, Patricia. *Trades and Crafts in Medieval Manuscripts*.
London: The British Library, 1990.
A collection of plates from medieval manuscripts, with discussion
divided up according to, the following subjects: "agriculture and
husbandry"; "trade and commerce" (banking, transport, and fish
industry); "industry and crafts" (mining, building, cloth, and salt);
and "the professions" (law, church, and medicine). Select
bibliography and index.

1638. Ovitt, George, Jr. *The Restoration of Perfection: Labor and
Technology in Medieval Culture*. New Brunswick and London:
Rutgers Univ. Press, 1987.
Looking at medieval texts and later critics' views on medieval labor,
the author examines "what cultural imperatives existed in support of
the labor of human beings, labor that would in due course, transform
European and eventually global life" (x). A philosophical book,
studying the "intellectual and spiritual" framework offered by
medieval Christianity, by monasteries, and by other institutions to
see how these affected "the economic and technological
transformation of Europe," with an interest in whether, as Bacon
thought, labor could restore an original perfection (x). Bibliography
and index.

1639. Swanson, Heather. *Medieval Artisans: An Urban Class in Late
Medieval England*. Oxford: Basil Blackwell, 1989.
As Swanson explains, "details of manufacturing processes have only
been given to clarify the distinction between crafts; the emphasis is
on the political and social status of artisans, their place in the
industrial structure of the town and their contribution to the urban
economy" (1). Divided up into the following chapters: the
victualling industry, the textile industry, the clothing industry, the
leather industry, the metal-workers, the building industry, minor
crafts, artisans and the civic authorities, industrial investment, and
wealth and social status (including a table entitled "occupation of
craftsmen's sons taking out their freedom by patrimony"). Ends with
a lengthy bibliography and index.

1640. Whitney, Elspeth. "Paradise Restored: The Mechanical Arts from Antiquity through the Thirteenth Century." *TAPS* 80, no.1 (1990): 1-169.
According to the introduction, in which Whitney discusses past critical views on technology in the Middle Ages, "the present study examines the intellectual process by which medieval philosophers and theologians revised classical concepts of technology and its place in classifications of the arts and sciences in order to redefine technological invention as a full-fledged category of knowledge" (2).

DANCE

1641. Alexander, Jonathan J. G. "Dancing in the Streets." *JWAG* 54 (1996): 147-62.
Studies the negative medieval atttitude toward people dancing singly or in couples that is not presented in depictions of round and circle dances where the threatening sexuality of the first type of depiction is neutralized. Plates.

1642. Cheney, Liana. *The Symbolism of Vanitas in the Arts, Literature, and Music.* Freeport, NY: Edward Mellen, 1993.
Studies hair, mirrors, skulls, and other images of *vanitas* chiefly from the Dance of Death tradition.

1643. Friedman, John B. "'He hath a thousand slayn this pestilence': Iconography of the Plague in the Late Middle Ages." *Social Unrest in the Late Middle Ages.* Edited by Francis X. Newman. Medieval and Renaissance Texts and Studies. Binghamton, NY: State Univ. of New York Press, 1986, pp. 75-112.
Notes three and six in this article give a bibliography of studies on the Dance of Death motif.

1644. Künstle, Karl. *Die Legende der Drei Lebenden und Drei Toten und der Totentanz.* Freiburg im Breisgau: Herdersche, 1908.
Studies the motif of three worldly young persons who meet three skeletal figures who warn them of mortality. Relates this story to

legends of the apostle James. This motif was very common in medieval wall and manuscript painting. The book is accompanied by numerous in-text black-and-white pictures and some colored ones also.

1645. Storck, Willy F. "Aspects of Death in English Art and Poetry." *BM* 21 (1912): 249-56.
Studies "the legend in which the three Living (Kings) encounter three Dead (Kings), who warn them of the transience of the world" (249) in medieval art and literature and how this may be tied in to the theme of the Dance of Death.

1646. Williams, Ethel Carleton. "The Dance of Death in Painting and Sculpture in the Middle Ages." *JBAA*, 3d ser., 1 (January 1937): 229-57.
Examines the medieval origins and iconography in France, England, Germany, Austria, Italy, and Switzerland, of the image of life as a dance from which dancers are snatched away by death, that later becomes so popular in the works of Hans Holbein the younger. Ends with a list of "Dances of Death in Painting and Sculpture now Extant."

1647. _____. "Mural Paintings of the Three Living and the Three Dead in England." *JBAA*, 3d ser., 7 (1942) : 31-40.
A detailed description of how this scene is iconographically depicted in medieval English mural painting with only a few plates and including a useful annotated "list of paintings of the three living and the three dead formerly existing in churches in England."

DAWN AND NIGHT, IMAGES OF

1648. Baskervill, Charles Read. "English Songs on the Night Visit." *PMLA* 36 (1921): 565-614.

Studies the conventions of medieval songs dealing with the lovers' visit during the night (and their parting at dawn), quoting from a number of different English and Continental examples.

1649. Hatto, Arthur T., ed. *Eos: An Enquiry into the Theme of Lovers' Meetings and Partings at Dawn in Poetry.* The Hague: Mouton, 1965.
Essays by various hands, some of which may be useful to the medievalist, in particular "Classical, Later, and Mediaeval Latin," by John Lockwood; "Old Provençal and Old French," by B. Woledge; and "Mediaeval German," by A. T. Hatto. Index.

DIRECTIONS, LEFT AND RIGHT

1650. Dietmaring, Ursula. "Die Bedeutung von Rechts und Links in theologischen und literarischen Texten bis um 1200." *ZDADL* 98 (1969): 265-92.
Lefthandedness was from antiquity regarded with contempt and suspicion. For example, Aristotle, *De Partibus Animalium* 670 b. 15 associates the left with crookedness, darkness, evil, femininity, passivity, wetness, and cold, and with the back and bottom. Typically, religious art shows hell to God's left as with Michaelangelo in the Sistine Chapel ceiling. In medieval religious plays, hellmouth is at stage left, and unsympathetic characters like Judas were believed to be left handed. The right hand, typically, is a symbol of fidelity. This article focusses on the particular symbolism of the right and the left hands of God, chiefly in patristic commentary.

1651. Guillaumont, François. *"Laeva prospera:* Remarques sur la droite et la gauche dans la divination romaine." *D'Herakles à Poseidon: Mythologie et protohistoire.* Edited by Raymond Bloch. Centre de recherches d'histoire et de philologie, no. 3. Hautes études du monde gréco-romain, no. 14. Geneva: Droz; Paris: Champion, 1985, pp. 159-77.
Examines symbolic associations attached to right and left among the ancients, especially as concerns the divination of religious

matters. Some of these beliefs influence late antique and medieval conceptions.

* Pastoureau, Michel. "Rouge, jaune et gaucher." Cited above as item 1636.
Most of this article's documentation concerns left handedness rather than color. Some black-and-white plates.

1652. Wagener, Anthony Pelzer. *Popular Associations of Right and Left in Roman Literature*. Baltimore: J. H. Furst, 1912.
Discusses the right hand as active agent, as pledge of good faith, in the expression of emotion, the left hand as dishonorable member, association of the right with male, of the left with female (in dreams, in the determination of sex), the right side as the position of honor, and various superstitions based upon the derived associations of right and left.

DOMESTIC IMAGES

Armor and Weapons

1653. Ascherl, Rosemary. "The Technology of Chivalry in Reality and Romance."*The Study of Chivalry* (item 1657) pp. 263-311.
Discusses the technical production of the knight's armor, the mechanics of combat (including weapons), and military technology (including the portcullis, clocks, torture machines, and bathing facilities among others) in romances. Ends with a suggested reading list arranged by subject.

1654. Blair, Claude, et al., eds. *Studies in European Arms and Armor: The C. Otto von Kienbusch Collection in the Philadelphia Museum of Art*. Philadelphia, PA: Philadelphia Museum of Art. Distributed by the Univ. of Pennsylvania Press, 1992.
Essays by different authors all dealing with specific pieces or types of armor, accompanied by numerous plates of armor and of art work depicting armor or battle scenes from the fifteenth century onwards.

1655. Bolgar, R. R. "Hero or Anti-Hero? The Genesis and Development of the *Miles Christianus.*" *Concepts of the Hero in the Middle Ages and the Renaissance. Papers of the Fourth and Fifth Annual Conferences of the Center for Medieval and Renaissance Studies. State University of New York at Binghamton 2-3 May 1970, 1-2 May 1971.* Edited by Norman T. Burns and Christopher J. Reagan. Albany: State Univ. of New York Press, 1975, pp.121-46.
Discusses the concept of the soldier of Christ as it develops throughout medieval literature, with plates.

1656. Brewer, Derek. "The Arming of the Warrior in European Literature and Chaucer." *Chaucerian Problems and Perspectives: Essays Presented to Paul E. Beichner.* Edited by Edward Vasta and Zacharias P. Thundy. Notre Dame and London: Univ. of Notre Dame Press, 1979, pp. 221-43.
Examines the arming of the warrior motif throughout Western literature, starting with antiquity and the Bible and moving through medieval European literature, citing many passages from different texts, with specific interest in the different uses of this motif in Chaucer and in the *Gawain*-poet.

1657. Chickering, Howell, and Thomas H. Seiler, eds. *The Study of Chivalry: Resources and Approaches.* Kalamazoo, MI: Medieval Institute, 1988.
Contains items 1653 and 1664.

1658. Contamine, Philippe, et al., eds. *Histoire militaire de la France.* Vol. I: *Des origines à 1715.* Paris: Presses Universitaires de France, 1992.
Although this is a general historical introduction to the subject, it does include a large number of interesting plates of medieval and Renaissance art works concerning war and battle scenes that may provide a useful resource for scholars interested in investigating the iconography of armor and weapons.

  * DeVries, Kelly. *Medieval Military Technology.* Cited above as item 54.

1659. Gaier, Claude. *Les armes*. Typologie des sources du Moyen Age occidental, no. 34. Turnhout: Brepols, 1979.
Like other works in this series, this one aims at an overview of medieval weaponry with an extensive bibliography.

1660. _____. *Armes et combats dans l'univers médiéval*. Bibliothèque du Moyen Age, no. 5. Brussels: De Boeck, 1995.
Study for the beginner of forms of medieval hand-to-hand combat and the weapons used.

1661. Grancsay, Stephen V. "Medieval Armor in a Prayer Book." *BMMA*, n.s., 16 (1957-58): 287-92.
Examines armor appearing in the marginal illustrations of the fourteenth-century Hours of Jeanne d'Evreux, and links it with armor used in the period. Includes manuscript plates and pictures of contemporary armor.

1662 Herman, Gerald. "Unconventional Arms as a Comic Device in Some Chansons de Geste." *MLQ* 30 (1969): 319-30.
Looks at many examples of non-conventional weapons and manners of conducting battle and how these generally humorous scenes function in the narratives.

1663. Jones, George Fenwick. "'Christis Kirk,' 'Peblis to the Play,' and the German Peasant Brawl." *PMLA* 68 (1953): 1101-25.
Presents these two most popular and published Middle Scots works as examples of the tradition of the peasant brawl, which parodies courtly chivalric practices Looks at the costumes, appearance, weapons, and roles of the different participants, among other topics.

1664. Nickel, Helmut. "The Tournament: An Historical Sketch." *The Study of Chivalry* (item 1657), pp. 213-62.
A detailed historical discussion of the tournament accompanied by plates of its depiction in art and some pictures of armor. With select bibliography and appendices with translated texts concerning tournaments and their rules from different medieval works.

1665. Nicolle, David. *Arms and Armour of the Crusading Era 1050-1350*. 2 vols. White Plains, NY: Kraus International Publications, 1988.

This survey is divided according to geographical region, mostly medieval Christian and Muslim. Each section includes a number of illustrations of arms, armor, or plates of art works representing arms and armor in Volume Two. Volume One contains an introduction to each geographical region and then a commentary upon each of the illustrations in the second volume. Also provides a dictionary of terms relating to medieval armor and arms, bibliographies of "Arms, Armor and Art Sources" and of "Military, Cultural and Social Background," and an index, all in the second volume.

1666. Oakeshott, Ewart. *Records of the Medieval Sword.* Woodbridge, Suffolk: Boydell, 1991.
A catalogue of numerous swords with plates and descriptions, categorized according to type with an introduction on sword production and supply.

1667. Pfaffenbichler, Matthias. *Armourers.* Medieval Craftsmen Series: Toronto and Buffalo, NY: Univ. of Toronto Press, 1992.
As explained on the back cover, "From the evidence of documents and surviving armour, the author examines in detail the communities of armourers which flourished in Europe; the individual armourers whose names and work are known, and whose records show us the wealth and social position they achieved; the organisation of armourers into companies or guilds; and the processes of making and decorating armour, from early mailshirts to the splendid garnitures of sixteenth- and seventeenth-century princes." Many plates, bibliography, and index. Reviewed by Robert Calkins in *Speculum* 69, no. 2 (April 1994): 421-3.

1668. Schrader, C. R. "Handlist of Extant Manuscripts containing the *De Re Militari* of Flavius Vegetius Renatus." *Scriptorium* 33 (1979): 280-305.
This work is useful for finding illuminations of weapons and sieges.

1669. Stone, George Cameron. *A Glossary of the Construction, Decoration and Use of Arms and Armor Together with Some Closely Related Subjects.* New York: Jack Brussel, 1961.
An alphabetically arranged glossary of words and persons' names in any way associated with arms and armor with many plates

interspersed among the definitions, which include some history and dates. The book ranges across many different time periods and cultures but with references to medieval and later Europe. Useful for clarifying unfamiliar terminology.

Baths

* Gaignebet, Claude, and J[ean]-Dominique Lajoux. *Art profane.* Cited above as item 1615.
Discusses baths and "stews," Melusine in her bath, and the relationship between bathing and menstrual purification. The work offers an excerpt from a thirteenth-century regulation of "estuves" dealing with sexual misconduct in them, and publishes several choir stall carvings of such misconduct in baths.

1670. Spriewald, Ingeborg. *Literatur zwischen Hören und Lesen. Wandel von Funktion und Rezeption im späten mittelalter.* Berlin and Weimar: Aufbau, 1990.
This work offers some discussion and bibliography on baths and bathing in the fifteenth century in the context of Hans Folz's plague treatise, pp. 98-104.

1671. Vigarello, Georges. *Le propre et le sale: L'hygiene du corps depuis le Moyen Age.* Paris: Seuil, 1985.
Examines viewpoints throughout the ages on such subjects as bathing, location of baths, temperature of the water, the washing and cleanliness of clothes, the washing of face and hands, cosmetics, odors, perfumes, and vermin chronologically, with quotations from various sources, but no index or plates.

Beds

1672. Hoffmann, Marta. "Beds and Bedclothes in Medieval Norway." *Cloth and Clothing in Medieval Europe* (item 1683), pp. 351-67.

Discusses specific terminology and looks at art works depicting beds.

1673. Scheller, R.W. "The 'Lit de Justice,' or How to Sit on a Bed of Estate." *Annus Quadriga Mundi: Opstellen over middeleeuwse kunst opgedragen aan Prof. Dr. Anna C. Esmeijer.* Edited by J. B. Bedaux. Zutphen: De Walburg Pers,1989, pp. 193-202.
Discusses the iconography of the "lit de justice" (which originally meant the covering of the seat upon which a king sat in parliament) as well as aristocratic beds as seats in general and their coverings, focussing on fifteenth-century France. Plates.

Clocks

1674. Tuve, Rosamond. *Allegorical Imagery: Some Medieval Books and Their Posterity.* Princeton, NJ: Princeton Univ. Press,1966.
Considers manuscript illustrations of women wearing clocks on their heads as symbols of vanity.

Costume

1675. Anderson, Ruth Matilda. *Hispanic Costume 1480-1530.* Hispanic Notes and Monographs. New York: The Hispanic Society of America, 1979.
Organized by "Men and Their Dress Occasions" (bullfight, conquistador, capture of a king, wedding banquet); "Men's Dress" (hair style, headgear, body garments, leg coverings, footgear, accessories, furs); "Women and Their Dress Occasions" (Princess and attendants, Lady of Sevilla, Women in Church); and "Women's Dress" (hair styles, headgear). Full-color plates as well as numerous plates presenting details from art works showing a particular garment or body part. Very useful resource with index.

1676. Boucher, François. *A History of Costume in the West.* London: Thames and Hudson, 1967.
Three sections may be of use to the medievalist: "Europe from the Fifth Century BC to the Twelfth Century AD," "Europe Between the Twelfth and Fourteenth Centuries," and "Costume in Europe from the Fourteenth to the Early Sixteenth Century." Each chapter provides detailed description of the manner of dress in this period supplemented by numerous plates of surviving costume and of costumes represented in a variety of art works, with bibliography.

1677. Cunnington, C. Willett, and Phyllis Cunnington. *Handbook of English Mediaeval Costume.* London: Faber and Faber, 1952.
Proceeds by century from the ninth through the fifteenth for men and for women, providing descriptive notes under such topics as tunics, mantles, footwear, colors, hair, and the like, with line drawings taken from medieval art works (with sources of the drawings at back) Sections on children's and on working people's clothes at the end are followed by a glossary, bibliography, and index.

1678. Cunnington, Phyllis, and Catherine Lucas. *Occupational Costume in England from the Eleventh Century to 1914.* London: Adam and Charles Black, 1967.
Detailed discussion organized by occupation, with chapters on workers on the land; seamen and fisherfolk; miners, coal carriers, navvies; tradesmen and craftsmen; household servants; postal service; and the medical profession. With many quotations from various contemporary literary works and many plates and drawings from art works involving costumes associated with the different occupations. Bibliography and index.

1679. Cutler, Charles D. "Exotics in 15th Century Netherlandish Art: Comments on Oriental and Gypsy Costume." *Liber Amicorum Herman Liebaers.* Edited by Frans Vanwijngaerden, et al., eds. Brussels: Les Amis de la Bibliothèque Royale Albert 1er, 1984, pp. 419-34.
Discusses the exotic or orientalizing costumes such as turbans often found in Netherlandish manuscript illumination and religious panel painting, especially in scenes of the Passion. Among the wearers of

such costume were a group new to art, the gypsies, who introduced distinctive headgear and striped clothes. Numerous plates.

1680. Davenport, Millia. *The Book of Costume.* Vol. 1. New York: Crown, 1948.
A very thorough iconographical history of costume, with commentary (including detailed description of the types of costume, when it was first mentioned, describing what appears in the plate) based upon a large number of plates from many different works of art. Relevant to the medievalist may be the following chapters: "The Roman Catholic Church," "The Dark Ages: Feudal Power," "Knighthood in Flower: XIIth Century," "Feudal Lords and Kings: XIIIth Century," "The Rising Bourgeoisie: XIVth Century," and "The Renaissance Begins: XVth Century."

1681. Demay, G. *Le costume au Moyen Age d'après les sceaux.* Paris: Librairie de D. Dumoulin, 1880.
Starts with a discussion of what seals are and types of seals, then proceeds through type of costume represented on seals, for example (royal, types of feminine garment, types of armor and weapon, for hunting, naval, different ecclesiastical costumes, and garments found on the three persons of God, the angels, the Virgin, and the saints). Examines each chronologically and with discussion. Accompanying drawings of the seals and index.

1682. Drobná, Zoroslava, and Jan Durdik. *Medieval Costume, Armour and Weapons (1350-1450).* Selected and illustrated by Eduard Wagner. Translated by Jean Layton. London: Paul Hamlyn, 1962.
Drawing upon Czech art, this book discusses and provides pictures of Bohemian costume from 1350-1450; battle equipment, cut, thrust, and haft weapons; projectile and seige machines; firearms; flags and banners; the horse's harness and bardings; and battle wagons. Also includes a list of sources and bibliography. Well over half of this large volume consists of the drawings (each with a full description of the art work from which it was copied).

1683. Harte, N. B., and K. G. Ponting. *Cloth and Clothing in Medieval Europe: Essays in Memory of Professor E. M. Carus-Wilson.*

Pasold Studies in Textile History, no. 2. London: Heinemann
Educational Books, 1983.
Treats such issues as textiles, dyes, knitting, woolen industry, and
garments, in various periods and at various locations—although
many of the essays are archaeological in focus. With index.
Contains items 1635, 1672, and 1697-98.

1684. Houston, Mary G. *Medieval Costume in England and France: The
13th, 14th, and 15th Centuries.* London: Adam and Charles
Black, 1965.
Covers ecclesiastical, civilian, and academic costume in the fifteenth
century, armor and details from metal ornaments, and ornaments as
applied to textiles and embroideries. Includes many drawings from
medieval art works as well as line drawings showing how the
costumes are constructed, a glossary of medieval terms for costumes,
and a bibliography.

1685. Jones, George Fenwick. "Sartorial Symbols in Mediaeval Literature."
MA 25 (1956): 63-70.
Discusses in detail the presentation of peasant costumes in medieval
literature and how scholars must be wary of taking as historical
descriptions what may often be satirical or didactic.

1686. Madou, Mireille. "Cornes and Cornettes." *Flanders in a European
Perspective* (item 399), pp. 417-26.
A brief treatment with many plates of miniatures from manuscripts
of the female headress and hairstyle which bears a likeness to horns.

1687. Marly, Diana de. *Fashion for Men: An Illustrated History.* London:
B. T. Batsford, 1985.
Chapter One, "A Verray Parfit Gentil Knight," pp. 10-27, concerns
the medieval period, discussing what was considered masculine in
dress and appearance at this time and providing plates from medieval
art works to illustrate these points.

1688. Newton, Stella Mary. *Fashion in the Age of the Black Prince: A
Study of the Years 1340-1365.* Woodbridge, Suffolk: Boydell;
and Totowa, NJ: Rowman and Littlefield, 1980.
Treats fashion during this twenty-five year period in many different
levels of society: the court, the tournaments, the Great Wardrobe;

dress of actors, minstrels, and fools; among the poor; and in works of art. With plates from a variety of different art works, bibliography, and index.

1689. Ollier, Marie Louise, ed. *Masques et déguisements dans la littérature médiévale.* Montreal and Paris: Vrin, 1988.
A collection of brief essays, many relating to the theme of mask, disguise, and alteration of shape. Particularly interesting are the studies of *Tristan*, where the hero radically alters his appearance.

1690. Pastoureau, Michel. *L'étoffe du diable: Une histoire des rayures et des tissus rayés.* Librairie du XXe siècle. Paris: Seuil, 1991.
Studies striped clothing as a sign of infamy, prostitution, and the like in the Middle Ages. Some plates.

1691. Robert, M. Ulysse. *Les signes d'infamie au Moyen Age: Juifs, sarrasins, hérétiques, lepreux, cagots et filles publiques.* *MSNAF* 49, 5th ser., 9 (1888): 57-172.
Examines the different external symbols or badges that Jews, Saracens, heretics, lepers, and prostitutes were forced to wear in the Middle Ages, with diagrams and plates illustrating these, with discussion of the laws regarding this subject, and with passages quoted from particular texts treating this practice.

1692. Ruelle, Pierre, ed. and trans. *L'ornement des dames (Ornatus Mulierum): Texte anglo-normand du XIIIe siècle.* Université libre de Bruxelles travaux de la Faculté de Philosophie et Lettres, vol. 36. Brussels: Presses Universitaires de Bruxelles, 1967.
Provides the text and translation, with introduction, bibliography, and glossary, of this thirteenth-century French text which a lengthy subtitle describes as the oldest text in French with medical recipes for facial care. Interested in the making of facial powder, combatting dandruff and hair loss, how to dye hair or grow it long, killing lice, makeup, pimples, wrinkles, the whitening of the teeth, and other such topics.

1693. Scott, Margaret. *Late Gothic Europe, 1400-1500.* The History of
       Dress Series. London: Mills and Boon; Atlantic Highlands, NJ:
       Humanistic Press, 1980.
       Though this work studies costume in the works of the great Flemish
       panel painters like Memling, it is still very valuable for
       Netherlandish iconography of dress in manuscript painting.
       Bibliography and index.

1694. _____. *A Visual History of Costume: The Fourteenth & Fifteenth
       Centuries.* London: B. T. Batsford, 1986.
       A collection of plates from different types of art works from Europe
       in these two centuries with captions commenting on the dress in the
       plates, prefaced by an introduction. Also includes a select
       bibliography, glossary, and index.

1695. Shapiro, Susan C. "Sex, Gender and Fashion in Medieval and Early
       Modern Britain." *JPC* 20, no. 4 (Spring 1987): 113-28.
       Focusses on "the history of 'transvestism' in its widest sense: the
       affectation of fashions and coiffures (often accompanied by
       opposite-gender mannerisms) which label men 'effeminate' and
       women 'mannish'" (113); how effeminacy and mannishness are
       defined; the diatribe against such opposite-gender dressing and
       behavior; and its popularity in some courtly and aristocratic circles.
       Provides quotations from numerous medieval works.

1696. Song, Cheunsoon, and Lucy Roy Sibley. "The Vertical Headdress
       of Fifteenth Century Northern Europe." *Dress* 16 (1990): 4-15.
       A detailed discussion of the subject including the terminology and
       a number of plates of art works displaying headdresses.

1697. Turnau, Irena. "The Diffusion of Knitting in Medieval Europe."
       Cloth and Clothing in Medieval Europe (item 1683), pp. 368-
       89.
       Discusses the development of knitting, the types of items that were
       knitted in the Middle Ages, and their color, style, and provenance
       (relying on archaeological evidence) and the development of knitting
       as an industry starting in the thirteenth century. Contains plates of the
       remains of knitted items and of depictions of knitting in medieval
       works of art.

1698. Uytven, Raymond van. "Cloth in Medieval Literature of Western Europe. "*Cloth and Clothing in Medieval Europe* (item 1683), pp. 151-83.
Examines discussion of colors and types of cloth in medieval literature of different countries and centuries, with numerous quotations. Suggests that literary allusions "sum up, so to speak, the contemporary view of the place these cloths occupied in the economy of the time and the part they played in medieval life" (152).

1699. Zijlstra-Zweens, H. M. *Of His Array Telle I No Lenger Tale: Aspects of Costume, Arms and Armour in Western Europe, 1200-1400.* Amsterdam: Rodopi, 1988.
This curious book, in English, German, and Dutch, consists of six chapters with English summary, plates, notes, bibliography, and index. The work considers methodological problems; thirteenth- and fourteenth-century costume and armor, with a rather miscellaneous glossary of costume terms like words for shoes and jackets; changes of fashion around the mid-fourteenth century based on household inventories and detailed gifts of clothes and arms; an outline of costume dress and armor appropriate to the *Tristan* of Gottfried; and finally an inventory of Floris V of Holland's military equipment. The last two chapters deal with military undertakings against a town the size of Derventer and with a detailed study of a sword which might have been used in such a siege.

Cushion

1700. Friedman, John B. "Pandarus' Cushion and the *'pluma Sardanapalli.'" JEGP* 75 (1976): 41-55.
In the process of elucidating Pandarus' gesture of fetching a pillow for his friend at Criseyde's bedside, this article explores the iconography of cushions and pillows throughout medieval literature and art.

Distaff

1701. Ackerman, John Yonge. "On the Distaff and the Spindle as Insignia of the Female Sex in Former Times." *Archaeologia* 37 (1857): 83-101.
Collects from literature and art images of the distaff and spindle as insigniae of women, from ancient Egypt up until the seventeenth century.

1702. Holloway, Julia Bolton, et al., eds. *Equally in God's Image. Women in the Middle Ages.* New York and Bern: Peter Lang, 1990.
In addition to Laura F. Hodge's "Noe's Wife: Type of Eve and Wakefield Spinner," pp. 30-39, showing how Noah's wife is represented as a type of Eve, especially through imagery of spinning, Chapter One also contains two other treatments of the distaff image. "Appendix: The Recalcitrant Wife in the Ramsay Abbey Psalter," by Adelaide Bennett, pp. 40-45, looks at Noah's wife as type of Eve and an instrument of the devil; and "The Thread of Life in the Hand of the Virgin," by Gail McMurray Gibson, pp. 46-54, discusses the iconography of this distaff image.

1703. Turnau, Irena. See item 1697 "The Diffusion of Knitting."
Though chiefly a technical work, this article gives a number of pictures of distaffs in contexts with an iconographic signficance.

Feasting and Food

1704. Adamson, Melitta Weiss, ed. *Food in the Middle Ages: A Book of Essays.* Garland Medieval Casebooks, no.12. Garland Reference Library of the Humanities, no. 1744. New York: Garland, 1995.
This collection is primarily concerned with actual recipes and foods, but does contain several literary and iconographic essays, chiefly those of Frey, Farrier, and Everest. (Item 1550 above).

1705. Altenburg, Detlef, et al., eds. *Feste und Feiern im Mittelalter. Paderborner Symposion des Mediävistenverbandes.* Sigmaringen: Jan Thorbecke, 1991.
A large collection of miscellaneous essays on feasting and church festivals, mostly in German. Especially useful is Derek Brewer, "Feasts in England and English Literature in the Fourteenth Century," pp. 13-26, and the section "Tafelrundenfeste" on courtly festivities.

1706. Arn, Mary-Jo, ed. *Medieval Food and Drink.* Acta, no. 21. Binghamton, NY: The Center for Medieval and Early Renaissance Studies, 1995.
Nine essays on many aspects of medieval cooking and feasting. Of particular interest is Nadine Bourdessoule's piece on the taste of game in medieval French hunting treatises. **See also Hunting.**

1707. Aurell, Martin, et al., eds. *La sociabilité à table: Commensalité et convivialité à travers les âges. Actes du colloque de Rouen, 14-17 novembre, 1990.* Publications de l'Université de Rouen, no. 178. Rouen: Université de Rouen, 1992.
A group of essays treating eating and drinking in convivial social contexts such as private and municipal banquets.

1708. Bynum, Caroline Walker. *Holy Feast and Holy Fast: The Religious Significance of Food to Medieval Women.* Berkeley: Univ. of California Press, 1987.
A well-written, interesting, and scholarly treatment of food and the control of food as a crucial element in women's piety, discussing their distribution of food through charity, their religious fasting, food in the family, women as body and as food, and other issues on the subject. Including a number of plates representing such topics as miracles concerning food and women feeding others. Indices.

1709. Camporesi, Piero. *Bread of Dreams: Food and Fantasy in Early Modern Europe.* Translated by David Gentilcore. Chicago: Univ. of Chicago Press; Cambridge, England: Polity Press, 1989.
Reviewed by Randolph Starn in *Speculum* 67, no. 2 (April 1992): 389-91. A theoretical and psychologically based investigation into how food affects many attitudes and beliefs during the Middle Ages,

as Starn explains, "drawn from a patchwork of (mostly Italian) sources—theology, legislation, literature, lives of saints, songs, and tales" (390). Also discusses the imagery and imagination resulting from famine and ideas about food, with numerous quotations from medieval works and with such interesting chapter headings as "Sacred and Profane Cannibalism," "'They Rotted in Their Own Dung,'" "The World Turned Upside Down," "Ritual Battles and Popular Frenzies," "Collective Vertigo," "Poppyseed Bread," and "Putrid Worms and Vile Snails." Index.

1710. Fenton, Alexander, and Eszter Kisban, eds. *Food in Change: Eating Habits from the Middle Ages to the Present Day.* Edinburgh: John Donald Publishers in Association with the National Museums of Scotland, 1986.
A collection of essays arranged by country. Two focus on the medieval period specifically: "Fasting and Working Monks: Regulations of the Fifth to Eleventh Centuries" by Maria Dembínska, pp. 152-60, and "Obligatory Fasts and Voluntary Asceticism in the Middle Ages" by Johanna Maria van Winter, pp. 161-66.

1711. Guerrau-Jalabert, Anita. "Aliments symboliques et symbolique de la table dans les romans arthuriens (XIIe-XIIIe siècles). *Annales ESC* 47 (1992): 561-94.
Studies the descriptions of different combinations of food and of eating together in Arthurian romances, covering, for example, such topics as foods often mentioned together, cooked versus raw meat, celestial food, venison, fish, social relations at table, talking and sexuality at table, the Round Table, dining hierarchies, and the Grail.

1712. Henisch, Bridget Ann. *Fast and Feast: Food in Medieval Society.* University Park and London: The Pennsylvania State Univ. Press, 1976.
A practical book, explaining how feasts were performed in the Middle Ages, and covering mealtimes, fast and feast, cook and kitchen, methods and menus, laying the tables, manners, and entertainment, with numerous quotations and plates from medieval sources. Centers mainly on thirteenth- through fifteenth-century England, but does include sources from other countries and centuries as well. Includes "suggestions for further reading" and an index.

1713. Lambert, Carole, ed. *Du manuscrit à la table: Essais sur la cuisine au Moyen Age et répertoire des manuscrits médiévaux contenant des recettes culinaires.* Etudes médiévales. Montreal and Paris: Presses Universitaires de Montréal, 1992.
Thirty-one essays mostly in French on all aspects of medieval cooking from the fourteenth through the sixteenth centuries with a handlist of manuscripts containing recipes. Reviewed by Barbara Wheaton in *Speculum* 71, no. 2 (April 1996): 449-52 with a summary of each article.

1714. Mead, William Edward. *The English Medieval Feast.* London: George Allen and Unwin, 1931.
Discusses such topics as the preparation of food, cost, medieval drinks, the scene of the feast, serving the feast, food and health, and the like, with quotations from a number of different medieval works (translated into English for the general reader). Focusses on the food of the upper classes. Includes plates of representations of feasts in manuscript illustrations and other art works, mostly French. Some bibliography for reference and index.

1715. Mennell, Stephen. *All Manners of Food: Eating and Taste in England and France from the Middle Ages to the Present.* Oxford: Basil Blackwell, 1985.
The third chapter, "Pottages and Potlach: Eating in the Middle Ages" discusses eating and cooking across the different social classes, the distribution of food, and medieval cookery manuscripts, with quotations from numerous sources. Two chapters on cooking and eating in the Renaissance as well. Bibliography and index.

Games

1716. Aries, Philippe. *Centuries of Childhood.* Translated by Robert Baldick. London: Jonathan Cape, 1962.
Looks at the role of the family and in particular the child as it evolves from medieval times up to the present with sections on the idea of childhood (the Ages of Man, the discovery of childhood, children's dress, games, modesty shown children); the scholastic life

(medieval scholars, the college, and ages of pupils); and the family (pictures of the family and from the medieval family to the modern family). Some plates and index.

1717. Bett, Henry. *The Games of Children: Their Origin and History.* Reprint. Detroit: Singing Tree, 1968.
Full of interesting lore on games from classical Greece to contemporary America and everything in between, here arranged by theme of the game: weddings and funerals, springtime and verdure, sunshine and fire, fairies and goblins, and foundations and sacrifices. Quotations from many sources and an index.

1718. Carter, John Marshall. *Medieval Games: Sports and Recreations in Feudal Society.* Contributions to the Study of World History, no. 30. New York: Greenwood, 1992.
The place to start for any investigation into medieval games and sports for adults. Begins with a useful introduction discussing the state of scholarship on the subject and describing the most important works in the field thus far. Then proceeds with chapters on such subjects as society's perception of sports, sports in pre-feudal and in feudal Europe, sports for establishing a reputation in the high Middle Ages, sports in the church, sports as reflected in medieval art (with plates), sports and the social order, sports violence, and two medieval sportspeople. Concludes with a bibliographical essay, select bibliography, and index.

1719. Cunningham, Hugh. *Children and Childhood in Western Society since 1500.* London and New York: Longman, 1995.
A good summary introduction to childhood as seen in the ancient world, the changes that came with Christianity, and how childhood was viewed generally in medieval Europe, based on what recent critics have claimed about the topic. Some discussion of games.

1720. Hole, Christina. *English Sports and Pastimes.* London: B. T. Batsford, 1949.
Covers field sports; games of skill and strength; ball games; football, hurling, and cricket; martial exercises; leisure hours at home; country delights, fairs and wakes; shows and spectacles; the theatre; shrine and spa; and the pleasures of London. Index. Although the plates are

from later periods, many of the references in the text are to the medieval and Renaissance periods.

1721. Jonin, Pierre. "La partie d'echecs dans l'épopée médiévale." *Mélanges de langue et de littérature du Moyen Age et de la Renaissance offerts à Jean Frappier.* Vol. 1. Edited by M. J. C. Payen and M. C. Regnier. Geneva: Droz, 1970, pp. 483-97.
Looks at how chess games function in medieval literature, particularly in French epics, with passages cited from a number of texts.

1722. Legaré, Anne-Marie, et al. *Le livre des echecs amoureux.* Paris: Chêne, 1991.
A translation into modern French of this fifteenth-century allegory of chess as a game of love. Not a scholarly edition, but very attractive, with all the illustrations of the manuscript *en face.* Also with an introduction, a table explaining the symbolism of the different chess pieces, and a discussion of the miniatures.

1723. McLean, Teresa. *The English at Play in the Middle Ages.* Windsor Forest, Berks: Kensal, 1983.
A study heavily based upon art and textual evidence from the English Middle Ages of the out of doors; animal sports; hunting, hawking, and fishing; tournaments, jousts, and tilts; outdoor and house and garden games; board and table games; glee, medieval music, singing and dancing; medieval drama; and folk games. Numerous plates from medieval art works and index.

1724. Randall, Richard H., Jr. "Frog in the Middle." *BMMA*, n.s., 16 (1957-58): 269-75.
Compares marginal illustrations from the fourteenth-century Hours of Jeanne d'Evreux to those in contemporary manuscripts with a particular interest in the game called "frog in the middle" or "la grenouille" and to similar types of games. Plates.

1725. Strutt, Joseph. *The Sports and Pastimes of the People of England from the Earliest Period, Including the Rural and Domestic Recreations, May Games, Mummeries, Pageants, Processions and Pompous Spectacles, Illustrated by Reproductions from*

Ancient Paintings in Which Are Represented Most of the Popular Diversions. Reprint. Detroit: Singing Tree, 1968. This very thorough work, originally written in 1801, describes each sport, game, diversion, or pastime, discussing the first evidence of it in art or literature and its history. Provides numerous quotations, many from medieval literature, and drawings reproducing how these games appear in a variety of different works of art. Index.

Mill

1726. Rowland, Beryl. "The Mill in Popular Metaphor from Chaucer to the Present Day." *SFQ* 33 (1969): 69-79.
Explores the use of the mill and the grinding of corn as a metaphor for copulation in Chaucer's work and elsewhere.

Mousetrap

1727. Berg, Gösta. "Medieval Mouse Traps." *SEU* 26, Varia 2 (1966): 1-13.
Argues that the object Joseph is making in a panel of the fifteenth-century Mérode Altar-piece and the object in the window are mouse-traps. Examines a large number of mousetraps depicted in medieval and Renaissance art.

1728. Roth, C. "Medieval Illustrations of Mouse-Traps." *BLR* 5 (1956): 244-51.
Looks at the tradition of illustration of the manuscript entitled "The Ancient Parable," containing the animal allegories of the thirteenth-century Spanish poet, Isaac ibn Sahula, of Guadalajara. Picture cycles were regularly added to this work in the Middle Ages and Roth describes these, providing plates of, and discussing particularly, the illustrations of mouse-traps.

1729. Zupnick, Irving L. "The Mystery of the Mérode Mousetrap." *BM* 108 (March 1966): 126-33.
Treats the mouse-trap Joseph is supposed to be making in a panel of this fifteenth-century Altar-piece and the one in the window also in the picture, discussing other medieval representations of mouse-traps, and arguing that the object represented here is not, in fact, a mousetrap. With plates.

Windows and Doors

1730. Goldman, Bernard. *The Sacred Portal: A Primary Symbol in Ancient Judaic Art.* Detroit: Wayne State Univ. Press, 1966.
Studies the symbolic associations and origins of the sacred portal in Near Eastern art up into the early Christian era. With a number of photographs and drawings and bibliography and index.

1731. Gottlieb, Carla. *The Window in Art: From the Window of God to the Vanity of Man: A Survey of Window Symbolism in Western Painting.* New York: Abaris, 1981.
Part Two, The Christian World, includes sections discussing symbolism of the window in painting, manuscript illustration, actual windows, and other art forms related to Mary's conception, and the five senses as windows, with numerous plates, bibliography, and index.

FLIGHT

1732. Hart, Clive. *Images of Flight.* Berkeley: Univ. of California Press, 1988.
A wide-ranging study of upward and downward motion as well as true flight, seen in Greek antiquity through the Renaissance. Numerous plates and a bibliography.

GESTURE

1733. Baldwin, Robert. *An Interdisciplinary Bibliography of Body Movement and Body Symbolism.* 9th ed. Cambridge, MA: Harvard Univ. Fine Arts Dept., December, 1979.
A mimeographed typescript. This work contains some 2000 bibliographical entries on gesture in different historical periods; its focus is mostly art historical.

1734. Barasch, Moshe. *Gestures of Despair in Medieval and Early Renaissance Art.* New York: New York Univ. Press, 1976.
Examines the history of the depiction of gestures of despair in medieval and Renaissance art. Index.

1735. _____. *Giotto and the Language of Gesture.* Cambridge Studies in the History of Art. Cambridge: Cambridge Univ. Press, 1987.
A thorough investigation of the iconography of gestures in the works of this early fourteenth-century artist, organized by gesture: "the speaking hand," "awe," "prayer," "crossing the hands on the chest," and "the gesture of incapacity." Many plates and some discussion of medieval sources for his portrayal of particular gestures. Bibliography and indices.

1736. Benson, Robert G. *Medieval Body Language: A Study of the Use of Gesture in Chaucer's Poetry.* Anglistica, no. 21. Copenhagen: Rosenkilde and Bagger, 1980.
Examines Chaucer's use of gesture, by which Benson means "any expressive bodily movement, manner, bearing, posture, facial expression, or sound specified in the text" (10) in his different works in the light of literary traditions of the time, particularly the allegorical tradition. Also includes an appendix containing the "gestures existing in Chaucer's poetry"(101) by poem with the line number, character exhibiting the gesture, and the type of gesture.

1737. Bremmer, Jan, and Herman Roodenburg, eds. *A Cultural History of Gesture.* Ithaca, NY: Cornell Univ. Press, 1992.

Most relevant to the medievalist is Jean-Claude Schmitt's essay "The Rationale of Gestures in the West: Third to Thirteenth Centuries," pp. 59-70, which looks historically at gestures in this period. This collection includes a select bibliography with a lengthy section on history and art history in the Middle Ages and the Renaissance. Indices.

1738. Curschmann, Michael. "Pictura laicorum litteratura." *Pragmatische Schriftlichkeit im Mittelalter.* Edited by Hagen Keller and Klaus Grubmüller. Munich: Fink, 1992, pp. 211-29.
This article deals with the gestures of the Manesse manuscript. **See also items 345, 347-48, and 354..**

1739. Davidson, Clifford. "Gesture in Medieval Drama with Special Reference to the Doomsday Plays in the Middle English Cycles." *EDAM Newsletter* 6, no. 1 (Fall 1983): 8-17.
Calls for a reference work cataloguing the gestures alluded to in the directions for medieval plays. Discusses the gestures in the Doomsday plays. Covers God the Father, the Son, angels, and the saved and damned.

1740. Garnier, Francois. *Le langage de l'image au Moyen Age*: *Signification et symbolique.* Paris: Le Léopard d'Or, 1982.
This work deals with a variety of different gestures from early medieval art, such as the *orans* and various poses of the hands. It is illustrated by many small line drawings of gestures.

1741. Habicht, Werner. *Die Gebärde in englischen Dichtungen des Mittelalters.* Munich: C. H. Beck'schen, 1959.
Treats the use of gesture in a variety of Middle English romances as well as in some Old English poetry, though not from an iconographic point of view.

1742. Ladner, Gerhart B. "The Gestures of Prayer in Papal Iconography of the Thirteenth and Early Fourteenth Centuries." *Didascaliae: Studies in Honor of Anselm M. Albareda.* Edited by Sesto Prete. New York: Bernard M. Rosenthal, 1961, pp. 245-75.
Examines closely the depiction of popes in the attitude of prayer in medieval art works, with plates.

1743. Ménard, Philippe. "Les gestes et les expressions corporelles dans la *Chanson de Roland:* Les attitudes de commandement et de défi." *Guillaume d'Orange and the Chanson de geste: Essays presented to Duncan McMillan in Celebration of his Seventieth Birthday by his Friends and Colleagues of the Société Rencesvals.* Edited by Wolfgang van Emden and Philip E. Bennett. Reading: Reading Univ. Press, 1984, pp. 85-92.
Studies gestures of command and defiance in the *Chanson de Roland* as a reflection of medieval social rituals.

* _____. *Le rire et le sourire dans le roman courtois.* Cited above as item 1613.

1744. Schmitt, Jean-Claude. *La raison des gestes dans l'occident médiéval. Bibliothèque des histoires.* Paris: Gallimard, 1990.
Looks at gestures throughout medieval Christian and secular life, the language used to describe gestures, how they were represented in art and literature, what different gestures signified to different artists and writers, theories of gesture, and the like, with numerous black-and-white plates. Lengthy bibliography and index.

1745. _____, ed. "Gestures." *History and Anthropology* 1 (1984).
A volume devoted to the study of gesture from antiquity through the modern period by various authors. Several of the articles deal with Christ's gestures or with saintly postures in Romanesque art, for example Richard Trexler, "Legitimizing Prayer Gestures in the Twelfth-Century: The 'De Penitentia' of Peter the Chanter," pp. 97-126. Some plates.

1746. Warren, Glenda. "True and False Gestures in Jean de Meun's *Roman de la Rose." Iris: Graduate Journal of French Critical Studies* 2, no. 1 (1986): 29-37.
Examines the discussion of Faux Semblant, Ami, and La Vieille concerning "gestures appropriate to the adventures of the Lover" (29).

HERALDRY

1747. Bascapè, Giacomo C., and Marcello del Piazzo, with Luigi Borgia. *Insegne e simboli: Araldica pubblica e privata medievale e moderna.* Pubblicazioni degli Archivi di Stato. Rome: Ministero per i Beni Culturali e Ambientali, 1983.
Reviewed by Brigitte Bedos Rezak in *Speculum* 60, no. 3 (July 1985): 634-8. As Rezak explains, "despite its general title, this work is devoted to an exposition of Italian heraldry from its origins to the Napoleonic period. Its explicit dual purpose is to present the use of emblematics as a paradigm of Italian history and to provide a general guide for the scholarly study of heraldry in Italy" (635). Chiefly Italian but useful for good glossing of heraldic terms generally.

1748. Bedos, Brigitte. *Corpus des sceaux français du Moyen Age. Tome 1er: Les sceaux des villes.* Paris: Archives Nationale, 1980.
A catalogue of seals up to 1500 with plates, short descriptions of the iconography, wording on seals, date, and collection information, arranged alphabetically by city in France. Includes an introduction on the topic, bibliography, and iconographical index. Useful for images of an heraldic nature, especially those involving civic blazons. Many plates.

1749. Brault, Gerard J. *Early Blazon: Heraldic Terminology in the Twelfth and Thirteenth Centuries with Special Reference to Arthurian Literature.* Oxford: Clarendon, 1972.
Brault seeks "to trace the evolution of blazon from the earliest times down to about the year 1300" (1). He offers a useful description of the state of scholarship on heraldry, research tools, and critical works already existing, and then proceeds to describe early blazons. Much of the volume consists of "a Glossary of Heraldic Terms and Phrases in the thirteenth-century French and Anglo-Norman rolls of arms" and "twelfth- and thirteenth-century French literary texts." With a table at end entitled "Coats of Arms Identified by Name."

1750. Dalas, Martine. *Corpus des sceaux français du Moyen Age.* Vol. 2: *Les sceaux des rois et de régence.* Paris: Archives Nationale, 1991.

A catalogue like that of Bedos above except arranged chronologically by king or aristocratic person. Also includes more critical apparatus such as an essay specifically on iconography, various tables, color plates of some of the more impressive seals, a glossary, genealogies, and the like.

1751. Dennys, Rodney. *The Heraldic Imagination*. NY:Clarkson N. Potter, 1975.
For the medievalist, the appendix "Preliminary List of Medieval Heraldic Treatises," and Glossary of Heraldic Terms make this book especially useful.

1752. Jones, E. J. *Medieval Heraldry: Some Fourteenth-Century Heraldic Works*. Reprint. NY: AMS, 1983.
Publishes the important early heraldic treatise of Johannes de Badio Aureo, *Tractatus de Armis* (1395).

1753. Pastoureau, Michel. *Les Armoires*. Typologie des sources du Moyen Age occidental, no. 20. Turnhout: Brepols, 1976.
Begins with a bibliography and then covers such issues as definition of heraldry, different approaches to it, origins, genres and their evolutions, problems in criticism, and heraldic shields as historical sources. Like most of this author's work, the book makes little reference to medieval accounts of the subject.

1754. Wagner, Anthony. *A Catalogue of English Mediaeval Rolls of Arms*. Aspilogia, being materials of heraldry, no. 1. Oxford: Society of Antiquaries, 1950.
Describes in minute detail, classifies, and dates all known manuscripts of medieval rolls of arms.

1755. Wright, C. E. *English Heraldic Manuscripts in the British Museum*. London: British Museum Publications, 1973.
As explained in the preface, "after an introductory section describing the various kinds of heraldic manuscripts with an account of representative manuscript examples of each, the Department's four nucleus collections, Harley, Cotton, Sloane, and Royal, are examined in that order and then the Lansdowne, Stowe, and Arundel; the survey concludes with an account of the individual items or

collections to be found in the Additional and Egerton series" (3). Plates with descriptions and select bibliography.

MADNESS AND FOOLS

1756. Assirelli, Marco. "L'immagine della 'Stolto' nel Salmo 52." *Il Codice Miniato. Rapporti tra Codice, Testo e Figurazione. Atti del III Congresso di Storia della Miniatura.* Edited by Melania Ceccanti and Maria Cristina Castelli. Florence: Olschki, 1992, pp. 19-34.
Studies the "Dixit Insipiens" illustrations of the fool in a number of manuscripts from the Carolingian through the late Gothic periods and shows how the figure of the fool in such miniatures was adapted to other illustrative cycle, such as those showing Lancelot driven mad by love and the Franciscans hunted as mad men. Numerous in-text black-and-white illustrations and an up-to-date bibliography in the footnotes.

1757. Billington, Sandra. *A Social History of the Fool.* Sussex: The Harvester Press; New York: St. Martin's, 1984.
Looks at the role of the fool in England from the Middle Ages onward with the first two chapters discussing the medieval period, the second focusing on theological and philosophical attitudes toward him. Bibliography, and an Appendix presenting "A chronological list of Fool illustrations in English manuscripts" by century for the thirteenth through fifteenth, and index.

1758. Davidson, Clifford, ed. *Fools and Folly.* EDAM, no. 22. Kalamazoo, MI: Medieval Institute, 1996.
General essay collection on medieval and Renaissance fools, of which about half will be of interest to users of the present guide. Twelve plates.

1759. Dols, Michael W. *Majnun: The Madman in Medieval Islamic Society.* Edited by Diana E. Immisch. Oxford: Clarendon, 1992.

Provides an historical context for insanity and examines its significance, not only within the fields of medicine, theology, magic, and law but also within the social milieu of Islamic society, studying the medical context and its relation to the development of Islamic sciences and institutions; the practice of religious healing, particularly among Muslim saints; and the phenomenon of the holy fool as an expression of Muslim religiosity. The work concludes with translations of three treatises, two by Ibn Sina, the third by Sarabiyun ibn Ibrahim" (vii). Plates, bibliography, and index.

1760. Doob, Penelope. *Nebuchadnezzar's Children: Conventions of Madness in Middle English Literature*. New Haven and London: Yale Univ. Press, 1975.
Considers literary rather than chiefly medical presentations of, and explanations for, madness, including Nebuchadnezzar and many other characters as well as wild men as holy or evil, among other topics. With plates.

1761. Feder, Lillian. *Madness in Literature*. Princeton Univ. Press, 1980.
Discusses how "imaginative writers from the fifth century B.C. to the present have always been concerned with madness as a revelation of processes of the human mind" (xi), examining in the chapter on medieval attitudes toward madness Bartholomaeus Anglicus, Thomas Hoccleve, the *Malleus Maleficarum* and Renaissance treatises on madness. Index.

1762. Fritz, Jean-Marie. *Le discours du fou au Moyen Age, XIIe-XIIIe siècles: Etude comparée des discours littéraire, médical, juridique et théologique de la folie*. Paris: Presses Universitaires de France, 1992.
Examines definitions, discussions, and representations of insanity and insane persons in the literature, medicine, law, and theology of the twelfth and thirteenth centuries. Select bibliography and index.

1763. Garnier, François. "Les conceptions de la folie d'après l'iconographie médiévale du psaume 52 'dixit insipiens'." *Actes du 120e Congrès national des sociétés savantes (Limoges, 1977)*, vol. 2. Etudes sur la sensibilité au Moyen Age. Paris: Bibliothèque Nationale, 1979, pp. 215-22.

Shows how the iconography of the fool in this commonly illuminated initial changes from the end of the twelfth up until the fifteenth century, with plates.

1764. Gifford, D. J. "Iconographical Notes toward a Definition of the Medieval Fool." *The Fool and the Trickster* (item 1778), pp. 18-35.
Gifford explains, "in this short paper I have taken examples from Western European manuscripts in order to attempt some tracing of the fool's ancestry," starting with the fifteenth century and working backward through time, with plates, and focusing on, though not limited to, the fool carrying a stick and a 'white disk' who appears in the historiated initial *D* which introduces the psalm 'Dixit insipiens in corde suo non est Deus' (xiv and liii)" (p. 18).

1765. Gross, Angelika. *'La Folie': Wahnsinn und Narrheit im spätmittelalterlichen Text und Bild.* Heidelberg: Carl Winter, 1990.
Studies the religious and medical backgrounds of medieval madness in Hildegard of Bingen and Bartholomaeus Anglicus, and in the illuminations for the Jean Corbechon translation of Bartholomaeus and Conrad of Megenburg's *Book of Nature* and the *Sachsenspiegel*. Numerous plates of fools from tarot cards, madmen and of the *dixit inspiens* image from Psalm 52 as well as a lengthy bibliography add to the work's utility. Reviewed by Malcolm Jones in *Mediaevistik* 5 (1992): 252-54.

1766. Harvey, Ruth E. *The Inward Wits: Psychological Theory in the Middle Ages and the Renaissance.* Warburg Institute Surveys, no. 6. London: The Warburg Institute, 1975.
Harvey explains that the inward wits are part of "a traditional psychological theory, resting on the medieval commonplace that man belongs to two worlds: the external material world into which he is born, and the higher world of intellect and truth, inhabited by immaterial beings, to which he may attain. The inward wits stand at the point of communication between these two worlds in man, between body and soul, the realm of sense, and the realm of intellect" (2). Examines how this theory functions, looking at a number of medical and philosophical works from the period. Index.

1767. Lever, Maurice. *Le sceptre et la marotte: Histoire des fous de cour.* Paris: Arthème Fayard, 1983.

A historical examination of the development of the fool's role in medieval and Renaissance court society, looking at the idea of insanity in religious practices, the fool's carrying of a stick or club, his domestic and institutional roles, and the like. Plates containing images of fools from a variety of different art works. Bibliography.

1768. McDonald, William C. "The Fool-Stick: Concerning Tristan's Club in the German Eilhart Tradition." *Euphorion* 82 (1988): 127-49.

Examines the function of the club Tristan carries when insane in the twelfth-century *Tristan* poems of Eilhart von Oberge, and how this image was picked up by later *Tristan* writers. Also looks at how clubs function in other medieval works, usually to identify fools or outsiders, and possible sources for the image in *Tristan*.

1769. Ménard, Philippe. "Les emblemes de la folie dans la littérature et dans l'art (XIIe-XIIIe siècles)." *Hommage à Jean-Charles Payen. Farai chansoneta novele: Essais sur la liberté créatrice au Moyen Age.* Edited by Hugette Legros. Caen: Université de Caen, 1989, pp. 253-65.

Studies the iconography of insanity in twelfth- and thirteenth-century literature and art, with plates, and discusses particularly beards, hair, and clothing (or lack thereof), and the club and "fool's loaf."

1770. _____. "Les fous dans la societé médiévale: Le témoignage de la littérature du XIIe et du XIIIe siècles." *Romania* 98, no. 4 (1977): 433-59.

Looks at how fools were depicted, their rejection , and their integration into society in twelfth- and thirteenth-century literature, with numerous passages cited.

1771. Neale, R. E. "The Fool and His Loaf." *MA* 54 (1985): 104-9.

Discusses the change in the depiction of the fool in the illuminated letter *D* at the beginning of the psalm "*Dixit insipiens,*" examining especially the significance of the round white object in his hand often thought to be a loaf of bread.

1772. Neaman, Judith S. *Suggestion of the Devil: Insanity in the Middle Ages and the Twentieth Century.* 1975. New York: Octagon, 1978.
A detailed analysis from an historical perspective of views toward, and treatment of, insanity throughout the Middle Ages, presenting different theories, with quotations from authorities, definitions of madness, and canon and civil law on the subject of madness, looking at how medieval views came to form our present -day perspectives. Bibliography and index.

1773. Santucci, Monique. "Le fou dans les lettres françaises médiévales." *LR* 36 (1982): 195-211.
Covers the costume and attributes of a fool, his food, his behavior, social and medical views of fools, and love and insanity in French medieval literature.

1774. Sprunger, David. "Madness in Medieval Art and Romance." Ph.D Diss. Univ of Illinois at Urbana-Champaign, 1992.
Explores the cultural representations of madness in the Middle Ages in medical and theological thought, and in literary texts. Investigates depictions of madness in medieval art and particularly the moment in which a person goes mad, emphasizing ways in which the mad hero is transformed into a beast. Shows how the cure of Yvain's madness had ecclesiastical overtones to emphasize this symbolic restoration to a higher world, and contrasts the madness episodes of Tristram and Lancelot in Malory's *Morte D'Arthur*, demonstrating ways in which the madness sequence underscores character development. Including the useful appendix, "Medieval Depictions of the Insane: An Annotated Handlist," covering manuscripts, incunabula, and works of art. Plates and bibliography.

1775. Swain, Barbara. *Fools and Folly During the Middle Ages and Renaissance.* New York: Columbia Univ. Press, 1932.
Looks at presentations of the fool in medieval and Renaissance literature and culture with many quotations and the following chapters: "The Fool in Disgrace"; "The Fool Triumphs over the Wise Man"; "The Fool in Person" (describing his role in society, in festivals, and for entertainment); "The Joyous Societies"; "The Fool's Roles in the Sottises"; "The Ship of Fools" (by Brant); "The Praise of Folly" (by Erasmus); "Roles of Folly in English

Moralities"; and "The Fool Exhausted" (the loss of his symbolic importance). Index.

1776. Welsford, Enid. *The Fool: His Social and Literary History.* Gloucester, MA: Peter Smith, 1966.
Divided into four parts of which only the first two are relevant to the medievalist. The first concerns the parasite or buffoon, the type of fool most like the normal man, endeavoring to distinguish between his appearance in history and his popular transformation. Part Two is concerned with the fool proper, the man whose real or assumed infirmities have singled him out from his fellows. Bibliography and index.

1777. Willeford, W. *The Fool and His Scepter.* Evanston,IL: Northwestern Univ. Press, 1972.
General treatment of the theme with special attention to the way the scepter motif is adapted to other legends.

1778. Williams, Paul V. A., ed. *The Fool and the Trickster: Studies in Honour of Enid Welsford.* Cambridge: D. S. Brewer; Totowa, NJ: Rowman and Littlefield, 1979.
A collection of essays most focusing on medieval and Renaissance portrayals of fools, looking at such topics as iconography, Loki, and fools in England.

MAGICAL REPRESENTATIONS IN ART

1779. Alverny, Marie-Thérèse d'. "Surviance de la magie antique." *Antike und Orient im Mittelalters: Miscellanea Mediaevalia, Veröffentlichungen des Thomas-Instituts der Universitäts zu Köln.* Vol. 1. Edited by Paul Wilpert. Berlin and New York: De Gruyter, 1971, pp. 154-78.
Study of the late antique component of medieval magical texts by one of the great medievalists of this century.

1780. Betz, Hans Dieter, ed. *The Greek Magical Papyri in Translation Including the Demotic Spells.* 2nd ed. Chicago and London: Univ. of Chicago Press, 1992.
As Betz explains, "'The Greek magical papyri' is a name given by scholars to a body of papyri from Greco-Roman Egypt containing a variety of magical spells and formulae, hymns and rituals, many involving diagrams. The extant texts are mainly from the second century B. C. to the fifth century A. D." (xli). A critical translation of these spells with lists and tables of them for easy reference and bibliography.

1781. Burnett, Charles S. F. *Magic and Divination in the Middle Ages. Textes and Techniques in the Islamic and Christian Worlds.* London: Variorum, 1997.
Contains an introductory essay on magic and twenty essays on various magical and divinitory topics including cheiromancy. Indices of names, manuscripts, and initia of texts, with seventeen black-and-white illustrations.

1782. Chandès, Gérard, ed. *Le merveilleux et la magie dans la littérature.* Amsterdam and Atlanta: Rodopi, 1992.
Collects nine articles on magic in various period, of which the ones relating to the Middle Ages are on such subjects as white and black magic in Chrétien de Troyes, two on automata in the twelfth century, the werewolf, and alchemy.

1783. Cooper, Helen. "Magic that does not Work." *M&H,* n.s., 7 (1976): 131-46.
This articles surveys references to magic and magical representation in medieval romances.

1784. Dukes, Eugene D. I. *Magic and Witchcraft in the Dark Ages.* Lanham, MD: Univ. Presses of America, 1996.
As the title would suggest, uncritical study. No plates.

1785. Flint, Valerie I. J. *The Rise of Magic in Early Medieval Europe.* Princeton Univ. Press, 1991.
Examines the history of magic in the early Middle Ages, its rejection, and the acceptance of certain kinds, especially Christian magic, based upon wide-ranging textual sources from this period but

without plates. Examines such topics as love magic, the cross, medical magic, astrology, demons, and others. Bibliography and index.

1786. Hommel, Hildebrecht. "Die Satorformel und ihr Ursprung." *Sebasmata. Studien zur antiken Religionsgeschichte und zum frühen Christentum.* Edited by Hildebrecht Hommel.Vol. 1. Wissenschaftliche Untersuchungen zum Neuen Testament, no. 31. Tübingen: J. C. B. Mohr and Paul Siebeck, 1983, pp. 84-130.
Examines the history of this magical square of twenty-five letters that makes up the Latin words Sator Arepo vertically and horizontally in all directions and which was a popular visual image from ancient times, adapted later in medieval medical and quasi-scientific manuscripts.

1787. Kieckhefer, Richard. *European Witch Trials: Their Foundations in Popular and Learned Culture, 1300-1500.* Berkeley and Los Angeles: Univ. of California Press, 1976.
Drawing on a thorough investigation of the sources of these trials throughout Europe in these two centuries, this work provides a revisionist reading of them. Focusses especially on "the distinction between popular and learned notions of witchcraft, as these are revealed in the trials" (viii-ix), looking at the types of magic witches were accused of, and the social context. Calendar of Witch Trials and some bibliography with reference to other more extensive bibliographies. Index.

1788. _____. *Magic in the Middle Ages.* Cambridge Medieval Textbooks. Cambridge: Cambridge Univ. Press, 1990.
Concerns "magic, both natural and demonic, within the broad context of medieval culture. Covering the years c. 500 to 1500, with a chapter on antiquity, it investigates the way magic relates to the many other cultural forms of the time, such as religion and science, literature and art" (i). Some plates, bibliography, and index.

1789. Last, Hugh. "The Rotas-Sator Square: Present Position and Future Prospects." *JTS* 3 (1952): 92-97.
A brief summary of past, and possible topics for future, scholarship on this square of twenty-five letters that makes up Latin words. and

was a popular visual image from ancient times, adapted later in medieval medical and quasi-scientific manuscripts.

1790. Luck, Georg. *Arcana Mundi: Magic and the Ocult in the Greek and Roman Worlds*. Baltimore: Johns Hopkins Univ. Press, 1985.
A collection of ancient texts in translation with discussion, divided into the following categories: magic, miracles, demonology divination, astrology, and alchemy. Bibliography and indices.

1791. Molland, A. G. "Roger Bacon as Magician." *Traditio* 30 (1974): 445-60.
Focusses on two works, one of the fourteenth and one of the sixteenth century, describing Bacon as a magician, looking at what magic Bacon was purported to have performed and how it would have been considered in the period, with quotations from the work, and sections on "The Brazen Head," "Optical Devices," and "Forbidden Magic."

1792. Sherwood, Merriam. "Magic and Mechanics in Medieval Fiction." *SP* 44 (1947): 567-92.
Surveys fictional and factual accounts of machines from the Middle Ages with many descriptions of automata supposed to be operated by magic, with quotation and citation of numerous works.

1793. Thomas, Keith. *Religion and the Decline of Magic*. New York: Charles Scribner's Sons, 1971.
Considers magical beliefs held by people on every level of English Renaissance society and how these beliefs were a part of the religious and scientific assumptions of the time. Covers religion, magic, astrology, the appeal to the past, witchcraft, and allied beliefs such as ghosts, fairies, critical times, and omens. The book offers a useful backward glance at late medieval magical interests.

1794. Trachtenberg, Joshua. *Jewish Magic and Superstition: A Study in Folk Religion*. New York: Behrman's Jewish Book House, 1939.
"Offers a contribution to an understanding of folk Judaism, the beliefs and practices that expressed most eloquently the folk psyche—of all the vagaries which, coupled with the historic program of the Jewish faith, made up everyday religion of the Jewish people.

. . . The material here presented is culled from the literature of Germanic Jewry" (viii). Bibliography and index.

1795. Ulrich Ernst. *Carmen figuratum: Geschichte des Figurengedichts von den antiken Ursprungen bis zum Ausgang des Mittelalters.* Pictura et poesis, no. 1 Cologne: Böhlau, 1991.
His tenth chapter, pp. 429-59, with numerous illustrations, is entitled "Das Sator-Quadrat in Antike und Mittelalter" and studies the Sator-Arepo diagram.

MARGINAL GROUPS

1796. Anderson, George K. *The Legend of the Wandering Jew.* Providence: Brown Univ. Press, 1965.
Traces the origins and development of this legend mostly in folktales and literature, as well as other art forms, starting in the medieval period and moving up to the present day. Includes many quotations and citations from different medieval works concerning this figure. Index.

1797. Bériou, Nicole, and François-Olivier Touati. *Voluntate Dei leprosus: Les lepreux entre conversion et exclusion aux XIIème et XIIIème siècles.* Spoleto: Centro Italiano di Studi sull'alto Medioevo, 1991.
An investigation of twelfth- and thirteenth-century literary treatments of the conversion (since they were imagined as sinners) or exclusion of lepers, focusing on attitudes to them in sermons and accompanied by the edited texts of a number of sermons on the subject. Indices.

1798. Blumenkranz, Bernhard. *La représentation de Synagoga dans les Bibles moralisées françaises du XIIIe au XVe siècles.* Proceedings of the Israel Academy of Sciences and Humanities, no. 5 (1970): 70-91.
Examines the iconography of the allegorical personage Synagoga, representing the Jewish faith, especially as it appears in the *Bibles moralisées* of the thirteenth to fifteenth centuries, with plates.

1799. Brody, Saul Nathaniel. *The Disease of the Soul: Leprosy in Medieval Literature*. Ithaca and London: Cornell Univ. Press, 1974.
Studies the medieval "association of leprosy with moral defilement" (11) in society, in the church, and in literature, as well as offering some medieval medical views on leprosy. Index.

1800. Cohen, Jeremy. *The Friars and the Jews: The Evolution of Medieval Anti-Judaism*. Ithaca and London: Cornell Univ. Press, 1982.
Cohen explains how "this book seeks to bridge two scholarly disciplines . . . : the history of the medieval Church and the history of the Jews in medieval Europe." Examines the interaction between medieval Jews and Christians, and studies how, "at the same time that Christian theology affected the Jew . . . the particular character of the Jewish community—especially its reactions to the ideas and institutions of Christendom—reflected and even contributed to important developments in Christian society at large" (7-8). Large bibliography of primary and secondary sources and index.

1801. _____. "The Jews as the Killers of Christ in the Latin Tradition, from Augustine to the Friars." *Traditio* 39 (1983): 1-27.
Examines medieval views on the nature of Jewish "disbelief," focussing especially on their supposed role in the Crucifixion, with passages from a number of medieval writers on the subject.

1802. Cohen, Susan Sarah, ed. *Anti-Semitism: An Annotated Bibliography*. New York: Garland, 1987.
Three volumes have been published to-date. They contain a section on the medieval period.

1803. Cutler, Allan Harris, and Helen Elmquist Cutler. *The Jew as Ally of the Muslim: Medieval Roots of Anti-Semitism*. Notre Dame, IN: Univ. of Notre Dame Press, 1986.
Shows that "medieval Western European Christians tended, in their own minds, to associate Jew with Muslim, equating the two non-Christian groups and to consider the Jew an ally of the Muslim, as well as an Islamic fifth columnist in Christian territory" (2). Examines specific medieval papal attitudes toward Jews. Indices.

1804. Demaitre, Luke. E. "The Description and Diagnosis of Leprosy by Fourteenth-Century Physicians." *BHM* 59, no. 3 (Fall 1985): 327-44.
Discusses not only the description and diagnosis of leprosy, but also how it was contracted, its relation to syphilis and to sexuality generally, and how these fourteenth-century views relate to modern knowledge of leprosy and similar diseases. Includes a number of interesting accounts of leprosy from medieval manuscripts.

1805. Ell, Stephen R. "Blood and Sexuality in Medieval Leprosy." *Janus* 71 (1984): 153-64.
Studies two common beliefs about leprosy in the Middle Ages that do not apply to the disease as we now know it: that the blood of people with this disease was visibly different and that the disease was sexually transmitted. Discusses the spread of these beliefs in the Middle Ages and also looks at reasons, scientific and social, that they may have become popular.

1806. Hsia, R. Po-Chia. *The Myth of Ritual Murder: Jews and Magic in Reformation Germany.* New Haven and London: Yale Univ. Press, 1988.
Examines the accusations of Christians that Jews murder children in magic rituals but discusses mostly cases beginning in the fifteenth and moving up through the eighteenth centuries. Eighteen plates, bibliography and index.

1807. Jordan, William Chester. "The Last Tormentor of Christ: An Image of the Jew in Ancient and Medieval Exegesis, Art, and Drama." *JQR* 78, no. 1 (July-October 1987): 21-47.
Studies the medieval iconography of the bearer of the sponge full of "vinegar" (and also what this word really meant) and this whole scene viewed as a final torment to the thirsting, dying Christ, with some plates.

1808. Liebeschütz, Hans. *Synagoga und Ecclesia.* With an afterword by Alexander Patschovsky. Veröffentlichungen der Deutschen Akademie für Sprache und Dichtung Darmstadt, no. 55. Heidelburg: Lambert Schneider, 1983.
A reprint of a 1938 study by this author on the motif of Church and Syngague. No plates.

1809. Mellinkoff, Ruth. *Outcasts: Signs of Otherness in Northern European Art of the Late Middle Ages.* 2 vols. California Studies in the History of Art. Berkeley: Univ. of California Press, 1993.
A large very well-illustrated study of the iconography of outcasts in all types of medieval art, divided into two sections. Part One (text) on the costumes of outcasts, covers patterns, colors, headgear, and Hebrew and pseudo-Hebrew lettering. Part Two (plates) on the body, illustrates unusual physical features, physical distortions and deformities, red hair and ruddy skin, and skin blemishes. Bibliography and index.

1810. Moore, R. I. *The Formation of a Persecuting Society: Power and Deviance in Western Europe 950-1250.* Oxford and New York: Basil Blackwell, 1987.
Examines, with an historical focus, the persecution of heretics, Jews, and lepers in the Middle Ages, and the reason for this persecution. Bibliography and index.

1811. Pflaum, H. *Die religiöse Disputation in der europäischen Dichtung des Mittelalters, Erste Studie Der allegorische Streit zwischen Synagoge und Kirche.* Geneva and Florence: Olschki, 1935.
Considers the debate tradition between Synagoga and Ecclesia and looks at the literary use of the topos in Latin and vernacular literature. Many in-text plates but no bibliography.

1812. Richards, Jeffrey. *Sex, Dissidence and Damnation: Minority Groups in the Middle Ages.* London: Routledge, 1990.
This book devotes a chapter to leprosy, imagined as a sexual disease, tying lepers to other groups who suffered discrimination because of their sexual practices.

1813. Richards, Peter. *The Medieval Leper and His Northern Heirs.* Cambridge, England: D. S. Brewer; Totowa, NJ: Rowman and Littlefield, 1977.
Focusses on treatment of lepers in medieval English and Scandinavian society and then discusses how these attitudes persisted, with quotations from a variety of documents and with plates of manuscript illumination, coins, and other art work.

1814. Seiferth, Wolfgang. *Synagoge und Kirche im Mittelalter*. Munich: Kösel, 1964.
Rather miscellaneous chapters on the tradition of contrasting two women, one blindfolded and down cast and the other triumphant as, respectively, the Synagogue and the Church, the Old Law and the New, in art and allegorical exegesis. Many excellent black-and-white plates of such images down through the seventeenth century and a selective bibliography.

1815. Shatzmiller, Joseph. *Shylock Reconsidered: Jews, Moneylending and the Medieval Society*. Berkeley: Univ. of California Press, 1990.
Studies the treatment of the image of the Jewish moneylender, beginning with an early fourteenth-century trial in which Bondavid of Draguignan had to defend his reputation as Jewish moneylender in Marseille. The book then branches out to the attitudes, both hostile and sympathetic, toward Jewish moneylending in other European countries. No plates but includes a bibliography and index.

MARVELS

1816. Beaugendre, Anne-Caroline, ed. and trans. *Les Merveilles du Monde ou Les Secrets de l'histoire naturelle*. Paris: Bibliothèque Nationale; Anthèse, 1996.
A translation with reproduction of the miniatures of Bibliothèque Nationale MS fr.22971, a French version of a Latin work based on the writing of Pierre Bersuire. The manuscript, illuminated in Poitiers by Robinet Testard for Charles of Angoulême is one of the great treasures of French illumination and is a very good introduction to the "wonders" of fiftty-six countries arranged alphabetically. Each country is illustrated by a miniature. A modest afterword gives the history of the manuscripts of the work, its sources and possible authorship.

1817. Biow, Douglas. *'Mirabile Dictu': Representations of the Marvelous in Medieval and Renaissance Epic.* Ann Arbor: Univ. of Michigan Press, 1996.
Compares Virgil, Dante, Boccaccio, Ariosto, Tasso, and Spenser in terms of their treatment of the marvellous, beginning with the common image of a person metamorphosed into a bleeding branch which then speaks, and then considers numerous other marvellous images.

1818. Darré, René. *Géants d'hier et d'aujourd'hui.* Arras: Imprimerie de la Nouvelle Société Anonyme du Pas-de-Calais, 1944.
Uncritical but entertaining study.

1819. Dronke, Peter. *Dante and Medieval Latin Traditions.* Cambridge: Cambridge Univ. Press, 1986.
Chapter Two, "The Giants in Hell," pp. 32-50, analyzes the passages in which giants are encountered in Dante's hell with reference to sources for their iconographical depiction.

1820. Gervais of Tilbury. *Le Livre des Merveilles: Divertisssment pour un empereur (Troisième Partie).* Edited and Translated by Annie Duchesne. Preface by Jacques le Goff. La Roue à Livres. Paris: Les belles lettres, 1992.
A modern French translation of this thirteenth-century Latin work written by an Englishman for the Emperor Otto IV of Brunswick. It is an encyclopedia of marvels of the world and of nature, treating werewolves, dragons, fairies, magic water, religious objects with magic properties, and telling stories about these objects.

1821. Harward, Vernon J. *The Dwarfs of Arthurian Romance and Celtic Tradition.* Leiden: Brill, 1958.
In investigating the Celtic origin of the dwarfs figuring in Arthurian romance, Harward also ends up studying the role of dwarfs in medieval life generally and the ways in which they were presented in medieval literature.

1822. Idel, Moshe. *Golem: Jewish Magical and Mystical Traditions on the Artificial Anthropoid.* SUNY Series in Judaica: Hermeneutics, Mysticism, and Religion. Albany: State Univ. of New York Press, 1990.

Claims that the golem concept in Judaism confered an exceptional status on the Jewish elite by giving it supernatural powers deriving from a knowledge of the Hebrew and its traditional magical and mystical values. Includes a large section on the medieval period. Subject and author index.

1823. Kenseth, Joy. *The Age of the Marvelous*. Hanover, NH: Hood Museum of Art, Dartmouth College, 1991.
Reviewed by Scott D. Westrem in *Speculum* 68, no. 3 (July 1993): 812-16. An exhibition catalogue of plates with descriptions which Westrem calls "a learned and elegant book that records permanently a worthy exhibition of works of art, objects of many kinds, and illustrated texts." (814).

1824. Lecouteux, Claude. "Introduction à l'étude du merveilleux médiéval." *EG* 36, no. 3 (July-September 1981): 273-90.
Defines and describes the concept of the marvellous in medieval literature and focusses on the marvellous in Christian writings, and in the popular literature of diversion, as well as on learned marvels.

1825. _____. *Les nains et les elfes au Moyen Age*. Paris: Imago, 1988.
Treats dwarves and elves in antiquity and the Middle Ages, discussing some specific characters like Auberon and his parents and Alberich. Looks at a variety of myths concerning elves and dwarves. Bibliography and index, with some plates containing line drawings.

1826. Mayer, Maximillian. *Die Giganten und Titanen in der Antiken Sage und Kunst*. Berlin: Weidmannsche Buchhandlung, 1887.
The emphasis of this book is chiefly classical, with studies of the major scenes of giants like Polyphemus, and Titans at war with the gods in Greek literature and in Attic vase painting. A few plates.

1827. McAlindon, T. "The Emergence of a Comic Type in Middle-English Narrative: The Devil and Giant as Buffoon." *Anglia* 81 (1963): 365-71.
Examines how the devil is characterized as buffoon (a characterization giants also share) not only in Middle-English drama (as previously recognized) but also in saints' legends and in romance.

1828. Meurant, René. *Géants processionnels et de cortège en Europe, en Belgique, en Wallonie.* Tielt: Veys, 1979.
Several essays by the author on giants or gigantic figures in parades or processions in different European countries, with many pictures and some plates of art works. Most focus on the Renaissance or later, but there are many references to the medieval period.

1829. Palliser, Janis L. "Giants." *Mythical and Fabulous Creatures* (item 1341), pp. 293-324.
General study with select bibliography.

* Rouge, Gustave Le. *La Mandragore Magique, Teraphim, Golem, Androides, Homoncules.* Cited above as item 1556.
Studies how golems and androids were depicted or described especially in literature from antiquity up to the eighteenth century.

1830. Stephens, Walter. *Giants in Those Days: Folklore, Ancient History, and Nationalism.* Lincoln and London: Univ. of Nebraska Press, 1989.
Attempts to "trace a cultural history of the concept of the Giant, from Old Testament times to the early modern period" (1), with a special interest in Rabelais and the ancient, medieval, and Renaissance traditions that come to form his views of giants. Cites numerous passages from writers of each period concerning giants, taking a Bakhtinian approach to explain the ways in which giants are perceived. A few plates, bibliography, and index.

1831. Tietze-Conrat, E. *Dwarfs and Jesters in Art.* London: Phaidon, 1957.
A collection of plates from art works depicting dwarfs and jesters, most fifteenth through eighteenth century and from Europe and discussion of how they are represented.

1832. Wittkower, Rudolf. "Marco Polo and the Pictorial Tradition of the Marvels of the East." *Allegory and the Migration of Symbols* (item 272), pp. 75-92.
Studies the way Marco Polo manuscript illustrators reproduced the wonders in the text and how the author often conflated real observation with accounts of wonders from books about China and India.

MUSIC

General

1833. Bandmann, Gunter. *Melancholie und Musik. Ikonographische Studien.* Cologne and Opladen: Westdeutscher, 1960.
Considers the effect of music on the melancholy temperament.

1834. Bowles, Edmund A. "The Role of Musical Instruments in Medieval Sacred Drama." *MQ* 45 (1959): 67-84.
Examines several instruments mentioned in cycle plays.

1835. Brown, Howard Mayer, and Joan Lascelle. *Musical Iconography: A Manual for Cataloguing Musical Subjects in Western Art before 1800.* Cambridge: Harvard Univ. Press, 1972.
Proposes a method of cataloguing art works depicting musical instruments especially for an Index of Musical Iconography to be compiled at the University of Chicago, providing here guidelines and a number of sample entries with plates, some from medieval art works.

1836. Bukofzer, M. *Studies in Medieval and Renaissance Music.* New York: Norton, 1950.
A chronological history of the development of music and ideas about music from the Greeks up to the twentieth century. Two chapters, "Gregorian Chant and Romanesque Art," pp. 22-50, and "The Gothic Period," pp. 51-73, may interest the medievalist. Both examine the parallel developments of music and architecture in the period they discuss, treating different types of music and their qualities as well as ideas and quotations about music by contemporary writers.

1837. Carpenter, Nan Cooke. *Music in the Medieval and Renaissance Universities.* Reprint. New York: Da Capo, 1972.
A good overview study, though not concerned specifically with musical iconography. First looks at the study of music (the teaching of music, manuscripts and treatises about music and their dissemination, degrees, particular musicians, interests, theories, and the like), in antiquity and then medieval monastic and cathedral schools; then turns to look at medieval universities by country; and then Renaissance universities also by country. Index.

1838. Galpin, Francis W. *Old English Instruments of Music: Their History and Character.* 4th ed. Revised from the 1910 edition with supplementary notes by Thurston Dart. London: Methuen, 1965.
A detailed history arranged by instruments such as rote, harp, gittern, citole, mandore, lute, psaltery, and dulcimer with many plates and diagrams of the instruments themselves as well as of medieval and Renaissance art works depicting them, musical scores, and quotations from texts describing them. With index and list of books of reference.

1839. Hammerstein, Reinhold. *Diabolus in Musica. Studien zur Ikonographie der Musik im Mittelalter.* Berne and Munich: Francke, 1974.
After a general discussion of music theory, the author develops the associations of music, especially wind music, and the devil. He considers various instruments, (pipes, drums, and horns) and connects them with dances of devils and then moves on to examine the associations of instruments with animals, such as the ass and the lyre, the ape, especially in parodic contexts, and sirens. This material is chiefly a prolegomenon to his study of music and musical instruments, especially bagpipes, in the musical pandaemonia of Bosch. Illustrated by 199 black-and-white plates. Select bibliography.

1840. Harrison, Frank L. *Music in Medieval Britain. Studies in the History of Music.* London: Routledge and Kegan Paul, 1967.
This book studies church music—choirs, liturgy, and plain song—after the Norman Conquest up through the liturgical and institutional changes brought about at the Reformation. Bibliography, register and index of musicians, and general indices.

1841. Hollander, John. *The Untuning of the Sky: Ideas of Music in English Poetry, 1500-1700.* Princeton Univ. Press, 1961.
Though really beyond the time-frame of this guide, the book's introductory matter is excellent on the musical theory of microcosm and macrcosm.

1842. Hyatte, Reginald, and Maryse Ponchard-Hyatte, eds. *L'harmonie des sphères: Encyclopédie d'astronomie et de musique extraite du commentaire sur Les Echecs Amoureux (XVe S.) attribué à Evrart de Conty.* Studies in the Humanities, no. 1. New York: Peter Lang, 1985.
Critical edition of this fifteenth-century encyclopaedia of astronomy and music based upon the manuscripts of the Bibliothèque Nationale with introduction, notes, and copies of the diagrams.

1843. Mirimonde, A. P. "Les concerts parodiques chez les maîtres du nord." *GBA,* 6th ser., 64 (1964): 253-84.
Examines parodic concerts in which musicians are represented as animals, children, or carnival people, in northern art works, mostly painting, starting in the medieval period. Plates.

1844. _____. "Le symbolisme musical chez Jérôme Bosch." *GBA,* 6th ser., 77 (1971): 19-50.
Studies the iconographical treatment of music in the works of Bosch (particularly its satirical treatment) in the context of ancient and medieval views of music as uplifting the soul or conversely as associated with lust. Plates from Bosch and from other artists on this theme.

1845. Montagu, Jeremy. *The World of Medieval & Renaissance Musical Instruments.* Newton Abbot: David and Charles, 1976.
Treats different types of instrument such as string, percussion, and wind, as well as the use of the instruments, the role of musicians and the like during the early Middle Ages, the crusades, the Hundred Years War, and the Renaissance, with numerous plates of the instruments themselves and of art works in which they appear. Bibliography and index.

1846. Munrow, David. *Instruments of the Middle Ages and Renaissance.*
London: Oxford Univ. Press, 1976.
A history of instruments and their use, covering woodwind,
keyboard, brass, strings, and percussion in the Middle Ages and in
the Renaissance and including many plates of artifacts and of
medieval art works depicting the instruments. Index.

1847. Reuter, E. *Les représentations de la musique dans la sculpture
romane en France.* Forme et style: Essais et mémoires d'art et
d'archéologie. Paris: Ernest Leroux, 1938.
Treats the iconographic representation of various Biblical and
profane images having to do with music (such as, for instance,
David, the Annunciation of the Shepherds, the ass as musician, and
the hunt) in French Romanesque sculpture. Black-and-white plates
and line drawings.

1848. Schueller, Herbert M. *The Idea of Music: An Introduction to
Musical Aesthetics in Antiquity and the Middle Ages.* EDAM,
no. 9. Kalamazoo, MI: Medieval Institute Publications, Western
Michigan Univ., 1988.
Provides "an orderly presentation of works which furnish an outline
of the *idea* of music prior to the Renaissance in the West, especially
as this idea pertains to aesthetics" (ix) and their relation to each
other, covering the Middle Ages. Select bibliography and index.

1849. Winternitz, E. "Bagpipes for the Lord." *BMMA,* n.s., 16 (1958): 276-
86.
Treats the iconography of the bagpipe and other instruments such as
the mandola, the vielle, the bellows, the cymbals, the triangle, the
rattle, and drums in the early fourteenth-century Hours of Jeanne
d'Evreux. Plates.

1850. _____. *Musical Instuments and Their Symbolism in Western Art.*
New Haven: Yale Univ. Press, 1979.
Studies the symbolism of a variety of musical instruments including
the bagpipe.

Music by Instrument

[Bagpipe]

1851. Boenig, Robert. "The Miller's Bagpipe: A Note on *The Canterbury Tales* A 565-566." *ELN* 21, no.1 (September 1983): 1-6.
Proposes a new interpretation of Chaucer's Miller playing a bagpipe after investigating the iconographical associations of this instrument in medieval literature and art.

1852. Butts, Thomas E. "Bagpipes in Medieval Music." *AR* 14 (1973): 43-45.
While correcting the notion that the medieval bagpipe "was little more than a folk instrument appealing only to the lower classes" (43) and revealing its importance not only as a popular monophonic instrument, Butts looks also at its appearance in art and literature.

1853. Jones, George Fenwick. "Wittenwiler's *Becki* and the Medieval Bagpipe." *JEGP* 48 (1949): 209-28.
Studies the instrument's role in Heinrich Wittenwiler's fifteenth-century *Ring,* and reviews the history of the bagpipe and references to it in the Middle Ages.

1854. Ross, Lawrence J. "Shakespeare's 'Dull Clown' and Symbolic Music." *SQ* 17 (1966): 107-28.
Turns to earlier traditions in art and literature of symbolic music to explain how Shakespeare uses symbolic music, especially that of the bagpipes, before the appearances of the clown in Othello. Plates.

1855. Stephen, David. "History at the Margins: The Bagpiper in Medieval Manuscripts." *HT* 39 (August 1989): 42-48.
Examines the diverse iconographical representations of the bagpipe in marginal illustrations of medieval manuscripts, looking at how this instrument was used at various levels of society and at how "when bagpipes were objects of satire it was due precisely to their popularity and common association with earthly delights" (48). With plates.

*   Winternitz, E. "Bagpipes for the Lord." Cited above as item 1849.

[Lyre and Psaltery]

* Adolf, Helen."The Ass and the Harp." Cited above as item 1268.

1856. McKinnon, James W. "Musical Instuments in Medieval Psalm Commentaries and Psalters." *JAMS* 21 (1968): 3-20.
Examines first views on musical instruments in psalm commentaries and then turns to their iconographical depiction in illustrated psalters.

1857. Prideaux, Edith K. "The Carvings of Mediaeval Musical Instruments in Exeter Cathedral Church." *AJ* 72 (1915): 1-36.
Aims to offer a list of all the musical instruments that appear in the carvings at Exeter, with photographs of each along with discussion and comparison with illustrations of instruments from other medieval buildings.

* Stauder, W. "Asinus ad lyram." Cited above as item 1270. **See also item 1320.**

PILGRIMAGE

General

1858. Buridant, Claude. *La traduction de L'historia orientalis de Jacques de Vitry.* Paris: Klincksieck, 1986.
Edition of this text of circa 1221 describing, among other things, the landscape, flora, fauna, and people and their customs in the Holy Land, from the thirteenth-century French translation of the Latin original.

1859. Dansette, Beatrice. "Les pèlerinages occidentaux en Terre Sainte: Une pratique de la 'Devotion Moderne' à la fin du Moyen Age. Rélation inédité d'un pèlerinage effectué en 1486." *AFH* 72 (1979): 106-33.

Examines the changes in religious sensibility in the fourteenth and
fifteenth centuries that lead to the writing of all these pilgrimage
narratives, looking at developments relating to Franciscan spirituality
and the practice of religious devotion in the Holy Land and then at
changes in the practice of pilgrimages to Jerusalem. Ends with a
bibliography of fourteenth- and fifteenth-century pilgrimage
narratives.

1860. Davidson, Linda K., and Maryjane Dunn-Wood, eds. *Pilgrimage in
the Middle Ages: A Research Guide*. New York: Garland, 1993.
Offers material on all the major shrines as well as Jerusalem.

1861. Kriss-Rittenbeck, Lenz, and Gerda Mohler, eds. *Wallfahrt kennt
keine Grenzen. Themen zu einer Ausstellung des Bayerischen
Nationalmuseums und des Adalbert Stifter Vereins, München.*
Zurich-Munich: Schnell and Steiner, 1984.
A miscellaneous collection of essays on pilgrimage, virtually all of
them illustrated, by scholars such as Kurt Köster and Jean Richard,
in English, French, and German. There are English summaries of
French and German studies and some color plates as well as
extensive notes and documentation. An excellent intoduction to the
theme of pilgrimage in art.

1862. Ohler, Norbert. *The Medieval Traveller*. Woodbridge, Suffolk:
Boydell and Brewer, 1989.
Treats pilgrimage among other forms of travel.

1863. Peters, F. E. *The Holy City in the Eyes of Chroniclers, Visitors,
Pilgrims, and Prophets from the Days of Abraham to the
Beginnings of Modern Times*. Princeton Univ. Press, 1995.
The earlier part of this book gives a good account of how Jerusalem
appeared to early travellers. With eight color plates and forty-eight
in-text pictures.

1864. Richard, Jean. *Croisés, missionnaires et voyageurs: Les perspectives
orientales du monde latin médiéval*. London: Varorium Reprints,
1983.
A collection of twenty-one previously published essays by this
author concerning medieval travel, grouped under the following

headings: crusades and the Holy Land, the kingdom of Cyprus, Latins and Mongols, the missions, and voyages and voyagers.

1865. _____. *Les récits de voyages et de pèlerinages.* Typologie des sources du Moyen Age occidental, no. 38. Turnhout: Brepols, 1981.

A standard bibliographical study in this series by an eminent authority.

1866. Röhricht, Reinhold. *Bibliotheca Geographica Palaestiniae. Chronologisches Verzeichnis der von 333 bis 1897 verfassten Literatur über des heilige Land, mit dem Versuch einer Kartographie Neuausgäbe.* With a foreword by David H. K. Amiran. Jerusalem: The Universitas Booksellers of Jerusalem, 1963.

A photographic reprint of the 1878 edition. The first 160 pages of this work are chiefly useful as a chronologically arranged guide to writing on the Holy Land by various medieval visitors to 1500. Indices of authors and places.

1867. Schur, Nathan. *Jerusalem in Pilgrims and Travellers' Accounts: A Thematic Bibliography of Western Christian Itineraries 1300-1917.* Jerusalem: Ariel, 1980.

As Schur explains, this bibliography "does not cover historical writings but relies solely on the published works of [Western] Christian pilgrims and travellers who visited Palestine during the Mameluke and Ottoman periods. It draws on the original travel descriptions and tries to serve as a guide to some of the numerous subjects covered by them, relating to the city of Jerusalem and its inhabitants. Thus we have tried to select short or long passages referring to a particular subject from the text itself, somewhat like a Concordance" (5). Covering sites, city walls and gates, the temple area, the Jews, the Christians, the Moslems, and a section entitled "General," which includes historical events, pictorial records, ways of life, public services, intellectual pursuits, sickness and healing, crime, security forces, tourism, economics, and statistics. Indices and plates.

Badges, Devices, and Mottos of Pilgrims

1868. Beuningen, H. J. E van, and A. M. Koldeweij, eds. *Heilig en Profann 1000 Laat-Middleeuwse Insignes.* Cothen: Society for the Study of Pilgrim Badges, 1993.

A collection by various hands, all in Dutch with the exception of an article on secular badges by Malcom Jones. The pieces deal with various aspects of pilgrim badges and the catalogue at the back is divided into religious and secular badges. Many plates.

1869. Blick, Sarah. *A Canterbury Keepsake: English Medieval Pilgrim Souvenirs and Popular Culture.* Ph.D. Diss. University of Kansas, 1994.

Studies the practice of acquiring tin or lead badges at popular English shrines. Includes bibliography.

1870. Cohen, Esther. " *In haec signa*: Pilgrim-Badge Trade in Southern France." *JMH* 2 (1976): 193-214.

Looks at the function of badges in medieval tourism and how they changed the function of pilgrimages, with discussion of different shrines, the development and sales of their badges, and who had financial control of this industry. Appendix includes five excerpts discussing legal considerations on badges from thirteenth-century works.

1871. Köster, Kurt."Gemalte Kollektionen von Pilgerzeichen und religiösen Medaillen in flämischen Gebet-und Stundenbüchern des 15. und frühen 16. Jahrhunderts. Neue Funde in Handschriften der Gent-Brugger Schule." *Liber Amicorum* (item 1679), pp. 485-535.

A *catalogue raisonné* of new discoveries in prayer books and books of hours in major collections containing representations of pilgrim badges in the decoration. Many of these are in the Bibliothèque Royale in Brussels. Numerous plates.

1872. _____. "Kollektionen metallener Wallfahrts-Devotionalien und kleiner Andachtsbilder, eingenäht in spätmittelalterliche Gebetbuch-Handschriften." *Das Buch und sein Haus. Gerhard Liebers gewidmet zur Vollendung d. 65. Lebensjahres.* Vol. 1:

Erlesenes aus der Welt des Buches. Edited by Rolf Fuhltott and Bertram Haller. Weisbaden: Dr. Ludwig Reichert, 1979, pp. 77-130.

Similar in character to the item above, with many plates of medals sewn to parchment pages or impressions of where they have been with detailed descriptions of manuscripts containing such pages.

1873. _____"Religiöse Medaillen und Wallfahrts-Devotionalien in der flämischen Buchmalerei des15. und frühen16. Jahrhunderts." *Buch und Welt. Festschrift für Gustav Hofmann zum 65. Geburtstag dargebracht.* Edited by Hans Striedl and Joachim Wieder. Weisbaden: Otto Harrassowitz, 1965, pp. 459-504.

Studies the pilgrimage medallions obtained by travelers at shrines and how they were often attached to the pages of horae and later painted on those pages in the Ghent-Bruges school of manuscript illumination. Numerous plates and a catalogue of manuscripts containing such sewn-on medallions.

1874. Mitchiner, Michael. *Medieval Pilgrim & Secular Badges.* London: Hawkins, 1986.

An extremely useful catalogue of badges, both religious and secular, beginning with a bibliography relating to medieval England, then proceeding by century according to region in England or type (such as votive badges, horse harnesses, griffins, crosses, and the like) up to the sixteenth century, then continuing with Continental badges. A picture of each badge is provided beside the description. Index.

1875. Radowitz, Joseph Maria von. *Die Devisen und Motto des späteren Mittelalters. Ein Beitrag zur Spruchpoesie.* Stuttgart and Tübingen: J. G. Cotta'scher, 1850.

Arranges Latin mottoes and devices of eminent persons alphabetically, but without indicating the sources. Really more concerned with Renaissance than with medieval mottoes.

1876. Spencer, B. *Medieval Pilgrim Badges from Norfolk.* Norwich: Norwich Cathedral, 1980.

Studies, with plates, badges known to have been sold to pilgrims at Norwich Cathedral and in the city.

1877. _____. *Salisbury Museum Medieval Catalogue.* Part 2. Salisbury:
        Salisbury and South Wiltshire Museum, 1990.
        A catalogue with descriptions of tin, lead, and pewter badges
        recovered from the Thames as well as other English archaeological
        sites.

1878. Vignay, Jean de. *Les Merveilles de la Terre d'Outremer:Traduction
        du XIVe siècle du récit d'Odoric de Pordenone.* Translated by
        D. A. Trotter. Exeter: Exeter Univ. Press, 1990.
        Early account of the Holy Land and far east, different shrines, the
        development and sales of their badges, and who had financial control
        of this industry. Appendix includes five excerpts discussing legal
        considerations on badges from thirteenth-century works.

POLYMORPHIC FIGURES

1879. Anderson, William. *The Green Man. The Archetype of Our Oneness
        with the Earth.* London and San Francisco: HarperCollins, 1990.
        A coffee-table study of the green man, broadly interpreted, with
        excellent photos. Not all of them are of wodewoses, as the author
        takes virtually any face in foliage as a green man. But a large
        selection of representations from medieval works of art is presented
        here. Bibliography and index.

1880. Bartra, Roger. *The Artificial Savage: Modern Myths of the Wildman.*
        Ann Arbor: Univ. of Michigan Press, 1996.
        Studies the history of the myth of the wildman chiefly from the
        eighteenth century onward. Some useful medieval material. Fifty-
        seven illustrations.

1881. _____. *Wildmen in the Looking Glass: The Mythic Origins of
        European Otherness.* Translated by Carl T. Berrisford. Ann
        Arbor: Univ. of Michigan Press, 1994.
        The wildman idea provided a useful lens through which to examine
        alien peoples of the period of European colonial expansion. Largely

a reprise of Bernheimer's book on the subject, the author's most useful contribution is the early section on the Greek types of wildmen. Discussions of literature and visual images are somewhat superficial and images aren't analyzed but used as "illustrations." Some plates.

1882. Bernheimer, Richard. *Wild Men in the Middle Ages: A Study in Art, Sentiment, and Demonology.* Cambridge: Harvard Univ. Press, 1952.
   Divided into chapters covering "The Natural History of the Wild Man," "His Mythological Personality," "His Theatrical Embodiment," "The Learned Aspect," "The Erotic Connotations," and "His Heraldic Role," with reference to his appearance throughout literature and art and plates from a number of different medieval art works. Indices.

1883. Druce, George C. "Some Abnormal and Composite Human Forms in English Church Architecture." *AJ* 72 (1915): 135-86.
   Traces the history and attempts to provide an explanation for the presence of some of these polymorphic creatures in church architecture.

1884. Ellis, H. D. "The Wodewose in East Anglian Church Decoration." *PSIASNH* 14 (1912): 287-93.
   Briefly touches on the history of this name for the wild man and then turns to medieval mentions of the word "wodewose" and to numerous examples of the wodewose in East Anglian church decoration, seeking their provenance and the reason for the interest in them.

1885. Husband, Timothy. *The Wild Man: Medieval Myth and Symbolism.* New York: The Metropolitan Museum of Art, 1980.
   A handsome museum exhibition catalogue with an overview essay and many excellent color prints of wild men and women in a variety of different art forms.

1886. Mazur, Oleh. "The Wild Man." Ann Arbor, MI: University Microfilms International, 1980.
   A detailed study with sections on "The Wild Man as an Evolving Concept in Europe and in Spain" (survey, types, history from

antiquity to after 1500, evolution of the idea from antiquity to the twentieth century); "Physical and Spiritual Characteristics of the Wild Man including the *Barbaro* and the Indio" (geographical location, habitat, physical characteristics, clothes, food, personality and sociological traits, theological aspects and the like); and "The Wild Man as a Dramatic Device in Spain, 1522-1700." Bibliography and index.

1887. Sprunger, David. "Wild Folk and Lunatics in Medieval Romance."
The Medieval World of Nature: A Book of Essays. Item 1148, pp. 145-63.
Attempts "to understand better the perplexing madness sequence common in romance" by studying "the iconographic tradition of wild folk and realiz[ing] the multiple implications suggested by this single symbol"(145). Plates.

1888. Tchalenko, John. "Earliest Wildman Sculptures in France." *JMH* 16 (1990): 217-34.
Studies the wildman in French Romanesque capital and tympannum sculpture with a very good assortment of plates.

1889. Wells, D. A. *The Wild Man from the "Epic of Gilgamesh" to Hartmann von Aue's "Iwein": Reflections on the Development of a Theme in World Literature.* New Lecture ser., no. 78. Belfast: The Queen's University, 1974.
Examines the medieval wild man and older sources for this image

1890. White, Hayden. "The Forms of Wildness: Archaeology of an Idea."
Tropics of Discourse: Essays in Cultural Criticism. Baltimore: Johns Hopkins Univ. Press, 1986, pp. 150-82.
Traces a sort of "genealogy of the Wild Man myth, to indicate the function of the notion of wildness in premodern thought" (150), looking at antique, early Christian, and medieval writing and then continuing up until the present with a theoretical and psychological focus.

1891. Williams, Charles Allyn. "The German Legends of the Hairy Anchorite." *Illinois Studies in Language and Literature* 18 (1935): 1-140.

Discusses the German legend of an ascetic (based on a thirteenth-century account) who rapes a virgin princess, imposes penance upon himself by behaving as a beast, and grows hair. Looks also at versions of the story in art, with plates. Provides an edition of two German and one parallel Latin text of the story.

1892. _____. "Oriental Affinities of the Legend of the Hairy Anchorite: The Theme of the Hairy Solitary in Its Early Forms with Reference to *Die Legend von Sanct Johanne Chrysostomo* (Reprinted by Luther, 1537) and to Other European Variants." *Illinois Studies in Language and Literature.* Part 1: "Pre-Christian" 10 (1925): 187-242; Part 2: "Christian" 11 (1926): 429-510.

A detailed study of this figure in pre-Christian and Christian works, investigating the connection between early Oriental and later European versions, citing numerous passages describing him, and touching also on holy women solitaries. Bibliography and index.

PROVERBS AS SOURCES OF IMAGERY

1893. Frank, Grace, and Dorothy Miner. *Proverbes en Rimes: Text and Illustrations of the Fifteenth Century from a French Manuscript in the Walters Art Gallery ,Baltimore.* Baltimore: Johns Hopkins Univ. Press, 1937.

An edition of this fifteenth-century illustrated French book of proverbs with plates of the illustrations included along with an introduction discussing the manuscripts, the illustrations, and their place in the tradition of French proverbs.

1894. Jones, Malcolm. "The Depiction of Proverbs in Late Medieval Art." *Europhras 88: Phraseologie Contrastive. Actes du Colloque International, Klingenthal, Strasbourg, 12-16 mai 1988.* Edited by Gertrud Greciano. Strasbourg: Université des Sciences Humaines, Département d'études allemandes, 1989, pp. 205-24.

Examines the appearance of proverbs and proverb themes, chiefly Flemish, in medieval art, especially woodcarving and metal badges. Some plates.

1895. Taylor, Barry. "Medieval Proverb Collections: The West European Tradition." *JWCI* 55 (1992): 19-35.
"This study offers a survey of the proverb genre in medieval western Europe, concentrated on texts written wholly or partly in Latin"(19), looking at definitions, the range of the genre, the development of books of proverbs, and their purpose.

SHIPS

1896. Friel, Ian. *The Good Ship: Ships, Shipbuilding and Technologies in England 1200-1520.* Baltimore, Johns Hopkins Univ. Press, 1995.
Excellent introduction to the design and iconography of the early ship.

*   Unger, Richard W. *The Art of Medieval Technology.* Cited above as item 1063.
Both a work on art history and the history of technology with many plates of Noah shipbuilding from the third century AD up through the seventeenth century. Examines the changes in the technology of shipbuilding and the manner of depicting it. Bibliographical references, index, and forty-seven pages of plates.

Index

Abeele, Baudouin van den,1446-
7, 1479

Abraham, Claude K., 1324

Abrahams, Israel,1046

Abt-Baechi, Regina, 1113

Achilles, 744

Acker, Paul,1616

Ackerman, John Yonge,1701

Ackerman, Phyllis, 224

Adam and Eve, 1021-28

Adamson, Melitta Weiss, 1704

Adeline, Jules, 437

Adhémar, Jean, 37

Adolf, Helen, 1268

Aerts, W. J., 526

Aesthetics, 21-22

Ages of Man, 795-8

Agnel, Emile,1253

Ainalov, D.V., 38

Alabasters, 159-60

Albert, L., 996

Albert, P., 1366

Alchemy, 573-85

Aldrovandi, Ulisse,1210-13,1388,
1419,1558

Alès, Adhémar d', 1325

Alexander, J. J. G., 23, 239,141,
240, 274, 318,1621,1641

Alexander, Paul J., 959-60

Alexander the Great, 799-805

Allen, Don Cameron,
586,1059,1436,1620

Allen, Judson Boyce, 724

Allen, J. Romilly,1256

Allenbach, Jean, 1051

Allmagne, Henri-René d', 167

Altenburg, Detlef,1705

Alton, E. H., 725

Alverny, Marie-Thérèse d',
870,1779

Ameisenowa, Zofja,1443,1580

Amelli, A. M., 523

Amira, Karl., 336

Amos, Thomas L., 543

Amsler, Mark, 902

Ancona, Mirella Levi d',
1009,1525

Ancona, P. D,'275

Anderson, Flemming G., 240

Anderson, George K., 1796

Anderson, Jørgen, 439

Anderson, Mary D., 58, 445,
1257-58

Anderson, Ruth Matilda,1675

Anderson, William, 1879

Andseron, W. S., 720

Animals:Fables of, 1242-4; in
Heraldry,1245-6; Imaginary,
1333-41; Specific:
Amphisbaena, 1342, Ant-lion,
1508-9, Basilisk, 1343,
Caladrius, 1468, Centaur,
1345, Chimera, 1347,
Cynocephalus, 1348-9,

1348-9, Draconopede, 1350, Dragon, 1351-5, Griffin, 1358-60, Manticore, 1361, Minotaur, 1362, Phoenix, 1469-76, Roc, 1477-8 Satyr,1363-4, Siren, 1411-18 Sphinx, 1365, Unicorn, 1366-76, Werewolf, 1377-9, Woman-headed snake, 1380-4, Yale, 1385-7; Impregnated by wind, 1255; Marine: Barnacle, 1390, Conch, 1391, Crab, 1392, Crocodile,1393-4, Cuttlefish, 1395, Oyster, 1396-7, Pike, 1398, Pilot-fish, 1399, Scallop, 1400-5, Serra/ Sawfish, 1406,Whale, 1407-9,Sea serpent, 1410; Medicine using,1247-8; Naming of,1249; Trials of, 1253; Specific: Ape, 1263-5, Asp, 1266-7, Ass,1268-71, Beaver,1272, Boar,1273, Cat, 1274,Deer/Stag,1275-7, Dog, 1278-82, Elephant, 1283-91, Fox, 1292-97, Giraffe, 1298-9, Goat, 1300, Hare, 1301, Horse, 1302-10, Lamb, 1311, Lion, 1312-17, Lynx, 1318, Ox,1319, Pig, 1320-23, Rabbit, 1324, Rhinoceros, 1325-6, Salamander, 1327, Snake, 1328, Tiger, 1329, Toad, 1330,Tropical; 1254; Weasel, 1331 ; Wood and stone carvings of , 1256-62;

Birds: 1419-35, Bird of Paradise, 1458, Cock, 1436-40, Crow, 1441, Dove, 1442, Eagle, 1443-5, Goldfinch, 1451, Hoopoe, 1452, Lark, 1453, Nightingale, 1454-7, Partridge, 1459, Peacock, 1460, Pelican, 1461-4, Raven, 1465, Robin, 1466, Thrush, 1467, Insects: Bee, 1500-1, Fly, 1502-3, Scorpion, 1504-5, Snail, 1506-7
André, Lewis J., 1114-15
Andrews, M. C., 615
Anglo-Saxon art, 23-36
Antichrist, 931-6
Antique heritage, 37-42
Apocalypse illustration, 937-958
Apocrypha, 882-95
Apollo, 745
Aptowitzer,V., 1032
Architecture, 43-52
Arentzen, J.-G., 616
Ariès, Philippe,1716
Aristotle, 806-10
Armor, 1653-69
Armstrong, Edward A., 1420
Arn, Mary-Jo,1706
Arnulphus of Orleans, 687
Arthur, king, 811-15
Artists, female, 61-62
Ascherl, Rosemary,1653
Ashworth, William B., Jr.,1138
Assirelli, Marco,1756
Astrology, 586-605
Attitudes towards Art, 63-69

Aurell, Martin,1707
Aurenhammer, Hans, 1
Aurigemma, Luigi,1504
Avray, D. L.D,' 544
Azouvi, F. ,606

Babcock, Robert G.,136
Backhouse, Janet, 276, 389, 400-402
Baer, Eva,1365
Baert, Barbara, 990
Bagpipe,1851-5
Bailey, Richard N., 24
Baird, Joseph L., 1454
Baird-Lange, Lorrayne,1437
Baisier, Léon,1583
Baldwin, Robert, 1733
Baldwin, Spurgeon P.,1187
Baltrusaitis, Jurgis, 39
Bambeck, Manfred,1596
Bandini, A.,112
Bandmann, Gunter,1833
Bannister, A.T.,115
Barasch, Moshe, 1734-5
Barb, A. A.,1033, 1391, 1411
Barber, Richard,1333,1204
Barbier de Montault, Xavier,1200
Baring-Gould, S.,1116
Barkai, Ron, 587
Barkan, Leonard,1480
Barker, Nicholas,1182
Barley, Nigel F.,1622
Barnard, Mary E.,745
Barral i Altet, Xavier, 156, 961
Barrette, Paul, 512
Bartelink, G. J. M.,1084
Bartholomaeus Anglicus, 504-10

Barton, Tamsyn, 588
Bartra, Roger, 1880-1
Bartscht, Waltraud, 1358
Bascapè, Giacomo C., 1747
Basing, Patricia, 1637
Baskervill, Charles Read,1648
Baswell, Christopher, 743
Bataillon, Louis-Jacques, 533, 545
Bath, Michael, 1275-6
Baths, 1670-1
Bauer, J. B,1301
Bawcutt, Priscilla,1453
Baxandall, Michael, 456
Baxter, Ronald, 1245
Beards,1605-7
Beatus of Liebana, 987
Beaugendre, Anne-Caroline,1816
Beauty,1596-1604
Bechmann, Roland, 1559
Beckwith, John,207
Bedos, Brigitte, 1748
Beds,1672-3
Beer, Ellen J., 337
Beer, Jeanette, 1207
Beer, Robert Rüdiger, 1367
Behling, Lottlisa,1535-6, 1549
Behrends, R., 896
Behrends, Rayner, 937
Beigbeder, Olivier, 2
Bellew, G.,1400
Belon, Pierre, 1421
Bender, Margaret, 931
Benson, Robert G.,1736
Benton, Janetta Rebold, 1215
Berg, Gösta,1727
Bergamini, Laurie J.,1010
Bergman, Robert P., 208

Bergouignan, Paul,1021
Bériou, Nicole, 1797
Berlioz, Jacques, 534
Berman, Ruth, 1412
Bernabò, M.,1263
Bernard of Chartres, 688
Bernard Silvester, 689
Bernheimer, Richard,1882
Bernstein, Alan E.,1085
Berrurier, Diane O. le, 524
Bersuire, Pierre, 698-706
Berti, Giordano,168
Besserman, Lawrence L.,1049
Best, M. R., 1216
Bestiaries,1180-1209
Bett, Henry, 962, 1717
Betten, Francis S.,617
Betz, Hans Dieter,1780
Beuningen, H. J. E. van, 1868
Beyerle, K., 305
Bianciotto, Gabriel, 1139, 1205
Bible, 877-88; moralized, 896-
    901
Bieber, M., 799
Biedermann, Hans, 648
Billington, Sandra,1757
Bilson, John, 1086
Bing, Gertrude, 938
Binski, Paul, 277
Biow, Douglas,1817
Bisi, Anna Maria, 1359
Bivium or letter Y, 816
Black, W. H., 141
Blair, Claude,1654
Blanch, Robert J.,1623
Blankenburg, Wera von,1217
Blick, Sarah,1869

Bloch, R. Howard, 903
Bloomfield, M., 746
Blume, Dieter, 471
Blumenfeld-Kosinski,
    Renate,1117
Blumenkranz, Bernhard, 1798
Blunt, Wilfrid, 1531
Bober, Harry, 384, 511, 589
Boehm, Barbara D.,187
Boenig, Robert, 1851
Boer, C. de, 726
Boethius, 717-18
Boglioni, Pierre,1250
Boitani, Piero,1011
Bolgar, R. R.,1655
Bologna, Corrado, 621
Bolton, Diane K., 707
Boltz, Wiliam G., 1298
"Bombardier,"1422
Bond, Francis, 439, 477-8
Bonnell, John K.,1380
Borchardt, Frank L., 866
Borgehammer, Stephan, 991
Borland, C. A.,110
Born, Lester K., 695, 727
Borst, Arno, 863, 1029
Bouard, Michel de, 514
Boucher, François,1676
Bourgain, Louis, 546
Bovini, Giuseppe, 426
Bowers, R. H.,1052
Bowles, Edmund A., 1834
Braekman, W. L., 1448
Braider, Christopher, 241
Brain,1608
Brandl, Rainer, 338
Branner, Robert, 278

Brasses, 161-66
Bratschkova, Maria, 1401
Bratton, Susan Power, 1512,1560
Braude, Pearl F., 1034
Brault, Gerard J.,1749
Breasts,1609-11
Bréhier, Louis, 4
Breiner, Laurence A., 1343
Bremmer, Jan, 1737
Bremond, Claude, 535
Brendel, Otto J., 831
Bretèque, François de la,1312
Brewer, Derek, 1597, 1656
Bridaham, Lester Burbank, 452
Brieger, Peter H., 939
Brincken, Anna-Dorothee von
    den, 527, 618-20
Brody, Saul Nathaniel, 1799
Broek, R. van den,1469
Brown, A. K.,1520
Brown, Howard Mayer,1835
Brown, Michelle P., 279
Brown, Robert, Jr.,1368
Brown, Sarah, 192
Brown, T. J., 403
Brown, Virginia, 685
Brownrigg, Linda, 280
Bruning, E., 1567
Brusatin, Manlio, 1624
Bruyne, Edgar de, 21
Bruzelius, Caroline, 70
Bryce, Derek, 25
Bühler, Curt F., 281
Bukofzer, M., 1836
Bunt, Cyril G. E., 1313
Bunt, Gerrit H. V., 800
Burger, Edward K., 963

Buridant, Claude, 622, 1858
Burnett, Charles S. F., 712, 1781
Burrow, J. A., 795
Burton, T. L.,1393
Butkovich, Anthony, 1118
Butts, Thomas E.,1852
Bynum, Caroline Walker, 1708
Byrne, Donal, 282, 504-5
Byvanck, Alexander William,
    356-57

Cabrol, F., 5
Cahier, Charles, 1150
Cahn, Walter, 283
Cain,1032-42
Calkins, Robert G., 284
Callaghan, Mary, 781
Callisen, S. A.,1438
Camille, Michael, 24, 396, 427
Campaspe, 806-10
Campbell, Mary B., 623
Campbell, Sheila, 649
Camporesi, Piero, 1709
Canon and Roman Law, 817-19
Caplan, Harry, 547-8
Caprotti, Erminio, 1334
Caputo, Cosimo, 607
Carey, Hilary M., 590
Carmody, Francis M.,1151
Carpenter, Nan Cooke,1837
Carrol, William Meridith,1218
Carroll-Spillecke, M.,1526
Carter, John Marshall, 1718
Cassidy, Brendan, 243
Castles, 53-57
Cathedral and churches, 58-62
Cavallo, Adolfo, 225

Cave, C. J. P.,446,479-80
Cavendish, Richard,1069
Caviness, Madeline H.,193-99
Cazelles, Raymond,404
Céard, Jean,1030
Cella, Mariaserena,1413
Ceramics and tiles, 178-84
Cerberus, 746-8
Ceresoli, A.,1481
Cerulli, Enrico,1070-71
Chamot, M.,188
Champeaux, Gerard de, 6
Chance, Jane, 670-1
Chandès, Gérard,1782
Chandler, Albert R.,1455
Charlesworth, James H., 882-6
Charon, 749
Chastel, André,1120, 1502
Cheetham, Francis, 159
Cheney, Liana,1642
Cherry, John, 221
Cheyney, David R., 1361
Chibnall, Marjorie, 497
Chickering, Howell, 1657
Christ, Passion of, 999-1001;
    images of, 988-9
Christe, Y., 964
Church Feasts, 1108-11
Ciavolella, Massima,772
Cioffari, Vincent, 821
Circe, 750
City,1619
Clark, Anne, 1335
Clark, David L, 549
Clark, Willene B., 1152, 1423
Clarke, A. K., 693
Clarke, T. H.,1326

Clayton, Muriel, 161
Clébert, Jean-Paul,1140
Clément, Félix, 1269
Clier-Colombani, Françoise, 1414
Cliffs,1511
Clocks,1674
Cockerell, Sydney C., 1015
Cogliati, Luisa Arano, 1153, 1537
Cohen, Esther, 1870
Cohen, I. B., 1219
Cohen, Jeremy, 1067, 1800-1
Cohen, Susan Sarah, 1892
Cohn, Norman, 1060
Coldstream, Nicola, 43, 440
Cole, Penny J., 550
Coletti, Teresa, 1012
Colker, Marvin L., 107
Collections, 70-72; of
    manuscripts, 73-155
Collins, Arthur H., 1259,1292
Collins, Patrick J., 244
Collison, Robert, 498
Colnort-Bodet, Suzanne, 573
Color, 1620-32; Specific:
    black,1633, blue, 1634, red,
    1635-6
Colvin, Howard,44, 428
Cómez, R., 1482
Compass, 820
Compendium Philosophiae, 514
Complexions and Physiognomy,
    616-14
Contamine, Philippe,1658
Cook, Albert Stanburrough, 1154
Cooke, J. D., 779
Cooper, Helen,1783
Copenhaver, Brian P., 1399

Cornelius, Roberta D., 53
Cornell, Henrik, 472, 897
Costa, Dennis J., 965
Costello, Peter, 1336
Costume,1675-1799
Coulson, Frank T.,759
Coulter, Cornelia Catlin,1407
Courcelle, Pierre, 717, 823,1381,1415
Courtens, André, 358
Cox, Charles J., 481-2
Coxe, Henry O., 142, 940
Crafts, 1637-40
Crane, Thomas Frederick, 536
Creasy, William C., 1087
Crichton, G. H., 458
Crick-Kuntzinger, Marthe,1061
Cross legends, 990-5
Cross, J. E.,1283
Cummins, John, 1483
Cunningham, Hugh, 1719
Cunnington, C. Willett, 1677-8
Curley, Michael J.,1362
Curschmann, Michael,1738
Curtius, Ernst Robert, 904-5
Cushions,1700
Cutler, Allan Harris, 1803
Cutler, Anthony, 209
Cutler, Charles D., 359,1679

D'Hulst, Roger-A., 228
Dahan, Gilbert, 1035
Dainville, François de, 624
Dal, Erik, 796
Dalas, Martine,1750
Dalton, O. M., 210
Damisch, Hubert, 763

Dance,1641-7
Daniel, E. Randolph, 966
Dansette, Beatrice,1859
Danthine, Hélène,1581
Daphne,751
Darré, René, 1818
Dauphiné, J., 1351
Davenport, Millia,1680
David, Biblical king, 1043-5
Davidson, Clifford, 245,1002,1072,1088-89,1739,1758
Davidson, Linda K., 1860
Davies, Sioned, 1302
Davis, J. I.,1199
Davis-Weyer, Caecilia, 285
Davy, M. M., 551
Dawn, 1648-9
Dawson, Warren R.,1452
De Winter, Patrick M.,77
Dean, James, 871-2
Debidour, V.-H., 1260
Decalogue, 1046-7
Del Zotto Tozzoli, Carla, 1155
Delaissé, L. M. J., 2, 286, 360
Delbouille, Maurice, 806.
Delisle, Léopold, 940
Demaitre, Luke E.,1804
Demay, G.,1681
Dennys, Rodney, 1751
Deonna, W.,1392,1416, 1505
Derolez, Albert, 518-19
Deserts,1512
Deshman, Robert, 27
Desmond, Marilynn R., 728
Destombes, Marcel, 625
Deuchler, Florens, 942

Devil, 1084-1107
DeVries, Kelly, 54
Diagrams, 237-8
Diana and Actaeon, 1480
Dickins, Bruce, 845
Didron, A.,7
Diekstra, F. N. M., 1157
Dierbach, Johann Heinrich,1538
Dietmaring, Ursula, 1650
DiMarco,Vincent,1062
Dinzelbacher, P.,1073
Diringer, David,287
Distaff,1701-3
Distinctiones, 902-917
Doak, Robert, 1625
Dodwell, C. R, 28
Dogaer, Georges, 361
Dolezalek, G., 817
Dols, Michael W.,1759
Don, Gerard Le,1090
Donaldson, Ian, 753
Donati, Lamberto, 288
Donovan, Claire, 390
Donovan, Mortimer J.,1396, 1476
Doob, Penelope Reed, 834, 1760
Doors,1730-31
Doren, A., 824
Dove, Mary, 797
Drake, Maurice, 1121
Drawings, 185-6
Drobná, Doroslava, 306, 1682
Dronke, Peter, 710,
    1568,1627,1819
Druce, George Claridge,1157-8,
    1191,1220, 1284, 1300, 1314,
    1320, 1342, 1385, 1394, 1406,
    1424, 1461, 1468, 1508, 1883

Dubost, Francis, 1303
Dubourg.-Noves, Pierre, 1261
Duchenne, M. C., 528
Duchesne, Annie, 1820
Duchet-Suchaux, Gaston,
    246,1122
DuFeil, Michel-Marie, 1254
Dukes, Eugene D. I.,1784
Dumezil, Georges,1345-6
Dummett, Michael, 169
Duncan, T., 1331
Dunn-Lardeau, Brenda, 1251
Durand, Paul, 247
Dutschke, C. W.,105, 151
Dutton, Paul Edward,688
Duval, Yves-Marie, 1053
Dvorakova, Vlasta, 307
Dwarves, 1821,1831

Eames, Elizabeth,178-9
Eamon, William, 591
Earth,1513
Eberly, Susan S., 1577
Eckhardt, Caroline D., 782
Eco, Umberto, 63
Eden, P. T.,1159
Edsman, Carl-Martin, 836
Edwards, A. S. G., 506
Eemans, Marc, 362
Egbert, Donald D., 405
Egbert, V. W., 768
Ehltert, Trude, 801
Ehrenstein, Theodor, 1016
Ehrhart, Margaret J.,764
Einhorn, Jürgen W.,1369
Ell, Stephen R.,1805
Elliott, J. K., 887

Ellis, H. D.,1884
Emboden, William A.,1553
Emmerson, Richard K.,932, 943, 967-8
Emmerson, Robin, 162
Enamel, 187-91
Engels, Joseph, 698-701,729,906
Erffa, Hans Martin von, 1017
Erich, Oswald Adolf,1091
Ernault, Emile,1584
Ernst, Ulrich, 783
Erzgräber, Willi, 40
Esche, Sigrid, 1022
Esmeijer, Anna C., 248
Etymologies, 902-917
Euhemerism, 779-80
Euw, A. von, 78
Evans, David, 200
Evans, Elizabeth Cornelia, 1612
Evans, E. P.,1262
Evans, Joan, 157,423,453,1585-6, 1594
Evans, Jonathan D.,1352
Evans, Michael W.,185,1569
Evelyn, Charlotte d,' 933
Everest, Carol A., 1550
Exegesis, 918-930
Exempla, 533

Face, 1612-14
Fairies, 1356
Falkenburg, Reindert L., 1539
Faraci, Dora, 1181
Faral, Edmond, 1417
Farquhar, James Douglas, 289
Fawtier, Robert, 131, 898
Feast,1704-15

Feder, Lillian,1761
Fenton, Alexander, 1710
Ferrari, Mirella, 130
Fertility, 1067
Fierens, M. Paul, 363
Fiero, Gloria K., 429
Fischer, Nancy,1221
Fisher, A . S . T.,1458
Fisher, John Hurt, 1304
Fitzgerald, Wilma,73
Five Senses, 1617-18
Fleming, John V.,784
Flight, 1732
Flint, Valerie I. J., 515,609-10, 626-27,1785
Flores, Nona C., 1222,1285, 1382
Floyer, J., 155
Fontaine, Jacques, 516, 592, 907
Fontenrose, Joseph,758
Food,1704-15
Fools,1756-78
Forbes, Thomas, R.,1247
Forster, Richard, 608
Forsyth, Ilene H.,454, 1013,1439
Fortune's Wheel, 821-9
Fountain of Life, 830
Fouquet, Doris, 864
Fowler, James,1514
Frakes, Jerold C., 825
Frank, Grace, 999,1893
Freeman, Margaret B., 1370
French, Katherine L.,1605
French, Thomas, 201
Freyhan, R., 969
Friedman, John B.,152, 525, 609-10,650, 696, 747,760, 776, 820,1000, 1054-5,1278,

1305,1337,1350,1570,1587,
1643,1700
Friedmann, Herbert ,
1315,1451,1459
Friel, Ian,1896
Frinta, Mojmír, 308
Fritz, Jean-Marie, 1762
Fritzsche, Gabriela, 202
Fromm, Hans, 908
Frontain, Raymond-Jean, 1043
Früehmorgen-Voss, Hella, 339
Frugoni, Chiara,1619
Fulgentius, 719
Funerary art,426-36
Fyler, John M., 672

Gaborit-Chopin, Danielle, 211
Gaier, Claude,1659-60
Gaignebet, Claude,1615
Gaillard, Georges, 463
Galpin, Francis W.,1838
Games,1716-25
Gameson, Richard, 29,877
Gandilhon, René, 1277
Ganymede, 752
Gardens,1525-30
Gardiner, Eileen,1074-5
Gardner, Arthur, 430,447,455,483
Garnier, François, 8,1740,1763
Gauthier, Marie-Madeleine,189
Geerard, M., 888
Geijer, Agnes, 226
Génévoix, A.-M.,113
Genitalia, 1615
Geoffrey de Vitry, 693
Geography, 615-647
George, Wilma, 1160, 1386

Gerhardt, Cristoph,1462-3,1470
Gerhardt, Mia L., 757,1141,1395,
1509
Gero, Stephen, 889
Gesner, Conrad,1223,
Gesture, 1733-46
Gettings, Fred, 574, 593
Geurts, A. J.,365
Ghisalberti, Fausto, 694, 702, 730-
31
Giants,1829-30
Gibson, Margaret T., 878, 918
Gibson, Walter S., 366
Gieben, S.,703
Giet, S.,1353
Gifford, D. J., 1764
Gillerman, Dorothy W.,71
Gilligan, Janet, 785
Gilman, Sander L., 537
Ginzberg, Louis, 919
Giovanni del Virgilio, 694
Giraud, Yves F.-A., 751
Glass, 192-206
Glosses, 918-930
Göbel, Heinrich, 227
God as a Circle, 1068
Goffin, Arnold, 367
Goldman, Bernard,1730
Goldmann, B.,1360
Goldschmidt, Adolph, 212-13,499
Golem,1822
Goossens, Jan, 1224
Gosman, Martin, 628
Gosselin, Edward A.,1044
Gottfried, Robert S., 651
Gottlieb, Carla,1731
Goulburn, Edward Meyrick, 484

Grabar, André, 290, 1076
Grabes, Herbert, 837
Graham, Victor E.,1464
Grammar, 832
Grancsay, Stephen V.,1661
Gransden, Antonia,1142
Grant, Edward, 594-5
Graus, J., 997
Graus, F., 867
Green, Rosalie B., 1023
Greenhill, Eleanor Simmons, 1571-2
Greetham, D. C., 507
Grimm, Reinhold R., 1077
Grodecki, Louis, 1003
Grootkerk, Paul, 1363
Gross, Angelika, 1765
Grössinger, Christa, 485
Gueranger, Prosper, 1108
Guerrrau-Jalabert, Anita,1711
Guillaumont, François, 1651
Guldan, Ernst, 1024, 1092
Gumilev, L. N., 629
Gurevich, Aaron J., 249
Gurewich, Vladimir, 1001
Gutmann, Joseph, 1066

Habicht, Werner,1741
Haines, Francis, 1306
Hair,1605-7
Halleux, Robert, 575,1588
Hamburger, Jeffrey F., 406
Hamel, Christopher De, 291,920
Hammerstein, Reinhold, 1839
Hands,1616
Harbison, Craig, 368
Harf-Lancner, L., 1356

Hargrave, Catherine Perry, 170
Harley, J. B., 630
Harms,Wolfgang, 816.
Harries, Karsten,1068
Harris, Elizabeth Lee, 467
Harrison, F., 319
Harrison, Frank L.,1840
Harrison, Frederick, 1018
Harrison, Robert Pogue, 1561
Harrison, Thomas P., 1425-26
Hart, Clive,1732
Harte, N. B., 1683
Harthan, John P., 391, 1161
Hartlaub, G. F., 838
Harvey, John,1527
Harvey, P. D. A., 631-2
Harvey, Ruth E., 1766
Harward, Vernon J., 1821
Hassall, A. G., 944
Hassall, William O., 407,1019,1201,1532
Hassig, Debra, 1162
Hattinger, Franz, 408
Hatto, Arthur T., 1286,1649
Haureau, B., 732
Haussherr, Reiner, 899
Headdress, 1696
Heaven, 1069-83
Heckscher, William S., 250, 673,1287
Heffernan, Carol Falvo,1471
Heffernan, Thomas J., 552
Heimann, Adelheid, 186
Heinrichs, Katherine, 674
Heinz, Peter Ubach, 769
Heist, William W.,1004
Hell,1084-1107

Helleiner, Karl F., 633
Helsinger, Howard,1485
Henderson, Arnold Clayton, 1242-1243
Henderson, George, 945-8,1036
Henisch, Bridget Ann,1712
Henkel, Nikolaus, 1163
Henry, Avril, 900
Heraldry,1747-55
Herbert, J. A., 292
Herman, Gerald, 1662
Hermerén, Göran, 251
Hermon, Sharon, 309
Heron-Allen, Edward, 1390
Heuvelmans, Bernard,1410
Hexter, Ralph,733
Heydenreich, Ludwig H., 45
Hicks, Carola, 1225
Hieroglyphics, 833
Hill, Thomas D., 786
Hillgarth, J. N., 910
Himmelfarb, Martha, 890,1093
Hinckley, Henry Barrett,1427
Hindman, Sandra, 293, 369, 811, 899
Hippeau, C., 1192
Hoffeld, Jeffrey M., 1383
Hoffman, Detleff,171
Hoffman, Richard C., 1398
Hoffmann, Marta,1672
Hohler, Christopher,1402
Holbrook, R. T., 1226
Hole, Christina, 1720
Hollander, John, 1841
Holloway, Julia Bolton, 513,1702
Hollander, Robert, 777
Holmes, Urban Tigner, Jr.,

502,1338
Holt, Elizabeth Gilmore, 64
Holter, Kurt, 340
Holzworth, Jean, 687
Hommel, Hildebrecht,1786
Honorius of Autun, 515
Horae, 389-95
Horst, K. van der,153, 370
Houdoy, Jules,1598
Houlet, Jacques, 850
Houston, Mary G., 1684
Howey, Oldfield M.,1307
Hsia, R. Po-Chia, 1806
Hubaux, Jean,1472
Hughes, B., 787
Hughes, Robert, 1078.
Huhn, Vital, 1279
Hull. P., 921
Humphreys, H. H.,1371
Huneycutt, Lois, 859
Hunt, R. W., 503
Hunter, George Leland, 229-30
Hunting, 1479-97
Husband, Timothy B., 203-4, 1885
Husenbeth, F. C., 1124
Hutchinson, G. Evelyn,1143
Hyatte, Reginald, 1842
Hyde, J. K., 634

Iconography, 239-73
Idel, Moshe, 1822
Igarashi-Takeshita, Midori, 1316
Illumination: 274-303; Armenian 304; Bohemian 305-17; English, 318-31; French, 332-5; German, 336-

54; Italian, 355;
Netherlandish,356-83
Imbault-Huart, Marie-José, 652.
Incarnation as a Unicorn Hunt,
    996-8
Indergrand, Michel,1628
Ingersoll, Ernest,1428
Inglis, Eric, 409
Isaac, 1048
Isidore of Seville, 516
Iversen, Erik, 833
Ives, Samuel A., 1164
Ivory, 207-20
Izdorczyk, Zbigniew, 891

Jacquart, Danielle, 653
Jaffe, Irma B., 635
Jalabert, Denise,1418,1540-41
James, E. O.,1109, 1188-99
James, Montague Rhodes, 64, 65,
    79, 84-101, 124-126,132,181,
    892, 949-51, 1020,
Janson, Horst W., 1264
Jervis, Jane L., 596
Jesse, 1578-9
Jewelry, 221-23
Joachim of Flora, 970
Job, 1049-50
Jochens, Jenny,1606
John of Garland, 695
Jonah, 1051-5
Jones, E. J.,1752
Jones, George Fenwick,
    1663,1685,1853
Jones, Julian Ward, Jr., 686, 689
Jones, Karen Q., 788
Jones, Malcolm, 1227,1894

Jones, Peter Murray, 654
Jonin, Pierre, 1721
Jónnson, Einar Már, 839
Jordan, Leo, 611
Jordan, William Chester,1807
Joret, Charles, 1551
Jossua, Jean-Pierre, 1372
Joubert, Fabienne, 231
Jourdain, M. A., 232
Jung, Marc-René, 734, 868
Juvenal, 720-22

Kaeppeli, Thomas, O. P., 553
Kallendorf, Craig, 675
Kaplan, Paul H. D., 1005
Kaplan, Stuart R., 172
Karkov, Catherine, 30
Katzenellenbogen, Adolf, 851
Kauffmann, C. M., 320
Kaufmann, Lynn Frier,1364
Kaufmann, Thomas Da Costa, 371
Kearney, Milo,1321
Keenan, Hugh T., 922
Keiser, George R.,1589
Keller, John E., 252
Kellner, K. A. Heinrich, 1010
Kelly, Henry Ansgar, 1384
Kempter, Gerda, 752
Kenseth, Joy, 1823
Kent, J. P. C.,163
Keyser, C. E., 469
Kieckhefer, Richard, 1787-8,1125
King, David J. Cathcart, 55
King, Donald,233
King, Katherine Callen, 744
Kinter, William L., 775
Kirby, H. T.,1578

Kirsch, Edith W.,134
Kirsch, G. P., 431
Kirschbaum, Engelbert,10
Klein, P. K. ,971
Klein-Franke, F.,1590
Klemp, P. J., 789
Kletzel, Otto, 310
Klibansky, Raymond, 773
Kliege, Herma, 636
Klijn, A. F. J., 1064
Klinck, Roswitha, 910
Klingender, Francis D.,1228,1429
Knitting,1697
Knortz, Karl, 1328, 1498
Koch, Robert A., 1327,1542, 1548
Koechlin, Raymond, 214
Koehler, Wilhelm, 341-44
Köhn, Anna, 1599
Kollmann, Judith J.,1346
Konrad of Megenberg, 517
Konstantinowa, Alexandra, 1194
Koppenfels, Werner von, 988
Korte, Gandulf, 1126
Korteweg, Anne S., 372
Koschorreck, Walter, 345
Köster, Kurt, 1403-04,1871-3
Kramár, Vincent, 422
Krása, Josef, 311
Kraus, Dorothy, 486
Krautheimer, Richard, 46
Kren, Claudia, 576
Krey, Philip D. W., 972
Krill, Richard M.,713
Kriss-Rittenbeck, Lenz, 1861
Krochalis, Jeanne,74
Krofta, Jan, 312
Kronholm,Tryggve, 1037

Kügler, Hartmut, 637
Kuhn, Charles L., 321
Kulcár, Peter, 714
Künstle,Karl,11, 1644
Kuntze, F., 998
Kurtz, Otto, 655
Kuss, René, 656
Kutal, Albert, 313

Labande-Mailfert, Y., 852
Laborde, Alexandre De, 385, 901
Labors of the Months,1514-17
Labyrinths, 834-5
Lack, David,1466
Ladner, Gerhart B., 253, 992,
    1742
Laistner, M. L. W., 597
Lambert, Carole,1713
Lambert of Saint Omer, 518-22
Lamech,1056-7
Lampl, Paul, 47
Lanc, Elga, 468
Landscape,1510
Lane, Barbara G., 373
Lange, Hanne,790-1
Langlois, Charles, 1144
Langosch, Karl, 1573
Lantschoot, A. van, 1165
Last Judgement,1002-4
Last, Hugh, 1789
Latini, Brunetto, 512-13
Laufer, Berthold, 1299
Laurant, Jean-Pierre, 911
Lavedan, Pierre,48
Le Maitre, H.,767
Leach, Maria,1280
Lechner, Joseph, 1111

Leclercq-Kadaner, J., 1513
Lecouteux, Claude,1344,1348, 1518,1824-5
Lecoy, A. de la Marche, 554
Leeming, David Adams, 1347
Lefevre, Yves, 520
Left, 1650-2
Legaré, Anne-Marie, 1722
Lehmann-Haupt, Hellmut, 420
Lehmberg, S. E., 59
Lejard, André, 952
Lejeune, Rita, 182, 861
Lennep, J. van, 577
Leroquais, Victor, 294, 392
Lesnick, Daniel R., 555
Lever, Maurice, 1767
Levine, R., 735
Levy, B. J., 538
Levy, Brian, 1293
Levy, Mervyn,1609
Lewes, Ulle Erika, 1562
Lewis, Flora, 1127
Lewis, Suzanne, 973
Liebaers, Herman, 374
Liebeschütz, Hans, 697,1808
Light, Laura, 102
Lightbown, Ronald W., 222
Lindner, Kurt,1486
Lindsay, W. M., 912
Liniares, Armand, 1196
Lipscomb, William Lowndes, 893
Liturgy, 1108-11
Liver, Ricarda, 770
Llewellyn, Nigel, 432
Lloyd, Joan Barclay, 1288
Loffler, Christa Maria,1079
London, H. Stanford, 1281

Long, James R., 508
Longère, Jean, 556
Longhurst, Margaret H., 215-16
Longland, Sabrina, 1007
Loomis, Roger Sherman,183, 812, 846-47
Löther, Helmut, 1459
Lowrie, Walker,12
Luard, H. R., 101
Luck, Georg, 1790
Lucretia, 753
Lundberg, Erik, 473
Lurçat, Jean, 953
Lurker, Manfred, 3, 13,1574
Luscombe, David, 923
Lusignan, Serge, 529-30
Luzzatto, Aldo,135
Lyre,1856-7

MacDougall, Elisabeth Blair,1528
MacDougall, Hugh A., 869
MacFarlane, Katherine Nell, 676
Machielsen, Johannis, 557
Mackeprang, M., 106
MacKinney, Loren, 657
MacLean, Sally-Beth, 448
Macray, William, 143-5
Madan, Falconer,146
Madden, Dodgson Hamilton, 1487
Madness,1756-78
Madou, Mireille,1686
Magi, 1005
Magic, 1779-95
Maguire, Henry, 1128
Malaxecheverria, Ignacia, 1272
Mâle, Emile, 254-6,410
Malo, Henri, 411

Maltby, Robert, 913
Malvern, Majorie M., 1006
Man as an Upside-down Tree, 836
Manion, Margaret M., 82, 139,
    257
Manuscripts, facsimiles of, 400-
    19; films of, 407
Marchand, James W., 989
Marginal groups,1796-1815
Marginalia, 396-9
Marks, Richard, 205, 322
Marle, Raimond van,14
Marly, Diana de,1687
Marrow, James H., 258, 375-377
Marshall, Peter K., 708
Marsilli, Pietro, 807
Martianus Capella, 723
Martin, Ernest W., 1430
Martindale, Charles,736
Marvels,1816-32
Mary Magdelene,1006
Matejcek, Antonín, 314-15
Matheson, Lister M., 598
Mathews, Thomas F., 304, 677
Matthews, W. H., 835
Mayer, Maximillian, 1826
Mayo, Penelope C., 1582
Mayr-Harting, Henry, 346
Mazur, Oleh,1886
Mazure, André, 1025
McAlindon, T., 1095,1827
McCulloch, Florence, 1166,1266,
    1329, 1387,1397
McDannell, Colleen, 1080
McDermott, William Coffman,
    1265
McDonald, Sister Mary Francis,

1473
McDonald, William C., 1768
McGinn, Bernard, 974-6
McGurk, Patrick, 668
McKinnon, James W.,1856
McLaughlin, R. Emmet, 558
McLean, Teresa, 1529,1723
McMilan, Douglas J.,1474
McNamara, M.,894
Mead, William Edward, 1714
Means, Laurel, 599
Medea,754
Medicine, 648-65
Meer, Frederick Vander, 977
Meier, Christel, 1629
Meiss, Millard, 332-4,412-414
Mellinkoff, Ruth, 860, 1038,
    1058,1809
Melnikas, Anthony, 818
Mély, Fernand de, 378,1026,1591
Ménard, Philippe, 1377,1488,
    1613, 1743,1769-1770
Menhardt, Hermann,1554
Mennell, Stephen, 1715
Menner, R. J., 780
Merlin, Romain, 173
Mermier, Guy R., 1206, 1475
Messelken, Hans,1465
Meulen, Jan van der, 60
Meurant, René,1828
Meyer, H., 791
Meyer, Paul, 1592
Michel, Paul Henri,1039, 1229
Middleton, Henry J., 295
Milburn, R. L. P., 1129
Miles, Margaret R., 1610
Mill,1726

Millar, Eric G., 108, 323-4, 1180
Miller, Elaine, 658
Miller, Konrad, 638
Millet, J., 1167
Mills, James, 443-4
Miner, Dorothy, 61
Minerva, 755
Minkoski, Helmut, 1031
Mirimonde, A. P., 1511, 1843-4
Mirror, 837-44
Misch, Manfred,1500
Mitchell, H. P.,190
Mitchell, Sabrina, 296
Mitchiner, Michael,1874
Mittler, Elmar, 347
Mode, Heinz, 1339
Model books, 420-1
Mokretsova, I. P., 75
Molinier, Emile, 217
Molland, A. G., 1791
Mombello, Gianni, 297
Monson, Craig A., 62
Montagu, Jeremy, 1845
Monumental art: Bohemian,422;
    English,423; French,424;
    Netherlandish,425
Moore, R. I.,1810
Moralejo, Serafin, 464
Morand, Kathleen, 425
Morey, Charles Rufus, 15
Morey, James H., 924
Morgan, Alison,1081
Morgan, Nigel, 298,325,954
Morse, Ruth, 754
Morson, John, 1167
Morvay, Karin, 559
Moses, 1058

Mosher, Joseph Albert, 539
Mossé, Ferdinand, 1294
Mountains, 1518-19
Mousetrap, 1727-9
Mozley, J. H., 1271
Müller, Ulrich, 348
Mundy, E. James, 379
Munro, John H.,1636
Munrow, David, 1846
Müntz, M. E., 234 ,678
Muratova, Xenia, 1168-
    70,1195,1202,1249
Music, 1833-50
Musper, H. Th., 955
Mutherich, Florence, 349
Mynors R. A. B., 115,116,147
Mythology, 666-84

Narcissus, 756
Narkiss, Bezalel, 76, 111
Nash, Susie, 299
Neale, R. E., 1771
Neaman, Judith S.,1772
Neckham,Alexander, 502-3
Neptune, 757
Neubert, Fritz, 612
Newhauser, Richard, 852
Newlyn, Evelyn S., 1014
Newman, William R., 578-9
Newton, Peter, 206
Newton, Stella Mary, 1688
Nichols, Ann Eljenholm,1112
Nichols, Stephen G., Jr., 259
Nicholson, Marjorie Hope, 1519
Nickel, Helmut, 1664
Nicolle, David, 1665
Night, 1648-9

Nikolasch, Franz, 1311
Nine Worthies, 845, 849
Noah, 1059-63
Nolan, Edward Peter, 840
Noppen, J. G., 956
Norden, Linda van,1633
Nordenfalk, Carl, 31, 1130,1618
Nordström, Carl-Otto, 925-6
Norman, Joanne S., 854
Norris, Malcolm, 164
Norström, Folke, 466
North, J. D., 600-2
Norton, Christopher, 184
Nowotny, Karl A., 639
Numerology, 781-94
Núñez Rodríguez, M.,1489

O'Connor, Eugene, 1617
O'Neill, Ynez Violé, 1608.
O'Reilley, Jennifer, 855, 1563
Oakeshott, Ewart, 1666
Obrist, Barbara, 237, 580-1,
    1521-22
Odenius, O., 873
Oggins, Robin S.,1449
Ohler, Norbert,1862
Oldenburger-Ebbers, C. S.,1543
Oliver, Judith, 380
Ollier, Marie Louise,1689
Oman, Charles, 56
Omont, Henri Auguste, 150
Opsomer-Halleux, Camelia,
    1533,1544
Orbán, Arpád,1171
Orion,758
Orlandi, Giovanni, 1172
Orpheus, 759-61

Osten, Gert van der,457
Östling, Christine, 1027
Otherworlds, 1069-83
Ott, André G.,1600
Ott, Norbert H.,1096
Otten, Charlotte F., 1378
Overgäard, Mariane, 993
Ovid, 724-40
Ovitt, George, Jr.,1638
Owen, D. D. R.,1097
Owen, Dorothy M., 819
Owst, G. R., 560-1

Pächt, Otto, 148, 300, 386
Padoan, Giorgio, 690
Palliser, Janis L., 1829
Palmer, Barbara, 1098
Pandora, 762
Pannier, Léopold, 1593
Panofsky, Dora, 762
Paris, 763-4
Parkhurst, Charles, 1631
Parmelee, Alice, 1431
Pastoureau, Michel,1246,
    1317,1322, 1564, 1632,1634,
    1636,1690, 1753
Patai, Raphael, 582
Patch, Howard R., 826
Patrides, C. A., 978
Paulmier-Foucart, Monique, 531
Pearsall, Derek, 1490,1510
Pelletier, Monique, 640
Pépin, J., 66
Perdrizet, Paul, 1131
Pereira, Michael, 583
Pernoud, Régine, 260
Pesina, Jaroslav, 316

Peters, F. E.,1863
Pfaffenbichler, Matthias, 1667
Pfander, Homer G., 562
Pfeffer, Wendy, 1456-7
Pfeiffer, Rudolf, 679
Pfister, Kurt, 433
Pflaum, H., 1811
Phêbus, Gaston, 1484
Phillips, John A., 1028
Phillips, J. R. S., 641
Phipson, Emma, 487
Phyllis, 806-10
Pickering, F. P., 261
Pieper, Paul, 1132
Pigler, André, 1503
Pilate, 1007
Pilgrim Badges, 1868-78
Pilgrimage,1858-67
Pinder, E., 174
Pirani, Emma, 301
Planche, Aline,1373
Planchenault, René, 957
Plants and fruits:Pansy, 1549;
    Fleur-de-Lis, 1548;
    Mandrake,1554-7; Pea,1506;
    Pear,1550; Rose,1551;
    Strawberry,1552
Platt, Colin, 49
Playing Cards, 167-77
Plummer, John, 415
Poerck, Guy de, 914
Poesch, Jesse, 521
Poirion, Daniel, 1545
Polome, Edgar C., 1230
Polymorphs, 1879-1892
Polyphemus,765
Pope-Hennessy, John W., 459

Porcher, Jean, 416
Porter, Arthur Kingsley, 465
Porton, Gary G., 927
Potestà, Gian Luca, 979
Pouchelle, Marie-Christine, 659
Poulle, Emmanuel, 603
Pounds, N. J. G., 57
Preaching handbooks, 543-572
Presentation in Temple,1008
Prideaux, Edith K.,1857
Prinz, Otto, 934
Prior, Edward A., 449
Pritchard, Alan, 584
Prometheus, 765
Proverbs,1893-95
Prudentius, 741-2
Psichari, Michel,175
Psyche, 767
Psychomachia, 850-8
Pulsiano, Phillip J., 474,1523
Pygmalion, 768
Pyramus and Thisbe, 769

Quaquarelli, Antonio, 1354
Quénet, Sophie, 1379
Quinn, Esther Casier, 1065

Radowitz, Joseph Maria von, 1875
Raff, Thomas,1524
Rager, Catherine, 666
Rahner, Hugo, 994
Ramsay, Nigel,160
Randall, Lilian M. C., 83, 874,
    397-8,1506-7
Randall, Richard H., Jr., 1724
Randolph, Charles Brewster, 1555
Ratkowitsch, Christine, 67

Rauh, Horst Dieter, 935
Raven, Charles E., 1145
Rawcliffe, Carole, 660
Reames, Sherry L.,1133
Réau, Louis, 262
Reeves, Marjorie, 980-81
Reid, Davidson Jane, 667
Reinitzer, Heimo, 1476
Reinsch, Robert, 1193
Reiss, Edmund, 1057
Remigius of Auxerre,707
Remnant, G. L., 488
Renier, Rodolfo,1601
Reta, Jose Oroz, 915
Reuter, E., 1847
Reynolds, Reginald, 1607
Reynolds, William Donald, 704-5
Rhabanus Maurus, 523-4
Rhodes, James F., 1134
Ricci, Seymour de, 81
Richard, Jean, 1864-5
Richards, Jeffrey,1812
Richards, Peter,1813
Richardson, James S., 450
Richmond, Velma Bourgeois, 434
Rickert, Margaret, 326
Rico, Francisco, 563
Riding Backwards, 860
Ridwall, John, 696
Right, 1650-2
Ringger, Kurt, 1173
Robb, David M., 302
Robbins, Mary E.,1330
Robbins, Rossell Hope, 661
Robert, M. Ulysse, 1691
Robert-Tornow, Walter, 1501
Roberts, Gareth, 585

Roberts, Lawrence D.,1146
Robin, P. Ansell, 1231
Robinson, David M., 827
Robinson, Margaret W.,1340
Robson, C. A., 737
Rochelle, Mercedes, 1135
Rodari, Florian,1099
Rodley, Lynn, 50
Röhricht, Reinhold,1866
Roland, 861
Rombauts, E., 1295
Romi,1611
Romm, James, 1289
Roncière, Monique de la, 642
Roob, Helmut, 738
Rooney, Anne,1491-2
Rorimer, James, 417
Ross, David J. A., 802-3
Ross, Lawrence J., 1552,1854
Roth, C., 1728
Rouge, Gustave Le, 1556
Rouse, Richard, 564
Rowland, Beryl, 1232-3, 1308,
    1432, 1440,1726
Ruberg, Uwe, 1441
Rudolph, Conrad, 68
Rudwin, Maximilian,1100
Ruelle, Pierre,1692
Runeberg, J.,1408
Rushforth, G. McN.,17
Rushing, James A., Jr., 876
Russell, H. Diane, 848
Russell, Jeffrey Burton, 1101

Sacraments,1112
Saenger, Paul, 104, 393
Saints,1113-37

Salisbury, Joyce E., 1147-8,1244
Samaran, Charles, 706
Samarrai, Alauddin, 643
Sandler, Lucy Freeman, 327
Sanford, Eva M.,721
Sanoner, G.,1040
Sant, Jeannette Th. M. van't, 739
Santucci, Monique, 1773
Saperstein, Marc, 565
Saturn, 772-4
Saunders, Corrine J.,1565
Saunders, Elfrida O., 328
Savage, J. J., 748
Saxl, Fritz, 500, 669, 680-82
Sbordone, Francesco, 1174
Schapiro, Meyer, 32, 263, 1044
Scheiwiller, Vanni, 644
Scheller, Robert W., 421,1673
Scheve, D. A., 1296
Schilling, Michael, 828.
Schleissner, Margaret R., 662
Schmidt, G., 317
Schmidt, Gary,1102
Schmidt, Gerhard, 350
Schmidt, O.,18
Schmidt-Wiegand, Ruth, 351-2
Schmidtke, Dietrich, 1234
Schmitt, Jean-Claude, 1282,
    1744-5
Schmitt-von Mühlenfels, Franz,
    771
Schmolke-Hasselmann, Beate,
    1602
Schneyer, Johannes Baptiste,
    566-7
Schönbach, Anton E., 995
Schorr, Dorothy C., 1008

Schrade, H.,1575
Schrader, C. R., 1668
Schrader, J. L., 1175
Schreckenberg, Heinz, 264
Schreiber, Earl G., 691
Schreiber, W. L., 176
Schroeder, Horst, 849
Schueller, Herbert M.,1848
Schuler, Robert M., 663
Schur, Nathan, 1867
Schwab, Ute, 1267
Schwarz, Heinrich, 841-2
Schweickard, Wolfgang, 916
Schwenk, Sigrid,1493
Scott, E. J. L., 127
Scott, Kathleen, 329
Scott, Margaret, 1693-4
Sculpture,437-42:Danish,443-4;
    English, 445-51; French,
    452-5; German,456-7;
    Italian,458; Swedish,466;
    Spanish,463-5
Sears, Elizabeth, 798
Seasons,1510
Sed-Rajna, Gabrielle, 928
Seel, Otto, 1176
Segre, Cesare, 1208
Séguin, Jean-Pierre, 177
Seidel, Linda, 1309
Seiferth, Wolfgang, 1814
Seiler, Thomas H.,1103
Sermon collections, 543-572
Servius, 708
Seth,1064-5
Settis-Frugoni, Chiara, 804
Seven Deadly Sins, 1252
Seymour, Charles, Jr., 460

Seymour, M. C., 509-10
Seznec, Jean, 683
Shailor, Barbara,137
Shapes,geometrical, 831
Shapiro, Susan C., 1695
Shatzmiller, Joseph,1815
Sheingorn, Pamela, 1104
Sheldon, Susan Eastman,1444
Shephard, Odell, 1374
Shereshevsky, Esra, 929-30
Sheridan, Ronald, 489
Sherwood, Merriam, 1792
Ships, 1603, 1896
Shoaf, R. A., 1442
Sibyll, 775
Sicard, Patrice, 1576
Silk, Edmund T.,718
Sillar, Frederick Cameron, 1274, 1290,1323
Simonds, Peggy Muñoz, 265
Simpson, J., 875
Siraisi, Nancy, 664
Sjöström, Henning, 715
Skull, 862
Smalley, Beryl, 684
Smeets, Jean Robert, 880
Smeyers, M., 387
Smith, Alison M.,1048
Smith, Earl Baldwin, 51, 266
Smith, Forrest S., 1082
Smith, J . C. D., 490
Smith, M. Q., 491
Smith, Sharon O. Dunlap, 388
Smith, Thomas, 128
Smits, K., 381
Smoller, Laura Ackerman, 604
Söderberg, Bengt G., 475-6

Soleil, F., 394
Sollbach, Gerhard E., 517
Solms, Elisabeth de, 1177
Solomon, Biblical king, 1066
Song, Cheunsoon, 1696
South, Malcolm,1341, 1375
Spearman, R. Michael, 33
Specht, Henrik, 1515
Spencer, B.,1876-7
Spencer, Eleanor P., 418
Spencer, H. Leith, 568
Spriewald, Ingeborg, 1670
Springer, Otto, 808
Sprunger, David A., 124,1774, 1887
Squatriti, Paolo, 613
Squires, Ann,1178
Stange, Alfred, 353
Staniland, Kay, 235
Stannard, Jerry, 1534
Stapleton, Michael L.,740
Stauder, W., 1270
Stauffer, Marianne, 1566
Steger, Hugo, 1045
Steiger, Christoph von, 1185
Stephanson, Mill, 165
Stephen, David, 1855
Stephens, Walter,1830.
Steppe, J. K., 1405
Stettiner, Richard, 741
Stevenson, T. B., 355
Stevick, Robert D., 34
Stiénnon, Jacques, 461
Stokstad, Marilyn, 1530
Stone, George Cameron, 1669
Stone, L., 451
Stones, Alison, 72, 813-14

Storck, Willy F.,1645
Storost, Joachim, 809-10
Straten, Roelof van, 267-8
Stratford, Neil, 191
Strubel, Armand, 1484
Strutt, Joseph,1725
Stuart, Donald Clive, 1105
Stuart, Dorothy M.,1433
Studer, Paul, 1594
Styger, Paul, 435
Surles, Robert L., 793
Suther, Judith D., 1357
Swain, Barbara, 1775
Swanson, Heather, 1639
Swanson, Jenny, 569
Swarzenski, Hanns, 441, 522
Swords, 1653-69
Szonyi, György E., 269
Szovérffy, Josef, 1235
Tapestry, 224-36
Tatakiwicz, Wladyslaw, 22
Taylor, Archer, 1319
Taylor, Barry,1895
Taylor, John Prentice, 709
Taylor, Larissa J., 570
Tchalenko, John,1888
Temple, Elzbieta, 330
Terpening, Ronnie H., 749
Terrien, Samuel,1050
Terrien-Somerville, Beatrice, 138
Tervarent, Guy de, 19
Tescione, G., 1595
Tester, S. J., 605
Teyssèdre, Bernard, 238
Thérel, Marie-Louise, 856
Thibout. M., 1291
Thiébaud, J., 1495

Thiébaux, Marcelle, 1273,1496
Thomas of Cantimpré, 525
Thomas, Keith,1793
Thomas, Marcel, 335
Thomas, Ruth Stanford, 765
Thompson, Charles J. S., 1557
Thomson, Rodney M., 117
Thomson, W. H. G., 236
Thordstein, Arvid, 1209
Thorndike, Lynn, 614
Thurley, Simon, 52
Tietze-Conrat, E.,1831
Tilander, Gunnar, 1484, 1497
Tilley, Maureen A., 1499
Time, 863
Tinkle, Theresa, 744, 778
Tomlinson, Amanda,1614
Torti, Anna, 843
Toubert, Hélène, 303
Tower of Babel,1029-31
Toynbee, J. M. C., 1236
Trachtenberg, Joshua,1794
Tracy, Charles, 492-3
Trades, 1637-40
Trapp, J. B., 270
Trees and branches:
    diagrammatic, 1567-76;
    Specific: Hawthorn, 1577,
    Jesse Tree, 1578, Palm,1581-
    2,Tree of Life, 1580, Willow,
    994
Treu, Ursula, 1179,1332
Tristan, 864-5
Tristram, E. W., 470
Tristram, Hildegard L. C., 1083
Trivick, Henry H., 166
Trotter, D. A., 1878

Trousson, Raymond, 766
Troy Matter, 866-9
Tubach, Frederic C., 540
Tucci, Hannelore Zug,1389
Tugnoli Pattaro, Sandra, 1237
Turnau, Irena, 1697,1705
Turner, D. H., 331, 419
Tuve, Rosamond, 1516,1674
Tyson, Moses,133

Ugliness, 1596-1604
Ulrich, Anna, 1042
Ulrich, Ernst, 1795
Underhill, Evelyn, 830
Unger, Richard W.,1063
Unterkircher, Franz, 1183
Upton, Joel M., 382
Uytven, Raymond van, 1698
Van Os, A. B., 895
Varela, Gerardo Boto, 399
Varty, Kenneth, 1297
Vatican Mythographers, 712-16
Vaughan, R.,149
Venus, 776-8
Verlet, Pierre, 1376
Vernet, André, 881
Versluis, Arthur, 794
Vicaire, M.-H., 982
Vigarello, Georges, 1671
Vignay, Jean de, 1878
Villeneuve, Roland, 1106
Vincent of Beauvais, 526-32
Vincent-Cassy, Mireille,1252
Vinge, Louise, 756
Virgil, 743
Virgin Mary,1009-14
Virtues and Vices, 850-58

Vogel, Mary Ursula,1310
Volbach, Wolfgang Fritz, 218-19

Waal, Henri van de, 271
Wagener, Anthony Pelzer, 1652
Wagner, Anthony,1754
Walberg, Emmanuel,1203
Wall and panel painting,467:
        Austrian,468; English,469-70;
        Italian,471; Swedish,472-6
Walsh, Michael, 1119
Walther, Hans, 829
Walther, Ingo F., 354
Walworth, Julia, 865
Warburg, Aby M., 805
Warden, John, 761
Wardrop, James, 958
Warner, George F., 129
Warren, Glenda, 1746
Watson, Arthur, 1579
Webster, James Carson, 1517
Webster, Leslie, 35
Weijers, Olga, 501, 917
Weimann, Klaus, 1238
Weir, Anthony, 442
Weitzmann, Kurt, 41-2,1047
Wells, D. A.,1889
Welsford, Enid, 1776
Welter, J. -Th., 541
Wenzel, Siegfried, 542, 857
Wessner, Paul,722
West, Delno C., 983-4
Westra, Haijo Jan, 692
Westrem, Scott D., 645
Whitaker, Muriel, 815.
Whitbread, Leslie George, 719
White, David Gordon, 1349

White, Hayden, 1890
White, John, 462
White, Lynn, Jr., 1149
White, T. H.,1190
Whitney, Elspeth, 1640
Whittingham, Arthur Bensly, 494-5
Wickersheimer, Ernest, 665
Wieck, Roger S., 395
Wieland, Gernot Rudolf, 742
Wild, F., 1355
Wild Man, 1882-84, 1885-6,1889
Wilhelm, Friedrich, 1198
Willard, Charity Cannon, 858
Willeford, W., 1777
William of Conches, 710-11
Williams, Ann, 985
Williams, Charles Allyn, 1891-2
Williams, Ethel Carleton, 1646-7
Williams, John, 987
Williams, Paul V. A., 1778.
Williamson, G. C., 220
Williamson, Paul, 424
Wilpert, Josef, 436
Wilson, Bradford, 711
Wilson, David M., 36
Wilson, Jean C., 383
Windows,1730-31
Winds, 1520-4
Winston-Allen, Anne, 223
Winter, Patrick M. de, 158
Winternitz, E., 1849-50
Wireker, Nigel, 1271
Wirth, K.-A., 69
Wirth, Karl-August, 723
Wirtjes, Hanneke,1197
Wisbey, Roy A.,1603

Wisdom, 870
Wittkower, Rudolf, 272-3, 646, 755, 832, 862,1434, 1445, 1478,1832
Wolff, Phillipe, 1239
Wood, Casey A.,1450
Woodcarving:English, 477-96
Woodruff, Charles Everleigh, 103
Woodruff, Helen, 1186
Wooley, R. M., 118
Woolf, R. E., 1107
World Grown Old, 871-2
World Maps, 615-647
World UpsideDown, 873-5
Wormald, Francis,1136
Wright, C. E., 1755
Wright, Peter Poyntz, 496
Wright, Rosemary Muir, 936
Wright, Thomas,1240

Yankowski, S.V., 647
Yapp, Brunsdon, 1435
Yarnall, Judith,750
Young, John, 114
Yvain,876

Zambelli, Paola, 986
Zawart, Anscar, 571
Zender, Frank Gunther, 1137
Zijlstra-Zweens, H. M.,1699
Zink, Michel, 572
Ziolkowski, Jan, 1241,1409,1604
Zircle, Conway,1255
Zorzetti, Nevio, 716
Zucker, Wolfgang M.,844
Zupnick, Irving L,1729